齐家坪遗址与罗汉堂遗址考古报告

QIJIAPING YIZHI YU LUOHANTANG YIZHI KAOGU BAOGAO

本书为国家社会科学基金项目（21BYY067）阶段性研究成果

〔瑞典〕玛吉特·比林-阿尔提
（Margit Bylin-Althin）著

米亚宁 译　路东平 审订

兰州大学出版社
LANZHOU UNIVERSITY PRESS

图书在版编目（CIP）数据

齐家坪遗址与罗汉堂遗址考古报告 ／（瑞典）玛吉特·
比林-阿尔提（Margit Bylin-Althin）著；米亚宁译.
兰州：兰州大学出版社，2024. 12. -- ISBN 978-7-311-
06706-9

Ⅰ. K878.05

中国国家版本馆 CIP 数据核字第 20243K7Z36 号

责任编辑　梁建萍　张国梁
封面设计　汪如祥

书　　名　齐家坪遗址与罗汉堂遗址考古报告
　　　　　QIJIAPING YIZHI YU LUOHANTANG YIZHI KAOGU BAOGAO
作　　者　（瑞典）玛吉特·比林-阿尔提（Margit Bylin-Althin）　著
　　　　　米亚宁　译
出版发行　兰州大学出版社　（地址:兰州市天水南路222号　730000）
电　　话　0931-8912613(总编办公室)　0931-8617156(营销中心)
网　　址　http://press.lzu.edu.cn
电子信箱　press@lzu.edu.cn
印　　刷　甘肃发展印刷公司
开　　本　787 mm×1092 mm　1/16
成品尺寸　185 mm×260 mm
印　　张　20.5(插页4)
字　　数　213千
版　　次　2024年12月第1版
印　　次　2024年12月第1次印刷
书　　号　ISBN 978-7-311-06706-9
定　　价　150.00元

（图书若有破损、缺页、掉页,可随时与本社联系）

序　一

　　齐家坪遗址和罗汉堂遗址的考古调查者与最初研究者是瑞典学者安特生（Johan Gunnar Andersson），而其写作者是瑞典学者玛吉特·比林-阿尔提（Margit Bylin-Althin），她是安特生的学生和研究的协助者。筹备出版这本书的中译本的主要策划者，则是唐士乾先生。唐先生是甘肃省广河县文化局原局长，广河县是著名的齐家坪遗址所在地。唐先生是齐家文化有力的推动者，是地方文化事业建设的一位得力干将。他曾经发起并创立了齐家文化研究会，推动建起了令人惊叹的齐家文化博物馆。

　　这次出版这本译著，是他最新筹划完成的又一件大事。去年，唐先生退居二线并调整工作到政协部门，但他仍然不遗余力地贡献于文化遗产和齐家文化的公共事业。有一次，唐先生和我谈到了出版这本译著的事，他说有位学者已经把译稿大体完成了。我对他积极张罗该书的出版事宜深感高兴，但也怀疑，要做成或许遥遥无期。如今大功告成，自是感到欣慰，同时也很关心译稿的出版，和他还共同讨论过出版的事项，一度帮他联系了一家出版社，不料，最终因出版经费问题未能如愿。

　　如今，译著即将付梓，我由衷地为唐先生这位地方文化人所做出的贡献感到钦佩，这是我同意写这份序言的原因。再者，我作为齐家文化研究会的名誉会长之一，深为这项成果的功德无量而高兴，也必须为之说上几句。

　　原著 *THE SITES OF CH'I CHIA P'ING AND LO HAN T'ANG IN KANSU* 是安特生在甘青考古旅行调查后的第一手文献资料，具有重要历史价值，它的翻译出版，无疑是考古界，特别是甘青史前考古领域的大事，在学术史上，也具有重要而深远的学术意义。时值齐家文化发现百年纪念，这本译著的出版不仅具有学术献礼的深情，更有进一步推动齐家文化学术研究发展的积极作用，也是回味和反思安特生提出所谓甘肃史前文化"六期"说认识的最基础的资料。同时，该书为相关学者进一步挖掘早期的中国考古学，进一步探索学术思想发展的历史，提供了珍贵资料。

同样的资料，在不同的研究者那里，很有可能有着不同的解读，这源于研究者的立场和思想，以及看问题的角度和认识方法。在这本考古报告中，或许可以找到学术研究的规律性发展进步的主客观因素。这不仅是学术史，也是学术的思想史，以及是把考古学作为科学体系中的一部分的学科发展的技术方法史。

齐家坪遗址是甘肃的重要史前遗址，罗汉堂遗址是青海的重要史前遗址。译者在书中已经交代并说明了，作者把两个遗址放在一起的原因是，这两个遗址都是中国考古的学术圣地。两个重要的遗址，结果却不同，齐家坪的名气更大，因为它就是齐家文化的定名之地，是文化命名的来源。齐家文化也因为地方政府和研究学者们的共同努力，焕发出蓬勃生命力。

与齐家坪相比，青海贵德的罗汉堂遗址，除了在考古界有一定的知名度外，有很多普通人，甚至一些考古工作者，也不一定知晓。我也是做了甘青考古，到了青海，去过贵德，也才知道还有个罗汉堂遗址。不过并不是说罗汉堂遗址不重要，相反，它是中国考古学早期发现的非常重要的一处古遗址，在青藏高原的史前文化遗址中，具有特殊的意义。

安特生调查的青海几处古遗址，马厂塬遗址因为在民和县，也是我们后来发掘喇家遗址的甘青队相对比较熟悉的了，但实际去过遗址多次，并调查后才知道，马厂塬遗址也有很多问题，青海考古所的老先生高东陆老师，就对安特生的考古调查提出过质疑，甚至是怀疑。因为没有看到详细的报告，对它和现在遗址上的调查所见相比，有认识上的一些出入也就不足为奇。

安特生调查青海还有一个后来称为卡约文化的卡约（卡窑）遗址，是在塔尔寺所在的西宁市湟中区。卡约文化已经成为青海省很著名的史前文化了，但在公众中，知道卡约村的人并不普遍。不过，卡约文化却在青海高原大量发现，为数众多。据称，青海的卡约文化遗址，是青海独有的一个考古学文化，发现和发掘也都比较多。然而，对卡约文化的研究至今还是比较薄弱，有待深入，认识上也就还有很大的发展和提升空间。

贵德罗汉堂遗址，在本书中有了不少的资料，罗汉堂遗址内涵丰富，年代也比较早，主要是马家窑文化。罗汉堂遗址在青海没有受到更多关注和重视，是有些遗憾的，好在有本书关于罗汉堂遗址的一手资料。这极为重要，也是第一次为中国读者提供了阅读的便利。今后，罗汉堂遗址定会成为许多人都逐渐熟知的古遗址，也期望地方政府借国家大力发展考古学的契机，宣传好这一重要遗址。

　　总之，这本译著的出版，将为甘青史前考古增添一份考古学术史的珍贵资料，也为纪念齐家文化发现一百周年献上一份珍贵的贺礼。在此，我为这本译著终于能够付梓出版表示祝贺，也为本书译者的辛勤付出献上一份谢忱。

　　谨以为序。

叶茂林

2024年五一劳动节

序 二

　　翻译、文化记忆与国际文化传播是建构国家形象的关键。翻译与文化记忆是共生的关系，翻译促进文化记忆的生成，文化记忆又能进一步建构国家形象。把翻译与文化记忆引入中国新石器时代的彩陶文化研究中具有十分积极的意义。

　　中国新石器时代的彩陶文化基因在中国文化血脉中已经传承了数千年，是中国人最深刻的文化记忆，也是世界对中国最深刻的记忆。译者通过翻译来传播这一彩陶文化对于中国的国际形象建构是有积极意义的。地处甘肃的马家窑文化彩陶是中国彩陶甚至世界彩陶鼎盛时期的代表，齐家文化则代表了中国从彩陶到早期青铜文化的过渡，是中国青铜文化的开端，这两个文化类型对于中华文化的发展可以说都非常重要。《齐家坪遗址与罗汉堂遗址考古报告》正是齐家文化和马家窑文化的代表性遗址的首次发现和发掘的考古报告，该报告对于中国现代考古学的发端具有重要价值。在经过100年的考古研究后，上述两个遗址的首次考古报告的中文版本对于中华文明溯源、中国文化的国际传播等同样具有重要价值。

　　彩陶文化是考古学文化的范畴，翻译学与考古学文化的结合很好地体现了跨学科属性，是新文科思路在翻译领域的理想结合。新文科建设对于外语学科提出的要求是，外语学科不仅要培养懂外语及外国文化的人才，更需要培养能用外语讲好中国文化故事的人才，这就为翻译学界提出了翻译什么、如何翻译、为谁翻译的问题。答案很明确：我们要翻译中国传统优秀文化，以利于中国文化对外传播的方式来翻译，要为增强中国文化的软实力而翻译。因此，近年来翻译与中医药学结合、翻译与中国陶瓷文化结合、翻译与中国戏曲文化结合等跨学科专业翻译人才的培养越来越重要。这些专业翻译人员需要系统了解该专业领域的知识，又精通翻译理论，熟练掌握翻译技巧。目前，这类人才的培养难度极大，它就是一个系统工程，任何一个环节的缺失都可能导致人才培养的失败。考古学专业的翻译同样很具有挑战性，有志于该领域的翻译实践人员少之又少，遑论做翻译研究。

米亚宁在清华苦读6年，在我的严厉督导下，大量阅读，勤于思考，不断提升自己的学养，在翻译理论与翻译实践两个方面均取得很大的进步，这为她后来进行考古翻译研究奠定了基础。2020年6月，米亚宁从清华外文系博士毕业，后返回原单位工作。2020年底，她咨询我可否围绕彩陶文化开展跨学科翻译研究，我很赞成她的选题，并给予了一定的指导。2021年，该课题喜获国家哲学社会科学基金立项。2023年年中，我应邀去兰州文理学院讲学，其间阅读了她翻译的《齐家坪遗址与罗汉堂遗址考古报告》。当时仅仅是一部初稿而已，但我很快就通过阅读发现，这本书对于考古界很有价值，同时给跨学科翻译也提供了一个范例。米亚宁博士在翻译上下了大功夫，认真斟酌，反复修改，最终做到了译文流畅，意义明晰，可读性强，如下面一句："这些器物的用途始终是个问题，下面会给出一两种假设。陶器形态笔直，必定与器物用途有关。如上所述，这些陶器被切割成两半，这两部分可能是装在一起，组合成模具使用；如果是这样，里面会随意覆上草纤维、草、草席，或绳索、绳索做的粗糙编织袋。"再看全文译者注释情况，如"篦点纹（译者注：指花纹似梳齿所压，形成多数行列之点）""绳纹（译者注：齐家文化的绳纹、篮纹和席纹实际上指绳索、篮筐和席子在陶器表面留下的印迹）""如图版11中图13展示的陶器（可能是当地罕见的白泥）（译者注：此处或许为图版12中图13）"原文中，译者添加了三十多处注释，或添加了专业术语内涵，为普通读者扫除阅读障碍，或对原文个别处，文图描述不符之处做了说明。

《齐家坪遗址与罗汉堂遗址考古报告》的翻译是有挑战的。这首先与著作本身的专业性有关，译者除了要具有翻译专业的素养之外，又要对考古学、器物学等领域有较深的研究。尤其是原著所描述的文物的形态和纹饰情况，由于缺乏实物的支撑，可供参考的文献资料也不多，译者要读透原英文描述，反复揣摩实物的形态，才能开展翻译工作。另外，原著涉及大量的中外人名、地名、著作名等，这些名称均为历史史实，具有历史意义，但时过境迁，有的名称在历史的变迁中早已被彻底遗忘，有的已经更名，这些名称的翻译考证难度极大，很容易出错。还有作者本身为西方学者，在研究中国文化时，其视角和立场必然和中国学者有差异，这又给翻译增加了困难。因此，可以说这本著作的翻译属于冷门绝学研究，是有难度的。正因上述原因，该报告虽有价值，但学界很少有人有勇气投入时间和精力去翻译，由此可见这本译著的难能可贵。

是为序。

罗选民

2024 年 7 月 16 日于镜湖斋

前　言

　　1923 年至 1924 年，安特生在甘肃青海一带考古的过程中发现并首次发掘了齐家坪遗址和罗汉堂遗址（罗汉堂当时隶属甘肃，现隶属青海），后委托玛吉特·比林–阿尔提撰写齐家坪遗址出土文物的研究报告并负责研究罗汉堂遗址出土文物。1936 年，比林–阿尔提将研究报告《齐家坪遗址考古报告》寄往中国，计划在《中国古生物志》上发表。然而，1937 年 7 月 7 日，抗日战争全面爆发，该报告的发表计划中断。根据安特生与中央地质调查所的往来书信可知，1937 年 11 月 23 日，地质调查所的员工从南京撤到了长沙，《齐家坪遗址考古报告》的原稿也被安全地带到了长沙。之后，时任中央地质调查所副所长的黄汲清博士曾与香港的出版社商讨出版该报告未果，加之抗日战争持续多年，出版计划最终以失败告终。1946 年，作者修订原《齐家坪遗址考古报告》稿件后，与作者撰写的罗汉堂遗址的研究报告合并，发表在《远东古物博物馆馆刊》①第 18 期上，题名"齐家坪遗址与罗汉堂遗址考古报告"。

一

　　《齐家坪遗址与罗汉堂遗址考古报告》对齐家坪遗址和罗汉堂遗址考古所得文物进行了全面系统的论述，包括陶器、石器、骨器、哺乳动物遗骸、器物装饰及其象征意义等。报告通过研究指出，齐家文化应该处于早期青铜文化阶段，与殷商时期接近，因此不可能是甘肃远古文化"六期"之首。这一论断为后来齐家文

---

　　① "远东古物博物馆"，瑞典名称为"Östasiatiska Museet"，英文名称为"the Museum of Far Eastern Antiques"（简称 MFEA），中文名称前后有变化，2000 年前官方给出的中文名称为"瑞典远东古物博物馆"，2000 年后改为"瑞典东方博物馆"。该馆的馆刊"Bulletin of the Far Eastern Antiques"名称没有变化，本文仍采用"远东古物博物馆馆刊"。

化出土大量青铜器所证明。该报告为夏鼐确定齐家文化在甘肃远古文化"六期"中的位置提供了重要参考。

《齐家坪遗址与罗汉堂遗址考古报告》是对安特生在齐家坪遗址和罗汉堂遗址所得文物进行详细编目、分类和研究的最终报告。《齐家坪遗址与罗汉堂遗址考古报告》分"齐家坪遗址"和"罗汉堂遗址"两部分，外加图版描述。因安特生论断齐家文化是甘肃远古文化"六期"之首，因此作者比林-阿尔提首先论述了齐家坪遗址。作者指出，中国居址出土文物的研究工作相当艰难，因出土文物多又缺乏地层数据支撑，况且中国集约化的农业模式和梯田体系，导致不同地层的文物混合出现在同一地层，使得仅有的地层数据失去参考价值。除此之外，文物出土时受当时考古条件的限制，况且出土文物中完整器物较少，很难确定陶器的形状。因此，作者只能依据陶器的性质和工艺水准来分类并研究[1]。

报告前九章探讨了齐家坪遗址。第一章论述齐家坪遗址出土陶器，按照陶质和制陶技术水平，结合"安特生和他的助手从兰州及其周边区域购买的20个完整的陶器"，报告对陶器进行修复[2]、识别和分类（分为Ⅰ类、Ⅱ类和Ⅲ类）。比林-阿尔提标记了每类中每组陶片的数量，从陶质、技术水平、纹饰等方面进行了整体描述，之后又专门以"制陶技术细节""席纹和篮纹"为标题，对上述各类陶片进行了描述和对比分析。纹饰中探讨了篦点纹、附加堆纹、戳印纹等。第二章论述出土石器，主要分析了齐家坪出土的32把石斧和30把石刀。第三章论述出土骨器，共分析了31件，其中骨针13件。第四章杂项分析了一件灰色陶器的陶片，因烧制和上述几类不同而单独探讨。还分析了5个残缺的灰白色环状物，以及包括20片彩陶片。第五章是辛店丙址的发掘物，其中有6件不完整的陶器和15片陶片，还包括1个用烧过的黏土制成的平滑的蘑菇状的工具。第六章论述了齐家坪遗址出土陶器种类间的相互关系。第Ⅰ类和第Ⅱ类区别可能是用途不同。第Ⅰ类可能是用于储存和饮用的陶器，第Ⅱ类用作炊具，第Ⅲ类有着独特的装饰、精致的席纹和超薄的器壁[3]。作者在论述陶器类别之间的关系时，论述了齐家坪的篦点纹与俄罗斯-波罗的海带有篦点纹的陶器之间的联系，认为二者的共同点仅是装饰采用的技巧相同而已，二者之间没有直接的关联。第七章装饰及其象征性意义，

---

[1] 比林-阿尔提：《齐家坪遗址与罗汉堂遗址考古报告》，《远东古物博物馆馆刊》1946年第18期，第387页。

[2] 比林-阿尔提：《齐家坪遗址与罗汉堂遗址考古报告》，《远东古物博物馆馆刊》1946年第18期，第387页。

[3] 比林-阿尔提：《齐家坪遗址与罗汉堂遗址考古报告》，《远东古物博物馆馆刊》1946年第18期，第420页。

这里主要提到了精神象征。第八章为购买来的陶器，尤其分析了两件齐家文化的代表性陶盉。第九章显微镜照片分析，基本用以证实前面分类的合理性。

报告第十章至第十七章探讨罗汉堂遗址。报告中首先引用了安特生教授关于遗址地理位置的内容，其中提到"最重要的是此处发现的大量的仰韶彩陶是迄今为止我们在中国西北地区发现的数量最多、质量最完好的"[①]。报告交代了遗址地形的四大特征。随后，分Ⅰ类、Ⅱ类和Ⅲ类论述了罗汉堂的陶器。第Ⅰ类高质量素陶，论述了陶质、颜色和技术。第Ⅱ类粗糙的素陶论述包括陶质、烧制技术、器形几个方面。第Ⅲ类论述彩陶，包括其颜色、制陶工艺、器形三个方面。之后论述了石质工具、骨器、篮纹和绳纹，紧随其后是杂项、齐家坪和罗汉堂的哺乳动物遗骸、七里墩、榆中县小石峡（译者注：原著为 Yü Chung Hsien，Hsiao Shih Hsia，本书中译为榆中县小石峡）。

《齐家坪遗址与罗汉堂遗址考古报告》中，作者在第十八章"齐家坪遗址与罗汉堂遗址之间的关联性"中集中论证了齐家文化在甘肃史前六期文化中的顺序问题。报告指出，齐家文化陶器明显从造型上模仿了青铜文化，与殷商的青铜文化年代较近，齐家文化的年代不可能是安特生所说的甘肃史前六期文化的第一期。

作者主要通过对齐家坪遗址与罗汉堂遗址、朱家寨遗址、殷商文化等的出土文物的比较来说明齐家文化的年代较晚近。作者认为齐家文化一直与金属文化有接触，且金属影响了他们的陶器的造型，但齐家人在日常生活中并未使用金属器物，而是将金属器物作为他们制作陶器的模型。作者给出了数个理由，主要包括安特生对齐家文化沉积层"地表发现"的仰韶陶片的解释简单化了齐家文化的年代问题；齐家坪出土的陶器并不一定是安特生认为的"仰韶中期"，还可能是"仰韶晚期"[②]；齐家坪出土的双耳罐的品质明显先进，"这些双耳罐是模仿金属器物制作的"[③]；齐家坪遗址中没有金属或彩陶很少并不能说明齐家文化年代就更早[④]；齐家的哺乳动物遗骸种类比其他地方都更加齐全，可辨认的有狗、猪、牛、山羊和绵羊。而罗汉堂出土的猪骨不多，牛骨却很常见（当时牛可能已经被驯

---

① 比林-阿尔提：《齐家坪遗址与罗汉堂遗址考古报告》，《远东古物博物馆馆刊》1946年第18期，第430页。

② 比林-阿尔提：《齐家坪遗址与罗汉堂遗址考古报告》，《远东古物博物馆馆刊》1946年第18期，第464页。

③ 比林-阿尔提：《齐家坪遗址与罗汉堂遗址考古报告》，《远东古物博物馆馆刊》1946年第18期，第465页。

④ 比林-阿尔提：《齐家坪遗址与罗汉堂遗址考古报告》，《远东古物博物馆馆刊》1946年第18期，第466页。

养），且出土的动物骨骼多为野生动物骨骼。比较之下，马家窑出土的驯养的动物只有猪和狗。可见，三种文化中，齐家文化最为先进，由此判断齐家文化的年代最晚近。

该报告通过对出土文物的详尽研究，说明中国陶器与俄罗斯–波罗的海的带有篦点纹的陶器有某种联系，但二者之间没有直接的关联。齐家坪篦点纹陶器和两片黎波里文化的陶器存在一些细微的相似之处，主要体现在器形和纹饰上。针对出土文物的详尽研究也表明齐家文化年代在仰韶文化之后，属于早期青铜文化性质。

二

《齐家坪遗址与罗汉堂遗址考古报告》是齐家坪遗址和罗汉堂遗址研究的重要报告，对于甘肃远古六期文化年代顺序的修订以及齐家文化的后续研究都具有重要的参考价值。夏鼐1948年在《齐家期墓葬的新发现及其年代的改订》一文中修订齐家文化的年代时就提到了该报告。夏鼐在文中提到，《齐家坪遗址与罗汉堂遗址考古报告》是对安特生发掘的考古收获在近二十年后才发表的详尽的报告。这份报告为我们提供了齐家文化的相关知识，让我们更加了解齐家文化的事实，但是由于缺乏墓葬方面的材料，"大家总觉得有点欠缺"。夏鼐在文中提到，在《齐家坪遗址与罗汉堂遗址考古报告》中安特生仍然维持他关于齐家文化早于甘肃仰韶文化的观点，"但是瑞典的比林–阿尔提及友人刘燿（即尹达）先生对这一说法都加以怀疑，他们根据器物形制研究的结果，都拟加以修正"。"民国三十四年我们居然找到了齐家文化期的墓葬。新发现的结果，不仅对于齐家文化时代的埋葬风俗及人种特征方面，供给新材料；并且意外地又供给地层上的证据，使我们能确定这文化与甘肃仰韶文化年代先后的关系。"[①]也就是说，安特生提出齐家文化是甘肃远古六期文化之首的错误论断之后，是夏鼐纠正了这一观点，但实际上在夏鼐之前，比林–阿尔提已在《齐家坪遗址与罗汉堂遗址考古报告》中对此拟进行修订[②]。夏鼐1945年发现了齐家坪遗址的墓葬遗址，进一步确定了齐家文化在甘肃史前文化序列中的位置。

之后，国外学者在论述齐家文化的早期青铜属性时，引用比林–阿尔提的《齐家坪遗址与罗汉堂遗址考古报告》较多，如1995年胡博（Louisa G. Fitzgerald-

---

① 夏鼐：《齐家期墓葬的新发现及其年代的改订》，《中国考古学报》1948年第3期，第101–117页。

② 比林–阿尔提：《齐家坪遗址与罗汉堂遗址考古报告》，《远东古物博物馆馆刊》1946年第18期，第383–496页。

Huber）在《古代中国》发表《齐家与二头里：远距离文化互动的讨论》，提出了东亚与中亚或西亚青铜时代文化远距离互动的可能性①。同年，法国学者戴寇琳（Corinne Debaine-Francfort）（1995）出版了一本齐家文化专著②，胡博（1997）为其撰写了长篇书评，书评中指出戴寇琳通过研究指出齐家文化年代处于新石器晚期和早期青铜时代之间。该书评中引用了比林-阿尔提的《齐家坪遗址与罗汉堂遗址考古报告》③。胡博（2003）论述齐家文化的东西走向时，提出齐家文化属于早期青铜文化性质。文中引用了《齐家坪遗址与罗汉堂遗址考古报告》的观点，即"安特生的假设首先受到他的研究生比林-阿尔提的挑战，她（比林-阿尔提）的任务是发表齐家坪的发现结果，她认为一些齐家陶器明显模仿了金属模型，这一观点彻底改变了人们对齐家文化的认识，即齐家文化不是中国最早的新石器文化，而是最晚近的"④。

当年，安特生在中国西北甘青一带的考察就是为了印证他有关渑池县发现的仰韶文化是从西方传播而来的这一观点，因此，当他在齐家坪遗址仅发现"极为特别的"单色印花陶器时⑤，便据此推断齐家文化排在甘肃史前六期文化的第一期，比仰韶文化更早，从而确认了他的"中国文化西来说"的观点。《齐家坪遗址与罗汉堂遗址考古报告》对齐家文化在甘肃远古文化中的位置进行了修订，这意味着对安特生有关中国文化源头错误论断的部分依据的否定。

自1924年齐家文化遗址被发现以来，中国考古学界曾多次发掘和考察齐家坪遗址。然而，大部分发掘和考察的第一手资料报告记录都不够详尽，且对出土文物的研究也不充分，或等待出版。目前针对齐家坪遗址公开发表的考古报告或权威论文，除了陈玼的博士学位论文，大部分篇幅不超过1000字，而比林-阿尔提的《齐家坪遗址与罗汉堂遗址考古报告》是对1923年至1924年齐家坪遗址和罗汉堂遗址发掘所得文物最为详尽的考古研究报告。

概括而言，《齐家坪遗址与罗汉堂遗址考古报告》通过充分的论证说明齐家文化不可能是甘肃远古六期文化之首，齐家文化明显受到青铜文化的影响，部分陶器可能与殷商青铜器有关联。《齐家坪遗址与罗汉堂遗址考古报告》对齐家文化年

① 胡博：《齐家与二里头：遥远文化接触问题》，《早期中国》1995年第20卷，第17-67页。

② 戴寇琳：《从新石器时代到中国西北的青铜时代：齐家文化及其联系》，载《法国中亚考古代表团论文集》第六卷，巴黎：文明研究出版社，1995，435页。

③ 胡博：《评〈从新石器时代到中国西北的青铜时代：齐家文化及其联系〉》，《早期中国》1997年第22卷，第246-270页。

④ 胡博：《齐家文化：东西之路》，《远东古物博物馆》2003年第75期，第54-77页。

⑤ 安特生：《甘肃考古记》，乐森璕译，文物出版社，2011，第3页。

代的修订具有重要的价值，对于齐家文化及其与夏文化的关系研究等都具有重要价值，应该受到学界的重视。《齐家坪遗址与罗汉堂遗址考古报告》对齐家坪遗址和罗汉堂遗址出土文物的研究的谨慎态度也值得敬佩与学习，同时，安特生允许自己的学生挑战自己的学术思想的开放态度和豁达的胸襟也值得肯定。

三

时至今日，《齐家坪遗址与罗汉堂遗址考古报告》距原文发表时间已经将近90年，距离当初安特生发现并发掘齐家坪遗址已经100年。在纪念齐家文化发现100周年之际，该报告的中文版在中国出版，对于中华文明探源研究，对于中国现代考古学的进一步发展和齐家文化研究等都具有重要意义。然而，该书的出版同样波折重重。

《齐家坪遗址与罗汉堂遗址考古报告》的中文版，是中国社会科学院民族学与人类学研究所易华研究员倡导翻译的，是甘肃省齐家文化研究会唐士乾会长积极筹划出版的，是笔者在主持国家哲学社会科学基金项目"文化记忆与黄河彩陶术语翻译研究"的过程中耗费心血完成的。该书能够出版，也是作为齐家文化研究会正在开展的齐家文化双语出版工程的成果之一，得到以唐士乾会长为倡导者的齐家文化研究会的大力支持。

翻译该报告也是讲好中华优秀文化故事的一部分。2020年底，笔者从讲好中华文化故事的角度出发，着手申请有关黄河彩陶文化翻译研究的国家社科基金项目，为此，笔者同课题组人员曾登门拜访郎树德先生，了解该领域的研究现状及研究成果等，包括重要的研究专家及其著作。2021年5月，笔者在黄河文化研究会上有幸认识了马家窑文化研究会的王芳女士，并经介绍认识了易华研究员。2021年9月，笔者申请的国家社科基金项目立项。随后，易华研究员寄给笔者这份研究报告的原英文版，并说明该报告的重要性，希望笔者能翻译成中文。因齐家文化也是笔者主持的项目研究内容的一部分，于是，笔者就着手翻译。2023年4月，该报告的中文版初稿基本完成。2023年5月，中国考古学会等主办、甘肃省齐家文化研究会等协办的"文明汇聚·光耀河州——史前文化临夏论坛"召开，唐士乾会长邀请笔者参加了本次会议，并提议将该报告的翻译和出版工作纳入齐家文化研究的双语出版工程。就此开始，唐会长着手筹集出版资金，联系出版社，并邀请业内专家审校书稿、撰写序言等。2023年9月，本书的出版事宜正式被提上日程。后经唐会长多方协商，终于在12月底敲定了出版社和出版经费等事宜。

该报告的翻译过程也并非一帆风顺。因该报告涉及许多100年前的人名、地名等，并以威妥玛式拼音书写，考证难度极大。况且文中涉及大量的地质学、考古学、彩陶文化等领域的专业术语，还有对各类器物形状的细节描述，初稿翻译时笔者并未见到器物图片，仅凭文字描述来想象器物形状，笔者查阅并参考了大量的资料，包括《甘肃考古记》（乐森璕译）和《中华远古之文化》（袁复礼译）等的中英文版本，以及齐家文化研究、彩陶文化研究等各类文献，反复请教相关专业人士，并与兰州大学外国语学院路东平教授反复探讨，最终才确定上述内容的中文翻译。初稿出来之后，笔者将存疑之处交给考古学领域专家校对，然而，术业有专攻，直至笔者与出版社探讨修改数易其稿时，才收到专家们给出的一些关于地名、人名、文献名等的修改意见。后续笔者又请教了中国社会科学院考古研究所所长陈星灿研究员、甘肃省考古研究所郎树德研究员、远东古物博物馆的司汉研究员、甘肃省文物考古所考古研究一部主任周静副研究员等，反复校对了一些地名、人名，尤其是专业名词的翻译问题。经过反复打磨修改，才最终完成翻译工作。笔者认为这部报告对于考古学领域、齐家文化研究领域、甘肃文化对外宣传等均有价值，有必要翻译，故耗费心血不求回报地做这件事，希望学界能看到这本译著的价值和对考古界的重要意义，并能鼓励更多的学者潜心做有意义的学术研究。

在本书出版之际，笔者在此感谢参与本报告翻译和出版的各方人士，尤其感谢发起并指导此项翻译工作的易华研究员和唐士乾会长，感谢为本书提供专业指导和修改意见的陈星灿研究员、郎树德研究员，感谢为本书撰写序言的叶茂林研究员和罗选民教授，感谢我的搭档路东平教授在翻译中的指导和帮助。

在此特别鸣谢广河县文体广电和旅游局、甘肃省齐家文化研究会的大力支持，并将本书作为齐家坪遗址发现100周年献礼图书。

译者　米亚宁
2024年1月25日于兰州雁乐家苑

目　录

中文部分

英文部分

附录部分

第一部分
齐家坪遗址

甘肃宁定县(今甘肃广河县)

1931年，安特生教授委托我发表他在甘肃齐家坪遗址的发掘成果。

1936年，我将手稿寄往中国出版，该手稿详细描述了安特生教授在齐家坪遗址中的考古发现。此后中国人民抗日战争爆发，战争阻断了这一出版计划。直到最近，我才重启这项工作，修改原稿件，以便在瑞典出版。同时，我还承担了罗汉堂遗址发掘成果资料的研究工作。因此，本文包括了两个部分，但这两个部分彼此联系紧密。在此，我诚挚地感谢安特生教授对我的帮助以及对我工作的关注。

甘肃宁定县，靠近黄河支流洮河的中游。在洮河西岸陡峭的深沟边缘，有一处大面积的文化堆积，被称为"齐家坪"，是以附近的一个村庄命名的。1924年夏，在安特生教授的指导下，他的考古团队对这一居址的一小部分进行了发掘。安特生对这次发掘作了如下报告：

　　齐家坪遗址绘制在比例尺为1∶8 000的草图（插图1）上。其中有一条路，沿着洮河西岸低矮的近代10米台地延伸了约20里，穿过一条深沟，升至马兰高地顶部。这在地图上西侧74米处可以看到。这条路穿过齐家坪村，然后越过南面与村庄接壤的一条巨大深沟，继续向南延伸到排子坪。

　　该遗址位于齐家坪遗址现在村落的北面、东北面和东面。西北面是一条大深沟，标志着高原以北的尽头；遗址东北面文化堆积暴露最明显，紧邻的是洮河对面高峻陡峭的悬崖。东南面，地形条件相当复杂：从洮河陡坡向西南方向延伸出一条深沟，还有一条更大的深沟，其入口位于地图东面所示区域范围之外的陡坡处，与前面所提到的较小的深沟几乎相连。它们之间只有一条不到100米宽的未被侵蚀的高原通道。该通道通向一个未被侵蚀的高原裂口处，高原延伸至齐家坪东近1000米处，裂口之上也发现有零散的彩陶片，但未见黑灰色土层堆积。

如地图所示，西边和东边的深沟在村庄以西彼此接近，这里地面攀升，向西南方向的高山上延伸。如图上数字114和125处，是上坡起始处的缓坡地段。

前面提到过，在数字86（译者注：图中无数字86，根据文中描述，此处应为数字85）和数字102之间的大路上，有大面积的暗灰土层暴露。此外，从位置86（译者注：此处应为数字85）开始，向南沿着断崖边缘一路有大面积的暴露。第三组大面积的暗灰土层在村庄东南面低矮的断崖上，其中一个断崖标记了"袋状灰坑"，指下面要描述的灰坑。在村庄正北，道路以西，也发现了一些小型的文化堆积。在村庄北面和东面的田地里还发现了陶片，但我们没有发掘平坦的耕地，因为现存的暴露点已经为我们提供了大量的发掘机会。此外，有充足的证据表明这里有一处几乎连续的文化堆积，从西北向东南方向延伸500米，从东北向西南方向延伸250~350米。这是一处相当大的古代历史遗址。

文化堆积层在洮河之上90~100米，朝向河流的断崖边缘高80~90米。遗址靠近村庄较高的地方在100米左右处。我们可以看到，该遗址的地理位置与该地区其他遗址（例如辛店遗址和灰嘴遗址）大致相同，都位于断裂的高原上，由陡峭难及的深沟峭壁保护。但遗址与外界并非完全隔绝，因为在西南面，有一个深沟连接着齐家坪和高原。如前所述，在村庄的东面，还有一条深沟通往一处大的裂片。但这个裂片可以视为该遗址的一部分，因为它完全受北部的悬崖和南部的东侧深沟保护。

这个遗址中文化堆积物的厚度在甘肃实为罕见，但与河南仰韶村的大型废弃物堆积相似。在此处，标有数字86（译者注：此处应为数字85）的地方，测得厚度为2.5米，在遗址南部的一个地方测得为2米。这里还有一个真正的灰坑，和仰韶村的那些灰坑非常类似。

该遗址的陶器大部分是粗糙的单色类型，且经常被火烧黑，但在这里发现了少量精致的单色陶器，上面有非常迷人的压印纹，这在中国遗址中非常少见。

我多次在遗址表面观察到仰韶类型彩陶的小陶片。人们可能会认为这些

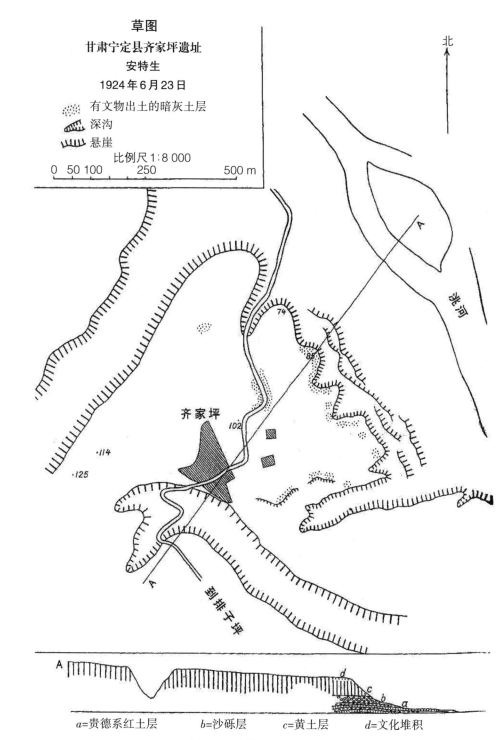

草图
甘肃宁定县齐家坪遗址
安特生
1924 年 6 月 23 日

有文物出土的暗灰土层
深沟
悬崖

比例尺 1:8 000
0　50 100　　250　　　　500 m

北

洮河

齐家坪

到排子坪

a = 贵德系红土层　　*b* = 沙砾层　　*c* = 黄土层　　*d* = 文化堆积

插图 1　甘肃宁定县齐家坪遗址

384

陶片是后来出现在遗址表面的，因为该文化堆积中彩陶是非常少见的。尽管如此，至少有一件文物是在这个堆积中发现的，因此，可以考虑它是属于这个文化堆积的器物。那就是李氏（译者注：此处原文只有人物姓氏，根据安特生的《黄土的儿女——中国史前文化研究》，应该为一位叫"小李"的朝鲜族采集人员）在1.5米深处发现的仰韶棋盘格纹的大陶片，以及该遗址独有的粗糙熏黑的陶器。该遗址可能要比其他含有大量彩陶的典型仰韶遗址略早，但上述发现（可能还发现有其他彩陶片）表明两者年代的区别不是很大。

最后一次考察齐家坪遗址，我在遗址上的麦田里散步时，注意到好几片典型的仰韶陶片散落在地表。由此推断，齐家文化遗址表面很可能混杂了少量仰韶陶片，之所以在更深的地层中发现了仰韶陶片，是因为农民在修建梯田时搬运了大量的土壤。

白万玉（译者注：此处原著只有姓氏，根据安特生的《黄土的儿女——中国史前文化研究》，此处应为安特生考古团队人员白万玉）发掘到一个陶轮制作的灰色高足陶片，其年代很可能更近。据说是在地表附近发现的。

在其中一个1米深的暴露点，我注意到一片现代黑彩瓷片。这些发现提醒我们，在处理这些遗址时要非常谨慎。

齐家坪居址出土了大量丰富的文物，包括陶器、骨器、石器以及大量的兽骨。

该遗址区并未发现金属。就中国居址而言，其文物毫无例外，均出现在文化堆积层，这确实和人类未开垦过且未分层的黄土区别非常明显。由于中国农业推行集约化发展模式和梯田系统，不同土壤层通常混合为一体，这在其他地方很少见。因此，多个不同阶段的文物可能在同一堆积层被发现，如在齐家坪遗址1米深处发现了一片现代黑彩瓷片。

以上观测结果证明：中国居址出土文物的科研工作可谓艰难。通常情况下，地层学知识往往价值不大。尤其是在齐家坪，由于特殊原因，能提供其文物出土时具体情况的数据寥寥无几[①]。上文提到，发掘工作由安特生带领的考古团队进行，他们同时也忙于附近其他考察工作。因此，他们发掘齐家坪的时间非常有限，主要目标是在短时间内收集到尽可能丰富且具代表性的文物材料。

随后，安特生将这些文物运往瑞典，并在那里编目、拍照。其中一半文物，根据协议返还了中国，另一半则保存在斯德哥尔摩的远东古物博物馆。

---

① 这批材料含34件石器、骨器和陶器，根据器身上的标记，它们有的是在地表上采集得来的，有的是在当地采集或购买。材料用字母来标记，以区别于其他用连续数字标记的材料。

第一章　陶器

由上文可知，在本次研究中，以地层学知识为依据，对这些各式各样的陶器划分年代，是绝无可能的。因发掘的文物中只有两个完整的器物，其他均是大小不一的陶片和器物残片，由此推测器物可能修复的形状，从而开展研究，这是不合理的。

鉴于以上情况，我认为只能根据陶器的陶质及其技术品质来开展研究，正是基于此，我对文物进行了分组、分类。事实证明，这批文物种类繁杂，很难纳入一个普通的类型演化系列之中。

于是，我将陶器划分为三类①，其中两类又进行了再分类。首先，依据器物做定性分类，只需要使用显微镜或肉眼就可以，无须化学分析或采用专门方法来断定。其次，依据器物的品质或技术水准进行分类。这两个因素，是分类系统建立的依据。以上分类通过贡纳·贝什科博士的显微镜照片分析得到了证实，其结果发表在下文第427页（译者注：即本书的第39页，第九章部分）。

因彩陶主要是大小不一的陶片，多数情况下都无法拼成完整的器物，因此很难对器形做出正确判断。幸运的是，在修复器物的过程中，我得到安特生教授和他的助手从兰州（甘肃）及其附近地区购买的20个完整的器物。

借助居址出土的陶器，我们能够辨认出其中大部分属于齐家文化器形的器物。反之，根据完整的器物又能为各种修复提供有力的支持。其中最重要的器物将在后面章节中描述并举例说明。然而，由于该批器物缺乏来源和发掘环境的确切资料，需要谨慎对待。没有进一步的证据，是不能分组、分类到齐家坪遗址出土文物里的。也就是说，其中一些器形无法确定的陶片，或许与齐家文化并无关联。

一、齐家坪Ⅰ类（约390片）

该组陶片数量最多，技术含量也最高。陶器形态设计在三类中最丰富多样且复杂多变，只有Ⅲ类在纹饰方面超越了该组。

该组中，陶质和制陶技术水平差异较大，为了更加详细地说明，我又进一步

---

① 标记为齐家坪Ⅰ类，齐家坪Ⅱ类，齐家坪Ⅲ类。

将它们分为三个子类①。这些子类别之间关联密切，但并无确切理由将它们单独划分类别，且次分类没有像大类别那么界限分明。

（一）齐家坪 I a 组（约90片）

该组陶片数量较少，但其中一些标本代表了目前所了解的齐家文化制陶技术的最高水平。

陶质。就陶质而言，该组统一性很高且质量最好。陶土混合均匀，且添加了生石灰（译者注：羼和料）来降低土质柔性（尽管从显微镜照片来看并不明显），生石灰颗粒在器表的膨胀效果清晰可见，器物烧制坚固（参见原著，第408页）。陶片色泽不一，在鲜艳的砖红色和各种深浅不一的淡褐色或灰黄色之间变化。器表往往比陶胎色泽暗淡。由于氧化不均匀或陶泥成分分布不均匀，陶器外壁通常会有颜色深浅不一的红色斑点。陶器外表比陶胎要灰暗，这种现象有可能出现在整个陶器上，或仅仅是陶器的部分区域。前者是氧化不均匀，后者则是土质本身成分差异造成的。

陶衣。多数陶片施有陶衣（参见原著，第407页）。陶衣通常是淡黄色，和陶器本身颜色相近，有时甚至无法确定是否有陶衣。有些情况下（如图版1中图2）陶衣的厚度不一，导致器表斑斑点点。如此，陶衣最薄的地方陶器本身的颜色就清晰可见了。有十几片陶片有较厚的白色陶衣，使其与该组其他陶片格格不入。这些陶片的陶衣太厚，下面的器表完全被覆盖了（图版1中图6）。器物厚度不一，平均约4毫米，测量到的最大厚度为7毫米。

器形。该组以及下一组器物中，漏斗状双锥形长颈陶罐最普遍、最典型，且有两种变体。第一种，器身由两个椎体相接而成（类型1A）；第二种，罐身轮廓略圆（类型1B）。罐颈高4～7厘米，且和上腹部一样光滑，通常饰同心线纹，且清晰可辨（参见原著第406页）。器口有时倾斜（图版1中图2），个别器物器口外侈（图版1中图4）。器腹中部有两个对称的短器耳，下腹部则通常有席纹或篮纹（参见原著，第411页；译者注：原著所说的绳纹、篮纹、席纹实际上是指绳索、篮筐、席子在陶器表面留下的印迹，本书翻译时按国内统一表述，译为"××纹"），但也有光滑无纹饰的（图版1中图6）。带圈足器底，器底底面偶尔有编织纹（图版2中图12）。该组器物类似于所购买器物中的较大者（见图版21和图版22），但有2片是器物上腹部的陶片，似乎来自非常大的标本。

除此之外，有3片宽碗陶片也属于这一组器物（图版1中图1），环形器口。

① 遗憾的是，未能按照设想的清晰程度，在图版中显示二次分类类别的质量差异。

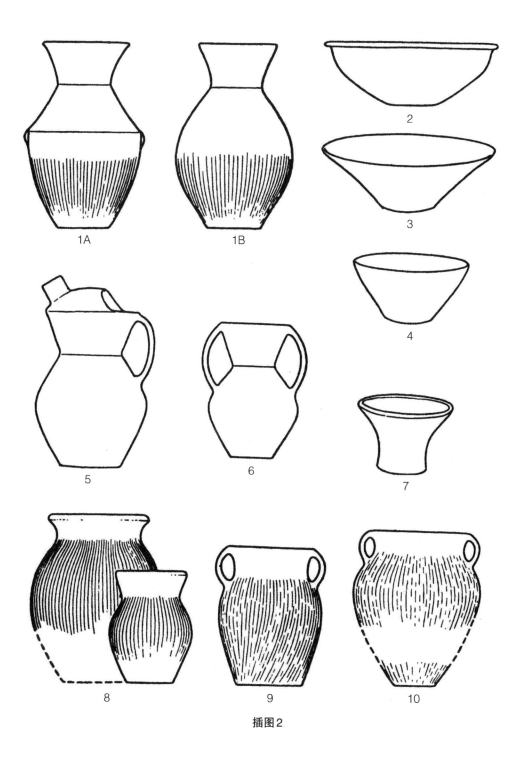

插图2

据其技术推测，这些器物必定是该居址出土的最完美的器物。内部光滑，完工良好，饰同心条纹，这和粗糙的碗体下侧形成对比。下侧刮痕和褶皱很明显。因只有靠近器口的陶片，不好确定器物是否有器底，但考虑Ⅰ类的其他陶片均有器底，推测它们也该有器底（类型2）。

该组还有一片器口外侈的陶片，可能是一个宽陶碗的陶片（图版2中图4）。内部做工精细，部分薄边折叠并贴于下方，且有篮纹①（类型3）。

图版2中图2和图版2中图3是两片器口，二者都带有较明显的器颈。前者器口实际边缘显然是扁平的，腹部较宽。后者只留有短颈和宽边，器颈向器身过渡处刻有一条方格纹带。器腹形状不好确定，但或许是Ⅰ类中较普遍的双耳罐（译者注：安弗拉）种类。

器颈陶片（图版1中图3）器形和质量均最精致。器颈和器身相接处，有凸起的编织带纹，陶器外壁施一层白陶衣，但和上文讨论的白陶衣不一样。

这一组还有3片宽大的环状器耳陶片（图版1中图11至图13），其中2片（图11和图13）属于淡白陶，其陶胎颜色较深，材质可能是白泥。器耳外侧有刻纹，图版1中图13有装过器耳的痕迹，是在器物毛坯制作好后、器形还未固化的时候固定在器壁和器耳之间的，因为器耳外部的纹饰上有手指印，和器耳固定的位置在同一高度。第三个器耳（图版1中图12）呈淡黄红色，且外侧有平行刻纹。这些器耳，至少图版1中图13，很可能是拱形器口陶盉系列，类似于图版22中图5。应该注意的是，这些陶器与其他陶器明显有差异，虽然并无充分的理由证明这些器耳不属于齐家文物。

（二）齐家坪Ⅰb组（约245片）

Ⅰb组是Ⅰ类中陶片含量最多的一组，器形和纹饰与Ⅰa组相似，但技术较为粗糙，比不上前一组。

陶质。陶器土质相对较好，黄土含量高，石灰石含量相当丰富，因添加了碱性长石和石英石，从而降低了土质的柔性。烧制温度比前一组低，色泽与Ⅰa组相同，但和Ⅰa组相比，砖红色色调运用不那么泛化。器物外部条带纹和火烧状也和Ⅰa组一样。

约50片陶片上有陶衣。通常是灰黄或褐黄色，一般都和器物本身颜色一致。有些器物的灰黄色陶衣未施均匀，大片砖红色器表裸露出来。不仅器盖上覆盖了陶衣，通常器颈内也施一层薄陶衣，但有时只在口沿周围。有些器物内部也有一

① 图2是在远东古物博物馆保存的出土于河南仰韶村的两个同类型陶碗的辅助下修复的器形（K.6417和K.6247）。

层陶衣，宽口浅碗尤为明显。

　　器形。这一组器形与上一组区别不大，但制作时器形工艺不精。未发现类型2和类型3的陶片。而且，该组出现了新的器形，但出现最多的代表性的器形还是漏斗状器颈双锥形器腹或圆腹陶罐，器耳置于腹部中部（类型1A和类型1B）。它们在该组中的变体比前一组多得多。从器口和器底的尺寸来看，这些陶罐中有一些体积相当大，器口通常很宽。直径平均15厘米，有一个器口口径的剖面直径达23厘米。罐颈一般7～8厘米高，但也有器颈更高或较低的。器颈向上扩，上延呈漏斗状。器口边沿偶尔倾斜。器颈或许毫无痕迹地过渡到器身，通常情况下，是用图版3中图2的线或带状斜刻纹来衔接。有几片陶片上出现了一排锯齿状交叉纹（图版4中图2）或斜方格纹（图版4中图5），有的出现在器颈与器身相连处，有的就在器颈下面。有时斜方格纹两边有深沟痕迹。另一种装饰是与上面提到的如图版4中图4的纹饰相近，器身上半部分装饰双排小三角，尖角朝下。

　　只有几片陶罐罐身上半部分陶片保存了下来，但整体光滑，显示出同心线纹。双耳置于器身中部，长度和宽度与陶器大小相称。

　　罐身下半部分通常带有各种特色的席纹或篮纹（比如图版3中图3、图版4中图13至图16，参照席纹和篮纹的章节）。一些罐身下半部分用平行的犁沟纹，这确实与席纹相似，但或许是模仿席纹压印在陶器上的（图版14中图12）。

　　如同Ⅰa组，器底界限分明，但制作比较粗放，接口和底座也未经打磨（图版4中图18）。

　　Ⅰa组缺失的几个器形成了这一组的新样式。几片陶片代表了新类型的陶碗（类型4）。图版3中图5直边均匀地扩大到器口，器壁显著地向器底增厚，是本组的典型。

　　有两片非常小的陶片（其中一个如图版4中图3所示）根据从兰州购买的一件陶器（图版23中图1）鉴别了出来。该陶片属于一种罕见又奇特的拱顶类型陶盉（类型5）。这些彼此类似的陶片是壶颈陶片和部分拱形顶陶片。其中一片上能清晰辨认出一小片陶器口（参照正文插图3的复原图）。

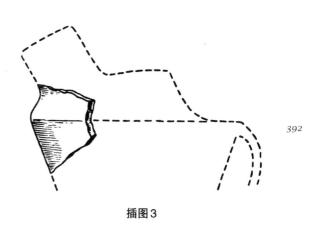

插图3

图版4中图6很显眼，因其是该组独一无二的一个陶器盖（残片状），如图所示，保留的部分有一个扁平圆纽。

文化堆积层中发掘的陶壶陶片中，有一个小型大双耳罐（图版3中图1），上面有两个从罐口延伸到罐身上半部分的半环形器耳（类型6）。罐身高12.4厘米，宽8.3厘米。从其与当地购买的小陶器（参见原著，第426页）的极度相似性来看，我们有充分的理由相信这是齐家文化陶器，因此，该大双耳罐将格外受到重视。

该组小型陶器几乎都属于上面提到的双耳罐类型（图版4中图7至图9）。除此之外，就是属于极其相似的变体，购买的陶器中也有这类变体（对比图版23）。陶器的厚度一般与器物的大小成正比，双耳罐越小，其器壁越薄。

装饰。如前所述，只有大型陶罐有装饰（类型1A和类型1B），而其他所有陶器均无任何形式的装饰或功能性的图案。而一些小型的陶器（如图版3中图5）器表有刻意抹去席纹的痕迹，这与上面模仿类似纹饰的案例形成鲜明对比（图版4中图12）——我们认为后者实际上不是真正的席纹，这一点很难根据现有的证据确定。

（三）齐家坪Ⅰc组（约53片）

从一些陶器的形态和纹饰细节上来看，Ⅰc组和Ⅰb组非常相近，区别是Ⅰc组质量较次，制作技术相对较差，且出现一些新的器物样式。整体来看，很难将Ⅰc组明确区分开来，因为Ⅰc组和Ⅰb组有部分相似，而且在某些方面处于Ⅰb组和齐家坪Ⅱ类的过渡阶段。

陶质。相对而言，该组陶器明显缺乏统一性，但共同点是它们均是低温烧制（事实上，比Ⅰb组烧制温度低得多）。陶土中添加的降低土质柔性的物质，其数量和性质都参差不齐，但整体上添加量比Ⅰb组要多。该组陶器和前几组相比，色度明显较深暗（通常是土褐色，但也有灰色和淡红褐色）。

陶衣。只有几个陶片有陶衣，这里是灰黄色陶衣。

器形。用为数不多的陶片，只能修复出几个器形。

有3片颈部陶片（图版5中图1至图3）与陶罐形状相似（类型1），这种陶罐在前几组中非常普遍，但其装饰不同且尺寸极大，属于另一类，在罗汉堂文化中常见[①]。图版5中图2颈部相对较低（33毫米），器口口沿稍外侈。器颈与器身相接处是方格刻纹附加堆纹带。图版5中图1有刻十字纹带。图版5中图3与其类似，但是这里的双排十字纹，形成一种方格纹，且两边各有一条浅沟（上面提到的大

---

① 这些陶片与罗汉堂遗址的一件超大型瓮非常相似，见图版25中图2。

双耳罐种类，只留下一两片器身陶片，一片器底陶片，以及几片较典型的低、宽双耳罐的耳部陶片）。

此外，这一组器物中还有一些上面提到的类型4陶碗的陶片。

图版5中图10所示是一个陶器的口沿陶片，很难判断其原来的尺寸和器形。但是可以推测，陶器尺寸很大，器形较直，类似花盆，敛口。陶器外侧装饰一种编织纹。如果我们的修复无误，那么这就是齐家文化的一种新的器形。

还有若干圈足小陶碗（类型7），也是新器形。图版5中图4所示标本高5.5厘米，内外都有红色痕迹。从形状来看，这些陶碗似曾用作油灯。这一假设得到了证实，因陶碗内侧有黑色物质，很可能是油痕。

这一组的另一个特点，是有一组种类、大小不一的器物盖（类型7）。直径在6~15厘米，一些表面光滑（图版5中图5），但器盖上边沿偶尔也有装饰，图版5中图7所示陶器有两两相向的新月纹，图版5中图6所示器物用简单的斜犁沟纹。所有器盖都有圆纽，图版6中图8（译者注：此处应为图版5中的图8）所示器物饰有编织刻纹。图版15中图6所示的大型圆纽也有类似装饰，可能是该组的器盖陶片。

最后，我们可以参照齐家坪Ⅰc组中3枚圈足陶片（图版15中图7）和1个小型陶鬲足（图版15中图8）。

装饰。该组有两种装饰：刻纹和附加堆纹。从上文推测，刻纹出现在器颈部，标记器颈向器身的过渡（图版5中图1和图3）。刻纹也是器盖边缘的修饰。应该注意，刻纹总是出现在上侧，说明该器物是器盖，而并非上文所推测的小陶碗。

刻纹和附加堆纹同时出现在图版5中图2的器物上，颈部有一圈宽带，上面有方格刻纹。

最后，图版5中图11所示的陶片必须归到带有附加堆纹的陶器中，它和我们的齐家研究有重要关联。我们在短宽类器耳上发现了盘旋而上的蛇形附加堆纹。在其中一个边沿破损处，有蛇头标记的附加堆纹，表明蛇头的方向。从陶片的外部来看，这明显应该放在上面。深印迹标出了蛇身曲线，这样就显出了爬行动物的蜿蜒形态。

一种难以辨别的编织纹出现在另一个相同形状的器耳上（如图版5中图9）。这或许是另一种装饰。

纯席纹和类似纹饰出现在一些陶碗陶片上，但这对于归类到齐家期Ⅰc组的文物没有多少价值。

图版5中图13，是一片超薄的褐色陶器的器口陶片。它似乎是一片又高又直

的颈部陶片。器口边缘中间向内收缩，使器边呈双圆弧形。

和这一构造最相近的是一个独特的小壶，［来自河阴县（译者注：今荥阳一带）池沟寨，见安特生：《中国史前史研究》，图版35中图1①］该器物薄如蛋壳，有不合比例的非常高的直颈，土坯经两次捏制，形成陶器嘴（出水口），和上文的类似。图版5中图13是类似形状陶器的陶片，但比刚才描述的壶尺寸要大。

图版5中图13的陶片形状独特，器壁极薄，不同于齐家遗址出土文物。但没有其他证据的话，还不足以将其排除到齐家文化之外。因此，这些陶片最适合与齐家坪Ⅰc组一起分组处理。

（四）齐家坪Ⅰ类增补

该类中有些文物并非陶器残片，很难将其归入相应的陶片细分类中，因此，这里单独探讨。

图版15中图2是一片动物雕塑，破损相当严重，除了主体部分，颈部和腿部也有残余。

此外，还有6个烧过的黏土球（图版15中图3）。其用途不详，可能用于研磨颜料或类似功用。

图版15中图1是个带孔的块状物，孔未穿过中心，不太可能是纺轮。另外，图版15中图9和图版15中图10都是半个纺轮的图。前者有席纹，后者虽在此处提及，实际上归于齐家坪Ⅱ类，这从其粗糙程度可知。

二、齐家坪Ⅱ类（266片）

该组非常整齐，但也有理由将其划分成两组，第一组，Ⅱa组，其陶片装饰独特或器物质量上乘，或兼而有之，明显不同于这一组的大部分陶片。其余的一起构成Ⅱb组，容纳了齐家坪遗址文化大部分质量较一般的日常家用陶器。

（一）齐家坪Ⅱa组（约65片）

陶器。该组器物和Ⅱb组相比，还原性物质含量较少。以浅色系为主，通常淡黄色，也有淡砖红色或褐色。外观色泽通常很均匀，也有像齐家坪Ⅰ组中发现的艳红色。相比下一组，该组器物质地疏松，但裂缝相当光滑。由此推断，其烧制温度可能相对较低。但有几片陶片，其烧制温度肯定高约900摄氏度，除了所含的石灰石颗粒大小不寻常之外，与齐家坪Ⅰ类a和b组器物高度相似。

陶衣。有一两片陶片上面有淡黄色陶衣，有的只在陶片外部，有的内外都有。

---

① 安特生：《中国史前史研究》，《远东古物博物馆馆刊》1943年第15期。

器形。轮廓略圆、颈部低矮又略上延的陶罐（类型8）是该组和后一组的标准形态。罐身饰绳纹或席纹（参见原著，第412页）。该组陶罐破损严重，无法判定尺寸，但似乎比齐家坪Ⅰ类（类型1A和类型1B）的罐要小，颈部要低，且罐身全部饰有席纹或绳纹。

罐颈高度各不相同，平均约3厘米，通常素面，也有带纹饰的。

极个别陶罐有器耳。图版6中图3有一个不完整的器耳，几乎无实用价值。

有4片器口陶片（图版7中图3至图5）显示出一种新的陶器，但现在很难估计该器物的完整样式。从陶片轮廓推断，该陶器侧面笔直，可能像花盆。所有器物口沿都很厚实（参见图版7中图3），也都有纹饰。

图版6中图1是另一种新型的复杂陶器。器物口沿内侧有一个宽凹槽，大概是放器盖的。该器物装有器嘴，且器嘴与凹槽的环线部分相交。因此，如果此处要安装器盖，就必须切除相应的凹槽。口沿下有一个环形的器耳。紧挨口沿处十分光滑，且开始出现绳纹，绳纹顶部饰有新月形脊边。

最后，权宜过后，将一堆11片陶片（图版8中图4至图9）整个放在了这一组，但其中有两片处于该组和Ⅱb组之间。这些陶器因被特殊处理过，所以放在一起，归为一组①。它们在烧制之前，整个或部分器身被薄薄的切割工具切开。断裂处有光滑的切痕，可以清楚地看到这把"刀子"是如何切过湿黏土的（图版8中图5和图7）。从所示陶器，可以清楚地观察到器具的尖端是如何沿着器身和底座的界线，一次次地从两边向下切割（图版8中图4），最终穿过底座内壁。底座外壁未被穿透，但有粗糙的断裂痕，由此推测，该器物可能后来断裂为两半。有9片陶片，都是内侧断裂。图示口沿陶片，切面在外面（图版8中图6）。另一片器底陶片，正穿器壁切开（图版8中图8）。还有一片最常见的器底陶片，最初被误切，随后得到修正，但最初的切痕未作细致抹平处理（图版8中图9）。除了一片陶片有轻微隆起（图版8中图6），其他的表面轮廓都是平直的。此外，所有陶片外壁都覆有绳纹，有些绳纹沿器壁向上，甚至超过扁平的器物口沿。图版8中图6所示陶片有类似弧状的器口。

这些器物的用途始终是个问题，下面会给出一两种假设。陶形笔直，必定与器物用途有关。如上所述，这些陶器被切割成两半，这两部分可能是装在一起，作为模具组合使用；如果是这样，里面会随意覆上草纤维、草、草席或绳索、绳索做的粗糙编织袋（参见制作技术细节那一节）。另外，也不排除该组器物与某种仪式习俗有关，比如陶器的切口能使其在仪式上更容易被破坏。我认

①河南仰韶村也出土了一片类似的带器耳的灰陶片（K.6446）。

为这不太可能，因为这些器物出土于居址，况且齐家人的丧葬习俗如何，我们并不知晓。需要指出的是，这些不可能是装有木质或类似木质材料隔板的双腔陶器的陶片，因为切口的宽度不足以插入隔板，而且，有一片陶片其切割面在外面。

装饰。该组纹饰仅限于器口和器颈部，或器颈和器身相接处，大多是刻棒雕成的刻痕或纹饰。单独作为纹饰的附加堆纹并不常见。刻纹部分是交叉纹带（图版7中图1），或呈斜沟状（图版7中图2）。这些纹饰也可以和附加堆纹带结合（图版7中图7和图9）。以上装饰在齐家坪 I 类中也有发现，但图版7中图4的口沿装饰独属于齐家坪 II 类。这里器物边缘有刻划棒的刻痕，使器边有了波浪纹。类似式样在图版7中图3和图5也出现了。

附加堆纹边缘呈锯齿状。有一个陶片，其器物口沿上有锯齿边附加堆纹，而图版7中图10附加堆纹则下行到颈部。图版7中图1所示陶片口沿正下方能看到一副点缀着菱形花纹的精美附加堆纹。

该组有一两片陶片制作时留下的纹饰起到装饰作用。图版7中图4纹饰极度简易，器口正下方被刻意抹平了，显得较为光滑。图版7中图2和图5采用了同样的思路，绳纹带被犁沟纹或线条截断。这些图形结构作为装饰纹路被保留了下来。

（二）齐家坪 II b 组（约201片）

该组囊括了齐家坪遗址大部分最粗糙的陶器。

陶质。制作这种陶器的黏土中混合了沙粒，土质柔性大大降低。器壁内侧能够清楚地看到沙粒，外壁则偶尔也能看到。剖面呈层理状纵向分布。一些陶片似乎由多层不同黏土制作而成。颜色多呈土褐色或土灰色，也有砖红色和黄色，但不常见。其烧制温度一定很低，可能在500摄氏度到600摄氏度之间。

该组陶片大部分有烟炱痕迹或斑点，或很厚的烟炱涂层。炱迹一般出现在器物外壁，偶尔内外壁都有或只在内壁出现，有时也出现在裂缝处。烟炱如此厚，足以断定这是在烹饪或类似操作过程中产生的。因沙粒可以防止陶器高温破裂，可以联想到黏土中出现大量沙粒也可能与该陶器用于烹饪有关。

器形。如上所述，该组中最常见的陶器也是陶罐，轮廓略圆，颈部低矮光滑且略微外侈。整个罐体覆有绳纹或席纹（类型8）。这属于齐家坪遗址发掘出的两件完整陶器中的一件（图版6中图6）。它是相对较小的一个（类型8），但显然，由陶片可知，同一种类的大型标本也曾出现了（图版6中图5）。

一种十分相似的陶器样式（类型9），带有两个从口沿延伸到器身上部的宽短

398

器耳。器身和器耳外侧饰有绳纹。在齐家坪遗址中只发现该类型的陶片（图版 8 中图 2），但与齐家密切关联的辛店丙址中，发现了相当完备的标本（参见原著，第 419 页）。这个陶罐，在图版 20 中图 5 有过说明，但尺寸相对较小。

　　另外，有一个小型陶碗，其厚度大，沙砾含量较高，和大量家用的厚实又匀称的陶碗不同，因此必须放在这一组。该陶碗有圈足（图版 5 中图 14）且足上饰有倾斜凹痕，与齐家坪 I 类中的小陶碗类型（类型 4）不同。

　　图版 8 中图 3 是个厚边器口陶片，可能是演变自辛店丙址的器物种类，参见原著的第 419 页和图版 20 中图 1。该陶器尺寸一定很大，器壁笔直，且可能向上延伸（正文插图 4 是修复图）。

插图 4

　　该组还包括 3 片三足陶器的陶片。图版 7 中图 16 是个实心器足，实心外面还包裹一层泥片，泥片上有席纹。另一片（图版 7 中图 14）是一个三足陶器的器足与器身相接的部分，外侧饰有柳编工艺留下的篮纹。

　　图版 7 中图 13 的器口陶片，其篮纹和陶器与上文描述的三足陶器的陶片非常相似，但这些相似点不足以证明它们是同一件器物。

　　最后，还要提到两片穿孔器底（图版 7 中图 18）。孔内边缘不平，说明是用工具从外部刺穿制成的。这些陶器器身饰有绳纹。安特生教授在《中华远古之文化》（第 61 页）一书中解释了它们的用途，推测是与三足陶鬲一起用来蒸煮食物，也可能用作火盆。

　　本章中，我们还会探讨两片带有牢固器耳的大型陶器器身陶片（图版 7 中图 6）。两片陶片构成的陶器比较相似，因此它们有可能来自同一个陶器。我们不知道该陶器完整时的样子，只知道安装器耳的部位被打断，器身上半部分可能很光滑，下半部分则有精细的席纹。在灰嘴居址也发现大量相似类型的陶片，它们彼此形状相似，陶质和席纹也相似。它们和其余材料区别不大，地层学数据也无区别，因此不需要分类。

三、齐家坪 III 类（大约 93 片）

　　该组陶片数量少但统一性高，其纹饰、器形、技术质量和陶质都与前一组区别明显。

陶质。根据显微照片显示，该组陶器黏土中含有不同量的黄土和云母，且均匀地混合着含有长石成分的沙粒，沙粒的岩相学特征使这一类别与前一组陶器完全区分开来。该组陶器质地疏松，似乎烧制温度相当低。其色调多样，在暗褐色和砖红色之间或浅黄色和灰黄色之间变化。那些淡黄色的陶器表面常有火焰痕迹，有时有砖红色斑点。有几片上有烟炱，有一些器壁内外和裂缝上都有。

这些陶器器壁非常薄，厚度只有几毫米。器颈无手工痕迹，外观优雅，虽然最好的标本明显是精心制作而成的，但总体上让人感觉技术不够完美。

器形。器形方面该组很少有变化。有一种特例器形，是一个高 30～40 厘米的低颈陶壶（类型 10）。这种陶壶偶有短而宽的器耳，器耳从器口延伸到器身上部，器耳中间宽度约 3 厘米，整个器耳从头到尾长约 4 厘米。器底包括圈足（图版 12 中图 6 和图 8），但这与其余的齐家陶器不同；通过挤压器壁下半部分形成器底（图版 14 中图 11）。这种制作器底的方法同样在辛店期和沙井期采用过。

图版 14 中图 1 所示陶器与该组最常见的器形不同：一方面是因为尺寸较小，且颈部轮廓不显著；另一方面，这种器形与齐家坪Ⅱb 组中的一种器形（类型 9）有相似之处（同样参见图版 8 中图 2 和图版 20 中图 5）。

纹饰。该组陶器大多数都有某种纹饰。只有几片显示完全没有纹饰的陶器存在（图版 13 中图 6 和图版 14 中图 2）。有纹饰的陶器可以划分为两类：第一类的特点是带有极为繁杂的篦点纹（译者注：指花纹似梳齿所压，形成多数行列之点）和戳印纹，并与附加堆纹和刻线相配合；第二类在陶器口沿上有简单的附加堆纹。所有纹饰都覆盖在整个器物表面的草或植物纤维的印迹上面（可能
401 是编织的粗席纹），这种席纹有实用功能，如果有装饰意义，那也纯粹是次要的。

在篦点纹组中，所有花纹都是根据特殊的纹饰体系应用的，包括将器颈和器身上半部分水平划分成若干区域。器身下半部分则垂直划分成若干区域。

篦点纹。篦点纹可能仅出现在陶器上部，有的单独出现，有的与其他纹饰组合。只有两三片陶片的篦点纹单独出现（图版 13 中图 1 和图版 13 中图 8 至图 10），用在陶器的条饰上，有的环绕器颈，极宽，标志颈部和腹部的过渡，有的则用在器腹的横带装饰上（图版 13 中图 8）。图版 13 中图 9 模糊的附加堆纹上有不常见的篦点纹。

该组中篦点纹与其他类型的一种或几种花纹相结合出现。篦点纹本身可能有多变的特点，因此，我们发现横线的（图版13中图4）或斜线的（如图版13中图2和图4），连续三角形条饰（图版12中图12）的或填充刻线贝壳方格纹的（图版13中图5）。篦点纹条饰或与其他纹饰相伴出现或彼此组合，从而使器身上半部分出现水平分区（例如图版13中图5）。最后，我们发现一些附加堆纹上有细线条篦点纹（图版12中图1至图3）。

附加堆纹。也有附加堆纹上没有篦点纹的。它们本身就有装饰功能，这和之前提到的那些附加堆纹不同。一般来说，如图版12中图2和图3，它们垂直下行通过器腹，呈明显的脊状突起。它们成组分布，有规律地划分器腹。陶器中部，突起的附加堆纹偶尔形成直角（图版12中图5、图8）或锐角（图版12中图4）的折线，中间再用之字形附加堆纹填充（图版12中图2）。

附加堆纹也可以呈奇怪的圆纽状，成对出现在器耳和器颈周围（图版13中图3）。通常有个中央圆纽，周围一圈圆形切口形成边界（图版13中图3和图4）。图版13中图5圆纽上装饰有模仿贝壳的新月纹。图版14中图1显示了一种独特的形式，中间的圆纽有压痕。

另一组较简单的陶器，仅器口周围有一圈附加堆纹。它们或呈圆纽器耳装饰锯齿状纹饰（图版14中图3至图5），或演变成一圈齿状镶边（图版14中图8），或呈波浪形或拧绳状纹带（图版14中图6和图7）。

刻纹。刻纹用简单的直线（图版12中图13和图版13中图11）和楔形（图版13中图2）或斜角线（图版13中图11）刻出，可能会组合成一个纹饰体系，如图版13中图11所示。刻纹也有可能是模仿海贝的双半月形式，有时与篦点纹结合（图版13中图5）。

戳印纹。以水滴或玉米粒的形式出现，无一例外都是尖角相对（图版12中图1），也有菱形和角形戳印纹（图版12中图10）。

彩绘。在两三片器颈陶片上我们发现了完全不同的装饰类别。陶片内侧饰有偏红或偏褐色的紫色系彩绘。图版13中图5b显示了器颈内壁垂直的宽线条。该陶器口沿外壁和器耳的上半节外壁上有红紫色痕迹。其他外部区域覆盖一层厚厚的烟炱。图版13中图7b和正文插图5的陶片，装饰尖端朝下的三角形。色泽和前面的陶片相同。

有一两片陶片上，整个外表都覆盖一层红紫色的陶衣。图版12中图1仅限于器颈内侧，而图版13中图3外侧也有痕迹。

插图5

制陶技术细节

在有关陶器的论著中，制陶方法往往被完全忽视或被三言两语带过，因为这一领域研究难度极大，或费力不讨好。我也认识到探讨这一主题的风险。因为关注太少，所有结论或多或少都是猜测性的，尽管如此，对于齐家坪陶器的技术问题我还是要说几句。

所有有关烧制温度等的数据都是大概数据，我没有机会做任何化学分析，但我从一些咨询专家、工匠和其他参与现代陶器制作的人那里获得很多有价值的信息。我们的调查到目前为止非常富有成效，因为我们研究陶器制作的技术程序时，不同类别的陶器生产技术程序差异体现得非常明显。

一、齐家坪 I 类

黏土质地精细，且淘洗得很好。每组陶片中都添加了降低陶土柔性的物质，但 I a 组添加量相当少。整体上看，I 类中黏土与其他类相比，仅含有少量的羼和料。

在某种程度上，陶器制作过程中所采用的技术方法自然取决于器物的形状和尺寸。提高技术能力的一个强大动力可能是制作新的复杂形态器物的雄心。

从保留下来的制作技术的少量痕迹来判断，大部分陶器的制作过程与石器时代陶器常用的泥条盘筑法是不同的。我们发现，齐家最小的陶器中出现另一种新石器时代常用的陶器生产技术，即陶器由一整块黏土制成，如图版5中图4。有一些陶碗可能就是这样制作的。图版2中图4的陶器是用大拇指在篮子上面按压制作的，因此在另一面的边缘外侧留有痕迹。然而无法确定，黏土是直接涂抹上去的，还是一层层涂上去的。小陶器的器身可能是一整块黏土成型形成的，但从现有的小陶片中不能得出明确的结论。

但是，其他陶器却采用了另外的技术。陶工首先擀出一条条宽度与预期陶器大小成比例的黏土条，然后将泥条一条垒筑在另一条上面，接口处用大拇指或某种抹刀封住。

当然还有一种可能：一些小陶器的下半部分可以用一个宽泥条制成。但从标记、印痕和裂隙来判断，它们通常是分层制成的。我们很难确切地了解这种制陶方式或模具的性质，但陶器上的印迹，有时器物下半部分多多少少的连续性印迹，证明当时确实使用了某种生产方式或支撑框架。如果这些印迹是在垫子或类似的东西上擀制一层层泥条时产生的，那么泥条接缝处就可以辨识出来。我们已经指出，这些陶器很可能是由若干层泥条叠加制作的。

模具的材料性质很难确定。另外，齐家坪Ⅰ类陶器很可能只有下半部分器身是用模具制作的，再接上上半部分。上半部分有些地方的印迹被抹平了，说明这 404 是用来压泥条的席子或类似材料留下的。

模具轮廓可能非常平直，这样，陶工就能将泥条压在模具器壁上。模具可能是用未烧制过的黏土制成的，这样就容易敲碎并与制成的陶器相分离。但模具本身也可能是陶制品。那么，上述分裂的陶器（参见原著，第397页）实际上可能是陶模。这就很自然地解释了它们笔直的轮廓和陶片独特的特点。

然而，无论模具是否是烧制的，其上面都附上了某种材料，这是为了让黏土黏附在器壁上。齐家坪Ⅰ类和Ⅲ类（参见"席纹和篮纹"一节）中使用了植物纤维或一些简单的编织篮子，而Ⅱ类中绳子被压在模具器壁上，使其黏附上去。

但是，还可能是另一种模具。这些编织材料，在个别情况下本身可以起到模具的作用。如果这样，我们就必须解释它们是如何达到必要的硬度的。有可能是把黏土涂抹在外面，但这样是否就足够使内模达到所要求的硬度，这很让人怀疑。因此，有真正的模具的观点似乎更可信。

可以看到，图版5中图12靠近底部的内侧有一排三角形凹陷，这可能是给编织物上压制黏土的工具留下的。压制过程中，让陶器转动，从而形成斜向的印迹。如此，器身完全干燥后，就达到了所需的硬度，而且器身收缩后，器壁和覆盖物能够分离，这时就会拆掉覆盖物和模具[1]。

值得注意的是，器底并非在模具中制作的，而是单独塑形的，是器身脱离模具后再从外部接上去的。器物底部可以清楚地看到与器身连接而产生的痕迹（如图版2中图10和图版4中图18），极个别才刻意抹平过接缝。一些器身光滑的陶器就是这种情况，我们很难确定它们最初是否有模具的印痕；如果有，印迹被去除，就是为了让陶器外观更加美观。

和器底一样，器颈也是单独制作后与器身相接的。特别是Ⅰa组，器颈形状非常规则，几乎是环形的。无论如何，最好的器颈是用模具制作的，形态比较规整。Ⅰa组一些陶片内侧，在陶器口沿处有三重轮廓（图版2中图1），从不同标本的相似处可以推断，它们都用同一工具制作而成。大多数颈部陶片和器身上部最好的陶片都饰有同轴条纹。乍一看，似乎是摔泥团法过程中留下的，但仔细观察就会发现，它们并不完全同心，而且条纹经常没有方向，因此，不可能像真正意义上的摔泥团法那样，通过快速旋转而产生同心纹，因为这会留下绝对有规律的同心痕迹。从上面关于陶器制作的探讨可知，用一整块黏土按照现代的摔泥团法制作陶器是不可能的。然而，或许这里是摔泥团法的早期阶段，与C. L. 伍利[2]所称的"手转陶器"最为接近，即，陶器是在一个近似圆形的底盘上制作的，在制作过程中它是旋转的。类似制作过程很知名，例如费拉科庇遗址中[3]，圆形编织席

---

[1] 祖尼印第安人会使用类似黏土陶器制作方法，库兴在《印第安普韦布洛陶器的历史之旅》中有描述（史密森尼美国民族学局第4份年报），华盛顿，1886，第497页起：陶器底部是在篮子里面塑形的，篮子内壁铺满了沙子，陶器其他部分则用黏土圈一层层建造起来，直到最后超过篮子模具边缘。陶器在干燥缩水的过程中脱离开篮子，黏土和篮子之间的沙子促进了这一脱离。另见瑞典科学家古斯塔夫·诺登斯基尔德：《梅萨维德的悬崖居民》，斯德哥尔摩，1893；霍尔姆斯：《美国东部原住民陶器》，《史密森尼美国民族学局第20份年报》，华盛顿，1903，第58-59页；亨特：《密西西比河以西几个印第安部落的风俗习惯》，费城，1823；Th. A. 乔伊斯：《墨西哥考古学》，《西班牙属之前的墨西哥和玛雅文明考古学概论》，纽约和伦敦，1914，第185页；林奈：《南美陶器技术》，系列4第29卷第51期，哥德堡，1925，第93页。因此，我们可以追踪到，从北美、墨西哥和安第斯山脉地区直至巴西，按照这种原理（篮模制陶法），制作陶器的证据。

[2] H. 法兰克福：《近东早期陶器研究》，伦敦，1924，第8页。

[3] 《雅典英国派费拉科庇遗址发掘》，伦敦，1904。

子作为旋转底座，在陶器底部表面留下了印迹[①]。

在齐家坪，陶工可能用了木块、碎裂的壶底或类似的东西（图版2中图12），
因为只有一个陶器器底外部有清楚的磨砂印痕，而且以明显的斜纹形出现。奇怪
的是，有一片器底陶片内壁上出现了一种编织纹，但编织纹不完整，无法得出任
何结论（图版2中图9）。该器物用了某种工具来抹平器表。齐家坪遗址没有发现
任何专用于抹平器表的工具，但图版15中图5修复的物体可能被使用过。远东古
物博物馆保存了一些收集自中国其他史前居址的新月形贝壳刀和陶壶陶片制成的
长方形刀。它们太容易破碎，不可能被用作普通刀具，但很可能用于制陶器。当
然，可能也使用了简单的木质或竹子工具。

应该提一下，较小的陶器完工时都刮削过，且通常整个陶器上（除了器身中
部呈水平痕迹之外）都会留下垂直痕迹。

有一两片陶片表面光亮，表明它们被抛光处理过。

器耳都是简单地贴上去的。一只手压住器物内侧，另一只手将器耳粘贴在器
壁外面，可以看到，手指印处器壁微微凸起。这种情况下，器耳必定是器壁相对
可塑时贴上去的。

该类目前发现的装饰、附加堆纹或刻划纹，均是陶器未完全干燥时完成的。

有一些陶器烧制之前，会涂一层薄泥浆，即陶衣。其中一些通过在泥浆池里
浸泡，内外都上了泥浆；另一些则用手或其他工具涂抹在器壁外侧或器颈内侧。
通常是黄褐色，但Ⅰa组部分陶片是白黄色，与众不同（参见原著，第390页），
这不是石灰石，可能是白泥导致的。陶衣颜色偶尔和陶器色调一致，这就很难
判定是否真的有陶衣。应该注意，陶衣并不一定是专门涂的，因为湿手或湿物在
未烧制的陶器上摩擦时，就会形成某种陶衣。这种陶衣是功能性的还是装饰性的，
很难判定。无论如何，这些陶片中陶衣颜色和器物颜色相差不明显，视陶衣颜色
为功能性的就很自然了，而白陶衣可能是装饰性的。同一颜色的陶衣可能是为了
使陶器看起来是同一材质而刻意涂上去的，如图版11中图13展示的陶器（译者

---

① 美国也有类似陶工陶轮的原始替代品。库兴（参见上述引文第504页）提到，生产过程中，
陶器被放置在一个破裂了的陶器的部分器底上（参见鸟居龙藏：《台湾的高山族》，《东京帝国大学
理科大学学报》第18卷第6条，图版LXⅢ B）或祖尼印第安人中发现的（《美国印第安人手册》第
2卷，第295页）专门制作的木块上。在北尤卡坦半岛，人们使用一个用脚转动的木块（亨利·查普
曼·默瑟：《尤卡坦半岛的山洞》，费城，1896）。类似的程序方法今天在南美印第安人中也有（林
奈：《南美陶器技术》，第9页）。

注：此处参照实物图应为图版12中图13；可能是当地罕见的白泥①）。

从这些陶器通常具有的深砖红色和坚硬的质地来判断，它们无疑是在封闭的烧窑内高温下通过通风调节温度来烧制的，其结果是发生了氧化。最硬的陶器的烧制温度可能在900摄氏度至1000摄氏度，无论如何，超不过1000摄氏度。当然，不同的陶器烧制温度是不同的，但平均温度无疑是900摄氏度或略低于900摄氏度。空气供应不规律，氧化过程有时不均匀，有时甚至完全停止，导致可能出现去氧化现象。有些彩陶片的条纹带中就能看出这种变化，这在前面提到过（参见原著，第388页）。陶器表层的艳红色也是空气不连续导致的，当然，这是烧窑建造有缺陷引起的。我们对于烧窑仍然一无所知，但可以设想它是非常原始的——如模仿木炭烟囱的样子（参见L.弗兰切特：《原始陶瓷制作术》，巴黎，1911）。

二、齐家坪Ⅱ类

该类和Ⅰ类相比，其采用的技术过程似乎没有本质上的区别，陶器制作的基本原理是相同的。该类黏土中通常有丰富的沙砾混合物，气孔多，尤其Ⅱb组，断裂处外观呈灰色。

虽然这里和前一组一样，陶器是在模具或用于支撑的篮筐内制作的，与Ⅰ类相反，Ⅱ类中，模具或篮筐在整个陶器外部留下了印迹。这些印迹（后文探讨）和Ⅰ类完全不同。

此处讨论的这一类充分证明这些陶器是泥片贴筑法制作的。从类型学出发，图版6中图4是Ⅰ类和Ⅱ类之间的陶器形态。该陶片内侧有一个长35毫米的水平裂缝，代表两泥片层之间的裂隙。现在这一片泥片厚度似乎不超过25～30毫米。从内侧看，裂隙明显不是沿器壁水平延伸的，而是斜向下的。但是，这个孤例提供的证据还不足以证明这一推断的正确性，即泥片与泥片相连接的表面是以某种方式相贴合的，尽管通常可能都是这样，因为这促进了泥片与泥片之间的连接。任何情况下，相邻泥片一定是相互推挤在一起的，这或许产生了上述裂痕。其中一个裂成两半的陶器，同样在两层泥片之间出现裂隙（图版8中图7），但这种情况下，裂隙是水平穿过器壁的。辛店丙址中收集到的与Ⅱ类相关的标本，为这种制陶方法提供了进一步的证据。我们在一个陶器内侧（图版20中图1）发现了长130毫米的直口裂隙。这个异常大的陶器似乎是用60毫米厚的泥片贴筑起来的，

① 阿恩在河南发现的彩绘陶器上也发现了类似的仿造。《河南石器时代之着色陶器》，《中国古生物志》，第1号第2册，北京，1925，第15页。

从而进一步证实泥片高度与陶器的大小成正比的理论。

Ⅱ类陶器和前面的类别不同，其器颈有时也是从外部贴附上去的。这在图版8中图1清楚可见，该图中，器颈和器身连接处未经细心挤压处理。图版10中图1和图版9中图2说明，该器颈陶片是在陶器还在模子中时就塑形的。这些以及类似的陶片上器颈和器身之间是看不到接合点的。器腹部的纹饰一直延伸到器颈。但上面提到的第一片陶片上，器口贴了一个单独的条饰，而且通过一个深深的裂缝，可以清晰地看到饰有锯齿状附加堆纹边的接合点。通常单独做器颈时，有时器颈接在器身上之后，会将其削平和磨平。除此之外，器物口沿塑形成细长的轮廓（如图版6中图5）。器颈抛光过程产生的痕迹经常会留下模糊的同轴条纹。

少数带耳的陶器，器耳连接方式与Ⅰ类相同。这也适用于图版7中图6的标本，尽管其尺寸超乎寻常的大。黏土层的接茬口界面上，有与器身相同的席纹，这可从一片断裂的器壁上清楚地看到。这些印迹的产生可能是由于陶工想要扩大接触面，或者是由于器耳是在垫料上做成的。顺带提一下，有几件买来的陶器上，长圆盘器耳的下侧有类似席纹，其中一个器耳上面的席纹显然来自一张未经处理的兽皮。该类中，也有一些器底陶片，它们是从陶器内侧或外侧连接上去的（参见图版7中图15和图版7中图17）。从内侧连接时，器壁下沿被折叠到器底，这从底部的圈足可以看出。这种情况下，器壁上的席纹或印迹就会延伸到器口下方。如果是从外部贴的器底，其过程和Ⅰ类相同，但连接处要粗糙得多。从陶片来看，两种方法都很常见。

该类中有时也出现陶衣。陶衣通常色泽不明显，厚度大，尤其内部，说明该陶衣是纯实用性的，即预防陶器孔隙太多而吸收太多水分。

如前所述，Ⅱ类陶器普遍带有烟炱。烟炱通常出现在外侧，有时内侧或断裂处也会出现。如果烟炱非常厚，且紧紧地黏附在器壁上，那可能是该陶器用于烹饪造成的。裂缝上的烟炱可以解释为陶器正在使用时出现了裂缝。通常情况下，该组陶器的烧制温度绝对比Ⅰ类陶器要低。Ⅱa组的陶片显示出淡黄色，偶尔带有砖红色色调，我们因此可以假设，它们是在陶窑中烧制的。Ⅱb组陶器呈褐色和灰色，且不坚实，表示是在明火上烧制的，温度不超过600摄氏度。

三、齐家坪Ⅲ类

很难确定这类陶器的制作技术过程，大部分结论都是假设。

除了图版14中图1，拇指按压泥层的过程中没有留下可辨识的明显的接点或痕迹。

其他陶片显示出另一种制作方法。器壁只有几毫米厚，内侧光滑平整，没有任何接缝或指印印迹。因此，这些器壁超薄的陶器可能采用了某种拉坯成型技术。陶泥可能没有做成泥片，而是直接涂抹在模具或支撑性的篮子制品上。陶器内壁偶尔也会出现与器身外壁相同的轻微印迹。可能为了使陶泥附着在器模上，器壁上用手挤压上了同样的材料。器颈单独制作，但有时只是口沿下面一个条带而已。口沿实际边沿扁平，通常和其他细节一样，处理粗糙。器颈内侧表面磨平了，但并未留下前面几类中所发现的有规律的同心纹。器颈外侧和器身一样，都有席纹。

至于4片器底陶片，其中两片器底表面明显不同（图版12中图6、图8）。松动的器底是从内侧贴上去的。另外两片器底陶片（图版14中图11）其外观让人想起辛店遗址的陶器。这些陶片器壁和器底似乎都是一体的。凸起的器底表面看起来好像是被挤压形成的，这大概是由于模具是由柔软的材料折叠放在器底制成的。席纹从器身延伸覆盖器底，这进一步证明陶器是由一整块陶泥制成的。精心制作的器耳，用手贴在器颈和器身上，但所有连接处都被抹平了。有时，就像器身上所发现的印迹一样，器耳的外侧，有时还有器底，都能发现同样的印迹。

陶器是在陶泥足够坚硬、支撑材料能够移除时装饰的，这时支撑材料会在外面留下清楚的印迹。整个装饰设计是叠加在这些印痕上面的（见图版14中图9）。有些陶器的器颈壁非常薄，支撑材料移除后，表面会涂上一层薄薄的泥浆，在泥浆上有时会做附加堆纹和篦点纹。尽管这种装饰的背景通常都是席纹。附加堆纹由厚度不同的条形和椭圆组成，且经常以刻划纹勾边。居址出土材料中，未发现可能用于制作篦点纹的工具。

两片器颈陶片（图版13中图5b和图版13中图7b）内侧的彩绘装饰，是烧制前完成的，红紫色可能是二氧化锰。一些器身上半部分外侧（图版13中图3）和器颈内侧呈红色。这显然是氧化铁，是烧制之前涂上去的。

陶器明显是在陶窑里烧制的，从色泽看，温度大约和Ⅰ类相同。一些陶器外侧有厚厚的烟炱。

席纹和篮纹

在陶器制作过程中的某些阶段，围在陶器周围或覆盖在模具上的支撑材料留下的印迹，其外观取决于支撑材料编织或缝制的方法。总体来说，不同类别的支撑材料留下的印迹是不同的。为了有一个适合它们的技术术语，我们给这些印迹起了一个共同的名字"席纹"，当然不能视之为横线和经线有规律地交叉织成的真正的纺织品，而是稀疏地连接在一起的经线。

一、齐家坪 I 类

I 类中，编织纹最常见，其经线是又宽又光滑的植物纤维，没有特定的排列顺序，隔一段用捆绑线或捆绑带捆在一起。捆绑技术可以与梅森①所说的"包裹"相提并论，但实际上，捆绑线是以直线型的纬线的方式做成的②。有时能看到经线铺设时的漫不经心，如图版 2 中图 7 至图 8。为了使捆绑或包裹印迹显而易见，有必要拉紧纬线或捆绑线，最后，经线的纤维中会有轻微的凹陷。大多数印迹中缺失纤维交叉的痕迹，一方面可能是因为缝得很松垮，另一方面是线本身很细或是扁平的，像韧皮或类似的材料。

安特生教授在《中华远古之文化》图版 16 中图 1 显示了仰韶村的一个陶器，器身上部和下部显示出捆绑留下的印迹，很难说这是不是粗纬线，或者是某种工具制作的装饰用印迹。也无法确定这种织物是不是篮子状，有无底，或者是缝制成袋子或暖手筒形状的垫子。然而，后一种假设因以下事实而不可信：整个陶器上没有任何接合或缝合的痕迹，尽管从整体印象来说，这种假设是最可能的。有一种织物的变体形式（图版 3 中图 3，图版 4 中图 14 至图 16），留下了紧密的横向线条印迹，但很难从外观上观察到纬线的印迹。后一种在辛店丙址或购置的陶器上未发现。

一件器底底面上留下的席纹证明齐家文化也有普通意义上的席子（图版 2 中图 12），它是典型的斜纹织法，经线为窄纤维，纬线为宽韧带。

二、齐家坪 II 类

下文（参见原著，第 420 页）提到的陶器是 I 类和 II 类之间的一个过渡形式，其席纹较粗糙且覆盖整个器身，但明显与 I 类（图版 6 中图 4）中最典型的席纹很相近。我们发现辛店丙址（图版 20 中图 4）的一个陶器上有类似的席纹，也比较粗糙，也覆盖整个器身，但从其形状和陶器质量来看，必须归到 II 类中。

II 类中陶器上最常见的印迹（见图版 7），是大量密集的绳纹，沿陶器纵向延伸，覆盖了整个器身，一直延伸到器颈部，消失进涂抹到器颈上的黏土中了（图版 6 中图 3、图 5 和图 6；图版 8 中图 1）。从外面贴上器底的陶器底座上也有类似

411

412

---

① 梅森：《美国土著篮子编织技术》，《史密森学会年度报告》（第二部分），1902，第 230 页。

② 我们通过"无色透明胶"翻模获得了一些最典型的纹饰，得到了最初印在黏土瓶上的构造的正面图片。

情况（图版6中图2和图6；图版7中图17）。都可能是绳纹。印迹非常规律，可能是绳索连接在一起，做成套筒或袋子。鸟居龙藏[1]用来自韩国的一种至今还存在的麻袋来说明。麻袋是由一条长经线与比较稀疏的缝合线交叉而成的——实际上与原始的草席编织原理相同。因此，我们这里关注的并不是真正意义上的经纬线织成的织物。韩国麻袋的缝合方式是经线水平运行，而齐家坪遗址则是垂直运行。此外，从印迹来推断，齐家坪的针脚距离很远（参见图版6中图3，图5至图6；图版7中图4；图版9中图3）。图版11中图1a和图1b的印迹来自类似材料，只是绳子拧得更紧。这些绳纹也不完全排除另一种解释，即采用手工缝制篮子（见梅森《美国土著篮子编织技术》，1902）技术制作的篮子造成的，但我们的绳纹比这种技术中的线条更直。

Ⅱ类中有几个篮子样例。例如，有两个柳编工艺（见梅森所述，第228页），图版9中图7显示了这一工艺。

我们还发现材料中出现了用泥条盘筑法制作的陶器陶片。给人印象最深刻的是来自辛店丙址的标本，见图版10中图3a和图3b，以及图版20中图2（见梅森所述，第244页）。这两种纹饰也可能来自简单的亚麻布织物，但从支撑材料在器壁上留下的凹痕来看，它们似乎是一些相对坚硬的东西制作的，因此不太可能是真正的布料留下的印迹。齐家坪遗址也提供了这种篮子的典型标本（图版9中图2a和图2b；图版10中图2a和图2b）。通常很难判断这到底是绳纹还是篮纹（比如图版10中图2a和图2b）。

有一两种印迹的来源无法确定。图版9中图4是呈网状、有些不规则的编织纹，其材料和结构无法确定。图版11中图3同样展示了一种性质无法确定的印迹。可能是篮纹，其工艺最接近盘绕的篮子，但也有必要考虑另外一种可能性。这片陶片也可以被视为"纹饰陶器"的代表性标本，这样，印迹可能是波浪状的工具在湿泥表面加工产生的痕迹。

413

三、齐家坪Ⅲ类

该类在印迹方面，以及其他方面都是异常统一的。只一件（图版14中图1）的印迹和制作方法与Ⅲ类有些不同，与其他期（辛店期和沙井期）有些联系。

---

① 鸟居龙藏：《东蒙的原始居民》，《东京帝国大学理科大学学报》，第36卷第4篇，1914，第60页。

除了刚提到的印迹，该类中只有一种印迹，且无明显变化。从图版14中图12能看到该印迹的整体外观。考虑图案的统一性，我们用无色透明胶翻模获得了一些印纹（图版9中图5a和图5b）。如图所示，陶片上的印迹由许多细小的、紧密联合的沟纹组成，在无色透明胶正面类似于纤维或稻草的印纹。可以想象，如果这些纤维和稻草形成了席子，纬线肯定是隐藏起来的，或者以相当大的间隔铺设的。构造如何很难说清，但当我们意识到齐家先民制作陶器的过程中席子起到的重要作用后，我们很难完全否定这样的思路，那就是席子是陶器生产过程中唯一的支撑材料。但可能还有另一种解释。如前所述，这些陶器壁非常薄，似乎是某种拉坯成型技术制作的。那么，有可能为了使泥土粘在壁上，在模具内侧覆了一层细纤维或稻草。这种情况下，烤制时里面放有或松散地铺放了稻草，就能解释没用连接线的问题了。

陶器制作过程中使用了模具，这无可厚非，问题是，陶器坚硬到不需要支撑时，模具是如何移除的？支撑材料在烧制过程中被破坏的解释是站不住脚的，因为连接器耳和器底，以及添加附加堆纹都是移除支撑材料后、烧制陶器前完成的。如果支撑材料是柔软的席子、麻袋或类似材料，理由就很明显，因为可以很简单地切断器颈最近处的连接线，然后移除陶器。但如果支撑材料是坚硬的篮子或黏土烤制的模具，那么唯一的解释是模具在陶器干燥的过程中收缩了（参见原著，第405页）。

第二章　石器

总的来说，这些石质材料并没有什么独特的吸引力。它们和其他中国居址发现的石质手工制品无明显区别，且一些石制品特征十分刻板，几乎在任何石器时代居址中都能看到类似标本。

石器主要是简陋的斧子和长方形石刀。石斧有32把，大部分都是残片，因此，很难想象它们最初的外观。制作也是粗枝大叶，似乎大多数用作简单的砍伐斧头。材料大部分是青石。方法是敲打石块成型，整个或局部地进行打磨。一般只打磨斧刃，但一些石斧似乎整个表面都被打磨过。斧头大小不一，最大的完整的标本（图版17中图1）全长180毫米，宽57毫米（在边缘处）；最小的（图版18中图5）长不超过84毫米，宽35毫米。一般来说，这种石斧都明显较薄。整个斧头斧刃处最宽。有一个极奇怪的变体，其上半部分明显变窄，类似把手状（图版

414

17中图2)。该类型的斧头明显固定在一个带孔的把手上，劈砍时，由上半部分变窄形成的斧肩支撑。但也不能忽视直接用手挥舞斧头的可能性。这种类型的唯一代表是一个颈部残片，与来自柬埔寨索姆龙·森国王的一把斧头有些相似（由H.曼苏伊发表）①。后者是印度新石器时代特有的有肩石斧的原型。而齐家坪遗址发现的标本太过零碎，而且类型不够明确，因此不能视为有肩石斧的代表。但是有一种颈部较薄的斧头，似乎属于这一种类（图版18中图8）。它由抛光的精矿制作，变窄的颈部有点像有肩石斧的颈部（参见H.曼苏伊，同上，图版Ⅱ中图13）。

另一种令人好奇的斧柄见图版18中图3。斧子上有一个孔，用于安装斧柄。孔起初或许呈椭圆形，不过斧子的破损状态让人不易得出一个明确的结论。

还发现了少量的凿子（图版18中图6和图7）。一些凿子的刃向两侧开，而有一种凿子只有一侧开了刃。

图版18中图9是一件石英制品，其刃经自然打磨而成。此工具或许是个铲子。

没有箭头，但有两个石板制作的匕首或矛头凿子（图版18中图1、图2）。

图版18中图2呈等腰三角形，两侧磨成锋利的斧刃。图版18中图1的斧刃比前一个更宽，安装了一个宽而略微不规则的柄刃。柄刃中上方可以看到一个双锥形孔的开端，可能表明该工具用作鱼叉。该类型在中国尚未发现过，但类似标本出现在中国台湾地区（见《远东古物博物馆馆刊》第4期105页起）和中南半岛②。

齐家坪遗址还出土了约30个长方形石刀标本，其中8件有孔。没有孔的刀在短边上经常有相应的凹槽，似乎是用来系绳的（图版19中图2）。长边则打造成刀刃。那些没有凹槽的标本可能因为还未完工（图版9中图1）（译者注：此处参照实物图应为图版19中图1）。

有孔的刀，孔在刀的垂直中线上，或许一开始孔在中心位置，但经过磨损及研磨，许多刀的刀刃越来越靠近孔了（图版19中图6）。

正如安特生教授所指出的（《中华远古之文化》，第4页和第5页），该类型以铁刀的形式存在于中国北方的"高粱地区"（参见安特生：《中国史前史研究》第

---

① H.曼苏伊：《中南半岛史前史研究论稿》（三），《中南半岛地理部门备忘录》第10卷第1册，图版中图12a及图b。

② 比林–阿尔提：《关于在台湾发现的一些新石器时代文物的说明》，《远东古物博物馆馆刊》第4期；H.曼苏伊：《中南半岛史前史研究论稿》（二），《中南半岛地质服务公报》第7卷第2册，图版4中图4至图6。

223页及其后）。

这种长方形刀和与之密切相关的月牙形刀的分布区域，远远不限于中国（见鸟居龙藏，同前文，第41页）。

图版19中图8是一个椭圆形的石制品，其中间有两个交叉在一起的凹槽，凹槽可能是用于固定物体的。该器物功用不详。

另一件物品，其功能很难猜测，由多孔的砂岩制成的不规则的小齿轮构成，中间有一个斜行的孔，应该不是纺锤。

图版18中图10是一个纺锤，用漂亮的白色大理石制成，形状奇特而规则。

最后，齐家坪遗址的材料中包括杵。

第三章　骨器

齐家坪材料中包含（图版16）31件骨制文物，它们是：

13根大小不同的骨针。其中4根有相当精细的针眼（图版16中图10至图12）。其余的无针眼，但造型同样优美，非常引人注目（图版16中图1至图7和图9）。

8根骨针（图版16中图13至图20）。图版16中图13的针根底上有一个凹槽，用于拴系，且最初有一个斜针尖儿，但后来断了，又重新制作了一个尖儿。针尖磨得闪亮，这表明第二个针尖儿是使用过的。其他的穿孔针中保留了原始的尖端。

5件骨器（图版16中图22、图24至图26），应该是用来编织的编织棒（图版16中图24至图26），陶拍（图版16中图22）或类似物。类凿子状的工具（图版16中图21、图23）功能可能类似，但也可能并未用作骨凿子。

除非一个中间有洞、形状不规则的骨盘不是装饰物，否则这个小圆柱形的骨头珠子就是在齐家坪遗址发现的唯一的装饰品，其显示在图版16中图27。

以上精致的骨针和编织工具是高度发达的纺织艺术的证据，显示了相对较高的文化水平。但这些骨制材料数量稀少，特征一般，虽说中国和毗邻区域都发现了类似工具，但还是无法从中得出任何关于齐家坪遗址年代位置以及文化关系的结论。

第四章 杂说

首先，我们要记录一件灰色陶器的17片陶片。鉴于它们数量稀少，不能把它们单独列为齐家坪遗址材料的一个类别。尽管它们与Ⅰ类非常相似，但由于其烧制过程与上面讨论的其他陶器有所不同（还原焰）（译者注：还原焰是一种在燃烧过程中由于氧气供应不足而产生的火焰）。我没有将它们归于上面所描述的任何类。

在这些陶片中，我们观察到一片，可能是一个部分陶器器底的陶片（图版24中图1）。上面残余的空洞比较独特，直径一英寸（译者注：2.54厘米），可能是用棍子刺入湿黏土制成的，棍子从一边移到另一边，就形成了凸圆形的孔壁，压出来的一小部分黏土在孔洞边缘周围凸起。这片陶片上有两个孔洞遗迹，但无法确定原器底有多少个孔洞①。

图版24中图2是另一片带孔的陶片，来自一个光滑的灰色陶器。孔相对较小（直径为6~7毫米），是在陶器烧制后制成的。

图版24中图3可能显示了一个小陶器的器颈陶片。灰色薄壁陶器，外部刻划方格纹，两边以平行线为界。这种装饰让人联想到辛店遗址的陶器。图版24中图4显示的是另一件小型灰色陶器的器颈陶片，外部有席纹（见《辛店丙址》，第419页）。

此外，还应提及5个残缺的灰白色环状物（图版15中图11至图15）。它们的直径都不够大，不能戴在成人的手上。如果用作手镯，那么肯定是童年时就戴上了。其中有4个手镯标本的剖面是三角形的（图版15中图11至图14），有一个剖面是圆形的（图版15中图15）。

最后，齐家坪遗址还出土了20个带彩绘装饰的陶片。其中4片（图版24中图6、图13、图23、图24）收集自土壤表面或购置于附近。该彩绘陶片将在下面探讨。居址中还发现了一个汉代器物的器盖（图版24中图27）和器足（图版24中图26），后者是在地表附近发现的。

_417_

---

① 参见远东古物博物馆，K.6549：仰韶村出土的一件红色高陶碗，碗口边缘轮廓清晰，带球状把手。底部有直径为一英寸的六个洞，其中一个在中间，其他五个围绕在其周围。

第五章 辛店丙址的发掘物

在洮沙县（译者注：现为临洮县太石镇）被称为辛店丙址中，出土了一批类似于齐家坪遗址陶器的材料。根据安特生教授的报告，这些发现"由庄永成收集在一个装有灰黑色泥土的小袋子中"。

该批文物包括6件不完整的陶器和15片陶片，还有一个蘑菇状的用于抹平器表的工具，由烧过的黏土制成（图版15中图5）。

该批材料没有一件齐家坪Ⅲ类型的标本，但却可以并入齐家坪遗址发掘物的相同体系中，这很让人诧异。

因此，辛店丙址中发现的陶片中，齐家坪Ⅰ类以2件残缺的陶器和12片陶片为代表。其中一个陶器明显是双锥形陶罐（图版22中图1），罐的上半部分光滑，下半部分则覆盖稀疏的席纹。

图版3中图4是一个器身光滑的陶罐，其陶质与齐家坪Ⅰ类相似。

12片陶片是器颈和器身陶片，其中一些一定属于具有明显的双圆锥形器身的巨大陶器。器身下部陶片，与齐家坪Ⅰ类具有相同的席纹（参见图版1中图5、图版1中图9和图版22中图1）。

有3片陶片上带有齐家坪Ⅰa组中观察到的独特的白色陶衣。刚才提到的所有陶片都是非常精致的陶器，色调呈砖红色或浅黄色，技术质量高，因此可能与齐家坪Ⅰa组有直接关联。

齐家坪Ⅱ类陶器以4个残缺的陶器和3片陶片为代表。Ⅱb组中所有类型的陶器在这里都有对应的实物。这里有一些类型8（图版20中图2至图4）的陶罐的标本。图版20中图3罐身布满了绳纹，而已经探讨过的与齐家坪遗址关联的图版20中图2（参见原著，第413页），器身则显示是盘绕的篮纹。这种纹路也有可能来自一些简单的纺织品，但从凹陷的深度和独特性来判断，这些印迹可能是一些较硬的材料造成的，因此，篮纹解释更可取。上面提到的罐的变体在图版20中图4也有显示。刚好在口沿下方的罐颈上，装饰一条齿状带。罐身非常奇怪，覆盖一层类似于Ⅰ类陶器的稀疏痕迹，但其器物和形式都属于Ⅱ类。这与Ⅰ类和Ⅱ类之间过渡的陶器形式（图版6中图4）比较像。

Ⅱ类中的类型9，也有一个具有代表性的、相对完整的标本（图版20中图5）。图版20中图1是一个大型陶器的上半部分，其器壁向器底部可能有所收缩。其宽大扁平的器口口沿下方有一个紧紧地压在器壁上的纹饰带，部分纹饰现在看不到了。器身覆盖绳纹[1]。

如上所述，Ⅱ类还包括2片陶片，其中1片为三足陶器器身与器脚之间的过渡部分。所有的陶片都有细绳纹。

最后，还有一小片灰色陶器的陶片。该陶片在各方面都与图版24中图4的陶片一致，后者是在齐家坪遗址发现的陶片的一部分。

辛店丙址发现的陶器中，虽然不含齐家坪Ⅲ类的陶器，但仍然与齐家坪陶器非常接近。这里顺便说一下，还有一个事实进一步确定了两个遗址之间的相似性，即符合Ⅱ类的陶器和陶片上有烟炱，但Ⅰ类的陶器和陶片上没有。我们进一步观察到，这两类陶器的出现频率与齐家坪大致相同。然而，由于辛店丙址尚未得到详尽的研究，资料存在不足，还不能完全验证这一事实。

第六章　齐家坪遗址出土陶器种类间的相互关系

由于缺乏能够为我们提供支撑的地层数据，我们上面确立的不同分组的陶器是年代不同，还是使用方式不同（不同用途的陶器），还没有确切的答案。

我们发现齐家坪Ⅰ类和Ⅱ类在陶质、造型和席纹上有所不同。然而，图版6中图4的陶器是两个类属之间的过渡形式。尽管它们有所不同，但Ⅰ类和Ⅱ类必须被视为一个时间组。辛店丙址文物形成了一个明显的统一体（全部在一个小的灰坑中发现，参见原著，第418页），其中包含了按比例分为两类的陶片和陶器，这一事实就强调了这一点。

两个类别的差异可能是用途不同造成的。齐家坪Ⅰ类可能用于储存和饮用陶器，而齐家坪Ⅱ类陶器粗糙，壁厚，无疑最适合用作烹饪器具。齐家坪Ⅱ类陶器陶片上存在的大量的烟炱就是证明。

从年代上来说，如果这三类中有一个和其他两类不同的话，那肯定是Ⅲ类，该类独特的装饰、精致的席纹和超薄的器壁，使其区别于其他两类。图版14中图1的陶器确实与Ⅱ类中的陶器（参照图版8中图2和图版20中图5）有一定相似性，但这一标本在器形和席纹上都是Ⅲ类中独一无二的。Ⅲ类中其他陶器，无论是整体品质还是独有的特色，都与其他两类无实质性的相似之处。虽然Ⅲ类的装饰先

----

[1] 我们可能在山西阳曲县阳曲镇B（K.5932）的陶器中找到与此陶器相对应的器形，并借助此发现可以重建陶器。

进，但它的技术水平相对较低。这里又用到辛店丙址陶器的一个重要证据——所有的陶片是一个整体，因为都是在一个灰坑中发现的。这些陶器没有一个是Ⅲ类中的代表陶器，但全部都对应于Ⅰ类和Ⅱ类。

尽管和其他中国史前时期有某种关联，但关联很少，且无足轻重①。

首先，陶器的制作技术和质量与辛店期（安特生的第四期）和沙井期（安特生的第六期）的大部分陶器有惊人的相似之处，从整体上看，这些文物材料的质量标准低于其他期。另一方面，从器物形态来看，这里的陶器和辛店期或沙井期的陶器之间没有明显的联系②。

其次，灰嘴居址文物最显著的特征之一，就是和齐家坪Ⅲ类的部分标本有同样类型的附加堆纹带。相似性太高了，可以说，两个遗址的某些陶片完全是同一类型，无法区分。然而，除过圆纽装饰之外，第四期（辛店期）和我们Ⅲ类中的装饰没有其他相似之处。有一个灰嘴陶器（K.11240：23）的一片陶片靠近口沿的地方有圆纽装饰，且中间凹陷（参考我们的图版14中图1）。该陶片具有和Ⅲ类中所发现的同样的席纹（灰嘴遗址的小三足陶器上出现无凹陷或切口的圆纽状装饰）。其他方面，灰嘴遗址的素陶和齐家坪遗址的材料没有可比性。

第六期（沙井期）的发现，除了已经引证过的席纹之外，还提供了更进一步的关联点。沙井期发现的陶片和齐家坪Ⅲ类陶片中精致的附加堆纹很接近（尽管缺少典型的箟点纹）；该陶片的陶器与齐家坪Ⅲ类陶器相似，但该陶器器壁极厚；外部覆盖常见的席纹底纹，在席纹的衬托下，附加堆纹（现在部分被抹去了）很突出，布局和Ⅲ类一样（图版12中图2、图3、图5）。原著第403页描述的彩绘涂层，作为一种特色又在第六期出现了。齐家坪Ⅲ类中的几件陶器上发现的彩色三角形让人想起第六期的简单几何装饰，这种装饰在器颈内侧也有出现。但是，这些彩绘太过简单，无法得出任何有关历史关联的明确结论，更何况Ⅲ类和第六期的陶器和颜料都不同。

有一种理论认为，齐家坪居址和灰嘴遗址（第四期）、沙井（第六期）居址之间没有某种联系，后二者都是青铜时代的文化。针对这种理论，一个强有力的论据结论是：齐家坪遗址没有发现任何金属，因此，应该将其定性为新石器时

420

---

① 无论如何，除了齐家坪遗址，中国没有发现与箟点纹类似的纹饰。

② 在未来，详细研究这几个阶段的材料后，这一观点可能会得到修正。可能要指出的是，齐家坪Ⅲ类中有2片器底，凹面和器身未分开，这同辛店期和沙井期的类型是一样的。Ⅲ类中的其他器物，其底面更明显，同样与Ⅰ类和Ⅱ类中器底的构造是完全不同的。

代文化。但这一论点可能不是绝对正确，因为该遗址整个文化堆积层区超过了500米，而研究过的区域只是其中一小部分，因此，目前未发现金属或许只是碰巧而已。

齐家坪Ⅲ类陶器中的篦点纹和俄罗斯-波罗的海带有篦点纹的陶器有某种联系。这一论点是安特生教授提出的①。他发现齐家坪带有篦点纹的陶器和北欧类似的陶器之间有极高的相似性②。

但就我而言，我觉得这种相似性不具有说服力。在我看来，它们的共同点仅限于装饰时采用的技术方法，即使用了篦点纹。就其性质而言，中国陶器很细腻，这和俄罗斯-波罗的海的篦点纹陶器以及其在西伯利亚的分支是有本质的区别的。首先，陶器形态无任何共同点。其次，中国陶器更薄、质量更高。再次，我们在中国陶器上未发现粗糙的孔洞装饰，而俄罗斯-波罗的海的篦点纹普遍有这样的特点。最后，纹饰的设计和整体构造没有本质的相似之处。而且事实上，这些器物总体上也没有表现出任何共同的特征。然而，所有这些都不排除一种可能性，即波罗的海西伯利亚和中国的篦点纹陶器虽然没有任何直接的文化内在联系，但也可能代表了一个或多个谱系的不同分支，亦或是发源自同一个思想体系。

我也斗胆反对一下孟辛的观点。他认为"在其他方面，黄河文化的人类学研究常常让人联想到早期的北极圈和寒武纪圈"③。

他认为，石器大多是用板岩制成的，这尤其能够提供证据。然而正如石器章节所言，至少就齐家坪遗址而言，情况并非如此，因为这里青石（译者注：青石是一种灰色或灰白色的沉积岩，属于石灰岩类目）标本占多数，只有少数凿子和矛头是用板岩制成的。

艾里奥④认为，篦点纹的影响"在乌兰哈达（译者注：位于现内蒙古自治区赤峰市）的中国长城上找到了影子"。但艾里奥的著作出版时，安特生教授的发掘工作还未开展，因此，他的著作中不可能考虑齐家坪遗址独特的篦点纹陶器。就齐家坪遗址篦点纹陶器和真正的俄罗斯-波罗的海的篦点纹没有直接关联而言，艾里

---

① 《初步报告》，第12页；安特生：《中国史前史研究》，第80页。

② 作为比较材料，他引用了艾里奥的《俄罗斯石器时代的问题》中的图14和图15。参见艾里奥：《俄罗斯石器时代的问题》，《芬兰古物学会杂志》XXIX：1，插图14和插图15。

③ 孟辛：《石器时代世界史》，1931，第290页及其后。

④ 艾里奥：《俄罗斯石器时代的问题》，《芬兰古物学会杂志》XXIX：1，第68页。

奥是正确的[①]。

在这一点上，齐家坪遗址篦点纹陶器和一两片属于黎波里文化的陶器陶片有一些细微的相似之处。这些陶片可以参考艾里奥的"混合风格"，即奇沃伊卡的类型Ⅰ，陶器口沿饰一周精致的锯齿带或珍珠带[②]。器颈下方有成排的点状印迹，可能是用类似篦点纹的工具制成的[③]。仅从正文插图来推断，这些陶器与齐家坪Ⅲ类的篦点纹陶器表现出一些共同特征，这种相似性主要体现在器物形态和纹饰上。但或许只是一种偶然的相似，没有任何更深层次的意义[④]。

第七章　装饰及其象征性意义

仔细研究这里所讨论的陶器装饰，我们发现这种装饰有两种类型。首先，齐家坪Ⅰ类和Ⅱ类中都出现了这种装饰，且除少数例外，这种装饰都是单纯的装饰目的；其次，Ⅲ类中也有这种装饰，且整体上来说，似乎是象征性的。这里概述的不同类别陶器装饰的本质区别，也进一步突出了我们已经强调过的齐家坪Ⅰ类和齐家坪Ⅱ类与齐家坪Ⅲ类之间的差异。

齐家坪Ⅰ类和Ⅱ类中发现的器颈装饰，如果不是单纯用作装饰，那么就可能是一种原始的制作方法的遗迹，这可以追溯到器颈和器身制作材料不同的那个时

---

① 另一方面，也可能和西伯利亚的一种特殊的篦点纹陶器相提并论。这在艾里奥上面引用的作品（第66–67页）中有提及。关于西伯利亚的篦点纹陶器，他说，在伊尔库茨克附近也发现了以同样方式凹槽、与梳齿状陶不同的陶器库克（译者注：此处指一本考古学、地理学研究档案文献集，准确名称不确定）。在同一背景下，应该提到在离托博尔斯克不远的库瓦斯基米斯发现的漂亮的、用细粒灰黄色黏土制成的悬臂式陶器，这些陶器的上部有规则的甚至是漂亮的梳齿状纹饰，部分是根据梳齿状风格的传统。在乌拉尔山脉沿线的喀山省和俄罗斯南部也发现了类似的陶器，但从未在梳齿状陶瓷文化区发现过；它们一定属于更南部的文化区。在塞米巴拉金斯克地区的卡拉扎尔，发现了由细粒黏土制成的黏土陶器陶片，上面装饰有梳齿和宽大的凹槽装饰物，这些陶片指向黎波里文化的深层装饰陶器；从同一地区还发现了一些让人联想到梳齿状陶瓷的陶器，但其黏土是烧红的，其器形是平底状，不能归为梳齿状纹饰陶器。我很遗憾没有机会看到这些发现，而且据我所知，这些发现还没有发表，我只能大胆地指出，这里可能存在一种让人联想到齐家坪的陶器（齐家坪Ⅲ类）。

② T.帕斯克：《黎波里陶瓷》，莫斯科，1935，图版10：图12至图13。

③ 参见艾里奥，同上，插图31。

④ 阿恩教授很善意地提请我注意这样一个事实，即基辅七子博物馆里（第16506条）保存着一片黎波里的陶器陶片，该陶片来自基辅市政府，利波韦茨区，上面有真正的篦点纹，尽管从我所见的草图来判断，这些纹饰排列的方式完全不同于齐家坪的纹饰。

代。制作过程中，器颈是以某种方式贴在器身上的。这种方式产生的痕迹被保留了下来，从而引发了和北欧"领圈"瓶子类似的发展[1]。

还有一种可能的解释：附加堆纹（图版5中图2）上的编结图案等装饰是编结皮带或类似物品的最后的痕迹。这种皮带在更早期，曾被系在这种陶器的器颈上。

我认为其他简单的刻纹要么是刚才提到的装饰类型的退化（例如图版4中图2），要么是纯粹的装饰（例如图版1中图12或图版4中图10）。

当研究上述器物制作时留下的印迹时，人们可能会问，为什么在齐家坪Ⅰ类中，这些纹饰只出现在陶器的下半部分[2]?

对此可能有一个简单又实际的解释：在斯德哥尔摩的民族志学博物馆的中国藏品中，有一些篮子的整个内侧和外侧上半部分覆盖有沥青，因此，只有下半部分才能看得到篮纹。如果我们设想齐家坪Ⅰ类的陶器最初是由篮子制品演变而来的，我们就可以想象得到，陶器下半部分留下的制作时产生的纹饰仅仅是早期生产方法留下的装饰印迹。

另一种可能是陶器下部的纹饰故意做得不光滑，波纹状的表面更方便握持。

很难解释这类陶器上半部分的纹饰被消除了，而齐家坪Ⅱ类陶器中却没有。这种情况其实进一步突出了不同类别陶器的差异。

如上所述，很明显，"齐家坪"中的一些装饰本质上象征着原始生活的某些重要方面。

这几乎完全适用于齐家坪Ⅲ类陶器。然而，前两类中有一个独例，其装饰可能追溯到某种象征主义。如图版5中图11（参见原著，第395页）所示的蛇可能与原始生育崇拜有某种联系。这条蛇与苏萨二世[3]时代出土的几条蛇有惊人的相似之处（特别是《埃塞梅特古代》，《代表团的波斯回忆录》第12卷图415和图416。浮雕蛇也同样见于阿苏尔[4]的古老伊什塔尔神庙中烧制的黏土房屋模型上）。

应该指出的是，齐家坪的附加堆纹蛇并不是中国史前出现的附加堆纹蛇的唯一代表。远东古物博物馆有一个人头器盖，器盖背后是一条蛇（巴尔姆格伦：《半山及马厂随葬陶器》，图版19中图9。也参见A. 萨尔莫尼：《中国新石器时代的人

① 参见舒查特：《艺术早期的技术装饰》，载《史前时代报》，1909年。

② 在中国其他遗址中发现的彩陶上，其装饰一般仅限于罐型陶器的上部。同样值得注意的是，有少数手杖（罗汉堂）下部是用混有砂砾的厚陶器制成的，且带有制作时产生的印迹，而上部是由精细的黏土制成，且饰有彩绘。不过，下部的质量和上面的印记和齐家坪Ⅱ类最相近。

③ 安德烈：《亚述古伊什塔尔神庙》。

④《内容提要》，《东方考古手册一》，插图159。

类形象》,《丝绸之路》,第5卷,1929),萨尔莫尼发现了这种表现形式和印度文化之间的关系。

与齐家坪Ⅰ类和Ⅱ类的装饰相反,Ⅲ类的装饰可以看作是象征性的,有关的装饰或是附加堆纹(线纹和乳头状的圆纽),或是篦点纹和其他印迹,其象征理念似乎指向生育和繁殖力。如图版13中图5a带符号的器耳可能有这样的含义:三角形(用篦点纹制成)两两相对排列,且和贝壳纹组合,经常被解释为性的象征。这种组合再配上可能象征女性乳房的乳头,更加证实了生育崇拜的解释。同样的三角形和乳房形堆纹组合见图版12中图14。

有时,三角形和广义上象征生殖力的图案相组合,如图版13中图2,我们发现三角形和闪电、丰沛的雨水相组合[①]。

第八章　购买的陶器

如前所述,在兰州及其邻近地区购买或出土了20件陶器,但陶器的确切出处和发现环境尚未可知。

作为齐家坪的文物材料,它们的重要意义在于帮助重建齐家文化的陶器类型。通过对比陶器特征、制作技术和陶片样式,购买的陶器可能会被归入Ⅰ类。在对这些陶器进行分类时,我们只能考虑把它们归入Ⅰ类,这一事实很让人奇怪。

上述购买的陶器是罐,存在几种变体。同严格意义上的齐家坪材料一样,购买的陶器中有两种类型的罐(类型1A和类型1B)。1A类型的罐,其纵向轮廓或多或少折向两端,陶器最宽的部分有器耳相连(如图版21中图1)。这些器耳似乎还未完成,器身下侧有席纹,但几乎都被抹掉了。如图版22中图2(1B类型)的罐,它的轮廓柔和圆润,器耳位于陶器中部,这种类型的罐还有几个。图版21中图2和图版21中图4是一种宽腹罐,席纹,但席纹没有到罐身的中部。其中一个没有器耳,另一个有较先进的器耳连接在颈部位置。

425

_____

① 齐家坪Ⅲ类的蜿蜒曲折纹不同于中国其他时期的同类纹饰,可以解释为是对倾盆大雨的描述;请注意,这种蜿蜒曲折纹是垂直穿过器腹的,而且并未形成连续纹饰。另外,还有之字形线条(图版13中图2)可能描述的是闪电,波浪线描述的要么是水,要么是蛇。同样的纹饰组合在辛店期也有(第四期),参见安特生:《中国史前史研究》,图版137。苏萨(古波斯城市)的多彩陶器上有象征水的之字形线条。

9件小型陶器中，有8件显示在这里（如图版23中图2至图8）。较为确定的一点是，我们也许可以按照陶器种类对它们进行排列。以图版23中图2所示陶器为出发点，可以得出两条发展脉络。在第一组陶器中，我们观察到随着陶器颈部的增长，器身变得越来越简陋；此外，器耳也随着颈部的变化而增长（如图版23中图2至图5）。沿着第二条发展脉络，陶器的腹部越来越圆润（如图版23中图6至图8），最后发展到图版23中图9所示，陶器形状收窄，器身完全呈梨形，颈部几乎消失，而器耳在整个发展过程中保留了下来。

我们可以观察到这些小型陶器同Ⅰ类陶器一样，没有篮纹或席纹。图版22中图7（译者注：此处参照实物图，应为图版23中图7）所示陶器带有一个蓝紫色的彩绘装饰图案，图案由几组指向下方的尖角构成，自陶器颈部和器身的分界线开始延伸。在另一件陶器上，这条分界线由于一条切痕具有了装饰作用（如图版22中图8）（译者注：此处参照实物图，应为图版23中图8）。

有两件陶器的器耳上也带有装饰图案。如图版22中图5的陶器的图案由一个形似沙漏的压印装饰和环绕周围的四个圆点组成。另一件陶器如图版22中图2（译者注：此处参照实物图，应为图版23中图2）的花纹则由两组刻线构成，在这两组刻线之间有三条装饰性的笔画。

购买的陶器中还包含另一种类型（类型5），Ⅰ类陶器中有两片陶片同属于此类（参见图版4中图3和原著的第392页）。这种类型的陶器是壶，壶身呈柔和的圆形，壶颈呈漏斗状，一直延伸到壶口，壶颈占据了器物高度的三分之二，壶口处有一个斜向上的水口。壶上还有一个宽大的环状器耳，从壶颈和壶身的轮廓以及技术质量来看，该壶很容易让人联想到之前介绍的小型陶器。

就设计而言，刚才提到的所有陶器似乎都源自金属原型，然而在齐家坪遗址尚未发现任何金属文化的遗迹。

如图版22中图5的陶器虽然从类型学来看出现较晚，但它与上文提到的壶样式相似。该陶器与其他陶器的不同之处在于它表面光滑且呈灰色调，这种特征不禁让人想起上文原著的第417页描述的陶片。整个陶器的表面都带有浅浅的红色痕迹。与上文描述的壶（类型5）相比，它的形状显得有些失调。口沿延伸，覆盖了大部分壶口，只留下一个狭小的肾形开口，在开口前方靠近边缘的地方，有一个斜向上的水口，上面带有铆钉状的圆形硬块装饰。壶身由于壶颈的延伸而遭到压缩，给人一种圆鼓鼓的肿胀感，壶口的遮盖部分也同样因此显得圆钝肿胀。虽然壶身膨胀，壶腹的下半部分却没有跟着膨胀，而是形成了一个足状的底座。另一方面，当壶颈向下延伸时，宽大的环状器耳也跟着向下伸长。器耳连接在从

426

拱形边缘突出的部分，这部分还带有两个类似于铆钉头的圆纽装饰，这一事实有力地说明了该陶器整体上是直接模仿金属陶器塑造的。

最后，买来的陶器中有两件（图版22中图3和图版22中图4）无法参照我们的陶片材料进行分类。它们材质疏松，颜色呈深黄褐色和砖红色，但还是与齐家坪的陶器有些不同。这两件陶器大腹宽口，边缘有四个器耳，圆底上带有四个孔。从类型学上讲，我倾向于把图版22中图3的陶器放在图版22中图4的陶器之前，因为前者外观明显是折腹型。

第九章　显微镜照片分析

贡纳·贝什科博士
下面是最明显的特征：

一、混合沙土

a）含沙量；b）粒度；c）颗粒形状；d）矿物成分。

二、黏土块

a）自然混合：黄土粒，有机物质；b）结构和光学特征。

（一）齐家坪Ⅰa组

K.11242：90号、285号、101号以及Ⅰb组的232号。

特征非常一致的一组（尤其是90号和285号极为相似）。

特征：

a）夹杂物：极少。所有的显微镜照片几乎都完全不含矿砂。101号含有大量褐色、非晶质、大密度的块状物，尺寸约为1毫米，其他标本中混合物极其稀少。427

b）黏土块。富含尺寸在0.05～0.04毫米和0.02～0.01毫米之间的石英砂粒，其中0.02毫米左右的颗粒最多。这种尺寸的颗粒在黄土土壤中最常出现，因此，这里的石英颗粒应当是黏土在沉淀过程中被嵌入的，是黄土中的物质（风积物）（译者注：经风力搬运后沉积下来的物质）。

在90号和285号标本中，黏土物质具有细小的团聚结构，并含有丰富的云母或云母矿物鳞片；黄土含量极高，其中285号所含黄土最多。

另一方面，101号标本含有一个几乎完全不透明且无结构的黏土块，黏土中仅含有少量云母鳞片，标本的黄土含量也同样较低。

Ⅰb组的232号标本与Ⅰa组关联密切。这片陶片同样不含沙砾，但黏土块中含有大量的黄土。该标本实际黏土物质的结构和丰富的云母含量与90号和285号完全一致。

因此，扩展出来的Ⅰa组是相对统一的一组，其特点是混合砂土的含量极低或完全没有，而且黏土中的黄土物质含量也相对较高。90号、285号和232号在各方面都极为相似，特别是黄土含量高，黏土微观结构细致，且黏土中富含云母。101号与上述几个标本的不同之处在于它的黄土含量较低，而且黏土质地致密，几乎没有结构。

（二）齐家坪Ⅰb组（两个标本）

特征非常一致的一组，特点是含沙量极高。沙砾主要由石英砂组成，但也含有大量的碱性长石。外观十分独特，颗粒多棱角，只略呈圆形。

两个标本的黏土块都含有丰富的黄土颗粒，黏土物质结构轻盈，因为黏土中含有非常小的云母鳞片，且数量适中。有一点引人注意，标本中方解石（译者注：方解石是一种碳酸钙矿物，天然碳酸钙中最常见的就是它）的含量很高，形状为圆形颗粒，与黄土颗粒大小相同（大多为0.05～0.02毫米）。

（三）齐家坪Ⅰc组（214号、265号、84号）

特征不太一致的一组。

最典型的特点是粗沙含量高，颗粒圆度远超Ⅰb组。此外，粗沙成分也与Ⅰb组不同，因为从岩相学的角度来看，Ⅰc组的沙子是一种更加不均匀的混合物。另一个突出特点是3份显微镜照片显示都含有砂岩（译者注：砂岩是一种沉积岩，主要由各种砂粒胶结而成）颗粒。

关于沙砾的成分和分布，214号和265号非常相似。84号与其他两个标本的不同之处在于，沙砾成分存在很大的差异。84号中石英石和长石颗粒的含量很低，不同种类的小块沉积岩含量极高。

这一组的3个标本中，黏土的成分有很大差别。

214号和84号黏土中黄土石英石颗粒占比极高，但是84号中所含黄土石英石颗粒尺寸偏小（多数为0.02～0.015毫米；很少出现大于0.025毫米的颗粒）。265号的黄土石英石含量非常低，但富含细黄土粒大小的圆状石灰粉。

428 云母含量及黏土物质结构也有所不同。

（四）齐家坪Ⅱa组（642号和503号）

特征相当一致，其砂混合物非常粗糙（2～4毫米），颗粒非常圆润（河砾石）。

其岩相学成分也类似：砂岩、石英砂和生石灰（类似于彩色、细粒的方解石）。

虽然黏土特征几乎相似，但还是有区别。黄土颗粒为常规大小，642号中黄土含量较多，503号中含量较少。在普通光线下，几乎看不出黏土成分有何不同；而在交叉棱镜下，642号接近黑色，云母含量极低；503号颜色更深一些，但其结构清晰可见，云母含量丰富。

（五）齐家坪Ⅱb组（591号）

该组中沙砾与Ⅱa组完全不同。大量的沙砾混合物由极细的颗粒组成（最大粒径为0.5毫米），主要为磨圆度不高的石英砂。

黏土中含有大量黄土颗粒，还有粒径为0.01毫米左右的细黄土以及相当比例的石灰粉。黏土物质似乎完全由云母组成。

（六）齐家坪Ⅲ组（729号和738号）

就沙的混合物而言，两张照片中，它们的特征几乎一致，都含有粗糙（粒径大于1毫米）的不规则状（非圆形）沙砾，以及长相新奇的长石。但有一点不同，除粗沙之外，729号含有大量粒径从中等到小（低至0.1或0.2毫米）的沙，这是738号所不具备的。

黏土成分也有所不同，738号的黄土颗粒含量较高，而729号的黄土颗粒含量较低。但它们的黏土质地非常相似，尽管738号中的云母含量更高。

但这一组有一个鲜明特征，使它与其他组有质的不同，那就是砂岩的岩相学性质。在这两个标本中，除了风化程度不高的长石外，还含有一种非常典型的富铁辉石，颜色因铁含量而不同，有浅绿色的，也有褐色的，有一部分已转变为深褐色的黑云母，此外还有一些绿帘石的小颗粒。

将陶器根据不同性质分成若干的自然组，显微镜观测结果显示，每组特征虽大致相似，但这一组却在多维变量系统中，具有不同于其他所有组的明显特征。

第二部分

罗汉堂遗址

甘肃贵德县（今贵德县隶属青海，原隶属甘肃）

安特生教授对罗汉堂遗址这样描述[1]：

罗汉堂遗址位于甘肃省省会兰州市以西240公里，地处黄河由青藏高原流经甘肃的平原河段。由于落差较大，其附近在黄河下切作用下形成了一个约800米深的峡谷，穿过相间排列的古老结晶岩地垒及下陷的柔和的上新世贵德岩层床。

说得更精确一些，该遗址位于黄河北岸的阶地山坡上，位于贵德县罗汉堂乡以西大约20公里。

安特生教授发布了罗汉堂遗址的地理位置及周边环境的照片[2]。该遗址位于安特生考察时住的两个白色帐篷后面的一处陡峭的悬崖的顶部。

1923年夏末，安特生教授和他的中国助手前往该遗址进行考察，并将此次实地调查结果记录在手稿中：

1923年8月16日，在罗汉堂村扎营时，我的助手陈氏从藏族人那里听说，山谷对面西北方向，距离营地几里处，有保存较好的史前陶器。第二天陈氏前往该处查证，发现的确很有研究价值。18日，我们一同前往调查，发现该遗址的陶器出土量将远超我们的想象。最重要的是，此处发现的大量的仰韶彩陶，是迄今为止我们在中国西北地区发现的数量最多、质量最完好的，无出其右。此地位于罗汉堂村西偏北35°方向，距离营地3里，我将之命名为罗

---

[1] 安特生：《中国史前史研究》，第48页。

[2] 安特生：《中国史前史研究》，引前书图版1。

汉堂西。《远东古物博物馆馆刊》第15期第83页刊登了现场环境的地图，该地图测量比例为1:5 000，等距等高线为10米。

我们分别在两个不同时段发掘该遗址，即8月18日至19日，8月29日至9月10日。

在地图的东侧，有一个狭窄的三角形山脊，隔开了从西藏的草原下来的主山谷和遗址所在的山脊西面的侧谷。罗汉堂村则位于主山谷的东侧，主山谷的东南部在地图上有显示。该村所处的台地与上述山脊一起构成了这个主山谷的马兰冲积平原。

在我们第二次更长时间的逗留期间，我们在距离遗址更近的地方安营扎寨，这个地点在地图上被标记为"营地"，并以此作为我们考察的起点。该地有四大地形要素：

1. 冲积平原，相对平坦，砂石散布，向下游倾斜的坡度比为1:30。

2. 马兰阶地，多险峻的悬崖，高达20～30米。有些区域，如大山脊的东侧，悬崖几乎是垂直的。悬崖的三分之二是贵德岩床层、沙砾层和类黄土物质。由此可以推断，该遗址以下三分之二的悬崖，是贵德岩层的黏土，而以上的三分之一则是沙砾，上面还覆盖了一层六米厚的类黄土物质，可能是贵德岩床的再沉积。

3. 马兰阶地平原，在地图上的东山脊上有清晰标示，该遗址本身也是这个古老的冲积平原的一部分。

4. 马兰阶地平原上升起的陡峭险峻、鳞次栉比的山坡。地图上只标出了一些相邻的山坡。这些由贵德黏土堆积而成的层层山丘，山坡上升到100米至150米的新高度，俯视着马兰阶地的支脉与史前遗址。山丘还要高很多。

如上所述，仰韶时代的人们曾生活在马兰阶地。实际上，罗汉堂遗址占地面积狭小，且周围到处是悬崖或斜坡。上文提到，面朝这个现代冲积平原的悬崖高31米，几近垂直。遗址南面和西南面的山坡也非常陡峭。只有遗址西北面最容易进入，但即使是这里，也有天然形成的陡坡作屏障。所有这些都表明，四五千年前，这里的仰韶聚落的地形和今天大致相同，而这片古老的马兰阶地正是集居住与防御于一身。

如图所示，该遗址东北—西南方向长90米，西北—东南方向长55米。遗址表土层内含器物，几乎不含砾石。表土层的厚度和地层可以通过以下几个部分来推断：

第一部分：

a.（顶层）灰黄色，质地均匀，无分层，有黄土状堆积物，多植物根系，不含器物，厚36厘米。

b.黄灰色沉积物与a层状态相似，但含有大量木炭块，和白色物质形成的斑块。该地层含有丰富的器物。其顶面和底层上都有一个似烧焦了的褐色巧克力的薄土地带，厚25厘米。

c.灰黄色黄土状堆积物。顶层沉积物粒径小，但质地粗糙，如细砂。该层不含任何器物，但依旧多植物根系。厚42厘米。

第二部分，在遗址西角：

1.（顶层）-（第一部分a层）灰黄色、质地均匀、无层状黄土状沉积物，底部有少量白色斑点，含有器物，厚66厘米。

2.与1号岩层沉积物相同，但多见木炭及白点，含有精美器物，厚72厘米。

此深度以下再无器物。

在这次发掘过程中，我们有一个新发现，即遗址中有两座烧制陶器的窑穴。文中插图6为其中一座。窑穴横断面长1.05米，窑头到窑身后段保存得较好，残长约0.61米。窑底残存部分13～22厘米厚，内部光滑、坚硬，表面有一些划痕。该窑有若干层窑壁，显然是由于烧窑过程中多次在内部重新涂层而形成的。窑底为炭黑色，窑壁为灰色，内层窑壁被烧成红褐色，厚度为7～8厘米。窑底燃烧已渗透至11厘米深，这一层为间隙均匀，砾石层10～20厘米。

第二个窑穴较小。除了窑基部砾石粒径仅7～10厘米，其余部分特征与大的窑穴相似。

此处是我们在贵德的峡谷中，发现器物出土最丰富的史前遗址。这里的器物陶片上饰有各种精美的图案，尤其是翼状石刀和直径为10～14厘米的粗凿的盘状石器。

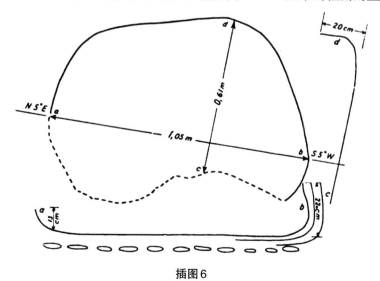

插图6

正如安特生教授上文所言，该遗址的整个文化堆积层还未得到系统的发掘，所以，除了上文引用的安特生教授的描述之外，我们无法获得关于不同地层或其他重要数据的规律性的记录，从而对文物进行分类。因此，我们对这些文物的研究结论必定是非常不确定的。尽管罗汉堂遗址的文化堆积层位于中蒙边疆牧区，没有受到农耕活动的影响，从而保存完好，而齐家坪遗址所在地，可能受到农耕活动的干扰。以上罗汉堂居址出土的器物中，陶器约1 500件[1]，但却只有少数是完整的。此外，石器约有108件，多数为工具，如长方形或半月形的石刀、石斧、燧石石片等。骨器约有90件，如骨镞、骨锥和骨针等。值得一提的是，该文化堆积层中还出土了大量的动物骨骼，这将在专门章节中加以论述。

第十章　陶器

由于上述发掘缺乏科学的地层调查数据，我们很难对罗汉堂遗址出土的陶器的确切年代下定论。如果研究这些陶器，则可以注意到三类主要情况：

432

Ⅰ.素陶，陶器品质上乘，塑形很好，外侧时有席纹或篮纹；

Ⅱ.粗制的素陶，外侧布满绳纹；

Ⅲ.品质上乘的彩陶。

一、罗汉堂Ⅰ：品质上乘的素陶（约178片）

陶质。该组陶器是由淘洗良好的陶泥在无大量添加任何羼和料[2]的情况下制成的。大部分陶片上有少量云母或石英砂混合物。只有几片陶片制作材料中掺入了大量的云母和石英砂，质地疏松。也有一些类似陶片被归到Ⅱ类，因为这些既小又无装饰的残片很难归类。

颜色。该组陶片颜色不一，有浅黄褐色、砖红色或各种色度的灰色。该组有三分之一的陶片多少呈灰色。

有鉴于此，我们应该注意，我们很难像吴金鼎博士[3]在他的著作《中国史前陶

---

[1] 一些较大的陶片由几个小陶片拼凑而成，只有一个日志编号，因此很难给出完整记录的准确统计数据。

[2] H.法兰克福指出，在有些情况下，纯净的黏土到底是自然净化的结果，还是人为刻意净化的，是很难决定的。见H.法兰克福：《近东早期陶器研究》，伦敦，1924，第5页及其后。

[3] 吴金鼎：《中国史前陶器》，伦敦，1938。

器》中那样，频繁地给陶器颜色下结论。这些陶器在数千年的储存过程中，可能吸收了土壤中的某些材料，这些材料会使陶器明显褪色。因此，罗汉堂器物中，有一个很多陶片拼凑出来的陶碗残片（如图版27中图2），其大部分陶片呈亮丽的黄红色，只有一片呈褐色。另一个（如图版28中图1）是由三片陶片修复的陶碗，也有同样的褪色现象。但遗憾的是，褪色在再现图中无法清楚地显示出来。其他褪色的陶片见图版28中图2和图版29中图6（注：3件）。上述所有例子中，陶器的变色不仅发生在表面，还渗透到陶胎中。因此，如果我们要给陶片的颜色下结论，就必须非常谨慎。整个材料长期埋藏地下，很可能在特定条件下便褪色了。

陶器颜色通常是均匀的，但有些陶器陶胎呈深灰色，器表较明亮。陶胎呈灰色是烧制过程中氧化不规则造成的（参见原著，第408页）。

技术。制陶方法似乎因陶器的器形不同而有所变化。小型陶器明显是用一整块陶泥按照理想的器形手捏而成的。

文物材料中出现很多陶碗和陶盆，可能是用模具制成的，但我们看不出任何模具的痕迹。正文插图7是一片饰绳纹的陶碗陶片，且部分绳纹被抹掉了。我的解释是，这些绳纹可能是敷在模具上的绳索留下的，因为绳索能够使黏土更容易附着在模具上。这些造型雅致的陶碗不可能是在无模具的情况下仅用一块黏土制成。倘若如此，陶器就应该又厚重又笨拙，且器壁薄厚不匀。也有可能是通过层层贴筑，再用拇指捏合接口来制成的，但层与层之间会有接合点。

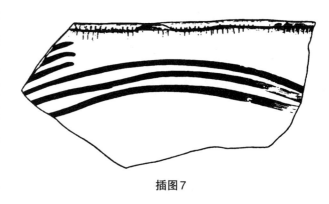

插图7

对于双锥形陶器，其上半部分必定是在底部脱离模具之后，再接合上去的。

我认为，图版25中图1的小型大双耳罐是以下面的方式制作的：罐腹部是两片不同的部分相接而成的，接点清晰可见。罐领单独制作，然后用拇指从罐身内部按压上去。罐领外侧可以看到清晰的垂直刮痕。罐领内侧饰有同心圆纹饰，这是模板在抹平内表面并矫正器物轮廓的旋转过程中产生的。模板应该长15厘米，模板边缘留下了非常清楚的痕迹。两个长器耳是在整个双耳罐完成后才贴上去的。较大的双耳罐（如图版25中图2）似乎也是以拇指按压的方式，层层垒筑制作的，而罐底可能是在模具中制作的（参见原著，第404页）。双耳罐的下半部分与我们在齐家坪遗址中见到的纹饰很相似。

制作完成后，陶工仔细地把器物表面抹平，有时抛光。只有底部印迹完整保留了下来。但我们很难知晓这些印迹到底是用于装饰，还是为了实际使用，比如为了抓握方便。

如上文所述，双耳罐的罐颈，有时还有陶碗，都是用工具抹平的。显然，在制作过程中，陶器保持旋转状态。

一些考古学家认为，中国不同居址发掘出土的双耳罐的罐颈上与陶碗上出现的同心条纹，是陶轮的痕迹。安特生教授[1]认为，仰韶村出土的大部分彩陶都是用陶轮制作的。他还认为，有一个来自池口寨的陶器也是用陶轮制作的[2]。阿恩教授也相信，河南陶器是以陶轮拉坯成型的方法生产的[3]。然而，我怀疑中国史前遗址上的居民是否熟悉陶轮。对于罗汉堂陶器，没有明显证据表明是使用了陶轮制陶法制作的。但有一些精致的陶器，其均匀的剖面，又很让人质疑它们的制作过程中，是否没有用过陶轮？在我看来，如果那时人们已经使用陶轮拉坯成型法，陶工却并未将这种方法应用在所有陶器的制作上，这几乎是不可能的。然而，毫无疑问，大部分陶器是以层层垒筑、手动挤压的方式生产的，这是与陶轮制陶法截然不同的另一种制陶方法。我认为考古学家在处理技术问题时，往往没有认识到，并非所有的同心条纹都是由陶轮产生的。层层垒筑、手动挤压捏制法制成的陶器和陶轮拉坯成型法制成的陶器截然不同，甚至采用前一种方法制成的陶器，在用工具抹平陶器表面的过程中，转动陶坯也会产生条纹带。陶轮生产的陶器，是用一整块黏土在离心力的作用下直接拉坯成型的，制作过程中整个陶器内侧会留下有规律的条纹痕迹。有时，陶轮制成的陶器器壁会被划分成几个部分。

吴金鼎[4]博士详细地研究了中国史前陶器的制陶技术，他认为同心纹是陶器在转盘上转动以塑形的过程中留下的。但是，吴博士又认为，史前陶器是通过层层盘筑或在模具辅助下制作的，因此，吴博士所说的"转盘"只是用来抹平陶器和抹除接合点的一种方式。这样的话，转盘并非制作陶器的工具。因此，陶器到底是手动转动，还是用特殊的转盘来推动转动的，这就无足轻重了。

---

① 安特生：《中华远古之文化》，《地质汇报》第5期，北京，1923，第53页。

② 安特生：《中国史前史研究》，第78页，图版35中图1。

③ 阿恩：《河南石器时代之着色陶器》，《中国古生物志》第1号第2册，北京，1925，第11页。

④ 吴金鼎，同前文第28、47、91页。

烧制。很难对烧制温度下任何明确的结论，我们只能与现代陶器相比较，采用近似的计算和概率理论来操作。我估计该组的烧制温度约为900摄氏度，无论如何超不过1 000摄氏度①。

435

无论如何，陶器烧制精良，多呈红色，表明黏土中含有铁，而且烧制温度相当高。这种高温只能在有强对流空气的烧窑内产生。罗汉堂发掘报告表明，罗汉堂居民明显使用了窑穴烧制陶器。有两座窑炉的遗迹（安特生教授在前文第431页对它们进行了介绍）被发现。

器物形态。该组中陶器形式如下：

第一种：小型大双耳罐，是齐家坪遗址的代表性陶器。除了几片陶片，仅发现一个完整的陶器，前文第434页已经分析过了，图版25中图1有展示。该类型似乎不是很普遍。

第二种：大陶罐，轮廓呈柔和的弧形，罐身中线上有吊耳。有一些标本或许与我们从齐家坪遗址了解的类型一样，器身呈双锥形。但是，由于该陶器本身残缺不全，所以很难就器物形态下任何确定的结论。我们只修复了一个该类型的陶器。

安特生教授已经发表过的大陶罐在图版25中图2有展示。这件陶罐是由很多陶片修复的，呈褐色，有淡褐色和红色斑点，部分是二次变色的。罐领稍微外侈，罐颈部紧挨罐身处有一条附加堆纹带，被对角线切口分成凸起的小菱形。腹部中线以下有两个吊耳（部分是修复的）。罐身上半部分光滑，下半部分布满席纹。席纹肯定是模具或布满在模具上的某种纤维留下的。陶器下半部分显然是在模具中制作的。罐腹上席纹出现处，可以看到一个对折或界线，明显是模具留下的。承受器身上半部分的压力，下半部分在接到器底底座上后，有些下陷，器底边缘部分稍微外侈。

该类型的陶罐有几片罐腹（约10大片）、罐领和底座的代表性陶片（如图版26中图1至图4，图版29中图10）。罐大小不一，有非常大型的，如上面提到的大型罐，也有中型的，如齐家坪的陶罐。罐体下半部分通常带席纹或篮纹，这也是齐家坪陶罐上典型的纹饰（约有10片腹部陶片有这样的纹饰）。但也有腹部光滑的，如图版29中图6和图版28中图5。如果完全从器底陶片来判断，那么大多数

①巴尔姆格伦博士认为，半山期陶罐的烧制温度约在900摄氏度至1 000摄氏度。见巴尔姆格伦：《半山及马厂随葬陶器》，《中国古生物志》丁种第3号第1册，1934，第5页。保罗·梅耶斯伯格博士对河南的史前陶器进行了化学分析，认为这种陶器的烧制温度在1 300摄氏度至1 400摄氏度。在我看来，这些数字之高令人惊奇。见阿恩：《河南石器时代之着色陶器》，第38页。

陶罐都会被认为是下半部分无纹饰，罐体光滑。但是，我们不要忘记，这些器底可能是彩绘罐的底部残存。无论如何，如图版29中图10所示，罐底部总是界限分明的。

　　该组文物材料中器领陶片仅存几片，形状各异，但边缘通常外侈，有时是环形的（如图版29中图5）。图版29中图1展示的大型器领陶片可能属于一个大型罐，正文插图8和正文插图9展示了其他器领的大陶片。图29中图2和图3展示的两片器领陶片，因其边缘扁平且外弯，比较有趣。该类型的器领在齐家坪材料中未出现过，但在马家窑材料中出现过[1]。

　　从标本如图版25中图2来推断，这些陶罐是带器耳的。图版29中图4是一片器耳陶片，饰有一条叠加的附加堆纹。通常情况下，器耳似乎并无装饰，但有一个形状未知的陶器器耳（图版29中图7），形状类似波浪状的凸脊。

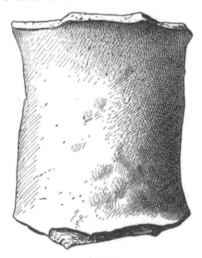

插图8　　　　　　　　　　　　　　　　　插图9

　　第三种：形状、大小各异的碗和盆。无完整标本，品质上乘，材质纯正，烧制良好。

　　一些陶片陶胎颜色较深。有几片陶片可能来自同一陶器，其器壁剖面显示陶器材质非常均匀，可以想象该陶器可能是用陶轮制成的。但正如我已经指出的，仅用陶轮制作几个陶器是非常不现实的。

　　有几个最好的陶碗展示在图版27中图2、图4，图版28中图1至图4，以及图版30中图3至图6。碗的轮廓和边缘各不相同：有些碗口部扩张，有些碗壁朝碗口收缩。碗身通常稍有弯曲。碗边有环形的，如图版27中图3，简单的，如图版30中图3，或扁平并外弯的，如图版30中图4至图6。只有一片上面带一片碗底，

---

　　① 参见安特生：《中国史前史研究》，图版56中图1至图2，图版62中图1。

如图版27中图4，碗底轮廓非常清晰。

有几个碗（图版27中图3和图版30中图1）的造型没有大部分碗片那么细致和整齐，无条纹，表面粗糙，刮痕和刻痕清晰可见。图版30中图1展示的小碗形状似花盆，是该组中唯——个该类型的陶碗，但从陶器形态来说，它和图版31中图1粗糙的陶碗非常相似。

图版30中图7是介于碗和罐之间的过渡形式。陶器呈双锥形，宽口，无领。遗憾的是，陶片上无器底残留，因此，无法完整修复。该陶器与一片大型宽口陶器的颈部陶片相似（图版27中图1），后者陶片上带有一个不成熟的器领，宽口，也是混合器形。

图版30中图2的一个小碗陶片，内部有两条红褐色的条纹，可能是测试用的，我不认为这是装饰。

图版26中图5和图6是两个独特的陶片。图版26中图5可能是一片小双耳罐或陶罐的陶片，腹部显著，窄领。褐色，陶器烧制良好，品质上乘。图版26中图6是由相对纯净的黏土制成，但烧制得不是很好。陶器形状不明，但器壁轮廓是直的，外侧装饰了叠加的波浪形黏土带。

最后，必须提到约50片深灰色或灰色陶器的陶片。它们大部分是碗的陶片或是无法归类的陶片。其余带有褐色或红褐色阴影的陶片，大部分是毫无特别之处的小片，也因此无法据此判断陶器的大小与形状。

二、罗汉堂Ⅱ：粗制的素陶（大约632片）

该组陶器器形、品质和装饰都很协调统一。大多数陶片是粗糙的黄褐色、黄色或红色，有时呈灰色或深褐色。许多陶片上布满烟炱。因只有边缘或陶器上半部分有烟炱（编号K.12003：962和K.12003：934），所以这可能不是烹饪产生的，或许是后来泥土污染了，或许是同时期的火灾留下的。该组的器底陶片外侧没有显示有烟炱痕迹，但有一个标本（编号K.12003：1120）的内侧，靠近器底部有烟炱，这一事实说明，烟炱不可能是烹饪留下的。

438

陶质。该组陶器通常品质不如前一组，由富含云母或石英砂的、不纯的黏土制成。

烧制。陶器烧制温度是一致的，从陶器疏松的材质来看，烧制温度肯定很低，可能在600摄氏度左右。

该组有一个破碎的陶罐，我们已经将之修复（图版31中图4）。这个陶罐似乎是该组中最常见的器形的代表，因此，研究该标本的制作技术意义非凡。

制陶技术。该陶器是在模具中制作的。器物下腹部单独用一种模具制作，上部则用另一个模具制成。之后，再将这两个独立的部分连接在一起，并在接口上涂上了黏土。由于接合点比较脆弱，后来裂开了，因此，接合点现在仍清晰可见。接合处上面有一条波浪形的附加堆纹带，可能是为了加固接合点。为了让器物表面外观对称，每隔一段就有波浪形附加堆纹。器领是在黏土干燥前，向外弯曲器口而形成的。器身外侧有绳索缠绕的扭绳花纹。该绳索可能布满模具，从而使得黏土更加牢固地附着在模具上，或者防止陶器在制作完成后还未干燥前破裂。无论如何，绳索移除之前，陶器上没有上述绳纹。该组文物材料中还有一个陶器，其下腹部外侧甚至都有这种清晰的绳纹。

图版32中图2的陶器，其制作过程留下的痕迹通过器身不同的泥条间的裂缝清晰可见。由此可见，超大的陶器的上部是用泥条盘筑法制作的。上述器物肯定不是模具制成的。看来其他的大型陶器也是采用泥条盘筑法制作的。

器形。如上所述，我们只能修复一个完整的标本，它是该组文物材料中最典型的器形，尽管每个陶器的轮廓略有不同。修复的陶器（图版31中图4）高235毫米，外形略微弯曲，低领，边缘稍外侈的陶罐。该陶罐最大直径258毫米，口径160毫米。罐口下方表面光滑，其他部分布满很有规律的绳纹，器身等距离间隔有波浪泥带。

这批材料中还有一些比这件陶罐大得多的陶器。我们已经修复了一个非常大的陶罐或双耳罐的一部分。该陶器上部光滑，下部布满垂直的交叉绳纹。陶器很硬，但也混合了一定量的云母和石英砂，呈红褐色。该陶器应该归到这一组还是第一组，这很难确定。其他大型陶器或许是罐，在图版33和图版35中图4有显示。

有两片器领陶片（图版35中图1和图2），也是大型陶器的，但很难判定它们的器身的形状。

有12片颜色各异（灰色、褐色、黄色）的碗口陶片，边缘设计简约，上部略微向内弯曲，碗口内敛。大多数陶片边缘下方区域质地光滑，且用一道深沟勾边。碗的其他部分布满了斜绳纹（图版34中图1、图2、图4和图6）。图版34中图4的碗内部有一层红色涂层，但非陶衣。尽管罗汉堂的陶碗没有彩绘装饰，且碗口可能更宽，但这些陶片可能和安特生教授在《中华远古之文化》中图版14中图3和图4展示的是同一种河南遗址的类型的陶碗。有7片不同颜色的陶片（图版34中图3、图5至图8）没有上述陶器轮廓弧度大。除了图版34中图8的陶器，其他几个似乎都是中等大小的陶器。图版34中图8必定是一个大型的粗灰陶器，陶器壁厚14毫米，其扁平的边缘和器身外侧均布满斜绳纹。边缘往下15毫米处，有一个破碎的器耳或环形器耳。图版34中图5口沿下面有一个波浪棱带，轮廓稍微弯曲，棱线以下的器身外侧布满了斜绳纹。图版34中图3和图5非常相似。棱带上有斜的窝状物装饰。图版34中图7的陶片上有一个环形器耳[①]。

归到该组的许多陶片属于该组中非常普遍的类型，即陶罐，形状很像图版31中图4修复的陶壶，这些陶片轮廓不好判断，且其中砖红色陶罐的质量相对较高。尽管如此，陶片中云母和石英砂颗粒还是清晰可见。器领稍外侈。器颈和器身外侧有两种朝向的绳纹（图版36中图1至图3，图版38中图11）。有些陶片来自薄壁小陶罐（图版38中图1），器身外侧通常在器颈和器腹下方装饰水平泥带，中间有一些小的对角线附加堆纹带（图版37中图1）。

虽然罗汉堂类型Ⅱ被定义为"粗制的素面陶器"，但是，我们还是不得不将一些不完全是素陶的、带一些彩绘装饰的陶器纳入其中。

有一些器口陶片（图版37）来自很精致的陶器，其上装饰了凸起的附加堆纹和蓝紫色的彩绘或刻线纹。毫无疑问，这些陶片都来自宽口、轮廓略微弯曲的陶罐。有些陶片带大小不一的器耳（图版37中图2至图5）。图版38中图1残缺的陶罐，让人对这些陶器的形状有了一些了解。它们在器形和大小上都与齐家坪的篦点纹陶器有关联：两组中的陶器颈部都出现同样的蓝紫色的彩绘（参见原著，第403页）。 *440*

图版37中图3的陶器向外弯曲的边缘一侧附有一个凸耳，器身布满斜绳纹，器颈下方有一条波浪形黏土带。薄器壁中掺杂了石英石和云母，但仍然很硬，烧制精良。厚度约4毫米。

图版38中图8的陶片来自灰色陶器，坚硬，混合了明显高比例的石英石。厚度5毫米。外侧有对角线绳纹。外侧弯曲的边缘内有倾斜的三角形蓝紫色的彩绘（正文插图10）。外侧装饰波浪形附加堆纹带。在下方，每隔一段距离，有几组小浮雕弦线，都绘制成同样的蓝紫色的三角形。

插图10

图版37中图7的器口陶片和上面提到的颈部陶片有相同的附加堆纹带，但看不出有彩绘。图版37中图5的陶片有明显的边沿轮廓，外侧有一个小凸耳。边沿内部有凸脊，我认为器口上有盖子。口沿以下，器身上半部分有两处水平横刻线

---

① 朱家寨遗址中也发现了同样的把手。参见《远东古物博物馆馆刊》，图版12中图18。

区域，之间有楔形的附加堆纹。该装饰系统和齐家坪的篦点纹浮雕陶器是同一类型，尽管没有篦点纹。

图版37中图9的边缘陶片是烧制得很结实的褐色陶器，边缘呈扇形，向外弯曲。紧挨边沿下方有水平和垂直带组成的装饰，含有刻线。水平区中心有一个圆纽。

这种刻痕装饰见于陕西府谷县吴兰沟[1]和山西巢县曹桥村（译者注：此处地名有待考证）。

图版37中图2是一个陶器的上部，或许来自一个小双耳罐。黄色。器耳下方有一个小白斑点。甚至器身表面都能看到云母和石英石颗粒。陶器内侧呈独特的双锥形，这与外侧柔和的弧线很不相符。外部有不清晰的绳纹。器耳上装饰许多小的波浪形黏土带。器颈和器腹周围有同样的波浪带。内侧有蓝紫色彩绘。由于陶器边沿可能较窄，我无法将内部的色斑解释为一种装饰，我认为这是保存在陶器内部的液体涂料。

441

在结束对有附加堆纹的小陶器的描述之前，有必要介绍一片深灰色陶器的陶片（正文插图11），外部磨光，带一个不成熟的器耳，并且有横脊装饰——这种装饰让人想起远东古物博物馆展出的鄂尔多斯铜器的装饰风格。

有两片器颈（图版35中图1和图2），口沿下方装饰有斜窝，显然和图版9中图1和图2以及图版10中图1是同一陶器

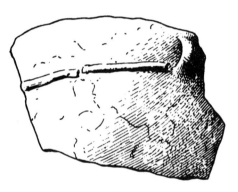

插图11

的陶片。另外一片器物边沿，有一附加堆纹，边沿下方有月牙形状的切口（图版35中图3）。

该组有大约70片器身陶片，可能是陶罐（参见原著，第440页），它们外部都有绳纹或类似纹饰。其中大部分有附加堆纹（图版36中图1、图3；图版38中图4、图9、图11）或宽扁彩带装饰（图版40中图2）。一些陶片有小器耳（图版35中图5、图7）。有时，波浪形附加堆纹形成了一种凸耳（图版35中图6），甚至凸耳上都有波浪形的附加堆纹装饰。

值得一提的是，有一片陶器的装饰饶有趣味。该陶片（图版36中图4）是砖红色陶器，表面有模糊的纹饰。我推测该纹饰是水平的，且装饰有浮雕蛇。遗憾

---

[1] 安特生：《中国史前史研究》，图版94中图6，图版98中图5。

的是，浮雕蛇残缺不全，蛇身上的黑点
用刻痕装饰（参见原著，第424页）。正
文插图12是另一片器体陶片，也似乎带
有蛇雕装饰。

插图12

　　该组陶器器底都是分开制作的（图
版38中图1、图4、图11，图版39中图
1、图4）。器底上经常出现绳纹，或者
在器底外表面带有清晰可见的真正的编
织纹，如图版41中图4。应该指出，即
使是类似于齐家坪的篦点纹的小陶器，如图版38中图1的带马鞍形器口的小陶
器，都有单独的器底，而对应的齐家坪的陶器器底通常处理得很随意，器底也
不很分明。

　　此外，我们必须注意到图版31中图2、图3显示的两片器颈陶片。第一片肯 442
定是斜喷嘴，属于巴尔姆格伦博士在他有关半山随葬陶器（图版20）的著作中描
述为"男人的夜壶"的类型。第二片来自一个中度大小的陶器的器颈，让人想起
朱家寨墓葬遗址中的一些陶罐[①]。我对比分析了安特生教授出版的两个陶器与罗汉
堂的器颈陶片。从器物、技术处理和外形方面看，这个器颈明显和朱家寨的陶罐
密切相关。

　　最后，应该提及5片鬲足陶片（图版38中图3、图5、图8、图10）。所有这些
陶片都是器腿底部陶片，没有残存任何腿部环状部分的陶片。

三、罗汉堂Ⅲ：彩陶（约630片）

　　罗汉堂彩陶在技术品质、器物形态和装饰三方面都非常统一。

　　陶质。该组所有的陶器都是用纯净的黏土制成的。这些黏土为制作精美的陶
罐和精巧的陶碗提供了上乘的材料。我们用罗汉堂文化堆积中的大大小小的陶片
能够修复出一些精致的陶罐和陶碗。

　　有一些陶片（8片）的制作技术相当独特（图版43中图4、图5，图版44中图
1、图2）。它们都是大型陶器的陶片，陶器上部的陶片部分由细黏土制成，而陶
器下部的陶片部分则用混有石英石的粗黏土制成。所有陶片上属于陶器上部的、
光滑的部分都有彩绘装饰，陶器下部则带绳纹或编织纹。图版43中图3的陶片与
其他陶片不同，它完全是用粗砂陶土制成的。该陶片的浮雕脊下方有黑色彩绘，

---

　　① 安特生：《远东古物博物馆馆刊》第17期，图版7中图7和图版8中图11。

而我们预计的是在脊形器耳上方能找到这样的彩绘。根据我从凸脊上的犁沟纹的方向判断，该黑色彩绘应该是应用于陶器下部的。但我认为这是个例外，意味着器耳上方未知的部分应是细陶土制成，并装饰了彩绘。因此，尽管位置偏下，脊状物下方的纹饰却一定是上部装饰系统的一部分。

我认为，这种用两种陶土烧制陶器的奇特技术很罕见。使用这种技术的所有陶片似乎都是宽大陶器的陶片。这种用粗陶土制作的器物下半部分较之用细陶土制成的上半部分，能够更好地承载上部的重量。

有一些无装饰的大型陶器的大陶片，和上述器物下部陶片来自同一类型的陶器，且上部纹饰也相同。因此，我认为它们也是用两种陶土制成的陶器的陶片。这些陶器的下部轮廓几乎是直线形的，尽管从器物下部向上部分有些许扩张。图版 39 中图 1 的器物下部陶片虽然外观呈灰色，但也可以归于这种类型。这些陶器的上部形状我们无法得知，但我猜测应该是大型陶罐。

制作技术。罐和碗是这一组陶器的主要类型，它们似乎和前一组陶器的制作技术一样。在研究这些彩陶碗的过程中，我没有发现有任何陶轮的痕迹。有些陶器的形状，如图版 46 中图 2 的陶片，并没有经过精心的设计。

在一片陶碗陶片（正文插图 7）的口沿外侧下方，能够看到被涂掉一半的绳纹，由此可见，这些陶碗是在模具或包裹物的辅助下塑形的。不管怎样，这些绳纹都是陶器制作过程中留下的。

陶器外侧面是做过抛光处理的。有些陶片腐蚀非常严重，因此，无法得出器物表面的原初特征的任何结论。

颜色。这些陶器似乎都是在相对高温下烧制的，大约 900 摄氏度。大多数陶片呈淡褐色或黄色。部分呈砖红色，有几片呈土褐色或灰色。有一些陶片，在颜色均匀的器表上有砖红色或灰色的斑点，可能由于煅烧过程中，火候把握不规律或陶土成分不均匀造成的。

彩陶的彩绘装饰整体是黑色，有些是蓝紫色或褐色。有一片陶片上，出现了黑色图案和厚重的白色的组合，但从未出现像半山遗址墓穴出土的材料中的黑色和蓝紫色组合的彩绘。

器形。大部分陶片都来自大型陶罐（图版 42 中图 1、图 3、图 4）或宽口碗。罐的大小不一，大多数宽大，但也有小标本（图版 44 中图 8）。遗憾的是，没有一件陶罐是完整的，我们也无法通过现有的小陶片修复出一个完整的，但如果观察马家窑遗址出土的陶器，我们就能了解罗汉堂出土陶罐的形状了[1]。大部分罐的颈

① 安特生：《中国史前史研究》，图版 56 中图 2，图版 57 中图 1 和图 15。

部似乎很高，口沿外侈（图版44中图5、图6、图11），但也有低领的（图版43中图1），即一些带有凸耳的陶器（图版45中图1至图4），显然也包括陶罐。

罐的大小不一，如图版42中的大型陶罐的陶片，也有如图版44中图7、图8中的小陶器的器颈陶片。

444

大多数罐体呈椭圆形。图版42中图4的大陶片的轮廓在水平彩绘图案带开始的地方有明显的折痕。比较该碎陶片上的彩绘装饰和附加堆纹带与由两种不同的黏土制作而成的陶器陶片（图版43中图4、图5，图版44中图1）上的装饰元素，我认为该陶罐的上部是用两种不同质量的黏土制作的。

除了陶罐的陶片，我们还发现一些陶碗或陶盆的陶片（图版45至图版48，图版50至图版51）。由于大多数材料都支离破碎，我们很难确定陶片到底来自陶碗还是陶盆。这些陶器的外形变化较大，有敞口也有敛口的。口部常有口沿（图版48中图3、图6）。许多陶片上的口沿都是向外弯曲，而且带有装饰（图版50中图7、图11、图13、图14、图15、图17、图18、图20、图21）。

图版44中图9的陶碗陶片上，碗壁向狭窄的碗口收敛，碗口没有口沿。它的设计独特，不同于碗口或多或少稍宽的普通陶碗。另一片口沿陶片（正文插图13）口部狭窄，但它上面有一个初具雏形的器领。这两片陶片密切相关，都是窄口陶器的陶片。我认为这是罐和碗的中间过渡形式。

插图13

这些陶片中约有15片器底陶片。图版51中图10至图13显示了其中一部分。器底表面总是与其他部分界限分明（正文插图14），且和马家窑的陶碗底部表面是同一类型。

插图14

前面提到过，一些陶罐，甚至还有少量的碗，都带有器耳。大型陶罐的器耳短而宽（图版45中图1、图4），小型陶罐的器耳非常小（图版45中图2、图3）。图版48中图4的陶碗陶片上，有一个横置的不完整的器耳。另一个陶碗陶片上有一个波浪状的凸脊，形成了一种短条器耳（正文插图15）。秦王寨出土的文物中也发现了同样的器耳，其中一些在阿恩教授

445

的出版物中有过介绍①。

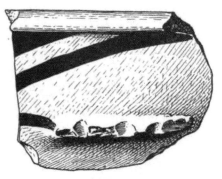

插图15

有6片陶片（参见原著，第457页）代表了一种完全不同的器耳。这些器耳均较长，扁平，且略有弯曲，宽度约在1.5厘米到3厘米之间。器耳外侧装饰有水平线（图版51中图15、图16）或交叉线（图版51中图14）纹饰。我认为它们是小型长柄双耳罐的陶片。安特生教授②曾发表过类似的马家窑陶器的器耳。

在结束对这些陶器的描述之前，我想指出图版51中图18的一个独特的陶器，它可能是一个陶碗的器耳。该器耳两面都装饰有黑色线条，内侧还装饰有椭圆形的点状物。就陶片本身来看，该器耳与安特生教授著作中提到的陶碗上的器耳形状非常相似③。

设计。陶罐和碗都带有不同特点的黑色装饰。除少数几个有杂色之外（稍后赘述），其余全部呈黑色。颜料涂在精心打磨和抛光的器物表面，当然，也有少数表面粗糙的器物上有涂颜料的痕迹（图版43中图3）。K.12003：1348展示的是一个未被修复的器身陶片，其粗糙的表面上布满了纵横交织的绳纹，且装饰有一条叠加的波浪形黏土带，器物表面涂有一层较宽的紫色的颜料带。这种涂色方式独具特色，也许和那些由两种不同的陶土制成的器物有关（参见原著，第443页）。

由于我们现有的材料中没有完整的陶罐，我们很难知晓这些器物的整体装饰理念。图版42中图1的器腹陶片上没有器颈残留，但我们推测它的器颈上可能装饰有横向排列的环状物或环带，类似图版44中图6、图7、图10的装饰。其他几片器颈陶片上的横线组合了圆点（图版44中图4）、椭圆形点（图版44中图5）或圆环（图版44中图11）。有一片粗陶的颈部陶片，上面装饰了横向条纹，条纹之间有一块竖纹区（图版44中图3）。图版44中图7的小片器颈陶片，其侈口口

---

① 阿恩：《河南石器时代之着色陶器》，图Ⅶ：20和Ⅸ：30。

② 安特生：《中国史前史研究》，图版52中图5。

③ 安特生：《中国史前史研究》，图版182中图2。

沿上有一种引人注目的装饰，由花环状线条和卷曲图形构成。器颈外侧装饰平行横线。再看图版42中图1的陶罐，其腹部的设计体现了罗汉堂最常见的图案元素，即横向排列的平行线组。这里，平行线与黑色带交替出现，且用椭圆点等距离分隔和镶边。在直线纹区域的中心，装饰有两条对角线。该陶罐身的下部无任何装饰。

这种水平线组以椭圆形点分隔的组合装饰，出现在一些陶罐和碗的陶片（图版50中图16和图23、图版51中图3、图18）上，有时是平行线、平行带或圈和圆点组合（图版49中图6、图7、图9）。有几片陶片上，水平线组区域以点状物图案分隔，又和网格纹图案组合在一起（图版49中图1。比较图版42中图1）。

图版42中图4的器腹陶片上，平行线的中心区域被几组对角线圆段和一个顶角加长的变形三角形替代。对角线圆段配三角形，有时还有刻印的圆点（图版43中图1），是陶罐和碗的图案中非常常见的元素，似乎和平行线带组合出现（图版49中图10、图14）。图版42中图5的器腹陶片上显示有一个大圆圈，中间有一条横线，并组合了一组圆圈。图版42中图2的器腹陶片装饰简单，器腹下部装饰宽竖线纹紧挨横线纹（有2片这样的陶片）。有些陶罐，最下边有横线区域，且用一个花环勾边（图版42中图4）。

有一些陶片仅用简单的平行线交替带状纹来装饰（图版49中图15、图16）。图版49中图15似乎和朱家寨出土的一片陶片非常相近[1]。其他腹部陶片上，则是一组组线条和带纹或三角形的组合（图版49中图8、图14）。

在结束对陶罐陶片的描述之前，我们要观察一下图版49中图2和图11至图13的一些非常重要的器腹陶片。它们都有齿状带纹，图版49中图2，齿状带组合了竖向辐射的线条组和大圆点，其他陶片则组合了圆圈纹。这些锯齿带与有名的丧纹（译者注：20世纪20年代安特生发现半山彩陶上的锯齿纹，认为这是一种特殊的与葬礼有关的丧纹）同类，但这里完全绘成了黑色。

如前所述，这些陶瓷材料支离破碎，有时很难知晓一片陶片到底是陶罐还是陶碗，但可以确定，这里检测的大部分都是陶罐的陶片。

就碗的装饰而言，有的陶片装饰非常简陋，仅在碗边上涂有黑彩（图版46中图2）。其他碗也仅是简单的横线装饰（图版51中图1），且有时集中在碗体上部（图版46中图1）。这些线条经常在碗外壁形成花环状纹饰（图版45中图5、图版46中图3至图5、图版50中图3）。有时花环用粗线绘制，粗线之间再绘制细线条（图50中图3、图6），这和马家窑出土的陶碗的装饰方式一样。两个花环的连接点

---

[1] 安特生：《朱家寨遗址》，《远东古物博物馆馆刊》第15期，图版101中图7。

447 有时装饰一个钩（图版50中图3）或者环（图版46中图4b）或者如图版50中图6上更复杂的装饰。有几片陶碗陶片上出现了马家窑有名的细长卷须纹（图版47中图1a和图2a）。

图版50中图2的陶片上，其口沿下方有斜线纹边界线。图版50中图1是一个设计独特而优雅的陶碗，展现出一套更加精致的线条装饰系统。该陶钵是典型的双锥形，器领低宽，且器边平整。陶器用黑色设计图案，装饰有平行带纹，组合更细的水平线、垂直线、大圆点，以及陶器偏上部分的三角形，三角形的长边紧邻一个浮雕器耳。除了刚才描述的黑彩之外，还有白色圆点和一条白线。该陶碗内部没有任何装饰。

边沿扁平的碗或盆通常边沿会装饰彩绘。最常出现的边沿彩绘参见图版50。彩绘组合变化多端。元素有斜线、直线、偶尔有波浪线、网格纹、圆点、圆圈、圆环和三角形形状的线条。

宽口碗或盆通常会带内部装饰，有的只是几条线（图版45中图6a），有的则是一系列丰富多样的平行线（图版47中图1b至图3b），许多陶片还组合了网格纹（图版47中图1b和图4）或圆点（图版50中图19和图22）。

有几片陶片内侧还有三角形纹饰，或单独出现（图版46中图5a）或结合系统的线条纹饰（图版46中图4a、图版50中图19、图22）。有些陶片装饰有非常独特的三角形图案（图版50中图4、图8、图12）。这些都装饰在陶器边缘附近。三角形的尖角被拉长，末端点缀圆点。三角形的角两侧还有许多圆点。

图版48中的陶碗陶片展现了罗汉堂设计的最高水平。图版48中图1的陶片的外部装饰了厚重的平行线，下方紧挨垂直线。内部无装饰。陶器边缘涂有黑彩，无装饰。图版48中图2略有弯曲的喇叭形的器沿上有一个三角形带。碗体绘制细长的卷须状纹饰，该图案前面也提到过。图版48中图3的图案绘制并不精细。纹饰中有一个圆圈，内刻有一个大圆点，圆圈周围是圆环，圆环两侧配三角形图案。边缘有黑彩。内侧装饰有两条大致平行的线条。图版48中图4的陶身外侧装饰有一条镶边，镶边上填满了竖直圆环，圆环中心有一个环形器耳。内侧呈砖红色，装饰有一个罕见的漏斗状的装饰，很明显，这个沙漏装饰是两个圆圈之间的空间，绘成黑色，圆圈内分别刻有成对的圆点（参见图版48中图6a）。图版48中图5外侧装饰和图版48中图4的装饰几乎都是竖直圆环，只是这里组合了三角形图案。内侧装饰有一组组横线，形成了一个棋盘格纹。图版48中图6的陶片被腐蚀的外侧由一个三角形、一组斜线和圆环组合的装饰。内侧有成对的圆圈，圆圈内是由
448 三条竖线分隔开的成对的圆点。圆圈组似乎和水平线带交替出现，水平线带又和

长条形点结合。类似的点带纹饰似乎出现在图版51中图4的小陶片上。

图版51中图6是一个砖红色陶碗的小陶片。陶片外部有个花环装饰，花环内里填充精美的平行线。花环和下端的横带纹之间有一个器耳陶片。内部有一个三角形边缘带。很明显，图版51中图7的陶碗小陶片，内外两侧都带有同样简洁的线性图形。

还有一些内侧有装饰的器物下部陶片。其中最重要的陶片显示在图版51中图10至图13。图版51中图10的陶片中心有前面描述过的圆圈图案（参见原著，第448页），圆圈内刻有圆点。圆圈内的线条组形成了一个十字，十字中心和十字周围都装饰有圆点，图版51中图13底盘上装饰有网格图案组合，而图版51中图11和图12装饰稀疏。前者只是圆圈或波浪线装饰，后者则带有从下部中心的圆环上辐射而成的圆环带。很明显，许多器物下部陶片和马家窑出土的完好无损的陶碗下部装饰相同，中心有一个圆点或一对弧线。

在结束对这些陶器的描述之前，我必须指出一些颜色与其他陶片相异的陶片。它们与之前陶片上的黑色涂料（偶尔呈黑褐色）差异较大，要么呈紫红色，要么呈红褐色。图版51中图17是一个黄白色陶碗的碗口陶片。陶片内外均装饰红褐色锯齿纹。图版51中图8的口沿陶片上，有一条紫色饰边带，饰边带下方内侧，有一条条竖线纹。有一片未列入主图版中的口沿陶片，其内侧有两条简单的紫色竖直线。图版30中图2的陶碗陶片内侧，有彩绘刷成的两笔紫褐色的涂料，但很粗糙，无法确定是不是装饰。其紫色的器耳则在原著第446页已经描述过了。

图版51中图19是一片小陶片，其外部呈浅黄色，其上带有浅红褐色彩绘，是由一个小圆点和一个带状物的痕迹组成的图案。正文插图16中显示有一片浅黄褐色陶器的陶片，其外侧装饰横线纹，上面有砖红色斑点。最低的一条水平线往下有四条垂直线，边上还有一个圆点纹。

449

插图16

最后，应该描述一下5片非常重要的陶片（正文插图17、正文插图18）。有4片灰色陶片，深褐色装饰（图17）。其器物形态和颜色都让人想起仰韶村和秦王寨有名的陶碗①。最后一片陶碗陶片，其外器表呈红褐色，装饰灰色图案，图案上有一个顶点拉长的三角形（正文插图18）。其器物形态和颜色设计

---

① 阿恩：《河南石器时代之着色陶器》，图版图Ⅱ和图版Ⅲ。

都与仰韶村非常有名的类型相同[①]。

插图17

插图18

　　研究发现，罗汉堂遗址中出土的一件残缺不全的陶器，和马家窑的彩陶关联密切。仔细研究罗汉堂遗址出土的材料，就会发现，罗汉堂遗址中出现的彩绘图案会反复地出现在马家窑出土的彩陶上。将这件陶器与安特生教授出版过的著作中的几个彩陶器和彩陶陶片相比较，或者与远东古物博物馆展览的陶器及陶片相比较后，我更加相信罗汉堂遗址与马家窑遗址之间有着密切的关联。我无缘研究马家窑出土的粗陶，因此，对于这些陶器之间的相互关系，我无法给出任何确切的说明，我也不知晓马家窑遗址的材料中任何一个双耳罐或大型陶罐上面的席纹。安特生教授的初步普查中没有这样的陶片。

　　罗汉堂陶器与朱家寨文化也有一些共同的特性[②]。如果我们研究朱家寨居址出土的彩陶，那么安特生称为"马家窑类型"（《中国史前史研究》，图版100中图1、图2、图4）的范畴，明显和罗汉堂陶器有亲缘关系；甚至安特生教授称为"仰韶晚期类型"的陶片也与罗汉堂的彩陶有一些共同特征（《中国史前史研究》，图版100中图9，图版101中图1、图5、图7、图8，图版103中图15、图17）。朱家寨的粗陶也和罗汉堂的粗陶有某种相似性。

　　让人震惊的一个事实是，朱家寨遗址中发现了3片齐家坪类型的彩陶片（安特生，《远东古物博物馆馆刊》第17期，图版11中图2、图8，图版12中图7）；同样引人注目的是，朱家寨遗址中还发现了真正的罗汉堂类型的陶器陶片。遗址中发现了有叠加的黏土带装饰的器体陶片（参见安特生，引自图版11中图1、图5，图版12中图2）。安特生著作中图版11中图1所说明的陶片和罗汉堂图版57中图2的器颈陶片几乎完全一致。还有，图版34中图7说明的带环状器耳的陶

　　[①] 阿恩：《河南石器时代之着色陶器》，图版图Ⅳ中图8。

　　[②] 安特生教授在《远东古物博物馆馆刊》第17期中论述过该遗址的出土材料。安特生的著作《中国史前史研究》中也概述过该文化居住遗址出土的彩陶，见第152-159页，图版100至图版106。

碗陶片（参见原著，第440页）。最后，我们还需要观察安特生在著作《中国史前史研究》中，图版11中图4和图版12中图4的两片黑彩绘陶片。第一片是罗汉堂黑彩陶碗的碗口陶片，第二片是和正文插图11中有同样脊状物装饰的器颈陶片。

如安特生教授指出的，甚至"带翼石刀"和带燧石片的骨刀，也是朱家寨和罗汉堂遗址有名的出土材料文物。上面举出的相似性足以证明，罗汉堂遗址不仅和马家窑遗址有某种关联，也和朱家寨有关联。至于这些关联所说明的遗址之间的年代学关系，还要等到马家窑遗址出土文物被彻底地考察和发表之后，才能下结论。

第十一章　石器

罗汉堂居址出土的石器并没有任何令人特别感兴趣的东西。其中大量的石质工具，如石斧、石凿、石刀和石盘等，在其他遗址中也多有发现。其中一些最好的器具，安特生教授在《中国史前史研究》的著述中有详尽的研究[1]。这里，我简单提一下，罗汉堂遗址出土了一把精美的银灰色玉凿，这是该遗址中出土的唯一一个半宝石制品。

最常见的石质工具（19件）中出现了盘状器，由闪长岩卵石硬性切割而成[2]。有时，其粗糙的外表保留了下来，同时，由于切削粗糙，也形成了某种边缘。其他卵石经过细心研磨或抛光处理，都成了椭圆形（图版53中图2）。

有3片花岗岩卵石，经过精心打磨成为扁平的圆盘状，但其功能不详。

图版52中图1是一个水晶岩权杖头，绕权杖头有两道槽，一道在边缘上，深一些，另外一道宽浅的槽与其交叉，明显是起捆绑作用的（参见原著，第416页，图版19中图8）。

安特生教授已经出版的著作中论述过的文物中有很多大石斧残片，但只有一个完整的石斧[3]。安特生将其归于半山类型，是他所界定的河南石斧和北方的圆形

---

① 安特生：《中国史前史研究》，第85–86页，第224–225页，第262页，第270页，图版40至图版41，图版73中图4，图版164中图1至图3、图7至图10。

② 安特生：《中国史前史研究》，第85页，图版40中图3。

③ 安特生：《中国史前史研究》，第85页，图版40中图1。

石斧之间的一种类型①。我们拥有的标本剖面呈椭圆形，颈部狭窄，材质为黑色片岩。

现存有许多带有剥片痕迹的石片或同样材质的残破石斧（图版52中图4）。有一把精心打磨的闪长岩石斧，图版52中图7有显示。图版52中图5、图6、图9都可能是黑色硬料做的石锛。所有标本的颈部都已断裂。材质的优美结构在图版52中图8有显示。

451

还发现了一些片岩凿子，其中两个是安特生教授发表的②。大部分石凿剖面显示是不对称的（图版52中图16至图18）。图版52中图19的凿一样的石器两边具有同样的刃缘。

有一个片岩石斧颈部，安特生教授称其为"方颈宽石斧"类型③。遗憾的是，该残片在安特生的著作中图版上是平放的，让人误以为是双孔石刀。虽然无边缘，且侧面收紧，但这确实是石斧的颈部。作为一种类型，这个标本是罗汉堂独一无二的发现。

这些石制品中还发现了26片石刀残片，其中最精美的石器已经由安特生教授在其著作中分析过了④。各种样式的石刀都有，既有无孔的粗糙块状石器（图版52中图15），也有安特生发表的最精致的石器。

有些石刀上没有孔，但短边上有对称的缺口（图版52中图11），这似乎是用来绑缚的。齐家坪遗址（参见原著，第416页）和其他中国遗址中，也发现了这种简单器形。其他标本上带有一两个孔（图版52中图12至图14）。图版52中图12的孔细长。有时，孔靠近边缘，有时在中心或器颈部位。大多数石刀的短边外侈，使石刀具有羽翼的形状。安特生教授称其为"带翼石刀"。安特生教授论述过的石刀中，有一些短边两侧都有很多缺口。我猜想，这些缺口使石刀起到锯子的作用，这显然是一项出于实用目的的发明。然而，这些缺口并不锋利。如果是出于实用而设计，那么肯定是用于柔软的材质的，因此，我们认为这些缺口很可能是便于捆绑或用于装饰。

据我所知，到目前为止，这些有翼有齿的石刀只见于罗汉堂遗址。

图版52中图15是一把不对称的半月形石刀，边缘锋利，只有一面光滑，刀背

---

① 安特生：《中国史前史研究》，第48页。

② 安特生：《中国史前史研究》，第85页，图版40中图10至图11。

③ 安特生：《中国史前史研究》，第85页，图版40中图13。

④ 安特生：《中国史前史研究》，第224–225页，图版40中图12，图版164中图1至图3、图7至图10。

厚实。安特生教授在他的著作《中国史前史研究》第223页中指出，这种长方形和半月形石刀非常重要，且分布广泛。

图版53中图1是一个独特的大器物。它也许是一把锄，两侧相对的缺口可能是用作绑缚。这把锄似乎和出土于中蒙边境的安特生教授称之为"宽大的北方类型"相关[①]。

图版52中图10是一个水晶做的半圆形残器，可能是穿孔石斧，但由于残缺太甚，难以作出肯定的结论。

图版52中图3的残石器，用途不详，中间有一条深槽，这也许是残损的研磨器。遗址中还发现了一个片状磨石，以及若干圆形砂岩残片，这些圆形砂岩残片可能也用于研磨。

另外，还需要注意2个板岩石坠，其中一个是安特生教授展示的[②]，另一个如图版54中图14所示。后者上面有一沟槽，用于系绳，但沟槽并未绕到石坠背面。在石坠的短边上，也有类似的沟槽。图版52中图2是一个类似盘状的小石坠，由白色大理石制成。

接下来记录的7件石器也是大理石制成的。图版53中（译者注：此处参照实物图应为图版54）的图3至图5，是最漂亮的标本，它们或许是臂钏。图3精美的残片，是用上好的大理石切割而成，且夹杂一丝温暖的黄玫瑰色。臂钏整体薄厚匀称，且中间略厚，边缘稍薄。外部打磨光滑，内部有红色颜料痕迹。臂钏上下边缘都有一组组细小的纹路，一侧边缘附近，有一个从外侧打的孔。图版53中（译者注：此处参照实物图应为图版54）的图5是用白色纹理大理石切割而成的，闪亮有光泽。内外两面向边缘延伸。因此，其横截面外侧呈凹面，相应地内侧呈凸面，内外侧都打磨光滑。其他臂钏，如图版53中（译者注：此处应为图版54）的图5和图版54中的图8，也是用白色大理石切割而成，上面有很多小孔，是典型的风化石。

有一个非常漂亮的小板岩环，这也可能是臂环（图版54中图6）。最后，我们还留意一个圆柱形的大理石质地的小珠子（图版53中图28）（译者注：此处参照实物图应为图版53中图29）。

安特生教授[③]公布过一个外形独特的石器，石器上部类似肩胛骨。明确这一点之后，我们再总结石器的具体内容。该石器出土于罗汉堂附近，但是，遗址上未

452

---

① 安特生：《中国史前史研究》，第58页，图版25中图1至图4。

② 安特生：《中国史前史研究》，第85页，图版41中图6。

③ 安特生：《中国史前史研究》，第56页，图版22中图5。

发现类似形状的文物。

第十二章　骨器（约90个残片）

安特生教授已经公布了若干至关重要的骨器①。为了挑选出其中的最佳之品，图版54再次展示了其中的一些标本。

其中最具特色的骨器当属骨刀，刀身有沟槽，用于加固燧石片（现有6片残片）。图版54中图12和图13的骨刀最为完整。图版53中图16、图25、图26和图27皆为其他骨刀残片。这些标本都带深槽，用于加固燧石片。每个标本的沟槽都延伸到刀尖。骨刀上部无槽，用作刀柄。某些标本的刀身弯曲。此外，我们还出土了大量的骨锥残片，图版53中图18至图25展示了其中一部分残片。

此外，这批中还有29根骨针，长短不同，型号各异，有些极其细小精致（图版53中图8、图9、图11），不少针眼制作精良。

图版54中，图10和图11是两个独特的骨器。图10是一片大骨中劈下来的薄板，有一端带两个孔，孔的上下有两个不对称的缺口；另一端还有一个孔。这些孔都是双锥形，由两面钻成。两边凹痕之间磨损痕迹明显。各孔到顶部或侧边的凹痕，都能看到同样的痕迹，看着就像丝带或绳子从这些孔中穿插，把该骨器缠绕起来，看起来似乎这些尖之间围绕一圈彩带或线束。我认为这是用于编织或编筐的工具。图版54中图11展示的是一个骨板，顶部有一个奇怪的孔，尖端部分带5个小洞。背面有一个类似的洞，比正面的那些小孔洞要略微高一些。这件骨器，以及图版53中图25的骨器残片可能都用于编织。图版53中图25的骨器与齐家坪出土的一些骨器（参见图版16中图24、图25和图26）高度相关，或许用于编织。

图版53中图6的骨器，制作精良，是一片由大骨切分后制作的锄头或斧头，前端凸起，后背凹陷，刀锋锋利。

从这些精良的骨针以及其他用于编织的骨器中，我们可以总结出，该地居民在织布、编席及其他家庭手工方面技术成熟。

---

① 安特生：《中国史前史研究》，第86-87页，图版41中图1至图4，图7至图9。

第十三章　篮纹和绳纹

鉴于篮纹和绳纹已经在齐家坪陶器章节一起做了研究，这里，我仅对这两种纹饰在齐家坪与罗汉堂陶器上最明显的差异做一概述，并在本章末尾，对出土于甘肃南部的一些齐家文化陶器，稍加补充说明（参见原著，第456页）。

罗汉堂第一组（罗汉堂Ⅰ类陶器）陶器有双耳罐、大型陶罐和细泥素陶碗，这些陶器上的纹饰，同齐家坪Ⅰ类陶器的纹饰（参见原著，第411页）一模一样。按照安特生教授给出的术语，这种纹理是真正的篮筐的印迹。我并不赞同这一观点，但我接受"篮纹或席纹"这一术语。我个人更倾向于认为，篮纹是由质地柔软的编织品或粗制的席子留下的，当这些编织品或席子被铺在模具里面，再用模具制陶时，陶器表面就留下了印迹，即篮纹或席纹。这种编织品并不指一种常规的或复杂的设计，我在描述齐家坪的纹饰时也提过，也有可能是些未经捆绑的纤维材料，只是覆盖在模具上，或者使用相同材料的线绳松垮地缚在一起。这种简单的编织品或席子在许多原始部落非常常见[1]。图版26中图1至图4显示了罗汉堂Ⅰ类陶器和齐家坪Ⅰ类陶器相对应的这种纹理。

在齐家坪，上述的简单席纹，仅在第一组陶器或陶器陶片中出现。特例是一个大陶罐的陶片（编号K.12003：1127），类似于图版25中图2的陶器。该陶器上部顺滑，下半部分覆有绳纹。图版28中图5陶罐的陶片上有绳纹或篮纹，位于重新安装的器耳处，这证明纹理具有实用功能。

罗汉堂第二组陶器（罗汉堂Ⅱ类陶器），质地粗糙。这些陶器不像第一组那样仅下半部分有篮纹，而是整个陶器都覆有篮纹，同齐家坪的篮纹样式一模一样，但具体形态各有千秋。

有些陶片的绳纹为垂直状，有些陶片的绳纹呈对角斜线状（图版31中图4；图版33中图1），同大多数齐家坪Ⅱ类陶器的绳纹高度一致（参见原著，第412页）。另外还有一些陶片同齐家坪Ⅲ类陶器中的精美绳纹高度一致（图版32中图1，图版35中图1、图2），但大多数陶片外部皆为如图版36中图1至图3以及图版38中图11所示的绳纹。显而易见，这些绳纹错综交织，纵横交错。图版40中图1b至图3b的泥塑模型正面的绳纹完整地显示了出来。我认为，这种绳纹出自制作

---

[1] 参见杰西·L.努斯鲍姆：《犹他州凯恩县制作篮子的洞穴》，《印第安笔记和专著》，美国印第安人博物馆，海伊基金会，纽约，1922，第18页及其后，图版L和图版LI。

粗糙、不太精良的编织技术，织物为交织线绳，网状结构也许是最佳表达。

另一种印迹，看起来与这种网状结构相关，出现在许多陶片中，其中3片为图版39中的图1、图2和图3，2片为图版41中的图2和图3。这种印迹可能与网状结构属于同一种，但是这种印迹呈片状，清晰可辨，我认为这是陶拍的痕迹，是用线绳包裹陶拍来拍打陶器而在器表产生的，虽然也可以解释为不规则的网纹。一些由两种陶土制成的彩陶，也可能使用陶拍处理过（图版43中图4，图版44中图1）。图版41中图1的陶片上部有简单的斜绳纹，下部覆盖交叉的斜绳纹。在任何情况下，都难以解决绳纹问题，我认为并不是所有的不规则绳纹都要解释为使用陶拍从而产生的印迹。

有的陶片上是水平状绳纹（图版31中图1；图版36中图4；图版39中图4），有些陶片的绳纹同在齐家坪中发现的篦点纹陶器，绳纹样式一样。图版31的陶罐，罐下部如图版41中图4所示，有真实的篮纹或编织纹。

七里墩和小石峡的陶片，为数不多，展示了一些真实的篮纹或绳纹（参见原著，第459页）。图版55中的图10和图12，具备真正的编织纹的特点。可能是篓筐的绳纹，倘若质地柔软，也可能是粗帆布料。图版56中图10是从小石峡出土的印有规则编织纹的陶片。

我们的调查结果显示，此地的甘肃居民编织技艺精湛，知道如何制作麻布袋子和如何织网。显然，他们能编织出质地粗糙的垫子、篮子，也许还会织布。精致的骨针证明，此处居民可以做针线活，甚至缝补软质布料。精细的针无法缝补皮毛或其他粗糙坚硬的布料，否则会断掉。

第十四章　杂项

下面展示的陶器，不属于上述任何一种类型。

罗汉堂出土了1个十分特别的器物，展示在图版25中图4。底盘两边顶部各有两个小孔，内空盛物，晃动瓶身，所盛之物于瓶内晃动。该器物可能是孩童的拨浪鼓，或是用于未知仪式中的物件。

还要再提3个小陶器，第一个是图版54中图7的器物。其中两个是陶罐形状，第三个为直壁陶器。这3个陶器都特别小，也许是小孩的玩具，也许是用来盛放珍贵液体的容器。

图版25中图3是另一种独特的灰褐色黏土陶器，呈圆柱形，另一头微细。我

认为，这件袖口状的陶器可能是手镯，也可能用来支撑其他物品。

此外，我们还可以看到，图版54中图2至图5有大概80个小型黏土环残片，它们大多呈灰色，也有褐色，剖面各不相同，有长方形也有三角形。它们直径并不大，约有30片可能是手镯的陶片，其余的呈扁平状，显然是一些小陶器器耳的陶片。

还有一些大小不一的黏土球，图版25中图5和图6呈现了其中两个，它们或许被用来当作研磨球使用。

最后，我们可以看到一个圆环状的褐色黏土陶器（见图版26中图7）。它的边缘极不规则，中心有一个不完整的小孔，可能被当作纺轮使用。

第十五章 齐家坪和罗汉堂的哺乳动物遗骸

伊利亚斯·达尔博士仔细研究了这些收集到的遗骸，并写了一份初步的调查报告，现保存在远东古物博物馆的档案中。经他允许，我在他的调查基础上发表以下意见：

齐家坪的动物残骸部分发掘于陡峭的洮河两岸，部分发掘于公路经过的峡谷。后者的地层条件极其复杂，其地面由于塌陷可能早已混合了不同的地层类型。那么，我们就极有可能同时发现不同年代的动物残骸。因此，这些骨头中可能存在一些近期的残骸残片，比如山羊和绵羊的下颌骨，它们仍然带有明显的羊肉味。

然而，除去一些残片标本，齐家坪的骨头遗骸与其他史前遗址的骨头遗骸保存状态相一致。

这些骨头遗骸整体呈白色，有的带一丝非常漂亮的淡黄色，也有的带点灰色。有些残骸表面还黏着一层土，十分牢固，且带有细沟纹，可能是植物的根茎盘踞所致。

这些骨头残骸大部分来自像狗、猪、牛、山羊和绵羊这样的家养哺乳动物。野生动物的残骸只有鹿和一些啮齿动物的头骨，且可能是最近才留下的，与之前的动物残骸混合在了一起。

狗的残骸大概有40片，可以看出，它们体型较小，可能与现代猎狐犬的体型相当，其中有一个保存完好的头盖骨，可断定是欧洲新石器时代的犬科动物。

猪的残骸大约有30片，特征十分有趣，一片保存完好的带有泪腺的面部骨头遗骸可称为货真价实的维塔利斯类型的遗骸。猪的大部分遗骸来自它们下颌骨的

457　其中一部分，低平单薄，牙齿（非獠牙）并不锋利，因此我们可以断定，这些猪已被人类驯化。

从牛的遗骸我们可以看出，它们体型较大，许多遗骸残片都有被人类加工过的痕迹，比如，一些从下颌骨的其他部分分离出来的残片，人们把它们磨尖当切割工具。另外，一些肩胛骨残片被用来制作锄头，或更确切地说，被用来制作斧头。

但有一点值得注意，牛骨过于柔软，并不适合用来制作工具。在欧洲石器时代，一些野生动物的骨头，尤其是鹿的骨头，常被用来作为制作工具的材料。因此，达尔博士认为，至少有一部分骨头可能是野牛的遗骸。

罗汉堂收藏的动物遗骸种类与齐家坪的相似，但它们的比例却大不相同。在罗汉堂，像羚羊和鹿这样的野生动物比比皆是。罗汉堂还有另一个特点，即猪骨头遗骸很少，仅有两片，而大部分骨头遗骸来自一些小型反刍动物，有300多片，其中牛的遗骸残片大约有40片，也有山羊和绵羊的骨头残片，这些动物可能都已被人类驯化。

大量的羚羊、鹿、野兔和旱獭的遗骸残片表明，这个地方的人大部分是技艺高超的猎手，甚至能追逐行动非常敏捷的动物。因此，这些骨头（约20片）很可能是猎狗的遗骸残片，从这么少的残片数量我们便可以看出，那时候的人们并不会把猎狗当作食物。

罗汉堂收集的哺乳动物遗骸有一个显著的特点，即它们均呈分裂状态。比如那些有蹄子的动物，它们的蹄子末端通常与其管状中心分离，管状中心被压碎以进入骨髓。此外，它们的盆骨均有规则地断裂，或许是曾被一种特殊的工具所屠宰或肢解所致。这些骨头表面非常粗糙，显然被某种原始的、不是很锋利的工具压碎了。

猪的遗骸残片很少，而野生动物的却很多，这说明，罗汉堂的居民是以狩猎为生或以养牛为生的游牧民族。毫无疑问，他们没有任何先进的农具，因为，以农耕为生的人会养很多猪，猪的遗骸也就会多得多。最后，值得注意的是，上述
458　两片残存的猪骨也可断定为猎人偶尔捕获的野猪的遗骸。

第十六章　七里墩

（天水县向东 3.5 公里）（译者注：天水县为今甘肃省天水市）

七里墩位于甘肃南部，是安特生教授的中国助手白万玉[①]所考察的其中一组遗址。

这里只收藏了 49 件文物（编号 K.2353：1-49），大部分是锅碗瓢盆，还有 6 个泥环、7 件骨器、5 个（贻贝）贝壳、1 件燧石器、半个石环和 2 件石器。

大部分陶器陶片与齐家坪 I 类文物类型相似，质量普遍较高。

有 5 片小型标本是齐家坪类型双耳罐的陶片（图版 57 中图 8）（译者注：原著无图版 57，参照实物图可能为图版 56 中图 8），还有一片细长的陶片，原型可能是一个体型较大的缸（图版 56 中图 4）。

有 1 片可能来自小双耳罐的器耳陶片（图版 55 中图 9），它的顶部有一个十字架的装饰，无疑是与买来的齐家坪类型的陶器之一相似（参照图版 23）。另一件残缺的双耳罐器耳顶端有一个狭长的凹槽，显然是为了装饰。

七里墩出土的陶碗中，有齐家坪非常有名的类型，共有 5 片碗沿的陶片，其中 4 片呈环状。

一些带有席纹的陶器底部可能与齐家坪 I 类文物有关（图版 55 中图 14）。

有一大片黄色陶器器耳的陶片（图版 55 中图 13）与齐家坪收藏的器耳陶片类型完全相同（参见原著，第 391 页）。

2 片器物口沿陶片（图版 55 中图 10、图 12、图 16）和 2 片质地疏松的深色鬲足陶片，上面疑似有真正的编织纹。现在提到的这些陶片与齐家坪 II 类文物的类型相同。

此外，还有 7 个灰色的黏土环，它们的剖面或多或少呈三角状，在齐家坪和罗汉堂也曾发现过同样类型的黏土环。

也有一些陶片与齐家坪没有关联。有一片陶片（图版 55 中图 3），貌似为某种尖底陶器的器口（参见安特生《中国史前史研究》图版 49 中图 1，其中记载了马家窑出土的一个类似的陶片）。

图版 56 中图 2 是另一片陶片，可能来自某种陶器的颈部或底部，上面有一些随意切割的横线，横线之间是一些大小不一的斜线。

第三片陶片的表面布满了网状的细线，这种线一般会出现在一些尖底的陶

[①] 安特生：《中国史前史研究》，第 99-102 页。

器上。

此外，图版55中图1的陶片，可能来自一个漏斗状的器物足部。其呈灰色，

表面有横向的划痕。

最后，还有5片彩陶陶片，其中4片我们可以忽略不提。第5片陶片（图版56中图1）是偏红的褐色彩绘，在河南遗址中非常有名。

第十七章 榆中县小石峡（译者注：此处地名有待进一步考证）

该遗址位于甘肃最南端，也是安特生教授的中国助手白万玉考察过的其中一组遗址。

该遗址共收集了33片陶片，其中大部分是大缸的陶片（齐家坪Ⅰ类），与在辛店丙址发现的陶片极为相似。

图版56中图10呈现的一件小型石器，有明显的篮纹或真正的编织纹。

一些带有绳纹的粗糙陶片，属于齐家坪Ⅱ类文物。

其中，有5片带有彩绘装饰的陶片，其中2片可能属于半山类型的陶器。还有一个小型的红色器耳，上面有一条条黑色的斜线，和马厂陶器上的花纹相似。

最后，我们回到图版56中图9的陶罐，其呈褐色，表面平滑。它的边缘下方和器耳上均有雕刻花纹。没有任何证据表明该陶器并非发掘于此地，但我想知道的是，它是否为人所购买而来，因为令人惊奇的是，它竟完好无损，而其他文物都只是一些小陶片。无论如何，它的类型与齐家坪那两个购买回来的陶罐很是相似（图版22中图3和图4）。

根据安特生教授的简要说明（《中国史前史研究》，第101页），在白万玉所考究的红山坡（礼县向南1.5公里）——甘肃南部的遗址之一，发现了1片与齐家坪遗址类型相同的小罐陶片。

综上所述，我们发现，在甘肃最南端的两个遗址处发现了齐家坪Ⅰ类和齐家坪Ⅱ类陶器，而篦点纹陶器却没有出现。虽然这些出土材料太少，我们无法得出更多的结论，但它们证明了这样一个事实，即齐家坪文化并不局限于齐家坪这一地区。我们或许可以期待，今后对整个甘肃地区的遗址的探索，将使我们明确地了解齐家期的来龙去脉。

第十八章　齐家坪遗址和罗汉堂遗址之间的关联性

　　讨论这个复杂的问题，我们首先要注意到，齐家坪和罗汉堂这两处遗址的不同地理位置。事实上，齐家坪遗址位于甘肃中部的平原农业区，而罗汉堂则位于汉藏交界处的石山中，这可能是研究齐家坪遗址与罗汉堂遗址的关系问题的关键所在。 *460*

　　总结齐家坪遗址和罗汉堂遗址出土彩陶的研究结果，我们发现了以下共同点：

　　两种文化中都出现了高领长耳小双耳罐，但齐家坪遗址比罗汉堂遗址更常见。同样，两个遗址都出土了一种陶罐，罐领呈漏斗状，器身轮廓有的是双锥形，有的呈椭圆形，但齐家坪遗址出土量似乎更多。除了修复的大型罐，罗汉堂遗址只发现了该类型陶罐的少数罐体陶片。此外，两个遗址中都出土了一些中型陶碗陶片，但该陶碗类型在罗汉堂遗址要比齐家坪遗址中更常见。

　　我们现在描述的两个遗址的陶器种类，都可以归到我们所说的第一类（齐家坪Ⅰ类和罗汉堂Ⅰ类）。结果，我们发现两个遗址中出土的陶罐都带有同一特征的篮纹或席纹，这种纹饰在罗汉堂遗址发现的大型陶罐上非常常见（图版25中图2）。

　　继续比较后，我们进一步发现，两个遗址都出土了一组较粗糙的陶器（齐家坪Ⅱ类和罗汉堂Ⅱ类），但两组器物的器形、装饰和制作过程中产生的纹理差异非常显著。一般来说，罗汉堂（罗汉堂Ⅱ类）出土的粗陶器更雅致，且腹部常饰叠加的波浪形泥带，这在齐家坪Ⅱ类中未曾见过的。罗汉堂Ⅱ类的一些陶器上，带有齐家坪Ⅱ类（例如图版31中图4和图版33）上独特的垂直绳纹，但大多数罗汉堂的陶片上都布满交叉的绳纹，使得陶器外部呈棋盘格纹。在讨论粗陶器时，我们注意到，鬲足和质地疏松的器物下部是两个遗址共有的特征，但这些类型在中国所有史前遗址中都出现了，因此，它们不能被当作齐家坪遗址与罗汉堂遗址相关联的证据。

　　我们将比较扩大到齐家坪Ⅲ类（以其精致的篦点纹陶器为特色），我们未发现罗汉堂文物有直接对应的花纹；然而，我认为图版37（参见原著，第440页）中的一组具有精美的附加堆纹或印花图案的陶器，与篦点纹陶器有关，虽然它们上面并未饰有纹图案。罗汉堂陶器与篦点纹陶器同样精致，器壁薄亮，饰有精致的

附加堆纹带或刻纹。一片陶片边缘内侧有一条蓝紫色凹痕（正文插图10），这与
齐家坪（图版13中图5b和图7b）的三角形彩绘有关。我认为，两个遗址的相关

461 类型的陶器上都出现这种边沿彩绘，说明这是一个非常重要的特征。

两个遗址出土的骨器和石器在许多方面都很相似，但这些器物的器形非常普
通，无法证明两个遗址有关联。

如果尝试确定这两个遗址之间最显著的区别，我们会发现，齐家坪的材料中
没有像罗汉堂那么丰富的彩陶。正如我们在原著第418页提到的，齐家坪遗址材
料中含有一小堆彩陶片，其中大部分可以确定为朱家寨（参见原著，第463页）
墓葬遗址或居址的陶器类型，而不是我们可能预期的马家窑居址的陶器；齐家坪
彩陶陶片中，没有一片典型的马家窑陶器陶片，但罗汉堂彩陶与马家窑彩陶密切
相关。

总结这些遗址之间复杂的关系，我们发现：很明显，齐家坪遗址和罗汉堂遗
址在小型双耳陶罐和席纹陶罐两种陶器方面是有联系的；另一方面，齐家坪没有
与罗汉堂相媲美的彩陶器具，也无罗汉堂特有的带翼石刀和带燧石片的骨刀。

依照安特生教授编制的年表，我在本文中首先描述了齐家坪，但我不认为齐
家坪能真正代表安特生教授发现的史前阶段的最早的文化。目前，在广泛的发掘
之前，我们无法确定齐家文化的确切的相对年代。因此，在下面的说明中，我仅
限于对本文所涉及的两个遗址略加评论。

安特生教授说道（《中国史前史研究》，第82页）："考虑这些非常先进的大
双耳罐，我们可能倾向于将这一文堆积的年代定为相对较晚近。另一方面，甘肃
有一条不间断的彩陶发展链，从仰韶到马厂、辛店、寺洼，再远到青铜时代，我
们清楚地意识到，不能将齐家文化置于金属时代。因此，我们不得不把它标记为
仰韶前文化。"[1]

462 毫无疑问，齐家文化没有金属残留痕迹，但这并不是将其置于年代上的第一
位的理由。出土文物中无金属可能只是个意外。我相信，齐家坪居民一直与金属
文化有接触，且影响了他们的陶器的造型。但是日常生活中他们并未使用贵重金
属物品，金属器物或许只是他们的模型。我会在下面继续讨论这一问题。

---

[1] 安特生教授把"甘肃仰韶"与"河南仰韶"联系起来。他所说的"甘肃仰韶"是指马家窑和
半山。这样，所有甘肃和河南的史前遗址都会因此而纳入这条完整的发展链条中。但在我看来，甘
肃马家窑和半山与河南仰韶之间的关联性是存在争议的。如果我们比较马家窑居址和河南仰韶村及
河南其他遗址，比较半山丰富的墓葬陶器和即将发表的仰韶村墓葬贫乏的出土材料，我们发现，河
南遗址和甘肃遗址有显著区别。

安特生教授认为（《中国史前史研究》，第82页），地层知识说明了他有关齐家是"前仰韶"的解释，因在"未受干扰的"齐家文化中从未发现仰韶陶片。他进一步指出，他在沉积层表面的耕地中，发现了大量的仰韶陶片。安特生教授的解释是，当仰韶人时不时地经过被遗弃的齐家定居点时，就在这里丢弃了一些垃圾，这曾是篦点纹陶器和双耳罐制造者居住的地方。

我冒昧地认为，安特生教授通过把他所说的仰韶彩陶陶片，解释为仰韶人随意丢弃的垃圾，从而使齐家坪遗址的年代问题简化了。

首先，我反对他的观点。因为，根据文物上所附的书面声明，一些彩绘陶片是在地表收集的，共有4片，且为了与出土材料相区别，它们上面都标记有字母，图版24中图6、图13、图23、图24给出了说明。其他彩陶片共有16片，由于它们并未被标记为"地表发现"，我们必须合理地看待它们，即，它们是被发掘出来的器物。无论如何，至少有1片棋盘格纹的陶器（图版24中图14），明确陈述是"小李"在1.5米深处发掘出来的。这些事实大大降低了"地表陶片"（其中只有3片是仰韶类型）的重要性[1]。

其次，我想强调一下，齐家坪彩陶陶片不一定对应于"仰韶中期"（安特生的术语），它们同样可以为"仰韶晚期"。如果研究这些陶片的设计，我们发现，其中大部分陶器可以被认定为是朱家寨文化中出现过的陶器。其中带有锯齿带的陶片（图版24中图6至10、图20）也可能来自《远东古物博物馆馆刊》第17期上图版1中显示的陶器类型。按照安特生的术语，这种陶罐是"仰韶中期类型"，但是，是朱家寨墓葬遗址（《中国史前史研究》，第26页）出土的。饰格子纹的颈部陶片（参见我们的图版24中图12）和《远东古物博物馆馆刊》第17期上，图版1中图4或图版2中图1（两个都是朱家寨）的罐领是同一类型。图版24中图14的棋盘格纹可以与《远东古物博物馆馆刊》第17期上，图版1中图4、图版2中图4、图版4中图4或《远东古物博物馆馆刊》第15期上，图版103中图18（均来自朱家寨）相比较。我们图版24中图15的边缘陶片对应于《远东古物博物馆馆刊》第15期上图版103中图21或图版101中图8（二者都是朱家寨陶片）。我们图版24中图23的曲折图案也出现在朱家寨文化中（《远东古物博物馆馆刊》第15期上图版103中图5、图版106中图2，《远东古物博物馆馆刊》第17期上图版3，中间的陶罐），尽管我怀疑朱家寨标本的颜色是否与齐家坪陶片的褐色色调一致。我们图版24中图11显示的小陶片的模糊设计，与《远东古物博物馆馆刊》第15期上图

463

---

[1] 事实上，提到未被翻动过的部分遗址就很让人怀疑，因整个堆积层位于甘肃的农业区，在过去的3000年间，任何一块肥沃的土地都有可能被翻动过一次或无数次。

版102中图6显示的陶片相似，我们图版24中图16的棋盘格纹与《远东古物博物馆馆刊》第15期上图版103中图12（都是朱家寨类型）相似。图版24中图21、图22、图24的陶片显然和安特生教授定义为马厂类型（《远东古物博物馆馆刊》第15期上第158、159页）的一组朱家寨陶片属于同一类型，都是外表呈红褐色，但图版24中图24带一丝紫红色。花纹设计成深蓝色或紫褐色。

　　经过详细地研究，我们总结到，有齿状带的陶片可以解释为半山类型的陶罐，但同样完全可以解释为朱家寨的陶罐。此外，有些陶片明显属于另一类型，与安特生教授定义为马厂类型的一组陶片相关。

　　如果我们将比较范围扩大到齐家坪遗址和朱家寨遗址的素陶上，我们发现朱家寨遗址中有3片陶片是典型的齐家坪类型（齐家坪Ⅰ类），《远东古物博物馆馆刊》第17期上图版11中图2和图8，以及图版12中图7。图版11中图8所示的器身陶片呈现了最显著的相似之处。

　　两个扁平器耳尤其值得注意。它们不见于齐家坪Ⅰ类中的陶罐上，却出现在一个购买来的陶器上（图版22中图5）。此外，《远东古物博物馆馆刊》第17期上，图版11中图7的陶片可能是齐家坪类型，虽然这不是很重要——或许《远东古物博物馆馆刊》第17期，图版10中图1、图2、图4至图6的器领陶片也是齐家类型。

　　最后，我们应该注意，朱家寨墓葬遗址出土的大陶罐（《远东古物博物馆馆刊》第17期上，图版1中图3）和图版22中图3和图4的购买来的齐家坪的陶器极度相似。显然，这些陶器也与来自榆中县小石峡（图版50）的一件陶器相关，但该陶器未注明是出土的还是购买的。

　　安特生教授在提到两片齐家坪陶片（《远东古物博物馆馆刊》第17期上图版11中图8和图版12中图7）时说道："我相信这两个标本实际上是齐家期的，也就是说，朱家寨人在此定居时，这两个标本已经被齐家人当作破旧的物品丢弃在这里有些年代了"（《远东古物博物馆馆刊》第17期第47页和63页）。我很怀疑，我们是否可以把朱家寨遗址中出现的齐家坪陶器当作纯粹的偶然。我更倾向于认为，这一事实表明，齐家坪遗址的年代比安特生教授所认为的年代要晚近得多。我可以从出土的双耳罐明显先进的品质来说明问题。在我看来，这些双耳罐是模仿金属模型制作的。这些双耳罐常有的高颈和长耳都不是彩陶的典型特征。图版22中图5的壶对金属的模仿最明显。该陶壶上部的长器耳上有清晰可辨的

464

连接处，用切痕和两个"铆钉"来标记。同样的"铆钉"也出现在壶嘴上[①]。甚至陶壶上层构造中的肾形开口、极高的器颈以及球腹和窄足都必定受到了金属模型的影响。

图版23中图1的陶器与上述陶壶相似，两个陶器的器领都通过一种上部构造做成了拱形，这种构造不见于中国其他史前彩陶时期。这两个陶器都购买自兰州，但毫无疑问，它们是齐家文化的真正代表，因具有这种上部结构的陶片在齐家坪遗址中也发现了两片，其中一件显示在图版4中图3（参见原著，第392页）。如果我们寻找这种有着拱形器领的陶器的原型，并考察历史上中国最早的青铜器，即殷商时期的青铜器，我们会发现有一种青铜器，其上部构造也是拱形的，也带有出水口，且出水口另一面还有一个孔。其器耳形状和齐家坪文化的陶器相同。这件陶器收藏于柏林博物馆，由库梅尔发表[②]，他认为该陶器的年代较早。这件铜器尤其与图版22中图5的陶器相似性非常高（尽管该铜器有三个球状腿）。如果我们研究其他早期青铜器，我们会发现图版22中图5的陶器腹部的球状弧度以及狭窄的足部是许多早期青铜器上出现的特征[③]。因此，这些特征同样可能出现在拱形的陶器上。

图版22中图3和图4是买来的陶壶，它们和朱家寨的大陶罐的腹部弧度都较大，都为窄足，这都具有青铜器的特征。因被发掘的堆积层中，出土的陶器或陶片，没有这种窄足部分，这就不排除买来的陶器比出土的陶器年代更近，但无论如何，它们都与居址出土的陶器密切相关。上面讨论的朱家寨标本和殷商铜器之间的亲缘关系实际上说明，我们必须把齐家坪文化的年代判定得更晚近一些（未来的发掘可能需要将其他文化的年代也定在更晚近的时期，目前定的时期较早）。无论如何，我确信，齐家文化不可能是中国史前陶器的最早时期。如果齐家文化与殷商文化不是同一时代，那么齐家坪和殷商必定有一些共同的原型，这一点说明，齐家坪文化年代相对较晚近。这一结论不可能因没有发现金属或彩陶稀缺而被推翻。正如上文第463页（译者注：此处指原著的第463页）所述，出土文物中无金属可能只是偶然：中国早期青铜时代的文化堆积中只发现了少数的青铜器[④]。至于彩陶，我已经在前面第463页（译者注：此处指原著的第463页）解释过了，

465

---

① 安特生教授在《远东古物博物馆馆刊》第15期，图版38中显示了该陶壶，壶把上的接头清晰可见。

② 奥托·库梅尔：《中国青铜器》，东亚艺术协会，柏林，1928，第9页，图版5和图版6。

③ 奥托·库梅尔：《中国青铜器》，图版2；容庚：《商周彝器通考》，《燕京学报》，专刊系列第17期，第2卷，1941，第323、335页。参照第256页被修复的标本和第412—413页的标本。

④ 灰嘴遗址只发现5件青铜器，辛店遗址仅有3件。参见安特生：《灰嘴遗址》，第171、177页。

有相当数目的陶片可以合理地被认为是从堆积层本身中发掘的（不只是地表发现）。因此，我不同意安特生教授的观点——该彩陶陶片是"被丢弃的陶器"。我无法解释为什么彩陶陶片数量如此之少，但我也不赞同安特生教授的观点，即这些篦点纹陶器上的彩绘三角形和购置的陶器中小型大双耳罐上的三角形带，都代表了远东陶器上最早的彩绘阶段①。

最后，应该提到的是，甘肃有两个青铜时代的遗址，即寺洼遗址和卡约遗址，还有一个可能年代比较晚近的河南省的遗址——不召寨遗址。该遗址中未发现一片彩陶陶片。安特生教授认为不召寨遗址比仰韶村更晚近（《远东古物博物馆馆刊》第15期，第66页）。此外，仰韶村附近，还有两个其他的遗址，即西庄村遗址和杨河村遗址，其中出现了较近年代的元素，但同样无彩陶（同上，第66页）。这些事实证明了我的观点，即没有或很少有陶器并不说明年代就早。这里有一个事实能证明我的观点，即中国考古学家在安阳附近的后岗进行考古发掘时，其中一个区域的最深处发掘出了彩陶，彩陶上面有一层黑陶，最顶层是白陶，白陶被认为可能与殷商时期的白器相关（D. G. Wu，同上21页）（译者注：此处可能为G. D. Wu，即吴金鼎）。这里同样是素陶出现在后，彩陶出现在前，素陶年代更接近现在。

还有一个特征表明齐家文化年代更晚近，即遗址中出土的哺乳动物遗骸发达的程度（比较原著，第457页）。安特生教授在谈到伊利亚斯·达尔博士对该遗骸的研究时说：

"该遗址出现的家畜种类比其他地方都更加齐全——在出土的诸多动物骨骼中，可辨认的有狗、猪、牛、山羊和绵羊。关于鹿，则仅有少量遗骸残片。"（《远东古物博物馆馆刊》第15期，第43页）

令人吃惊的是，罗汉堂出土的猪骨不多，而牛骨很常见，且牛有可能当时已被驯养，狗也如此。该遗址出土的动物骨骼多为野生动物骨骼，说明罗汉堂的居民是出色的猎手。

如果将这两个遗址与马家窑遗址相比，我们会发现，马家窑遗址驯养的动物只有猪和狗。

以上研究表明，齐家文化在三种文化中首屈一指，这一事实为我关于齐家文化年代更晚近的观点提供了有力的佐证。

---

① 巴霍芬将辛店期和齐家遗址相联系起来，认为齐家不是最早的阶段。我不赞同他的观点，但我承认齐家坪III类和灰嘴遗址之间可能有一些模糊的相似之处。我认为，在对灰嘴遗址进行研究之前，还是不能讨论这一问题。参见巴霍芬：《中国早期历史》，《1937年的世界历史》，第270页。

现有研究均表明，迄今为止，尽管齐家文化晚于罗汉堂文化，却与之有一定联系，具体表现在双耳高领罐、席纹罐及素面碗几个方面。显而易见，齐家文化受当时先进的青铜文化影响，部分陶器的原型可能与殷商青铜器有所关联。齐家文化很可能是受到安阳商王朝或其前身艺术影响的一个比较低级的文化。我认为，虽然时间差异不大，罗汉堂文化早于齐家文化，这种差异或许因地理和部族不同。无论如何，罗汉堂陶器并没有像齐家陶器般明显受到青铜器的影响。2号墓葬填土中发现的黑彩陶片显示在正文插图11，的确酷似鄂尔多斯陶器类型的形制和装饰①，但该陶片因独一无二而不具统一性，其意义不应被高估。

但是，即便我们不能假定青铜工艺对罗汉堂陶器有任何影响，具有特色的燧石片骨刀却极有可能有着金属的原型，它们与鄂尔多斯式的简朴刀具在外形上有相似之处，都有器耳，且刀身略有弯曲②。

高本汉教授指出，青铜小刀既普遍存在于西伯利亚和蒙古草原文化，又在早期中国的商文化中常见（《远东古物博物馆馆刊》第17期）。这些简朴的原型经历了漫长的发展，在中国边境最终形成了精巧的兽头或环柄弯刀。这种漫长的进化早已有之，高本汉教授认为，早在殷商时期（公元前13世纪）之始，兽头小刀就已存在。罗汉堂与上述原型显然有所联系，并非与晚期标本有关。

467

最后，关于工具我还得提及另外一件事实，那就是无论对齐家坪还是罗汉堂而言，均指向相对晚近的年代。图版52中图15是一把不对称石刀，这种形制在不召寨及安阳商王朝时期均有标本（《中国史前史研究》，第228页，图版165中图8至图10）。

---

① 安特生：《动物纹中的狩猎巫术的含义》，《远东古物博物馆馆刊》第4期，图版19中图2至图5。

② 比较图版53中图26、图27的标本，和安特生在《远东古物博物馆馆刊》第4期发表的文章《动物风格的狩猎力量》，图版1至图版4中的标本，以及B.卡尔格林发表在《远东古物博物馆馆刊》第17期上的文章《殷商时期的武器和工具》，图版27中图147，图版29中图158，图版30。

第三部分
图版描述

图版 1-19 和图版 24 是齐家坪的标本（图版 10，图版 15 有几个有特别标记的例外）。图版 20 来自辛店丙址，图版 21 至图版 23 是甘肃各地的标本。图版 25 至图版 54 是罗汉堂的标本。图版 55 和图版 56 是七里墩和小石峡的标本。

图版 1
（实物尺寸的一半）

1. 标号 K.11242：105. 浅褐色碗口陶片，陶胎呈灰色。内侧因抹平和修整而形成同心条纹。外侧除近碗口处，质地粗糙，布有划痕。齐家坪：Ⅰa 类。

2. 标号 K.11242：387. 褐色器物颈部陶片，陶胎呈砖红色。靠近器口处内壁及外壁陶衣分布不均，从而在表面出现凸带纹，陶衣呈灰黄色。齐家坪：Ⅰa 类。

3. 标号 K.11242：41. 砖红色器物口陶片。内壁及外壁陶衣呈浅黄褐色。齐家坪：Ⅰa 类。

4. 标号 K.11242：D. 浅砖红色陶罐的小陶片，两侧均有灰白色陶衣。齐家坪：Ⅰa 类。

5. 标号 K.11242：23. 砖红色器物器身陶片，外壁有偏白的黄色陶衣。器物下半部分有席纹。齐家坪：Ⅰa 类。

6. 标号 K.11242：159. 褐色陶罐陶片，外壁白黄色陶衣。罐体平滑，下腹部呈抹过的轻微席纹。齐家坪：Ⅰa类。

7.标号K.11242：300.褐色陶罐腹部陶片。外壁有典型席纹。齐家坪：Ⅰa类。

8.标号K.11242：30.砖红色陶罐腹部陶片，带浅褐色陶衣，外壁有席纹。齐家坪：Ⅰa类。

9.标号K.11242：281.砖红色器物腹部陶片，带浅黄色陶衣，外壁有席纹。齐家坪：Ⅰa类。

10.标号K.11242：298.浅褐色陶器器身陶片，外表光滑，也有部分抹去的席纹痕。齐家坪：Ⅰa类。

11.标号K.11242：282.白黄色陶器的器耳陶片。外侧饰有长刻线。

12.标号K.11242：24.淡褐色陶器器耳陶片。外侧饰有长刻线。齐家坪：Ⅰa类。

13.标号K.11242：22.白色陶器器耳陶片，陶胎呈灰色。内侧有席纹。这里还有一个起支撑作用的器耳的残片。外侧饰有刻十字纹。器口上有装饰用的槽口。齐家坪：Ⅰa类。

14.标号K.11242：60.带有环形器口的颈部陶片。器颈与器身过渡处有一个附加堆纹带，上面刻有方格纹。齐家坪：Ⅰa类。

图版2

（实物尺寸的一半）

1.标号K.11242：73.砖红色器物颈部陶片。器口内侧有三重轮廓。齐家坪：Ⅰa类。

2.标号K.11242：120.砖红色陶器器口陶片，灰褐色陶胎。口沿呈扁平状。齐家坪：Ⅰa类。

3.标号K.11242：396.砖红色陶器口部陶片。外部有褐色陶衣。口沿扁平。口沿向器身过渡到有条带装饰，条带上饰有方格纹。齐家坪：Ⅰa类。

4.标号K.11242：63.碗口陶片。砖红色。内侧光滑。碗口的外部有折叠边。下部隐约可见模糊的席纹。齐家坪：Ⅰa类。

5.标号K.11242：315.轮廓清晰的双锥形陶器的陶片。砖红色。外表色调部分呈褐色。器腹下半部分有席纹。齐家坪：Ⅰa类。

6.标号K.11242：290.砖红色陶器器身小陶片。外侧席纹。齐家坪：Ⅰa类。

7.标号11242：294.砖红色陶器器身陶片。外侧呈褐色，有篮纹。齐家坪：Ⅰa类。

8.标号K.11242：295.褐色陶器器身陶片。外侧有纹饰。齐家坪：Ⅰa类。

9.标号K.11242：356.砖红色陶器的器底陶片。外部有黄白色陶衣。底部外侧有模糊但精致的席纹或类似纹饰。内侧有较粗糙的篮纹。齐家坪：Ⅰa类。

10.标号K.11242：341.砖红色陶器底部陶片。外侧有粗糙的席纹。器底是从内部贴到器壁上的，图片上可以清晰地看到。齐家坪：Ⅰa类。

11.标号K.11242：370.有双锥形孔的器底陶片。浅褐色陶器。齐家坪：Ⅰa类。

12.标号K.11242：14.砖红色器底陶片。外表面有斜编织纹。齐家坪：Ⅰa类。

图版3
（实物尺寸的一半）

1.标号K.11242：818.浅褐色小双耳罐。器耳缺失一个，另一个上面有席纹。器底不分明。齐家坪：Ⅰb类。

2.标号K.11242：107.大型陶器的器颈和器身陶片。砖红色陶器，褐色表层，灰色陶胎。器颈和器身过渡处有长刻线纹。齐家坪：Ⅰb类。 *469*

3.标号K.11242：260.砖红色陶器器身大片陶片。外侧呈灰黄色色调，并带有红斑点。大部分器身覆有席纹。齐家坪：Ⅰb类。

4.标号K.11269：2.砖红色小陶壶。外部淡褐色，有红斑点。该陶器只有一个器耳。器身席纹明显，但已被刻意抹掉，几乎抹平了。壶底外侧也有席纹，壶底还可观察到另一种纹饰，似乎是木头的纹理。齐家坪：Ⅰb类。

5.标号K.11242：144.陶碗，砖红色，残缺不全。内外均涂有淡黄灰色陶衣。外侧有模糊可见的席纹，也几乎被磨平了。可以清楚地看到，碗的底座是从碗内部固定上去的，连接点很清晰。碗的质量很好，但生产工艺不精。齐家坪：Ⅰb类。

图版4
（实物尺寸的一半）

1.标号K.11242：166.浅褐色陶器器颈陶片。齐家坪：Ⅰb类。

2.标号K.11242：37.砖红色器物的颈部和器身部陶片，陶片内外都有黄白色陶衣。器颈向器身过渡处有刻十字纹。齐家坪：Ⅰb类。

3. 标号K.11242：380.第5类型陶盉陶片。浅褐色陶器。齐家坪：Ⅰb类。

4. 标号K.11242：283.器物器身上半部分的小陶片。褐色陶器，陶胎呈灰色。双排三角形戳印纹。齐家坪：Ⅰb类。

5. 标号K.11242：216.砖红色陶器陶片，涂褐色陶衣。器颈向器身过渡处有刻方格纹。齐家坪：Ⅰb类。

6. 标号K.11242：407.带平圆纽的器盖陶片。浅褐色器物。齐家坪：Ⅰb类。

7. 标号K.11242：377.小陶器陶片。浅褐色，陶胎色泽较暗。齐家坪：Ⅰb类。

8. 标号K.11242：381.器颈陶片，带残余的器耳。浅褐色器物。齐家坪：Ⅰb类。

9. 标号K.11242：431 小型陶器陶片。砖红色。外侧有褐色陶衣。齐家坪：Ⅰa类。

10. 标号K.11242：403 碗口陶片。砖红色陶器，带淡黄褐色陶衣。碗口饰斜切口。齐家坪：Ⅰa类或Ⅰb类。

11. 标号K.11242：398.陶碗口沿陶片。砖红色陶器，陶胎淡褐色。内外侧均有淡黄色陶衣。碗口有装饰性的齿状纹。齐家坪：Ⅰa类或Ⅰb类。

12. 标号K.11242：272.砖红色陶器器身陶片，胎心层呈灰色。外部布满深灰色陶衣，部分器表有烟炱。器身下腹部可能有纹饰。齐家坪：Ⅰa类或Ⅰb类。

13. 标号K.11242：293.浅褐色陶器器身陶片，陶胎呈淡褐色。外侧有席纹。齐家坪：Ⅰa类或Ⅰb类。

14. 标号K.1i242：312.砖红色陶器器身的小片陶片。外侧有席纹。齐家坪：Ⅰa类（陶器）或b类（技术）。

15. 标号K.11242：278.红褐色陶器器身陶片，灰色陶胎。外侧有浅灰黄色陶衣。席纹。齐家坪：Ⅰa类或Ⅰb类。

16. 标号K.11242：197.褐色陶器器身陶片。外侧席纹。齐家坪：Ⅰb类或Ⅰc类。

470

17. 标号K.11242：297.褐色陶器陶片。外侧有方格戳印纹。齐家坪：Ⅰb类或Ⅰc类。

18. 标号K.1i242：334.器身陶片，带有器底。红色陶器。外侧有浅黄色白陶衣。器身有席纹。器底是从外侧固定上去的。齐家坪：Ⅰa类或Ⅰb类。

图版5

（实物尺寸的一半）

1. 标号K.11242：B.褐色厚壁陶器颈部陶片。器颈向器身过渡处有方格纹。齐家坪：Ⅰa类。

2. 标号K.11242：57.褐色厚壁陶器器颈陶片。器颈向器身过渡处有方格纹。齐家坪：Ⅰc类。

3. 标号K.11242：25.厚壁陶器器颈和器身陶片。器颈向器身过渡处有方格纹。齐家坪：Ⅰc类。

4. 标号K.11242：859.带足小碗，可能是灯盏。褐灰色陶器。有红色痕迹。齐家坪：Ⅰc类。

5. 标号K.11242：268.砖红色陶器盖陶片，器表呈灰色。齐家坪：Ⅰc类。

6. 标号K.11242：269.带圆纽的器盖陶片。口沿饰有斜切的槽口。齐家坪：Ⅰc类。

7. 标号K.11242：812.淡褐色陶盖陶片。边缘有半月形的刻纹。齐家坪：Ⅰc类。

8. 标号K.11242：267.带圆纽的器盖陶片，边缘有一排凹纹。褐色陶器，器表呈灰色。有烟炱层。齐家坪：Ⅰc类。

9. 标号K.11242：150.带器耳的器身陶片。灰褐色陶器，红褐色陶胎。器耳上有方格纹。齐家坪：Ⅰc类。

10. 标号K.11242：103.碗口陶片。褐红色陶器。外侧有篮纹。齐家坪：Ⅰc类。

11. 标号K.11242：774.带器耳的器身陶片。器身上有附加堆纹蛇装饰。器身有席纹。褐灰色陶器。齐家坪：Ⅰc类。

12. 标号K.11242：336.器身和器底陶片。褐色陶器。器身布满席纹。底部内侧有织物留下的三角形纹。齐家坪：Ⅰb类。

13. 标号K.11242：99和29.褐色薄壁器物边沿陶片。边缘呈肾形，向内弯曲。齐家坪：Ⅰc类。

14. 标号K.11242：145.低足碗，饰有斜凹痕。黄褐色陶器。齐家坪：Ⅰb类。

图版6

（实物尺寸的一半）

1.标号K.11242：10.带器嘴的器口陶片。器物口沿内侧有一个用于安装器盖的宽凹槽。浅褐色陶器。外层有烟炱斑点。器口稍低处，还有器耳上有席纹。相邻处用新月形堆纹勾边，离器口最近部分很光滑。齐家坪：Ⅰb类。

2.标号K.11242：335.浅褐色器物器底陶片。有席纹。齐家坪：Ⅱa类。

3.标号K.11242：436.黄褐色陶器陶片。器身外侧布满绳纹，并带有一个圆纽。齐家坪：Ⅱa类。

4.标号K.11242：33.褐色陶器陶片。内外侧都有烟炱斑点。器身外侧布满篮纹。齐家坪：Ⅱb类。

4715.标号K.11242：815.褐色陶器陶片。器身布满纹饰。整个外侧布满厚烟炱层，内侧也有烟炱斑点。齐家坪：Ⅱa类。

6.K.11242：816.褐色小陶壶，外层有烟炱。陶身有绳纹。内侧向底部增厚。齐家坪：Ⅱb类。

图版7

（实物尺寸的一半）

1.标号K.11242：461.砖红色陶器陶片，两面都有褐色陶衣。器口饰有锯齿形纹饰。器颈和器身过渡处有环状物，上面刻有十字纹。器身布满绳纹。齐家坪：Ⅱa类。

2.标号K.11242：446.褐色陶器陶片，上有颜色基本相同的陶衣。口部饰有斜切的锯齿形装饰。器身有绳纹。离颈部最近的地方，绳纹被磨平了，但刻划的沟槽之间绳纹仍然保留，形成装饰性的脊线。齐家坪：Ⅱb类。

3.标号K.11242：36.口沿陶片，器口大大加厚，其外缘饰有斜切的锯齿形装饰。砖红色陶器，两面有淡黄色陶衣。外部有席纹。齐家坪：Ⅱb类。

4.标号K.11242：11.口沿陶片，器口大大加厚，器口外缘呈波浪状。外部有席纹。紧挨着器口下面的一部分很柔滑。砖红色器物，灰色陶胎，淡褐色表层。齐家坪：Ⅱa类。图b."无色透明胶取样"正面。

5.标号K.11242：462.口沿陶片，器口大大加厚，器口外缘呈波浪状。口部下方，有平滑的沟槽，沟槽之间有一部分席纹（其余部分布满在器身上），已经被抹去了。齐家坪：Ⅱb类。

6.标号K.11242：147.器身陶片，带大器耳。砖红色陶器，浅褐色陶衣。器身下半部分布满席纹，器耳下侧也有席纹。齐家坪：Ⅱb类。

7.标号K.11242：26.灰褐色陶器的器颈陶片。器颈与器身之间有一条附加堆纹带，上面刻有方格纹。齐家坪：Ⅱb类。

8.（原著缺第8条）

9.标号K.11242：53.砖红色陶器口沿陶片，外部有一丝淡褐色。紧挨器口下方有一个边框，上面饰有斜切口。齐家坪：Ⅱb类。

10.标号K.11242：35.浅褐色器物口沿陶片，陶胎呈红色。器口30毫米以下有锯齿装饰。齐家坪：Ⅱb类。

11.标号K.11242：574.褐色陶器陶片，浅灰黄色陶衣。内外均有大片的烟炱。器身和器耳外侧布满绳纹，虽然几乎被抹去了，但在器颈外侧还清晰可见。齐家坪：Ⅱb类。

12.标号K.11232：4.红黄色陶器陶片。器身外侧布满绳纹。齐家坪：Ⅱb类。

13.标号K.11242：52.浅褐色陶器陶片。内外均有灰黄色陶衣。器身外侧布满篮纹。齐家坪：Ⅱb类。

14.标号K.11242：249.砖红色三足陶器陶片，表面有褐色层。外部布满篮纹。齐家坪：Ⅱb类或Ⅱa类。

15.标号K.11242：718.褐色陶器器身和器底陶片。器底从内部连接上去，器身边缘折叠。器身布满绳纹。器底底面有模糊的席纹或类似的纹饰。齐家坪：Ⅱb类。

16.标号K.11242：202.砖红色三足陶器器腿部陶片。绳纹。齐家坪：Ⅱb类。 *472*

17.标号K.11242：715.褐色陶器的器底陶片。器底从外部连接到陶器上。器身有绳纹。齐家坪：Ⅱb类。

18.标号K.11242：366.带孔的陶器器底陶片。砖红色。外侧有褐色陶衣和烟炱痕迹。齐家坪：Ⅱb类。

图版8

（实物尺寸的一半）

1.标号K.11242：441.灰褐色器颈陶片。器身布满绳纹。器颈和器身连接处清晰可见。齐家坪：Ⅱb类。

2.标号K.11242：573.褐色陶器器颈陶片。外侧有烟炱斑点。器身和器耳布满绳纹。齐家坪：Ⅱb类。

3.标号 K.11242：493.陶口陶片，口沿上有附加堆纹来加固。外侧有席纹。齐家坪：Ⅱa类。

4.标号 K.11242：705.从内侧分两半的陶器的器身与器底陶片。褐色。器身有绳纹。齐家坪：Ⅱa类。

5.标号 K.11242：576.裂开的陶器器口陶片。器身外侧和器口扁平口沿上都有绳纹。浅砖红色。齐家坪：Ⅱa类。

6.标号 K.11242：555.裂开的陶器器口和器身陶片，轮廓微微凸起，从外面切割而成。浅砖红色陶器。器身外侧布满绳纹。器口口沿呈微微凹陷的轮廓。齐家坪：Ⅱa类。

7.标号 K.11242：577.裂开的陶器器身带器口陶片。外侧有席纹。陶片由两片小陶片连接在一起。裂缝在图中清晰可见。齐家坪：Ⅱa类。

8.标号 K.11242：707.裂开的砖红色陶器陶片，切口直接穿过陶器器壁。齐家坪：Ⅱa类。

9.标号 K.11242：717.裂开的陶器器底陶片。误切的切口，显示是从陶器内部切开的。褐色。外部有烟炱。齐家坪：Ⅱb类。

图版9

（实物尺寸的一半）

1.标号 K.11242：566.砖红色陶器器身陶片，两面都有厚厚的褐色陶衣。外部有绳纹（图2，无色透明胶翻转图的正面）。齐家坪：Ⅱb类。

2.标号 K.11242：478.浅砖红色陶器器颈陶片。外部有篮纹，该纹饰也延伸到了颈部（图b，正方形）齐家坪：Ⅱb类。

3.标号 K.11242：559.褐色陶器器身陶片。有绳纹。外侧有烟炱斑点，内侧一些地方也有。齐家坪：Ⅱb类。

4.标号 K.11242：4.浅褐色陶器器身陶片。外侧有编织纹（图b，无色透明胶翻转图的正面）。齐家坪：Ⅱa类。

5.标号 K.11242：727.褐色薄壁陶器陶片。外侧有席纹，上面有烟炱。内侧和裂缝上也有烟炱斑点（图b，无色透明胶翻转图的正面）。齐家坪：Ⅱb类。

6.标号 K.11242：567.黄褐色陶器器身陶片。外部褐色。有绳纹。齐家坪：Ⅱb类。

7.标号 K.11242：249.带褐色表层的砖红色三足陶器陶片。内侧布满柳编工艺篮纹（图 b，无色透明胶翻转图的正面）。齐家坪：Ⅱb类。

8.标号 K.11242：664.浅褐色陶器器身陶片。外侧有绳纹（图 b，无色透明胶翻转图的正面）齐家坪：Ⅱa类。

473

图版 10
（实物尺寸的一半）

1.标号 K.11242：16.砖红色陶器器颈陶片，器表呈艳丽的黄红色。器口下有锯齿状装饰。篮纹（图 b，无色透明胶翻转图的正面）。齐家坪：Ⅱb类。

2.标号 K.11242：558.褐色陶器器身陶片，外表呈红色。外侧有绳纹（图 b，正方形）。齐家坪：Ⅱb类。

3.标号 K.11269：27.辛店丙址，褐色陶器器颈和器身的小陶片。篮纹或编织纹（图 b，无色透明胶翻转图的正面）。齐家坪：Ⅱa类。

图版 11
（实物尺寸的一半）

1.标号 K.11242：7.砖红色陶器器身陶片，内外两侧都带黄褐色陶衣。外侧有绳纹。（图 b，无色透明胶翻转图的正面）齐家坪：Ⅱa类。

2.标号 K.11242：667.褐色陶器器身小陶片，外侧有烟炱层。绳纹（图 b，无色透明胶翻转图的正面）。齐家坪：Ⅱ类。

3.标号 K.11231：3.褐色陶器器身小陶片（图 b，无色透明胶翻转图的正面）。齐家坪：Ⅱb类。

图版 12
（实物尺寸的一半）

1.标号 K.11242：3.淡褐色陶器陶片。器耳下有一个黑斑点。器颈内侧呈紫褐色。外侧装饰篦点纹（还有一部分纹饰在附加堆纹上）和成对的戳印纹。齐家坪：Ⅲ类。

2.标号 K.11242：834.浅褐色陶器陶片。外部布满席纹；内部也存有类似纹饰。外部装饰有线形附加堆纹，有的还组合了篦点纹。齐家坪：Ⅲ类。

3.标号 K.11242：857.深灰褐色陶器陶片。外部有席纹和线形附加堆纹、篦点纹、角状的戳印纹。器颈下半部分戳印纹上的角的顶点上下交替。内外部都有烟炱。齐家坪：Ⅲ类。

4.标号 K.11242：848.浅褐色陶器器身小陶片。外部有席纹和蜿蜒的附加堆纹。齐家坪：Ⅲ类。

5.标号 K.11242：4.器身上半部分的小陶片。深褐色陶器。外部有线形附加堆纹和篦点纹。内外部均有烟炱痕迹。齐家坪：Ⅲ类。

6.标号 K.11242：845.陶器陶片，带器底。褐黄色陶器。器身有席纹和线形附加堆纹。齐家坪：Ⅲ类。

7.标号 K.11242：844.褐色陶器器身小陶片。外部有蜿蜒的附加堆纹。齐家坪：Ⅲ类。

8.标号 K.11242：846.灰褐色陶器器底和器身小陶片，器身带席纹和蜿蜒的附加堆纹。齐家坪：Ⅲ类。

9.标号 K.11242：777.暗褐色陶器器身小陶片。外部有席纹和线形的附加堆纹。齐家坪：Ⅲ类。

10.标号 K.11242：838.砖红色陶器，外部褐色。篦点纹线条装饰，器耳上有三角形和菱形戳印纹。齐家坪：Ⅲ类。

11.标号 K.11242：6.浅黄褐色器颈陶片。内侧整个涂有紫褐色。外侧有篦点纹和Ⅴ形戳印纹。齐家坪：Ⅲ类。

474

12.标号 K.11242：839.黄褐色陶器陶片。器身有席纹。器耳和器颈饰有篦点纹。器颈上也有三角戳印纹，三角形的尖角上下交替出现。外侧有烟炱痕迹。齐家坪：Ⅲ类。

13.标号 K.11242：842.灰褐色陶器器颈陶片。饰有篦点纹的附加堆纹，篦点纹之间有一排排短线。外部有烟炱。齐家坪：Ⅲ类。

14.标号 K.11242：841.褐色陶器器颈和器身陶片。外侧有席纹，并装饰篦点纹。器耳上有两个装饰性圆纽，其中一个已经遗失。齐家坪：Ⅲ类。

图版 13

（实物尺寸的一半）

1.标号 K.11242：858.黄褐色陶器陶片。外侧有烟炱和席纹，内侧也有模糊的席纹。装饰篦点纹。器耳残缺不全。齐家坪：Ⅲ类。

2.标号 K.11242：1.浅褐色陶器陶片。器身和器耳上有席纹和烟炱痕迹。装饰篦点纹、线形附加堆纹和短小的曲折线刻纹。齐家坪：Ⅲ类。

3.标号 K.11242：7.淡褐色陶器陶片。外侧有席纹。装饰附加堆纹带和篦点纹。器身和器耳上有两对带有圆形切口的圆纽，器颈两侧和器身上半部分表面涂成了紫红色。齐家坪：Ⅲ类。

4.标号 K.11242：835.浅褐色陶器陶片。器身有席纹。装饰有附加堆纹带和篦点纹。还饰有带圆形切口的圆纽。外侧有烟炱层。齐家坪：Ⅲ类。

5.标号 K.11242：8.浅灰褐色陶器陶片。外侧有席纹，装饰附加堆纹带和篦点纹。器耳和器颈也有双戳印纹，器颈上有两个饰有同样纹饰的装饰性圆纽。器颈内侧（见图 b）涂有紫褐色宽线纹。器耳上半部分也有紫褐色痕迹。其余表层有烟炱。齐家坪：Ⅲ类。

6.标号 K.11242：27.淡黄色陶器陶片，带红色斑点。外侧有篮纹。齐家坪：Ⅲ类。

7.标号 K.11242：843.褐色器颈小陶片。外侧饰线形附加堆纹、篦点纹和其他三条平行线形式的戳印纹。内侧涂有紫褐色彩绘三角形。外侧有一层烟炱。齐家坪：Ⅲ类。

8.标号 K.11242：847.褐色陶器陶片。外侧有席纹，装饰成带有短斜线篦点纹的附加堆纹。齐家坪：Ⅲ类。

9.标号 K.11242：855.黄褐色陶器器身陶片。外侧有席纹和带有篦点纹的附加堆纹。齐家坪：Ⅲ类。

10.标号 K.11242：854.与前一件同类型的器身陶片。深灰色陶器。齐家坪：Ⅲ类。

11.标号 K.11242：5.大型陶器器颈带器耳陶片。暗褐色陶器。锯齿纹上有连续的线条状装饰，器耳上也有两个装饰性圆纽。齐家坪：Ⅲ类。

475

图版14
（实物尺寸的一半）

1.标号 K.11242：575.浅褐色陶器陶片。外侧有相对粗糙的席纹。器颈和器身上半部分光滑。器耳上有两个圆纽，圆纽中间有凹痕。一个圆纽遗失。外侧有烟炱。齐家坪：Ⅲ类。

2.标号 K.11242：719.褐色陶器陶片。陶片外侧和器耳内侧有席纹。陶片内侧也有相同纹饰。齐家坪：Ⅲ类。

3.标号 K.11242：726.浅灰黄色陶器陶片。外侧呈艳丽的红色，并带有席纹。内侧也有相同纹饰。紧挨器口下方，有白色锯齿纹。齐家坪：Ⅲ类。

4.标号 K.11242：724.浅褐色陶器陶片。外侧有席纹。紧挨器口下方，有一条窝点装饰带。齐家坪：Ⅲ类。

5.标号 K.11242：12.砖红色陶器陶片。外侧呈灰色。器身和器颈外侧布满席纹。紧挨器口下方，有一条有窝点装饰带。外表有厚厚的一层烟炱。

6.标号 K.11242：758.浅灰色陶器陶片。外侧有席纹。紧挨光滑的口沿下方，有窝点装饰带。齐家坪：Ⅲ类。

7.标号 K.11242：771.砖红色陶器器颈陶片。外侧有席纹和烟炱痕迹。靠近器口下面有类似绳纹的附加堆纹。齐家坪：Ⅲ类。

8.标号 K.11242：721.黄褐色陶器陶片。外部有席纹。内侧也有相同纹饰的模糊印迹。器口下面有窝点装饰带。外部一层烟炱。齐家坪：Ⅲ类。

9.标号 K.11242：770.黄褐色器颈陶片。外面有席纹。器口口沿下面有窝点状附加堆纹，堆纹上有凹槽。齐家坪：Ⅲ类。

10.标号 K.11242：789.深褐色陶器的小陶片。外面有席纹。齐家坪：Ⅲ类。

11.标号 K.11242：783.器底陶片，与器身为一体。底部有席纹。齐家坪：Ⅲ类。

12.标号 K.11242：837.红褐色陶器陶片。外表显示有席纹，有一层烟炱。器颈装饰一圈附加堆纹，上面有窝点状装饰，上面用垂直的篦点纹勾勒了一条边，下面是V形戳印纹，V的方向上下交替出现。

图版15

（实物的大小）

1.标号 K.11242：798.淡黄红色黏土块。上有斜孔洞，但未穿过黏土块中心。

2.标号 K.11242：827.用烧过的黏土制作的动物雕塑，残缺不全。褐色陶器。

3.标号 K.11242：748.淡黄色的烧过的黏土块。表面不平整。

4.标号 K.11242：744.灰褐色黏土陶片。上侧有小孔，但未穿透。

5.标号 K.11269：10.辛店丙址蘑菇状黏土块。

6.标号 K.11242：205.陶片，带圆纽，圆纽上有锯齿状切口装饰。颜色呈淡黄褐色。

476

7.标号K.11242：207.环形器物足部陶片。砖红色。外侧有一层烟炱。

8.标号K.11242：203.小型陶鬲足部陶片。完全中空，残缺不全。淡褐色器物。

9.标号K.11242：749.纺轮陶片。品质上乘，砖红色。表层颜色比陶胎要浅。侧面有模糊可辨的席纹。直径70毫米。

10.标号K.11242：751.圆锥形的纺轮陶片。制作工艺相对不精。淡黄褐色。直径59毫米。

11.标号K.11242：821.黏土环残片。灰色陶器。剖面呈三角形。

12.标号K.11242：800.黏土环残片。灰色陶器。剖面呈三角形。

13.标号K.11242：824.黏土环残片。灰色陶器。剖面呈三角形。

14.标号K.11242：822.黏土环残片。灰黑色陶器。外表是黑色的抛光面。剖面呈三角形。

15.标号K.11242：825.黏土环残片。剖面呈椭圆形。

图版16

（实物的大小）

1.标号K.11242：f.骨针尖端。

2.标号K.11242：a.骨针尖端。

3.标号K.11242：e.骨针尖端。

4.标号K.11242：826.骨针或类似物品的残片。

5.标号K.11242：c.骨针残片。

6.标号K.11242：ö.残缺的骨针。

7.标号K.11242：Ä.残缺的骨针。

8.标号K.11242：Z.带眼的残骨针。

9.标号K.11242：b.骨针尖端。

10.标号K.11242：A.骨针针眼不全。

11.标号K.11242：d.带眼骨针。

12.标号K.11242：829 a.带眼骨针残片。

13.标号K.11242：832.带划痕的骨刀。

14.标号K.11242：T.骨刀。

15.标号K.11242：g.骨刀。

16.标号 K.11242：P.骨刀。

17.标号 K.11242：Q.骨刀。

18.标号 K.11242：V.骨刀。

19.标号 K.11242：X.骨刀。

20.标号 K.11242：819.骨刀残片。

21.标号 K.11242：828.骨器。

22.标号 K.11242：N.纺织用骨针。

23.标号 K.11242：831.似凿子的骨器。

24.标号 K.11242：S.纺织用骨板。

25.标号 K.11242：O.纺织用骨板。

26.标号 K.11242： R.纺织用骨板。

27.标号 K.11242：829.骨质珠子。

图版 17

（实物的三分之二尺寸大小）

1.标号 K.1383.石斧。边缘残缺但可能是打磨过的。长 180 毫米，边缘宽 57 毫米，中间厚 45 毫米。

2.标号 K.1338.石斧颈部残片。狭长的侧面被凿开。

3.标号 K.1384.小青石石斧。部分抛光。长 110 毫米，宽 50 毫米，厚 27 毫米。

4.标号 K.1379.抛光的青石斧头，残缺不全。狭窄面也经过抛光。宽 66 毫米，厚 30 毫米。

图版 18

（实物的三分之二尺寸大小）

1.标号 K.11242：6.石板矛头。矛刃中间有一个未完全穿透的双锥形孔。

2.标号 K.11242：801.石板矛头，三角形。

477
3.标号 K.1342.青石打磨的斧头，残缺不全。有穿绳的孔。

4.标号 K.11242：758.泥质石匕首尖。边缘锋利。

5.标号 K.1340.青石小石斧。边缘被磨尖。长 84 毫米，宽 35 毫米，厚 24 毫米。

6.标号 K.1327.磨制的片状岩石凿子。剖面规整。长 80 毫米，宽 11 毫米，厚

11.5毫米。

7.标号 K.1378.泥质砂岩凿子。剖面呈长方形，长86毫米，宽22毫米，厚18毫米。

8.标号 K.1324.泥质砂岩凿子。凿背面破碎。宽29毫米，厚18毫米。

9.标号 K.11242：754.石英石器具。

10.标号 K.1363.残纺轮。

图版19
（实物的三分之二尺寸大小）

1.标号 K.1331.未完工的砂岩石刀。长80毫米，宽50毫米，厚8毫米。

2.标号 K.1334.砂岩石刀。短边上有对应的凹槽。长61毫米，宽44毫米，厚11毫米。

3.标号 K.1355.砂岩石刀，已残缺不全。有钻孔。长65毫米，宽44毫米，厚10毫米。

4.标号 K.1385.抛光的青石刀。中间有双锥形孔。长79毫米，宽（中间部位）45毫米，厚9毫米。

5.标号 K.1335.青石刀。刀刃锋利。有双锥形孔。长82毫米，宽39毫米，厚6毫米。

6.标号 K.11242：H.板岩磨边刀。有双锥形孔。边缘明显向孔收缩。长100毫米，宽（中间）46毫米，厚6毫米。

7.标号 K.1364.打浆石。

8.标号 K.1330.石棒，窄边上有两个相互交叉的刻痕。宽65毫米，厚32毫米。

9.标号 K.11242：797.砂岩残片。中间有斜钻孔。

版图20

1.标号 K.11269：7-8.辛店丙址类型。残缺不全的大型直壁陶器。黄褐色。外侧带淡黄灰色陶衣，且有席纹。靠近陶器口沿处有大片断裂。实物的1/3尺寸大小。

2.标号 K 11269：5.辛店丙址类型。破碎的砖红色陶罐，表面呈褐色。外侧及内侧部分区域有烟炱。罐身外侧布满篮纹或编织纹，实物的1/2尺寸大小。

3.标号K.11209：6.辛店丙址类型。褐色陶器器颈和器身陶片。内侧和外侧都有烟炱痕迹。器身外侧布满绳纹。实物的1/2尺寸大小。

4.标号K.11269：4.辛店丙址类型。砖红色。陶罐。中等大小。底部内侧和外侧都有烟炱痕迹。外侧布满席纹。紧挨口沿下方，有锯齿状边框。实物的1/3尺寸大小。

5.标号K 11269：3.辛店丙址类型。残缺的陶罐。带两个器耳，其中一个已丢失。浅砖红色。罐外部和颈部内侧有浅灰黄色陶衣。颈部是从外部连接上去的，陶罐内外都有烟炱痕迹。罐身和器耳中部布满绳纹。器耳上方的器口边沿处有五个装饰性的指甲纹。实物的1/2尺寸大小。

478

图版21

1.标号K.5428.宁定县（译者注：今甘肃省广河县），八堡川（译者注：此处未考证到对应中文地名，根据此处威妥玛式拼音，疑为八堡川）购买。陶罐。漏斗状器颈，双锥形器身，带初步成型的器耳。呈淡黄褐色。罐身下半部分有微弱的篮纹。陶器高22.5厘米，最宽处13.6厘米，器口直径12厘米，底部直径6.1厘米。实物的1/2尺寸大小。

2.标号K.6042.狄道县（译者注：今甘肃临洮县）马家窑。浅黄褐色陶罐，轮廓柔和圆润，有两个器耳。罐身下半部带篮纹。器颈两侧都有厚厚的红色层。罐高29厘米，最宽处17.4厘米，器耳宽2.1厘米，口部直径12.2厘米，底部直径6.8厘米。实物的2/3尺寸大小。

3.标号K.5423.漏斗状长颈双耳双锥形罐。与罐身过渡处有一条切画痕。罐身下腹部布满篮纹。实物的2/3尺寸大小。

4.标号K.5433.购买于甘肃。陶罐。漏斗状颈部，双锥形罐身，罐身从圆润过渡到垂直面。砖红色。外侧黄灰色陶衣和油或类似东西的黑斑。罐身下腹部布满篮纹，一直延续到底部。罐高22.3厘米，最宽处14.8厘米，口部直径10.2厘米，底部直径7.1厘米。实物的1/2尺寸大小。

图版22

（实物的三分之一尺寸大小）

1.标号K.11269：1.辛店丙址类型。砖红色品质上乘的大型陶罐，残缺不全。外部呈艳红色。器身呈明显的双锥形，无器耳，下腹部有篮纹。

2.标号K.5426.购买于秦州（译者注：根据原文威妥玛式拼音，译为秦州）。中型陶罐。漏斗状器颈，双锥形器身，带两个器耳。高250毫米。最大口径155毫米，器耳宽20毫米，口部直径130毫米；底部直径90毫米。器颈以及器身上腹部有同心线纹，下腹部有不清晰的席纹。

3.标号K.5422.宁定县（译者注：今甘肃广河县），排子坪。购买。中等大小陶器，宽口，双锥形器身，最大宽度在陶器中部，环形器足上有四个孔。口部有两个大器耳和两个小器耳。明亮的黄褐色陶器；外表很光滑，但现在有些受腐蚀。陶器高190毫米，最大宽度212毫米，4个器耳宽度分别为19毫米、11毫米、18毫米和12毫米。器口直径140毫米；器底直径93毫米。

4.标号K.5963.榆中县小石峡。和前一件相同类型的中等大小陶器。然而，这个陶器器身轮廓是柔和的圆形。赤土陶器，上带黑色斑点，烟炱斑点或类似东西。高186毫米，宽178毫米，两个器耳宽分别是11毫米和16毫米，底部外直径91毫米。该陶器大部分是修复的。

5.标号K.5523.购买于兰州。陶壶。高颈，蹲身。带壶嘴，壶口有拱形顶，顶上有肾形孔。器颈向器身过渡处有一条刻线。宽器耳顶端有两个"铆钉头"。器物口沿高度19.8厘米，最大宽度15厘米，器耳宽4.6厘米。底部直径19.2厘米。深灰色器物，陶胎中间为灰色。外侧光滑，显示出红色的微弱印迹。器底底面和器耳，有不清晰的席纹。

479

图版23

（实物尺寸的一半）

1.标号K.5427.购自兰州。带深斑点的浅褐色壶。拱形顶盖占去器口三分之二，有一个高约18毫米的出水口。壶高156毫米，最宽处104毫米，器耳宽31毫米，底部直径58毫米。

2.标号 K.5487.购自秦州。小型大双耳罐。颈高 54 毫米，顶部加宽，双锥形器身。器高 131 毫米，最宽处 86 毫米，口部直径 82 毫米，底部直径 52 毫米，器耳 24 毫米。浅黄褐色。器颈内侧和器耳有微弱的红色痕迹。

3.标号 K.6563.陶器详细出处遗失。高颈小型双耳罐。光滑陶器，砖红色。高 125 毫米，最大口径 88 毫米，器耳宽 33 毫米，器口直径 90 毫米。底部直径 47 毫米。器颈和器耳明显有被磨光过的痕迹。其中一个器耳和部分器颈是修复过的。

4.标号 K.5429.购自兰州。浅褐色小双耳罐。带有红褐色斑点。器身明显是双锥形。器高 110 毫米，最大口径 86 毫米，两个器耳宽度分别为 26 毫米和 27 毫米。口部直径 98 毫米，底部直径 56 毫米。两个器耳都有四条双排装饰线，中间有三个装饰性切口，装饰很随意。

5.标号 K.5467.购自兰州。红褐色光滑小双耳罐。器高 108 毫米，最大口径 67 毫米，器耳宽 30 毫米，口部直径 90 毫米，底部直径 50 毫米。器耳上半部分有类似沙漏计时的戳印装饰，周围有 4 个孔。

6.标号 K.5606.皋兰县。非常小的双耳罐，砖红色。有大的灰色和灰褐色斑点。器高 74 毫米，最大口径 74 毫米。口部直径 62 毫米，底部直径 45 毫米，器耳宽度 22 毫米。器身与器底之间无明显界限，技术质量相比其他的要差得多。

7.标号 K.5430.购自兰州。类似双耳罐的小型陶器。褐黄色，光滑。器高 95 毫米，最大口径 80 毫米，器耳宽 28 毫米。口部直径 72 毫米，底部直径 40 毫米。底面分界线不像大多数买来的陶器那么明确。器身上腹部饰有紫色三角纹。一个器耳断裂，口沿有破损。

8.标号 K.5992.狄道县（译者注：今甘肃临洮县）阎家庄购买。浅黄褐色类似于双耳罐的小陶器。器高 94 毫米，最大口径 105 毫米，器耳宽 20 毫米，口部直径 104 毫米。底面凸起，器身与器底界限不很分明。器颈和器身过渡处有一条刻线。陶器的一小部分修复过。

9.标号 K.5469.购自榆中县。小陶器，类似于双耳罐。器身呈梨形。陶器光滑，呈深砖红色。器高 95 毫米，最大直径 93 毫米，器耳宽 25 毫米，口部直径 89 毫米。底部直径 68 毫米。底面有凹痕，可能是编织的席子纹饰。（参考图版 2 中图 12）

图版 24
（实物的大小）

1.标号 K.11242：802.灰色陶器陶片。陶片上有两个环形的孔洞。

2.标号K.11242：780.灰色光滑陶器陶片。陶片上有两个穿透的小孔。

3.标号K.11242：550.灰色陶器陶片。外部有方格纹。

4.标号K.11242：728.灰色器颈和器身小陶片。器身布满席纹。

5.标号K.11242：47.器口小陶片。黄色陶器。掺入了大量沙砾。

6.标号K.11242：I.彩陶片，呈黑色和褐色两种颜色。

7.标号K.11242：764.彩陶片，兼有黑色和褐色两种颜色。

8.标号K.11242：760.黑色彩陶片。

9.标号K.11242：813.彩陶片，兼有黑色和褐色两种彩绘颜色。

10.标号K.11242：807.彩陶片，兼有黑色和褐色两种彩绘颜色。

11.标号K.11242：812.彩陶片，兼有黑色和褐色两种彩绘颜色。

12.标号K.11242：762.黑褐色彩陶片。

13.标号K.11242：1.饰有较淡和较深褐色的彩陶片。

14.标号K.11242：761.褐色彩陶片。

15.标号K.11242：752.彩陶片，兼有黑色和褐色两种彩绘颜色。

16.标号K.11242：809.彩陶片，兼有黑色和褐色两种彩绘颜色。

17.标号K.11242：808.带器耳陶片，兼有黑色和褐色两种彩绘颜色。

18.标号K.11242：766.淡褐色彩陶片。

19.标号K.11242：810.褐色彩陶片。

20.标号K.11242：765.褐色彩陶片。

21.标号K.11242：814.外部有红色阴影的褐色陶片。绘有紫色装饰图案。

22.标号K.11242：811.外部有灰色斑点的红色陶器陶片。彩绘和上面的类型相同。

23.标号K.11242：K.褐色彩陶片。

24.标号K.11242：L.偏紫色的红褐色陶器，装饰蓝黑色彩绘。

25.标号K.11242：763.带深紫色彩绘装饰的陶片。

26.标号K.11242：104.淡灰色器物足部陶片。

27.标号K.11242：23.淡灰色器盖陶片。

28.标号K.11242：773.深紫褐色彩陶片。

图版25

1.标号K.12003：1549.小型高宽领双耳双锥陶罐。腹部和器口装有长耳。器高130毫米，外直径64毫米，器壁厚4毫米。褐色。表面抛光。部分领部后来脱了色。实物的1/2尺寸大小。

2.标号K.5824.大型陶罐。器领略外侈，领底有附加堆纹带，宽13毫米，被斜切口切成菱形。陶器上半部分光滑，无任何纹饰。下半部分布满席纹。中线以下有两个器耳。高460毫米，宽297毫米，外直径170毫米。实物的1/4尺寸大小。

3.标号K.12003：1550.残缺的烧焦的黏土制作的臂章，向一边缩小。深褐色。高90毫米，宽70～80毫米，壁厚6毫米。实物的1/2尺寸大小。

4.标号K.12003：1671.烧焦的黏土制作的空心泥块，或许是玩具。摇晃时内部有小球响动。灰褐色。实物的1/2尺寸大小。

5.标号K.12003：1676.烧焦的黏土制作的球状物。灰色。实物的1/1尺寸大小。

6.标号K.12003：1675.烧焦的黏土制作的球状物。灰褐色。实物的1/1尺寸大小。

图版26

1.标号K.2170：44.3片陶器器腹陶片。品质上佳，砖红色。外表黄色。上半部分光滑，下半部分有席纹。器壁厚7毫米。实物的2/3尺寸大小。

2.标号K.12003：629.砖红色器腹陶片。黄色器表。底部颜色较深。下半部分有席纹。品质上乘。器壁厚5毫米。实物的1/2尺寸大小。

3.标号K.12003：857.砖红色器耳和器腹陶片。黄色器表，带席纹。上半部分有器耳。器壁厚7毫米。实物的2/3尺寸大小。

4.标号K.2170：45.砖红色陶器腹部陶片。黄色外表。品质上乘。外部布满席纹。上半部分带器耳。器壁厚7毫米。实物的2/3尺寸大小。

5.标号K.12003：893.窄领小陶器颈部陶片。褐色，陶胎呈砖红色。器领外部，有垂直的刮痕。器表抛光。器壁厚度3毫米。实物的1/2尺寸大小。

6.标号K.12003：1456.2片大型褐色陶器的陶片。陶器外部布满很有规律的垂直绳纹，装饰叠加的波浪附加堆纹带。器壁厚度8毫米。实物的2/3尺寸大小。

7.标号K.12003：1672.黄褐色泥质纺轮或吊坠。中间有从两个方向同时向中心钻的孔，但孔未能完全穿透。图上显示的一面，有交叉绳纹。实物的1/1尺寸大小。

图版27

1.标号K.12003：927.大型陶器颈部陶片。粗糙的褐色陶器。宽低领。器壁厚12毫米。陶器边缘以下，有一条附加堆纹带，有不清晰的纹饰。实物的1/2尺寸大小。

2.标号K.12003：834.8片碗陶片。品质上乘的砖红色陶器。口沿外翻。其中一片脱色，从砖红色转变为深褐色。器壁厚度为4毫米，表面被仔细打磨过。实物的1/2尺寸大小。

3.标号K.12003：799.褐红色的碗口陶片，淡黄色表面。器壁厚5毫米，边缘倾斜。实物的1/2尺寸大小。

4.标号K.12003：836.13片口沿外侈的陶碗陶片，底部加强过。品质上乘的褐色陶器。平均厚度7毫米。实物的1/2尺寸大小。

图版28

1.标号K.12003：796.2片口沿外侈的陶碗陶片。品质上乘。砖红色，外部带浅色斑点。较小的陶片内侧因褪色而变成褐色。壁厚8毫米。实物的2/3尺寸大小。

2.标号K.12003：829.2片口沿外侈的陶碗陶片。品质上乘。砖红色。外侧苍白。较小的陶片由于褪色而外表呈灰褐色，这在图中清晰可见。壁厚5毫米。实物的2/3尺寸大小。

3.标号K.12003：687.陶碗陶片，带口沿。实物的2/3尺寸大小。

4.标号K.12003：820.陶碗陶片，带口沿。实物的2/3尺寸大小。

5.标号K.5959.4片陶罐陶片，外形呈弧度平缓的弯曲状。陶器材质中混合了石英石。浅黄色，带砖红色斑点。器耳遗失。壁厚6毫米。实物的1/2尺寸大小。

图版29

1.标号K.12003：915.大型陶器器领陶片。侈口。黄色。外表未做抛光处理（？）壁厚度11毫米。实物的2/3尺寸大小。

2. 标号 K.12003：679.侈口高领陶器陶片。褐色，器表未做抛光处理（？）壁厚7毫米。实物的1/2尺寸大小。

3. 标号 K.12003：680.侈口陶器陶片。褐色，品质上乘。壁厚7毫米。实物的1/2尺寸大小。

4. 标号 K.12003：706.带器耳的陶器陶片。灰褐色。器耳装饰有叠加的波浪带。壁厚8毫米。实物的1/2尺寸大小。

5. 标号 K.12003：810.黄色陶器器颈陶片，烧制较结实但混有石英石。外侧可能有陶衣。器领外侈，有边。器身厚8毫米，颈部厚6毫米。实物的1/2尺寸大小。

6. 标号 K.12003：756.2片双锥形陶器的陶片。黄褐色，陶胎呈灰色。上半部分由于褪色已经转为灰色。实物的1/2尺寸大小。

7. 标号 K.12003：859.砖红色陶器陶片，有附加堆纹带，上有三个斜窝，形成一个器耳。厚度5毫米。实物的1/2尺寸大小。

8. 标号 K.12003：755.砖红色陶器小陶片，灰色陶胎。两边钻有双锥形洞。壁厚5毫米。实物的1/1尺寸大小。

9. 标号 K.12003：749.上乘质量的黄色陶器陶片。从外侧钻有一个孔。厚度3毫米。实物的1/1尺寸大小。

10. 标号 K.12003：866.一个由53片不同小陶片组成的器底陶片，质量上乘。砖红色，陶胎呈灰色。壁厚7毫米。实物的1/2尺寸大小。

图版30

1. 标号 K.12003：892.3片黄褐色碗的陶片。其中一片（在图版右侧）由于褪色而变为深灰色。高82毫米。厚5~6毫米。实物的1/2尺寸大小。

2. 标号 K.12003：804.可能是碗的边缘陶片。浅红褐色陶器。内侧有两个红褐色彩绘色斑。厚度6~8毫米。实物的1/2尺寸大小。

3. 标号 K.12003：891.敛口碗口陶片。灰褐色陶器。该器物底部很独特。壁厚约6毫米。实物的1/2尺寸大小。

4. 标号 K.12003：701.口沿外侈的陶碗边缘陶片。灰色陶器，品质上乘，器表抛光。厚5毫米。实物的1/2尺寸大小。

5. 标号 K.12003：684.侈口陶碗碗口陶片。浅色灰褐色陶器，品质上乘。外表经过做抛光处理。厚度3毫米。实物的1/2尺寸大小。

6.标号K.12003：677.陶碗碗口陶片。浅灰色陶器，品质上乘。边沿和器身下半部分经过抛光。壁厚4毫米。实物的1/2尺寸大小。

7.标号K.12003：890.双锥形陶器上半部分陶片，无器领。砖红色陶器，陶胎呈浅褐色。外部经过抛光。壁厚9毫米。实物的1/2尺寸大小。

图版31

1.标号K.12003：116.掺杂了石英石和云母的黄色小盆。外表粗糙，有不清晰的纹饰。器边下面，有一片黏土被压在器壁上，可能是为了掩盖一个裂缝。形状不规则。高约75毫米，底部直径45毫米。实物的2/3尺寸大小。

2.标号K.12003：910.砖红色斜口器物，陶胎呈浅褐色，混有石英石。壁厚5～9毫米。实物的2/3尺寸大小。

3.标号K.12003：907.浅黄色粗制陶器的窄器领。外表云母颗粒清晰可见。厚度6～8毫米。实物的2/3尺寸大小。

4.标号K.12003：6309.粗制的褐色陶罐。陶器轮廓微弯曲，口部外侈。外侧肩部向下布满垂直绳纹。等距离间隔有叠加的波浪形附加堆纹带。底部有清晰可见的篮纹。高240毫米，器腹直径238毫米，口部直径116毫米，底部直径120毫米。实物的1/3尺寸大小。

图版32

1.标号K.12003：1455.一个大型陶器上半部分的11片陶片。黄色，有砖红色斑点。烧制精美，但混有一定量的云母和石英石。外侧布满垂直的绳纹，装饰叠加波浪附加堆纹带。壁厚7毫米。实物的1/2尺寸大小。

2.上述陶器的内侧。陶器的结构通过不同线圈之间的裂缝显示出来，这些线圈一个个垒叠在一起。实物的1/2尺寸大小。

图版33

1a.标号K.12003：913.大型陶器的器颈陶片。口沿外侈。粗制的黄色陶器。

陶器内外侧均混有石英石颗粒。外部和边沿布满有规律的斜线绳纹。壁厚11毫米。实物的2/3尺寸大小。

1b.上述器颈陶片的正面。

图版34

1.标号K.12003：1475.2片敛口陶碗陶片。质量好但掺杂石英石和云母。外部布满垂直绳纹，口部下方区域光滑。浅褐色。内侧有红色痕迹。壁厚7毫米。实物的2/3尺寸大小。

2.标号K.12003：985.敛口陶碗陶片。烧制精美，但混杂了石英石和云母。外侧布满深深的垂直绳纹。口沿下方有一道水平的沟槽。壁厚8毫米。实物的2/3尺寸大小。

3.标号K.12003：1002.器物边缘陶片。器身竖直的部分几乎垂直。粗制的灰褐色陶器。器表混有云母颗粒。外部饰模糊的垂直绳纹。器口下方部分有一个叠加的附加堆纹，上面有5个深窝，形成了一个器耳。壁厚9毫米。实物的2/3尺寸大小。

4.标号K.12003：1472.敛口陶碗陶片。灰色，烧制精美。器口以下区域光滑，被水平沟槽阻断。下面斜绳纹清晰可见。壁厚11毫米。实物的2/3尺寸大小。

5.标号K.12003：1008.2片器口陶片。竖直的部分几乎垂直。粗制的灰褐色陶器。外表混有云母颗粒。器口以下，隆起的堆纹形成了一个器耳。壁厚8毫米。实物的2/3尺寸大小。

6.标号K.12003：989.粗制的浅褐色陶器器口陶片。器物竖直的部分几乎垂直。外部布满绳纹。壁厚9毫米。实物的2/3尺寸大小。

7.标号K.12003：968.黄色陶器器口陶片，陶胎呈灰色。烧制精美，但混杂了云母和石英石。表面粗糙。器口下方有一个高度凸起的圆纽，形成一个器耳。壁厚11毫米。实物的2/3尺寸大小。

8.标号K.12003：1012.粗制的褐色陶器器口陶片，外侧灰色。表面混有云母颗粒。器物器壁竖直的部分几乎笔直。器口和器壁外部有斜绳纹。器口下方有圆纽留下的印迹。壁厚15毫米。实物的2/3尺寸大小。

图版 35

1.标号 K.12003：903.混有石英石的淡褐色陶器器颈陶片。器表有烟炱斑。外侧有绳纹。器口下方有附加堆纹带，装饰有斜窝纹。壁厚 7 毫米。实物的 2/3 尺寸大小。

2.标号 K.12003：904.器颈部陶片，与上文所述相同，可能是同一陶器的陶片。壁厚 7 毫米。实物的 2/3 尺寸大小。

484

3.标号 K.12003：905.混有石英石的褐色陶器颈部陶片。外部被烟熏黑。边缘周围有附加堆纹带，装饰新月形斜纹。壁厚 6 毫米。实物的 2/3 尺寸大小。

4.标号 K.12003：926.带凸缘的器颈陶片。粗制的灰色陶器。口沿和器身上有绳纹痕迹，但图中几乎显示不出来。壁厚 10 毫米。实物的 2/3 尺寸大小。

5.标号 K.12003：1016.带耳的器身陶片。砖红色，外表黄色。烧制精美，但掺有石英石。器耳装饰有叠加的波浪形附加堆纹带。壁厚 6 毫米。实物的 2/3 尺寸大小。

6.标号 K.12003：1302.粗制的砖红色陶器器身陶片。表面混有云母颗粒。外侧布满交叉的绳纹。有叠加的凸脊和斜窝，形成器耳。附加堆纹形成的，上面装饰有壁厚 9 毫米。实物的 2/3 尺寸大小。

7.标号 K.12003：1015.带耳的器身陶片。粗制的黄色陶器。外部有斜绳纹。器耳上有波浪形附加堆纹带。壁厚 6 毫米。实物的 2/3 尺寸大小。

图版 36

1.标号 K.12003：936.砖红色陶罐陶片，烧制精美，但掺和了石英石和云母。外部颜色较深，有烟炱斑点。轮廓呈微弧状，器颈外侈。外侧布满交叉绳纹。围绕器颈，有一个叠加的波浪形附加堆纹带。器腹有叠加的波浪形附加堆纹带。实物的 2/3 尺寸大小。

2.标号 K.12003：930.3 片带有红色斑点的粗制黄色陶罐颈部陶片。罐颈稍外侈。罐领和罐身之间有叠加的波浪形附加堆纹带。外部布满交叉绳纹。壁厚 6 毫米。实物的 2/3 尺寸大小。

3.标号 K.12003：1190.粗制的砖红色陶器器身陶片。外侧深褐色。器表布满不规则的、部分交叉的绳纹，装饰有水平或垂直的叠加的波浪形附加堆纹带。壁厚10毫米，实物的2/3尺寸大小。

4.标号 K.12003：1267.粗制的砖红色陶器器身陶片，表面带烟炱斑点。外部布满水平绳纹，装饰有堆纹盘蛇，蛇的头部缺失。蛇的皮肤用斜纹表示。厚9毫米。实物的2/3尺寸大小。

图版37

1.标号 K.12003：954.粗制褐色小陶罐陶片。罐领带边。罐身垂直部分呈微弧状。外侧布满粗糙的绳纹。罐颈和罐身下半部分有叠加上去的水平附加堆纹带。水平附加堆纹带之间有成对的斜向叠加的附加堆纹带群。壁厚8毫米。实物的2/3尺寸大小。

2.标号 K.12003：1019.粗制小陶器陶片。黄色，外部有白色斑点，口部有边沿。从口部延伸到器身上半部分的是一个宽大的器耳。器身外侧有模糊的绳纹。器颈和器耳下方，有叠加上去的波浪形附加堆纹带。整个器耳装饰有紧密连接的叠加上去的波浪形附加堆纹带。内侧有蓝紫色痕迹。壁厚4毫米。实物的2/3尺寸大小。

485

3.标号 K.12003：962.5片小陶器器颈陶片。薄壁，烧制精美，混合了石英石和云母。淡褐色。器颈稍微外侈，口部带边。从器口向器身上半部分延伸出去一个小器耳。器边和外侧有烟炱斑点。外部有模糊的绳纹。器颈有叠加上去的波浪形附加堆纹带。壁厚8毫米。实物的2/3尺寸大小。

4.标号 K.12003：935.小型粗制陶器陶片。浅褐色。器表粗糙。器领稍外侈。器壁轮廓稍弯，壁薄。上半部分陶器带小器耳。器颈上装饰叠加的波浪形附加堆纹带。壁厚5毫米。实物的2/3尺寸大小。

5.标号 K.12003：964.褐色陶器器颈陶片。薄壁，烧制精美，混合了石英石和云母。器表暗淡。侈口，里面有个凹槽。边缘以下有个小器耳。器颈上和边缘下有成对的水平犁沟，形成一种装饰。水平犁沟之间的光滑区域装饰有浮雕的楔子纹。壁厚4毫米。实物的2/3尺寸大小。

6.标号 K.12003：919.黄色陶器器颈陶片。砖红色陶胎。器领带口沿。器表粗糙。器身上半部分有两个圆纽形成一对凸起。厚度6毫米。实物的2/3尺寸大小。

7. 标号 K.12003：901. 浅褐色陶器颈部陶片。器领稍微外侈。器领边缘和器身下半部分有烟炱。外部布满交叉的绳纹。边缘以下有叠加的波浪形附加堆纹带，黏土带下面有几组凸起的短小附加堆纹带。壁厚5毫米。实物的2/3尺寸大小。

8. 标号 K.12003：902. 3片灰褐色陶器陶片。器领稍外侈，带有一圈边。器身稍弯曲，外侧布满绳纹。颈部有一条叠加的波浪形附加堆纹带，下面有几组凸起的短黏土条。浮雕装饰以蓝紫色绘制。壁厚5毫米，实物的2/3尺寸大小。

9. 标号 K.12003：900. 深灰褐色器颈陶片。质地疏松但几乎不含石英石和云母。口沿外侈。器颈有横线组与竖线组交叉的纹饰。纹饰中心有小圆纽。壁厚6毫米。实物的2/3尺寸大小。

图版38

1. 标号 K.12003：551. 粗制的灰褐色陶器小陶片。器口稍外侈。器身轻度弯曲，器身上半部分有一个小耳。器耳及底部都有绳纹。器颈周围和器耳上有叠加的波浪形附加堆纹带。器腹有几组呈对角线排列的小黏土条，黏土条下面，每一边带一个圆纽。器高105毫米，底部直径60毫米，壁厚6毫米。实物的2/3尺寸大小。

2. 标号 K.12003：948. 褐色陶器器颈陶片。掺有云母和大颗粒石英石。低领侈边。外侧布满交叉纹饰。环绕器颈有一条叠加上去的附加堆纹带，上面有几组窝状装饰。壁厚约7毫米。实物的2/3尺寸大小。

3. 标号 K.12003：1106. 褐色鬲足陶片。实物的2/3尺寸大小。

4. 标号 K.12003：1053. 粗制的黑褐色陶器器底陶片。底部平整。外侧有绳纹和叠加上去的波浪形附加堆纹带。器壁厚约8毫米。实物的2/3尺寸大小。

5. 标号 K.12003：1104. 褐色鬲足陶片。实物的2/3尺寸大小。

6. 标号 K.12003：1044. 带一个器耳的小型器物器颈陶片。粗制陶器，外部有一层烟炱。实物的2/3尺寸大小。

7. 标号 K.12003：1263. 两片砖红色陶器的陶片。烧制精美，但掺杂了云母和石英石。外侧由于褪色而转为褐色，且有一层烟炱。装饰有一条叠加的波浪形附加堆纹带。壁厚6毫米。实物的2/3尺寸大小。

486

8. 标号 K.12003：1104. 高质量褐色鬲足陶片。

9. 标号 K.12003：1060. 2片粗灰色陶器底部陶片，陶胎呈褐色。底部平整。器壁外侧和器物底部有绳纹。器身饰有两条叠加的黏土带。厚7毫米。实物的2/3尺寸大小。

10.标号K.12003：1103.鬲足陶片。陶质粗糙。浅褐色，带红斑。外侧有绳纹。实物的2/3尺寸大小。

11.标号K.12003：1112.9片粗制褐色陶器器底陶片。底部平整。外壁和底部布满斜向交的绳纹。外壁装饰有短小的附加堆纹黏土带。壁厚7毫米。实物的2/3尺寸大小。

图版39

1.标号K.12003：1110.浅灰褐色的质地疏松的器底陶片。外部和底部布满不规则的交叉绳纹。底部内侧也有清晰可见的交叉绳纹。壁上有一个从外面钻入的孔。壁厚8毫米。厚度非常匀称。实物的1/2尺寸大小。

2.标号K.12003：1075.粗制浅褐色蒸笼陶片。器壁向器口外侈，其中一片器边保存了下来。底部有穿孔，外部布满绳纹的斑点。厚11毫米。实物的2/3尺寸大小。

3.标号K.12003：1079.烧制很好的蒸笼底部陶片。外部有斜绳纹。厚8毫米。2/3尺寸大小。

4.标号K.12003：1480.粗制陶器浅灰褐色器底陶片。表面混有云母颗粒。外部有水平绳纹。壁厚11毫米。实物的2/3尺寸大小。

图版40

1a.标号K.12003：1196.3片粗制的褐色陶器陶片，外部有烟炱。外面有典型的对角线相交的绳纹。壁厚11毫米。实物的2/3尺寸大小。

1b.上述陶片的正面。

2a.标号K.12003：1388.混有云母的大型黄色陶器陶片。外部装饰宽大的附加堆纹黏土带，器身布满典型的对角线交叉绳纹。壁厚12毫米。实物的2/3尺寸大小。

2b.上述陶片的正面。

3a.标号 K.12003：1197.粗制砖红色陶器陶片。外表褐色。器表布满典型的对角线交叉绳纹。厚11毫米。实物的2/3尺寸大小。

3b.上述陶片的正面。

图版41

1.标号 K.12003：1143.褐色陶器陶片。砖红色陶胎。外表混有云母颗粒。外侧上半部分有稀疏的对角线绳纹，下半部分也有绳纹，但是是相互交叉的。壁厚10毫米。实物的2/3尺寸大小。

2.标号 K.12003：1070.烧制精美的砖红色陶器陶片。混有云母和石英石。外表可能覆了一层薄薄的陶衣。外侧有压印的网状纹。壁厚9毫米。实物的2/3尺寸大小。

3.标号 K.12003：1462.浅褐色大型陶器器身陶片。外部布满斜向交叉的绳纹。壁厚8毫米。实物的2/3尺寸大小。

4.标号 K.6309.是图版31中图4陶罐的底部。带有清晰的篮纹。实物的2/3尺寸大小。

图版42

1.标号 K.12003：305. 2片浅褐色大型双锥陶器器腹陶片。品质上乘。陶器上半部分（到器腹中线截止）经过抛光。器腹装饰有黑色彩绘，形成一个细小的同心线体系，同心线水平分组，以浓重的垂直笔触分组分界。水平区中间有两条斜线。水平线组以粗线为界。陶器下半部分未做装饰。壁厚6毫米。实物的2/3尺寸大小。

2.标号 K.12003：115.红褐色双锥陶器上半部分的陶片。器腹中线上用垂直粗笔彩绘，用两条水平线分界。壁厚5毫米。实物的2/3尺寸大小。

3.标号 K.12003：397. 2片浅褐色双锥形陶器器身陶片。品质上乘。外侧抛光，有黑色彩绘：上半部分有三条平行线和两个圆点。中纬线以四条同心线为界，下面有锯齿形线。壁厚7毫米。实物的2/3尺寸大小。

4.标号 K.12003：396. 8片陶片，构成了一个大型双锥陶器的上半部分，浅褐色，部分呈深褐色。外表已抛光至最低位置。黑色彩绘。上半部分有同心圆和各种数字，在器腹中线上以三条平行线分开，下面有波浪线。抛光又带彩绘的器身下方粗糙，上面有叠加的波浪形附加堆纹带。厚 10～12 毫米。实物的 2/3 尺寸大小。

5.标号 K.12003：160.器腹陶片。上面有一组同心圆装饰，同心圆中间有一条水平线。实物的 2/3 尺寸大小。

图版 43

1.标号 K.12003：171.浅褐色器颈陶片，局部褪色。品质上乘。低领，翻边。领子和器身外侧抛光。黑色彩绘。壁厚 8 毫米。实物的 2/3 尺寸大小。

2.标号 K.12003：255.砖红色陶器器颈陶片。品质上乘。外表苍白，随意抹平。黑色彩绘形成平行线区域，最低的横线上有一个斑点（？）。壁厚 8 毫米。实物的 2/3 尺寸大小。

3.标号 K.12003：896.粗制陶器陶片。混有石英石和云母。外侧有交叉的绳纹。附加堆纹带上有垂直的窝状点，形成器耳。附加堆纹带上还有绳纹。器耳下方，有两条黑色的平行线。壁厚度约 8 毫米。实物的 2/3 尺寸大小。

4.标号 K.12003：895.4 片大型陶器上的陶片。陶器上半部分由精心加工过的黏土制成；下半部分比较粗糙，混有石英石。黄色，有砖红色斑点。陶器轮廓不明显。上半部分外表被细心磨平，并装饰有平行线和圆环图案。上半部分向下半部分过渡处有一条犁沟：沟上方有一条凸脊，凸脊上有锥形工具形成的斜印痕；沟下方，有一排刻划出来的孔洞。下半部分布满交叉的绳纹。厚度为 7～8 毫米。实物的 2/3 尺寸大小。

5.标号 K.12003：405.由上述相同的两种黏土制成的陶器陶片。双锥形轮廓。上半部分装饰黑彩绘，形成圆环和平行线的图案。下半部分有垂直绳纹。壁厚 7 毫米。实物的 2/3 尺寸大小。

488

图版 44

1.标号 K.12003：894.2 片浅褐色陶器的陶片。上半部分品质很好，外表光滑，装饰有平行线和圆形图案。下半部分为粗陶。上半部分向下半部分过渡处，有一条棱带，棱带上有用梳子一样的工具制作的斜压痕。棱带下面，有几组压制的孔（？）。壁厚：上半部分5毫米，下半部分9毫米。实物的2/3尺寸大小。

2.标号K.12003：897.与上述同一种类的陶片。外表涂抹一层黏土，黏土下面绳纹明显。器耳现在丢失，但痕迹可见。壁厚7毫米。实物的1/2尺寸大小。

3.标号K.12003：244.混合了石英石的砖红色陶器颈部陶片。外表浅黄色，装饰有彩绘图案，由平行线构成，平行线之间有一条垂直线带。厚5～7毫米。实物的2/3尺寸大小。

4.标号K.12003：256.浅褐色陶器器颈陶片。外部装饰圆和点组成的彩绘图案。壁厚7毫米。实物的2/3尺寸大小。

5.标号K.12003：253.浅褐色陶器器颈陶片，灰色陶胎。外部光滑，装饰有平行线，平行线之间有水滴状的斑点带。壁厚6毫米。实物的2/3尺寸大小。

6.标号K.12003：143.浅褐色陶器器颈陶片。品质上乘。器口外侈。器颈装饰平行线。壁厚5毫米。实物的2/3尺寸大小。

7.标号K.12003：249.小型陶器器颈陶片。品质上乘。浅褐色。翻边外饰有黑色彩绘图案。器颈外侧有同心圆痕迹。壁厚5毫米。实物的2/3尺寸大小。

8.标号K.12003：246.品质上乘的砖红色器颈陶片。边缘外侈。领口外侧装饰粗大的平行线。壁厚5毫米。实物的2/3尺寸大小。

9.标号K.12003：389.陶器的边沿陶片，敛口，浅褐色。口部下面有一个孔，用于穿绳来系紧裂缝。质量很高。外部装饰有同心圆图案。壁厚5毫米。实物的2/3尺寸大小。

10.标号K.12003：254.粗制大型陶器的器颈陶片。浅褐色。外部色泽较明亮。表面粗糙。器颈外部装饰深黑色平行线。器身厚10～12毫米，器颈厚8毫米。实物的2/3尺寸大小。

11.标号 K.12003：240.大型陶器的颈部陶片，品质上乘。褐色。侈口。器颈外侧装饰由平行线和圆弧段构成的图案。壁厚7～8毫米。实物的2/3尺寸大小。

图版45

1.标号 K.12003：278.大型陶器的陶片，浅褐色。上半部分由高度净化的黏土制成，外部仔细磨平。下半部分为粗制陶器，外部粗糙，有绳纹。上半部分装饰黑彩绘。装饰带以下有一个凸起。壁厚8毫米。实物的2/3尺寸大小。

2. 标号 K.12003：281. 黄色陶器陶片。内侧褐色。黏土品质良好。外侧光滑，现在部分被腐蚀，装饰黑彩平行线和圆圈。小片器耳。壁厚6毫米。实物的2/3尺寸大小。

3. 标号 K.12003：282. 薄壁陶器的陶片。浅褐色。外部有一个小器耳。壁厚4毫米。实物的2/3尺寸大小。

4. 标号 K.12003：277. 带耳陶器。浅褐色。装饰叠加的波浪形附加堆纹带。器耳上下有彩绘的平行线图案。壁厚5毫米。实物的2/3尺寸大小。

489

5. 标号 K.12003：267. 砖红色小碗陶片。器表淡黄色。外部装饰同心圆组图案。壁厚6毫米。实物的2/3尺寸大小。

6. 标号 K.12003：367. 4片黄色陶碗的陶片。品质上乘。碗口有口沿。内外部都绘有平行线彩绘图案。有四个用于穿绳捆绑裂缝的孔。壁厚7毫米。实物的2/3尺寸大小。

图版46

1a. 标号 K.12003：158. 2片黄色陶碗的上半部分的陶片。品质上乘。侈口边沿上装饰圆圈和斜线图案。口沿下面也有平行线图案。壁厚6毫米。实物的2/3尺寸大小。

1b. 同一碗的内部。有装饰性彩绘痕迹。

2. 标号 K.12003：368. 一个陶碗的2片陶片。品质上乘，但表面未经仔细处理。碗口边缘绘有黑彩。壁厚6毫米。实物的2/3尺寸大小。

3. 标号 K.12003：217. 陶碗的陶片。质量很好。淡褐色。外部装饰黑色线条图案。内部装饰三角形和平行线。壁厚6毫米。实物的2/3尺寸大小。

4a. 标号 K.12003：219. 碗的内部陶片。品质上乘。浅灰白色。有楔子形和平行线彩绘。左侧有一个用于穿绳捆绑裂缝的孔。壁厚6毫米。实物的2/3尺寸大小。

4b. 同一陶片的外部。浅黄色。绘有几组线和圆。

5a. 标号 K.12003：209. 碗的内部陶片。浅褐色陶器。外表被磨光。内部装饰楔子形纹饰，绘成褐色。壁厚7毫米。实物的2/3尺寸大小。

5b. 外部相同。

图版47

1a.标号K.12003：203.8片侈口碗的陶片。质量较高。浅灰色。有褐色彩绘。边缘装饰圆点和斜线交替构成的纹饰。碗身外部有多组线条。壁厚5毫米。实物的2/3尺寸大小。

1b.同一个碗的内部。纹饰由弧线、平行线和格子构成。

2a.标号K.12003：191.浅黄色陶碗的陶片。品质上乘。外表磨光。侈口口沿和外部装饰成和图1相同的图案。壁厚5毫米。实物的2/3尺寸大小。

2b.同一个碗的内侧。纹饰由弧线或直线构成。

3a.标号K.12003：375.红褐色碗的陶片。品质上乘。外表被磨平。碗口和碗身外部饰有黑线条。壁厚6毫米。实物的2/3尺寸大小。

3b.同一个陶碗的内部装饰成斜向并行线。实物的2/3尺寸大小。

4.标号K.12003：103.口部收缩的碗的陶片。内部边缘带有平行线装饰，下面是格子纹。实物的2/3尺寸大小。

5.标号K.12003：234.陶器边缘的陶片，内部装饰红褐色三角形图案。实物的2/3尺寸大小。

图版48

1.标号K.12003：369.灰褐色碗的陶片。品质很好。碗沿装饰厚重的斜线。碗外侧装饰厚重的平行线，下面是斜线构成的纹饰。彩绘是黑褐色。内侧有彩绘线形成的花环。现在部分已被腐蚀（？）壁厚5毫米。实物的2/3尺寸大小。

2.标号K.12003：167.侈口碗的陶片。品质上乘。浅黄色。碗沿有黑彩绘制的三角形。碗身外部有平行线彩绘图案。壁厚6毫米。实物的2/3尺寸大小。

3.标号K.12003：170.2片带口沿的碗的陶片。品质上乘。淡褐色。口沿布满黑彩。外部有黑彩装饰，包括一个内部带圆点的圆圈，圆圈外部又环绕几组弧线。内部装饰两条重笔平行线。壁厚7毫米。实物的2/3尺寸大小。

4a.标号K.12003：275.碗的陶片。外部淡褐色，内部几乎是砖红色，陶胎呈灰色。内壁装饰计时器状图案，周围有几组斑点。实物的2/3尺寸大小。

490

4b.同一陶片的外部。边缘有黑彩装饰。器身在水平线之间有几组圆环段装饰。左侧有一个小圆钮。厚5～8毫米。实物的2/3尺寸大小。

5a.标号K.12003：228.带口沿的碗的陶片。品质上乘。灰黄色。内侧涂有灰色颜料。表面光滑。内侧装饰有成群的垂直线和平行线相交叉形成的棋盘格纹。壁厚5毫米。实物的2/3尺寸大小。

5b.同一陶片的外部。由多组圆环装饰。口沿以下有从外侧钻入的孔。

6a.标号K.12003：169.浅褐色碗的陶片。品质上乘。内侧装饰有水平线和斑点，与大圆圈组交替出现，圆圈内有三条垂直线分开的两对圆斑点。壁厚5毫米。实物的2/3尺寸大小。

6b.同一个碗的外部。表面有腐蚀的痕迹？有对角线组成的彩绘。实物的2/3尺寸大小。

图版49

1.标号K.12003：421.大型陶器的器腹陶片。品质上乘。灰褐色。上面用黑彩绘制图案，该图案由三种元素构成，即粗线条、细线条和格子纹。细线条与格子纹交替出现。壁厚5毫米。实物的2/3尺寸大小。

2.标号K.12003：404.大型陶器的器身陶片。品质上乘。灰褐色。外部装饰黑色锯齿带图案，锯齿带外侧辐射出细小的线条组；线条之间又有圆点。实物的2/3尺寸大小。

3.标号K.12003：603.灰色陶器的陶片。品质上乘。内部装饰黑彩格子纹。壁厚3毫米。实物的2/3尺寸大小。

4.标号K.12003：108.浅褐色陶器器腹陶片。质量良好。外部装饰交叉的粗线和细线组。壁厚5毫米。实物的2/3尺寸大小。

5.标号K.12003：466.浅黄色陶器陶片。品质上乘。外表抛光，装饰平行线和格子纹。壁厚5毫米。实物的2/3尺寸大小。

6.标号K.12003：97.砖红色陶器的陶片。品质上乘。外部装饰有粗平行线和圆点。壁厚4毫米。实物的2/3尺寸大小。

7.标号K.12003：114.浅褐色陶器陶片。品质上乘。外部装饰几组同心圆和圆点。有捆绑裂缝用的孔的痕迹。壁厚6毫米。实物的2/3尺寸大小。

8.（原著未标号）亮褐色陶器器腹陶片。品质上乘。外部被抛光，且装饰彩绘图案，图案由几组重笔线与对角线交替而成。壁厚6毫米，实物的2/3尺寸大小。

9.标号 K.12003：101.灰褐色陶器。品质上乘。外部被抛光，装饰同心圆和圆点。壁厚8毫米。实物的2/3尺寸大小。

10.标号 K.12003：116.淡褐色陶器陶片。品质上乘。外部被抛光，装饰斜线和横线。壁厚6毫米。实物的2/3尺寸大小。

11.标号 K.12003：422.灰褐色陶器陶片。外部被抛光，装饰弧线和锯齿带。壁厚8毫米。实物的2/3尺寸大小。

12.标号 K.2170：3.褐色陶器陶片。外部被抛光，装饰弧线和锯齿带。壁厚8毫米，实物的2/3尺寸大小。

13.标号 K.12003：530.黄色陶器小陶片。外部被抛光，装饰粗线和锯齿带。实物的2/3尺寸大小。

14.标号 K.12003：413.砖红色陶器陶片。外部淡黄色，装饰同心圆。壁厚7毫米。实物的2/3尺寸大小。

15.标号 K.12003：105.2片淡黄色陶器陶片。品质上乘。外部装饰不同粗细的同心圆。壁厚6毫米。实物的2/3尺寸大小。

16.标号 K.12003：418.淡褐色陶器陶片。品质上乘。外部被抛光，装饰平行线。壁厚6毫米。实物的2/3尺寸大小。

图版50

1.标号 K.2170：1.2片褐色碗的陶片。陶胎呈灰色。碗口口沿外侈。器身轮廓略微弯曲。平坦的口沿上装饰有斜线。碗身装饰设计独特，粗大的平行线黑白相间，其间有细线和带白色斑点的圆点交替出现。下方区域有白色横线与三角形交替出现，填满小弧线的区域，有三角形，周围有白色斑点。三角形下方，有一个小圆纽。壁厚5毫米。实物的1/2尺寸大小。

2.标号 K.2170：5.浅黄色碗的陶片。品质上乘。扁平的边缘外侈。表面被抛光。碗沿装饰斜线，与三角形和圆点交替出现。外部装饰有斜线区，以横线勾边。内部口边附近有一排三角形，下面是弧形线和圆点。壁厚5毫米。实物的1/2尺寸大小。

3.标号 K.2170：6.淡黄色碗的陶片。外部几乎白色，且装饰粗细不一的线绘制的花环。中心有弯曲的线。内部有随意绘制的三角形的痕迹。参照图版2中图

8。壁厚6毫米，实物的1/2尺寸大小。

4. 标号K.2170：4.淡褐色碗的陶片。品质上乘。扁平的口沿外侈，装饰有圆点图案（此处未能显示出来），圆点周围环绕锯齿圈、三角形和格子纹。内部装饰有三角形图案，以圆点结束，周围也有圆点。壁厚4毫米。实物的1/2尺寸大小。

5. 标号K.12003：189.灰褐色陶器的小陶片。品质上乘。边缘绘成褐色。外部设计成褐色的圆环段和圆点。壁厚5毫米。实物的2/3尺寸大小。

6. 标号K.2170：8.砖红色陶器的陶片。品质上乘。外侧灰白，装饰有由黑色图案和粗线构成的部分花环和圆圈。一条横线横穿圆圈。壁厚5毫米。实物的1/2尺寸大小。

7. 标号K.12003：163.淡黄色陶碗的陶片。品质上乘。外表被抛光。内部碗沿下装饰两条弧线，弧线下面有一条水平线的痕迹。口沿外侈，上有由圆点和斜线构成的黑色图案。碗体有曲线。右侧有捆绑裂缝的孔洞。碗体厚3毫米。实物的2/3尺寸大小。

8. 标号K.12003：222.品质上乘的黄色陶器小陶片。内部装饰三角形，角尖上有圆点。外部未装饰。壁厚6毫米。实物的1/2尺寸大小。

9. 标号K.12003：75.褐色陶器陶片。品质上乘。外部被抛光，且装饰有同心圆和斜线。壁厚4毫米。实物的2/3尺寸大小。

10. 标号K.2170：9.深褐色陶器器腹陶片。内部褐色。品质上乘。外部被抛光。饰黑色图案，由横线和波浪线带组成。壁厚5毫米。实物的1/2尺寸大小。

11. 标号K.12003：165.浅砖红色陶器的边缘陶片。品质上乘。侈口边缘装饰黑色斜波浪线和圆点。壁厚6毫米。实物的2/3尺寸大小。

12. 标号K.2170：12.浅黄色陶碗的陶片。品质上乘。外表被抛光。外部有一条黑色彩绘线。内部装饰三角形，角尖有圆点。三角形下面有平行线带。壁厚5毫米。实物的1/2尺寸大小。

13. 标号K.12003：180.褐色陶碗陶片。质量上乘。内部装饰平行线和圆点。扁平的边缘有锯齿形带和楔子。实物的2/3尺寸大小。

14. 标号K.12003：166.淡黄色陶器器边陶片。品质上乘。外表被抛光。内部装饰黑色图案，由圆环段组成。扁平边上，有斜线和圆点。壁厚4毫米。实物的2/3尺寸大小。

15. 标号K.12003：192.淡褐色陶器器边陶片。表面被抛光。扁平的边缘装饰锯齿状线条形成的不规则的三角形。实物的2/3尺寸大小。

16. 标号K.2170：2.淡褐色陶器器腹陶片。品质上乘。外部被抛光，装饰黑色水平线图案。上半部分，线条弯曲处有椭圆形点。壁厚4毫米。实物的2/3尺寸大小。

17.标号K.12003：196.灰褐色碗的陶片。碗边和外部抛光。扁平的边上有褐色格子纹。实物的2/3尺寸大小。

18.标号K.12003：161.淡褐色陶器器边陶片。外表被抛光。扁平的器边上装饰有黑色三角形带，其中刻有一个圆点。三角形图案的每一侧都有斜线组。实物的2/3尺寸大小。

19.标号K.12003：217.淡黄色陶碗陶片。内部装饰淡黑色图案：边缘有一个三角形，下面有一组平行线和圆点。外部装饰黑色线条（图版46中图3）。壁厚6毫米。实物的2/3尺寸大小。

20.标号K.12003：211.陶器器边陶片，装饰有三角形和斜带。实物的2/3尺寸大小。

21.标号K.2170：4.陶器边沿的陶片。品质上乘。黑色设计，有圆点，周围是同心圆段，左边是黑色，中间填充格子纹。实物的2/3尺寸大小。

22.标号K.2170：5.碗内侧的陶片。黑色设计，边沿上是尖角拉长的三角形，三角形下面是圆圈段和圆点。实物的2/3尺寸大小。

23.标号K.2170：7.淡黄色陶碗的陶片。品质上乘。外部装饰黑色图案，由几组水平线构成。上半部分线条之间有一些椭圆形点。下半部分有同样的圆点。厚5毫米。实物的1/2尺寸大小。

493

图版51

1.标号K.12003：238.淡褐色陶碗的陶片。品质上乘。外部被抛光，等距离装饰水平线，黑色。壁厚6毫米。实物的2/3尺寸大小。

2.标号K.2170：10.淡黄色陶器陶片。品质上乘。外部被抛光，装饰黑色图案，有圆圈区域和三角形，三角形内刻有圆点。壁厚5毫米。实物的2/3尺寸大小。

3.标号K.12003：7.灰褐色陶器的陶片。品质上乘。外部装饰黑色水平线，水平线与两个水滴状的点交叉。壁厚6毫米。实物的2/3尺寸大小。

4.标号K.12003：74.陶碗的陶片的内部。品质上乘。砖红色。内部装饰两个黑色水平带，中间有成对的线条。外部唯一的装饰是一条黑色带。壁厚4毫米。实物的2/3尺寸大小。

5.标号 K.12003：20.淡黄色陶器小陶片。品质上乘。外部被抛光，装饰黑色水平带和箭头形状图案。壁厚4毫米。实物的2/3尺寸大小。

6.标号 K.12003：383.小型碗的陶片。品质上乘。有两个用于捆绑裂缝的孔洞。厚4毫米。图a为外部，深褐色。黑彩绘设计的三角形图案，三角形内填充有平行线，三角形下面是平行带。三角形和平行带之间的角度里，有圆纽痕迹。图为内侧，砖红色。边缘黑色三角形设计，水平带勾勒边框。实物的2/3尺寸大小。

7.标号 K.12003：134.碗的陶片。深褐色。灰色陶胎。外表被抛光。内外均装饰黑色水平带和垂直线组。壁厚4毫米。图a为外部。图b为内部。实物的2/3尺寸大小。

8.（译者注：原文未描述）

9.标号 K.12003：79.陶器陶片。品质上乘。砖红色。内侧黑色装饰。壁厚4毫米。实物的2/3尺寸大小。

10.标号 K.12003：266.淡黄色陶器器底陶片。品质上乘。内部被抛光，装饰黑色设计：中心是一个圆圈，里面绘有一个由两组细线形成的十字，十字的间隙以及中间，有圆点。圆圈的外面有格子纹和垂直线。壁厚9毫米。实物的2/3尺寸大小。

11.标号 K.12003：259.淡黄色器底陶片。品质上乘。内部装饰黑色的弯曲线，弯曲线是从器底中间的一个大圆圈上辐射而成的。壁厚6毫米。实物的2/3尺寸大小。

12.标号 K.12003：268.器底陶片。质量上乘。外部红褐色。内部黄白色陶衣。内部装饰黑色弧线图案。壁厚6毫米。实物的2/3尺寸大小。

13.标号 K.12003：265.砖红色陶器器底陶片。质量上乘。内部装饰有格子纹的黑色区域。壁厚5毫米。实物的2/3尺寸大小。

14.标号 K.2170：29.淡黄褐色陶器器耳小陶片。外部有交叉斜线形成的棋盘格纹。实物的2/3尺寸大小。

15.标号 K.12003：624.粗制的黄褐色陶器器耳陶片。外部有褐色彩绘：上半部分斜线，下半部分竖线。实物的2/3尺寸大小。

16.标号 K.12003：625.淡黄色陶器器耳陶片。外部有红褐色线装饰。实物的2/3尺寸大小。

494 17.标号 K.12003：210.碗的边缘陶片，轮廓稍微弯曲，向口部收缩。黄白色陶器，陶胎呈灰色。内外部均饰红褐色锯齿状线条。壁厚7毫米。实物的2/3尺寸大小。

18. 标号 K.2170：11. 黄褐色陶器上的物件，可能是器耳陶片。表面被抛光。凹面有黑色粗平行线装饰，平行线之间有环绕椭圆形点的细线区。凸面上半部分有几组粗平行线。实物的 2/3 尺寸大小。

19. 标号 K.12003：80. 装饰红褐色点的小陶片。实物的 2/3 尺寸大小。

图版 52

1. 标号 K.2170：48. 花岗岩权杖头部。整个上面都有深槽，在一个边上还有一个横穿的宽槽，显然用于加固。壁厚 3 毫米。实物的 1/2 尺寸大小。

2. 标号 K.2170：46. 盘状的坠饰，大理石制成，紧挨边缘有双锥形孔。壁厚 3 毫米。实物的 1/2 尺寸大小。

3. 标号 K.12003：1771. 闪长岩残片？上侧有一道深沟。深沟底部有磨损的痕迹。实物的 1/2 尺寸大小。

4. （原著未标号）上面只标记了"L.H.T."（罗汉堂），未完工的斧头。边缘破。实物的 1/2 尺寸大小。

5. 标号 K.12003：1706. 深色紧致片岩小斧头。颈部断裂。外表抛光细致。剖面为方形。宽 18 毫米。壁厚 11 毫米。实物的 2/3 尺寸大小。

6. 标号 K.1524 和 K.1531. 两片深色紧密的片状岩石残片。颈部断裂。实物的 2/3 尺寸大小。

7. 标号 K.1519. 小而薄的片岩斧头，长 73 毫米，宽 39 毫米，厚 7 毫米。实物的 2/3 尺寸大小。

8. 标号 K.12003：1704. 粒状的片岩斧头残片。宽面被抛光。实物的 2/3 尺寸大小。

9. 标号 K.12003：1743. 片岩小斧头。颈部断裂。宽 40 毫米，壁厚 10 毫米。实物的 2/3 尺寸大小。

10. 标号 K.1549. 残缺的片岩制品？表面经过锤击。实物的 2/3 尺寸大小。

11. 标号 K.12003：1732. 石板刀。刀的侧身有两个用于捆绑的缺口。边缘呈圆形。壁厚 9 毫米。实物的 2/3 尺寸大小。

12. 标号 K.12003：1731. 中间有长方形孔的残缺的石板刀。壁厚 7 毫米。实物的 2/3 尺寸大小。

13. 标号 K.3220. 有两个双锥形孔的残缺的石板刀。翼形侧面。壁厚 6 毫米。实物的2/3尺寸大小。

14.标号 K.12003：1728.带双锥形孔的石板刀。外侧羽翼状。其中一个有十个狭窄的凹痕。壁厚4毫米。实物的2/3尺寸大小。

15.标号 K.12003：1746.深、片岩石制成的不规则的新月形刀。刀刃只有磨光面较锐利。刀背很厚。壁厚（中心）15毫米。实物的2/3尺寸大小。

16.标号 K.1520.残缺的石板凿子。壁厚5毫米。实物的2/3尺寸大小。

17.标号 K.12003：1757.凿子，不规则形状。实物的2/3尺寸大小。

18.标号 K.12003：1734.残缺的片岩凿子。实物的2/3尺寸大小。

19.标号 K.12003：1733.片岩长凿子。实物的2/3尺寸大小。

图版53

1.标号 K.12003：1690.残缺的大型闪长岩锄头（？）两个用于连接的侧面凹槽。壁厚33毫米。实物的2/3尺寸大小。

2.标号 K.12003：1786.砂石块制成的新月形磨石。表面细心打磨过。实物的2/3尺寸大小。

_495_

3.标号 K.2170：20.白色大理石制作的半个臂章，带有淡黄色的玫瑰色彩。切口规则。仅在边缘处略微变细。外侧抛光，内侧有红色颜料的痕迹。边缘有几组小切口。其中一边有一个由外钻入的孔。外部直径80毫米，壁厚6毫米。实物的1/2尺寸大小。

4.标号 K.270：21.白色大理石臂章残片。带有矿物被腐蚀后的无数个小孔。向边缘略微变细。剖面呈晶状体。壁厚约8毫米。实物的1/2尺寸大小。

5.标号 K.2170：23.白色糖粒状大理石臂章残片。剖面外部凹面，相应的内部凸面。壁厚7毫米。实物的1/2尺寸大小。

6.标号 K.5855：1.一块大骨头做成的斧子。外侧凸起，内侧凹陷。内侧边缘锋利。颈部断裂。边缘宽63毫米。实物的2/3尺寸大小。

7.标号 K.5855：2.带针孔痕迹的残缺针。实物的2/3尺寸大小。

8.标号 K.5855：3.精细完好的带眼针。实物的2/3尺寸大小。

9.标号 K.5855：4.小针的两片残片，带有从一侧钻出的针眼。实物的2/3尺寸大小。

10.标号 K.5855：5.针尖残片。实物的2/3尺寸大小。

11.标号 K.5855：6.残缺的针。实物的2/3尺寸大小。

12.标号 K.5855：7.针的残片。实物的2/3尺寸大小。

13.标号 K.5855：8.保存完整的双锥形孔型针。实物的2/3尺寸大小。

14.标号 K.5855：9.针尖残片。实物的2/3尺寸大小。

15.标号 K.5855：10.带有双锥形孔的针的残片。实物的2/3尺寸大小。

16.标号 K.5855：11.骨刀刀尖残片，带有栓系燧石片的沟槽。实物的2/3尺寸大小。

17.（原著未描述）

18—24.标号 K.5855：12—18.骨锥。实物的2/3尺寸大小。

25.标号 K.5855：19.骨器残片。尖端钝圆。实物的2/3尺寸大小。

26.标号 K.5855：20.骨刀。刀片的凸起面有固定燧石片的沟槽。反面是凹面。上半部分有一个狭窄的器耳。实物的2/3尺寸大小。

27.标号 K.5855：21.骨刀。直边有一条沟，用于固定延伸及整个侧面的燧石片。反面是弯曲的。实物的2/3尺寸大小。

28.标号 K.5855：22.残缺的骨制工具。圆纽形状的顶部下方是一个从一侧钻出的方孔。实物的2/3尺寸大小。

29.标号 K.5855：23.白色大理石珠子。实物的1/1尺寸大小。

图版54
（实物的大小）

1.标号 K.12003：1664.残缺的白色大理石环，上面有矿物质受腐蚀后留下的小气孔。

2.标号 K.12003：1638.残缺的黏土环。

3.标号 K.12003：1637.残缺的黏土环。

4.标号 K.2170：856.残缺的黏土环。

5.标号 K.2170：37.残缺的石板环。

6.标号 K.12003：1745.残缺的石板环。

7.标号 K.12003：1558.灰褐色黏土制作的小陶罐，有残缺。

8.标号 K.12003：1668.残缺的白色大理石臂章。表面有矿物质受腐蚀后留下的小孔。

9. 标号K.2170：30.带双锥形孔的骨针。针尖很细。

10. 标号K.2170：31.从一块大骨上分割下来的薄骨片制作的骨器。顶端有双锥形孔。下端有一个同类型的孔。在顶部的孔和四个边缘的压痕以及最低的压痕之间，磨损的痕迹清晰可见。

11. （原著中未给出标号）扁平骨器。顶部一侧钻有一个小孔。刀尖附近有5个孔洞。背面有一个同样的孔洞，位置稍微高一些。

12. 标号K.2170：26.细骨刀。带有用于固定燧石片的凹槽。图b中，凹槽清晰可见。骨刀上部用作手柄。

13. 标号K.2170：25.骨刀。带有用于固定燧石片的凹槽。刀刃略弯。把手顶部有一个孔。图b中凹槽清晰可见。

14. 标号K.2170：41.灰色石板坠。剖面呈矩形。两端都是钝尖。顶部处环绕三面切割出一个凹槽，长15毫米。短边有尝试刻划的痕迹，但底盘上几乎看不出这种痕迹。

图版55

1. 标号K.2353：10.天水县，七里墩。褐色陶器器领陶片。质量较好。外侧装饰一条切割的平行线带，平行线之间有疏密不同的垂直线。壁厚6毫米。实物的1/2尺寸大小。

2. 标号K.2353：7.天水县，七里墩。石环残片。剖面呈三角形。实物的1/2尺寸大小。

3. 标号K.2353：25.天水县，七里墩。亮黄色陶器的颈部陶片。黏土纯净细腻，可能没有经过高温烧制。狭窄的器口上设有双环。颈部有印迹。器颈厚7毫米。实物的1/2尺寸大小。

4. 标号K.2353：42.天水县，七里墩。陶碗内侧陶片。边缘内侧有环状装饰。浅褐色陶器，品质较高。壁厚7毫米。实物的1/2尺寸大小。

5. 标号K.2353：21 天水县，七里墩。浅褐色陶器陶片的内侧。质量上乘。边缘内侧呈环形。壁厚5毫米。实物的1/2尺寸大小。

6. 标号K.2353：23.天水县，七里墩。碗的内部陶片。质量上乘。外侧亮褐色，光洁，内侧淡黄色，有砖红色的斑点。壁厚7毫米。实物1/1尺寸大小。

7. 标号K.2353：8.天水县，七里墩。双耳罐陶片。高领，罐体曲线柔和。质量上乘。浅褐色。器耳饰有长凹槽。罐领高45毫米，器耳长75毫米，器耳宽33毫米。罐身厚6毫米。实物的1/2尺寸大小。

8.标号K.2358：43.天水县，七里墩。优质红褐色小双耳罐陶片。壁厚3~4毫米。实物1/2尺寸大小。

9.标号K.2353：24.天水县，七里墩。灰褐色陶器的器耳。外面有一个由两个交叉的新月组成的雕刻装饰。壁厚5毫米。实物的1/2尺寸大小。

10.标号K.2353：38.天水县，七里墩。鬲足，陶器粗糙。暗褐色。外侧有纺织品印迹。壁厚约10毫米，实物的1/2尺寸大小。

11.标号K.2353：22 天水县，七里墩。淡黄色陶器陶片，可见石英石颗粒。外侧刻有精细的相交的带痕。壁厚7毫米。实物的1/1大小。

12.标号K.2353：34.天水县，七里墩。灰褐色粗糙陶罐陶片。带边沿，陶罐身外侧覆盖纺织品印迹。壁厚5~7毫米。实物的1/2尺寸大小。

13.标号K.2353：9 天水县，七里墩。大器耳陶片。可以辨认出石英石颗粒。浅黄褐色。外面装饰垂直的犁沟纹。壁厚8毫米。实物的1/2尺寸大小。

14.标号K.2353：41.天水县，七里墩。浅褐色陶器的基部陶片。质量上乘。外侧有篮纹。厚度5毫米。实物的1/2尺寸大小。

497

15.标号K.2353：3.天水县，七里墩。灰色黏土环。横截面三角形。实物的1/1尺寸大小。

16.标号K.2353：37.天水县，七里墩。鬲足，很粗糙。灰黄色。厚度不统一，中间厚9毫米。实物的1/2尺寸大小。

图版56

1.标号K.2353：32.出土于天水县，七里墩。仰韶类型的亮褐色陶器小陶片。质量上乘。内侧有边沿，呈圆形。外侧经过细致抹平处理，并用灰色装饰呈花环状。实物的1/1尺寸大小。

2.标号K.2353：36.出土于天水县，七里墩。可能是漏斗形器物足部陶片。有孔但不粗糙。灰色。外侧有水平划痕。壁厚5毫米。实物的1/2尺寸大小。

3.标号K.2353：28.出土于天水县，七里墩。浅褐色陶器陶片，质量上乘。外部有不规则的绳纹带与光滑带相接。壁厚4毫米。实物的1/1尺寸大小。

4.标号E.2353：39.出土于天水县，七里墩。器物领部陶片。口沿外侈。材质中混有一定量的石英石。表面淡黄灰色，胎芯红褐色。壁厚5毫米。实物的1/2尺寸大小。

5. 标号K.2359：24. 出土于榆中县，小石峡。小双耳罐陶片。质量上乘。淡黄褐色。表面未经仔细抛光。器领高，口部略侈。器身略微弯曲。边缘以及腹部有长器耳的痕迹。器领上有水平划痕。腹部有模糊的篮纹（可能是柳条编织品的印迹）。底部也有篮纹。壁厚3毫米。实物的1/2尺寸大小。

6. 标号K.2359：25. 出土于榆中县，小石峡。3片双锥形陶器腹部陶片。陶器不是很粗糙，但在一定程度上混合了石灰和石英石。表面淡黄色，胎芯砖红色。中线以下有一个器耳。下半部分有篮纹。壁厚6毫米。

7. 标号K.2359：18. 榆中县，小石峡。一小片浅褐色的陶器陶片。外表被抛光，黑色花纹。壁厚4毫米。实物的1/1尺寸大小。

8. 标号K.2359：1. 出土于榆中县，小石峡。4片高领陶罐的上部陶片。边缘略微外翻。器物质量上乘，但表面未经仔细打磨。呈灰黄褐色。口径140毫米，罐领高90毫米。罐身厚5～7毫米。实物的1/2尺寸大小。

9. 标号K.5280. 出土于榆中县，小石峡。彭腹双耳罐。浅褐色。外表被仔细打磨过。罐体上半部分有一条切割的水平线，下面是一条曲折带。水平线上，有不规则间隔的环状切口。器耳的上部装饰有菱形凹槽，在一个器耳的底部有三个环形切口，在另一个器耳的底部只有两个环形切口。高178毫米，宽169毫米。罐口直径（从左侧器耳到右侧器耳）155毫米。壁厚5毫米。实物的1/3尺寸大小。

10. 标号K.2359：16. 出土于榆中县，小石峡。灰褐色陶器的小陶片。带粗纺织品的印迹，厚度5毫米。正文插图 a. "无色透明胶" 翻模成型的纹饰正面。实物的1/1尺寸大小。

11. 标号K.2359：32. 出土于榆中县，小石峡。腹部淡褐色陶器陶片，砖红色胎芯。质量上乘。外部上半部分经过抛光，并装饰黑色宽带。下方紧接一条波浪线。壁厚6毫米。实物的1/2尺寸大小。

498

THE MUSEUM

of

FAR EASTERN ANTIQUITIES

(Östasiatiska Samlingarna)

STOCKHOLM.

Bulletin N:o 18

STOCKHOLM 1946

THE SITES OF CH'I CHIA P'ING AND LO HAN T'ANG IN KANSU

BY

MARGIT BYLIN-ALTHIN

In 1931 Professor J. G. Andersson entrusted me with the task of publishing the results of his excavations in the site of Ch'i Chia P'ing in Kansu.

In 1936 a manuscript of mine giving a detailed account of the finds on this site was forwarded to China to be published there. The outbreak of the war between Japan and China prevented the realization of that plan, and it was only recently that I was in a position to take up the work again and revise my manuscript for publication in Sweden. At the same time I took upon me the task of investigating the materials from the site of Lo Han T'ang. In consequence the present paper consists of two separate parts, which, however, are intimately connected with each other. I take this opportunity of offering my sincere and respectful thanks to Professor Andersson for his invaluable aid and the interest he has taken in my work.

THE CH'I CHIA P'ING SITE, NING TING HSIEN, KANSU

In Kansu, Ning Ting Hsien, near the middle course of the T'ao, a tributary of the Huang Ho, there lies on the west river bank, at the edge of a steep ravine, an extensive cultural deposit, which is called Ch'i Chia P'ing after a village of that name in its immediate vicinity. A very small section of this dwelling-site was excavated in the summer of 1924 by Professor Andersson's collectors under the supervision of the professor himself, who gave the following report about the excavation:

»The Ch'i Chia P'ing site is illustrated by a sketch map on the scale 1: 8.000. (Fig. 1). The road which has run along the low modern ten-metre plateau on the west bank of the river for some 20 li here climbs to the top of the Ma Lan plateau through a ravine, which is shown on the map to the W of the figure 74 m. The road passes through the Ch'i Chia P'ing village, then crosses a big ravine bordering the village to the south and runs further south to P'ai Tzu P'ing. The site is situated to the N, NE and E of the modern village of Ch'i Chia P'ing. It is bordered to the northwest by the big ravine which marks the termination to the N of the plateau; to the NE where the culture deposit is best exposed the site is bordered by the steep and high cliff facing the T'ao river. To the SE the topographical conditions are rather complicated: from the T'ao river escarpment a ravine runs southwest, and a much bigger ravine, the mouth of which is at the escarpment to the east outside the area shown on the map, nearly joins the smaller ravine just mentioned,

383

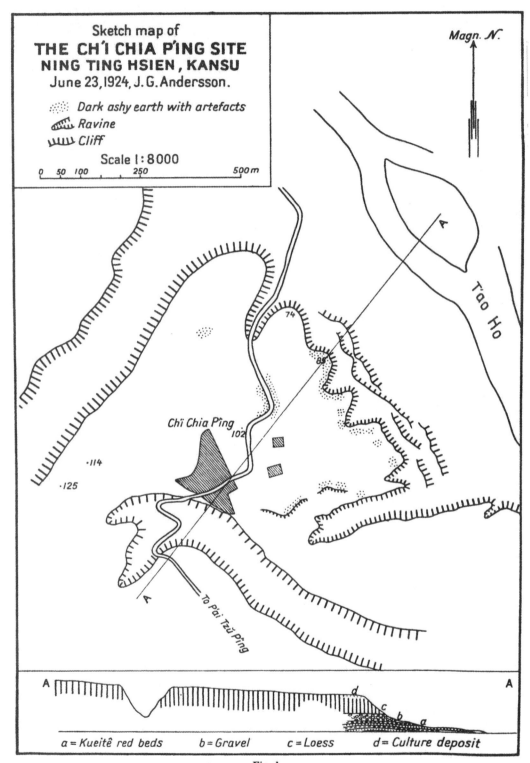

Fig. 1.

leaving between them only a passage of uneroded plateau less than 100 metres broad. This passage leads to a lobe of the underoded plateau, which extends to nearly one km. east of Ch'i Chia P'ing, and scattered over this lobe there were also seen fragments of pottery, but no deposit of dark, ashy earth was noticed here.

As shown in the map, the big western and the big eastern ravines approach close to one another west of the village where the ground rises to the high hills further SW, as denoted by the figures 114 and 125, which indicate only the gentle beginning of the upward slope.

It has already been mentioned that there are large exposures of the dark ashy earth in the big road between the figures 86 and 102. Another group of exposures is along the edge of the escarpment from the point 86 southeastwards. A third group of good sections occurs in some low cliffs E of the village, one of these cliffs being marked »pocket», referring to the pocket shown and described below. Some small sections in the culture deposit were also noticed due north from the village, W of the road. Fragments of pottery were also discovered in the fields N and E of the village. No diggings were undertaken in the level cultivated fields as the existing exposures offered ample opportunities for our excavations. Still, there is fairly good evidence that we have here a more or less continuous culture deposit extending 500 metres in the direction NW—SE and 250—350 metres NE—SW, representing an ancient monument of quite considerable dimensions.

The altitude of the deposit above the T'ao river is 90—100 m. The edge of the escarpment towards the river is at a height of 80—90 metres. The higher parts of the site near the village are at an altitude of about 100 metres. It will be observed that this site is topographically located much in the same way as other sites of this area, e. g. the Hsin Tien B and the Hui Tsui sites, upon a part of the dissected plateau which is largely protected by the steep and partly inaccessible cliffs of deep ravines. But in this case the isolation from the surroundings is less complete, as there is an isthmus connecting the Ch'i Chia P'ing lobe with the high land in the SW. As already mentioned, there is also a level isthmus leading to a big lobe E of the village, but this lobe might be regarded strategically as part of the site, as it is completely protected by the river cliff in the N and the big eastern ravine in the S.

Within this site the culture-deposit attains thicknesses that are uncommon in Kansu but resemble the big refuse deposit of Yang Shao Tsun in Honan. At the river cliff, the spot marked 86 metres, a thickness of 2.5 metres was measured and two metres was noted also at a place in the southern part of the site. Here was also noticed a real pocket very much resembling those at Yang Shao Tsun in Honan.

The pottery of this site is for the most part of the coarse monochrome type, very often blackened by fire. There were also found, though more rarely, fragments of monochrome vessels of a much finer type with very attractive *impressed* patterns, a type otherwise extremely rare in these Chinese sites.

Several times I observed small fragments of painted pottery of Yang Shao-type on the surface. These fragments might possibly be explained as a later surface addition, as painted pottery is very rare within the culture deposit. Still, at least one find may be said to have been made within the deposit under such conditions that it may be considered to belong to it. This is a large fragment of the Yang Shao chess-board pattern, which was found by Li at a depth of 1.5 m. together with the coarse sooted ware that is so characteristic of this site. It is possible that this site is slightly older than those typically Yang Shao sites containing an abundance of painted pottery, but the said find (and possibly a few other finds of painted fragments) seem to indicate that the difference in age cannot be great.

During my last visit to the Ch'i Chia P'ing site I took a walk across the wheat-fields

385

covering the site and noticed then several small sherds of typical Yang Shao-pottery scattered over the surface. From this observation it seems quite likely that here is a light surface infection of Yang Shao sherds over the surface of a pure Ch'i Chia site and that the Yang Shao sherds found in deeper levels are simply due to the farmers having moved masses of soil when laying out their cultivation terraces.

P'ai excavated a high grey foot made on the potter's wheel, which probably is of more recent date. It was said to have been found near the surface.

I noticed in one of the exposures a modern fragment with black glaze at nearly one metre's depth. These observations are mentioned to emphasize that the greatest caution should be exercised when dealing with these sites.»

The dwelling-site area has yielded a rich body of material consisting of pottery, artifacts of bone and stone, also a considerable quantity of animal bones.

The material discovered contains no metal whatsoever. As invariably where Chinese dwelling-sites are concerned, the artifacts occur in a cultural deposit that is distinguishable, it is true, from the untouched loess, but which is entirely unstratified. Owing to the intensive manner in which Chinese agriculture is carried on, with its terrace system, the soils are generally intermingled in a way that is less commonly found elsewhere, so that at the same level artifacts may be found dating from widely different periods. Thus, at Ch'i Chia P'ing there was discovered at a depth of 1 metre a modern sherd with a black glaze.

The above observations testify to the extreme difficulty involved in making a scientific study of the Chinese dwelling-site material. The stratigraphical data are often of but little value. As regards Ch'i Chia P'ing in particular, for special reasons there are extremely few data available as to the circumstances under which the objects were found.[1]) As mentioned above, the excavations were carried out by Professor Andersson's collectors, who at the same time were also engaged in other investigations in the neighbourhood, and consequently the hours at their disposal for excavating at Ch'i Chia P'ing were limited. The main object was to collect in a brief space of time as rich and representative a body of material as possible.

The collections thus brought together were subsequently shipped by Professor Andersson to Sweden, where they were catalogued and photographed. Half of the collection was then returned, by agreement, to China, and the other half is preserved in the Museum of Far Eastern Antiquities, Stockholm (MFEA).

I. POTTERY

It will be realized from what has been said above that in the present case it was *a priori* out of the question to make a stratigraphically substantiated division of the abundant and varied pottery finds into different chronologically determined

---

[1]) The material contains, *inter alia*, 34 objects of stone, bone and pottery, which according to the written particulars attached to them were picked up on the surface or bought in the district. This group has been marked with *letters* in order to distinguish them easily from the rest of the material, which bears consecutive numbers.

386

layers. Since the material which the excavations yielded contains only two entire vessels and for the rest consists merely of sherds of various sizes and fragments of vessels, it is hardly advisable to base the investigation of them upon the assumption of the existence of such vessel forms as it might conceivably be possible to reconstruct from them.

Under these circumstances I have considered that the only reliable premisses on which to base an investigation are the ceramic nature of the ware and the technical quality of its manufacture, and it is on this basis that I have grouped and classified the material, as it has proved to be far too heterogeneous to fit into an ordinary typological evolutional series.

Accordingly, the pottery has been divided into three different qualitative classes,[1]) and two of them have several sub-divisions. These qualitative classes are based, in the first place, upon the nature of the ware, so far as it can be judged microscopically or with the naked eye without being subject to chemical analysis or other special method of investigation, and in the second place upon its technically high or low standard of manufacture. These two factors, the quality and technical standard of the ware, have served therefore as the basis on which the following system of classification has been founded. The correctness of the grouping into classes has been confirmed by an analysis of microscopical slides carried out by Dr. Gunnar Beskow, the results of which are published p. 427 below.

Seeing that the pottery consists mainly of sherds and fragments of various sizes, which it has in most cases been impossible to fit together to make entire vessels, it would have proved somewhat difficult to form any true idea of what the different forms of vessels looked like. Fortunately, however, I have been greatly assisted in the work of reconstruction by having at my disposal a score of complete vessels bought by Professor Andersson and his assistants in the city of Lanchou (Kansu) and its vicinity.

Most of them are identifiable with the aid of the dwelling-site pottery as forms belonging to the Ch'i Chia culture, and the complete vessels have in turn lent strong support to the probability of the various theories of reconstruction. The most important of these vessels will therefore be briefly described and illustrated in a subsequent chapter, but as we have no exact data as to their provenience and the circumstances under which they were found, they must be treated with the utmost caution and cannot without further evidence be grouped and classified amongst the Ch'i Chia P'ing material. Some of them, that is to say, those whose forms could not be identified amongst the sherd material, may perhaps have little connection with the Ch'i Chia culture.

---

[1]) Denoted by the symbols CC: I, CC: II and CC: III.

387

CC: I.

About 390 fragments.

This class not only exhibits the highest standard of quality, technically speaking, but also comprises the greatest number of sherds. As regards the formal design of the vessels, it offers the greatest variety and shows the most complex forms. Only in the decoration of the vessels is it surpassed by CC: III.

Within the class itself there are fairly wide variations as regards both the character of the ware and the technique; consequently for the sake of clarity it has further been divided into three sub-divisions.[1] These sub-divisions are in many respects so intimately bound up with one another that there would be no justification in making individual classes of them; on the other hand, the lines of demarcation between these subdivisions are not so strict as between the main classes.

CC: I a.

About 90 fragments.

This group contains only a small number of sherds, but some of them represent technically the finest specimens that have come to light of the Ch'i Chia people's technical skill.

The Ware. In the matter of its ware the group is very uniform and is of extremely high quality. To the well-mixed clay has been added some lime in order to reduce its richness (though this is not apparent from the microscopical slide). The grains of lime have sometimes had an easily discernible expanding effect on the wall of the vessel. The ware is hard-baked (cf. p. 408.) and the colour varies on the different sherds between more or less pronounced brick-red and varying shades of light brown or pale yellow-brown. The exterior is frequently of a paler tone than the ware's inner layer. Owing to irregularities in the oxidation or an uneven distribution of the components of the clay mass, there are sometimes darker or lighter reddish spots on the exterior. For similar reasons there is sometimes a greyish core as against brighter surface layers. If, so, this phenomenon may concern the entire ware or else only certain sections of it. In the former case it depends on variations in the process of oxidization and in the latter case it is caused by disparities in the clay substance.

The Slip. Slip occurs on a number of the sherds (cf. p. 407). It has usually a pale-brown tone, which in some cases so closely resembles the ware that a doubt may arise as to whether any slip has been applied at all. In certain cases (e. g. Pl. 1,2) the surface has acquired a streaky appearance owing to the fact that the thickness of the slip layer varies, so that the ware's own colour is discernible beneath the thinnest parts. A dozen of the sherds differ strikingly from the rest of the

---

[1] Unfortunately the differences in quality between the subdivisions are not brought out in the reproductions as clearly as might be desired.

388

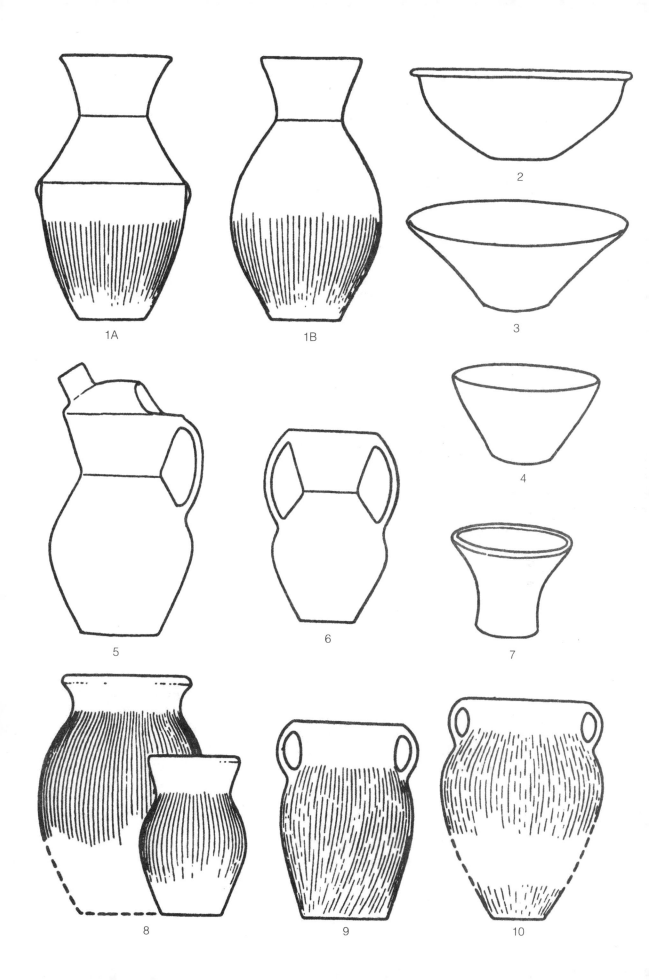

1A 1B 2 3 4 5 6 7 8 9 10

group in that they have a thickly applied whitish slip, probably of pipeclay, which completely conceals the underlying surface. (Pl. 1,6)

The thickness of the ware varies, but on an average it is about 4 mm. The maximum measured thickness is 7 mm.

Forms of vessels. The most common and most characteristic form of vessel within this and the following group is a bi-conical urn with a funnel-shaped neck, and it occurs in two different variants. In the one case the vertical plane of the body is distinctly broken (Type I a), in the other case the body's profile is slightly rounded (Type I b). The height of the neck varies between 4 and 7 cm. Like the upper part of the body, the neck is invariably smooth, and concentric striation is frequently discernible on these parts (see p. 406). The rim of the mouth is sometimes given a slight profile (Pl. 1,2) or in isolated cases is curved outwards (Pl. 1,4). Usually there are two short handles on the equatorial line. The lower portion of the body is generally covered with rush-mat or basket impressions (see p. 411), though there are also smooth forms (Pl. 1,6). The bottom surface is always clearly demarcated, and there are occasionally found on its underside the impressions of a woven mat (Pl. 2,12). In size the vessels appear to have most closely resembled the larger of the bought vessels (see Pl. 21 and 22), though two fragments of the upper part of a body seem to be remnants of very large specimens.

In addition, there belong to the group three fragments of wide bowls (Pl. 1,1), the rim of the mouth being annular, and these must technically have been the most perfect vessels in the dwelling-site. The interior is smooth and well finished, with concentric striations, and it is in striking contrast to the crudeness of the underside with its scratches and furrows. Whether these vessels had a demarcated bottom surface it is impossible to determine with any certainty, as the sherds only comprise parts nearest to the rim of the mouth, but considering that all the other vessels belonging to CC: I have a differentiated base, it is to be presumed that these also had a distinctly marked standing surface.[1]) (Type 2.)

To this group belongs also a fragment of a rim with its edge turned outwards, probably part of a large bowl. (Pl. 2,4). The inside has been carefully finished and a part of the thinned edge folded over and attached to the underside, which shows traces of basket impressions.[2]) (Type 3.)

Pl. 2,2 and 2,3 show two fragments of a vessel's mouth, both having a slightly pronounced neck. In the former the actual rim of the mouth is clearly flattened and the belly is wide. In the other, of which only the short neck with its broad rim is left, the transition to the body is marked by a belt of incised squares. It is not possible to form any definite opinion as to the shape of the body, but it probably belonged to the amphora type common in CC: I.

---

[1]) The shape of the vessels has been reconstructed in text fig. 2 with the aid of related types from other sites preserved in the MFEA.

[2]) The shape of the vessel has been reconstructed in text fig. 2 with the aid of two related bowls from Yang Shao Tsun, in Honan, which are preserved in the MFEA. (K. 6417 and K. 6247).

390

A third fragment of a neck (Pl. 1,3) is of a most exquisite shape and quality. The transition between neck and body is indicated by an interwoven band in relief. The exterior is covered with a thin white slip, which however is not of exactly the same kind as that discussed above.

To this group may also be referred three fragments of large, disclike handles (Pl. 1,11—13). Two of them (11 and 13) are made of a whitish ware with a somewhat darker, greyish-white core. The raw material was probably pipe clay. The exterior is decorated with an incised ornamentation. 1,13 shows traces of a supporting plug, which had been fastened to the completed but still plastic vessel between the handle and the wall, for the outside of the handle shows a finger-print in the ornamentation on a level with the point of attachment of the plug. The third handle (Pl. 1,12) is of yellowish red ware and has parallel ornamental incisions on the outside. These handles, at any rate the one illustrated in 1,13, have probably belonged to jugs with overvaulted mouth of a type resembling Pl. 22,5. It should be observed that the ware gives the impression of being to a certain extent alien to the milieu, although there are no convincing reasons to justify these handles' exclusion frome the Ch'i Chia culture.

CC: I b.

About 245 fragments.

This group, which comprises the largest number of sherds in CC: I, is closely connected in form and décor with the I a group but differs from it in its technically lower quality and its coarser ware.

The Ware. The vessels are made of relatively good clay material possessing a high loess content and a fair abundance of lime. Its richness has been reduced by the addition of sand of alkali feldspar or quartz. The baking appears to have been done at a somewhat lower temperature than in the case of the preceding group. The ware is of the same colour as that of the I a group, although brick-red tints are not so extensive as in the latter. Zonal striation and flaminess occur on the exterior, as in the preceding group.

Slip has been found on about fifty sherds. It is usually of a pale yellow or brownish-yellow tone, generally very much the same colour as that of the ware itself. Some fragments have a pale yellowish-grey slip so unevenly applied that large patches of the brick-red surface have been left uncovered. The slip covers the exterior of the vessels, a usually thinner layer of it being also applied to the inside of the neck, sometimes however only around the rim of the mouth. In a few cases the interior of the vessel has also received a thin coating, this being particularly the case with low bowls possessing a wide mouth.

Vessel forms. This group does not differ very much from the preceding one as far as the forms of vessel are concerned, although during manufacture the same care has not been expended on shaping the details. No fragments of types 2 and 3 have

391

been found; on the other hand, some new forms have emerged, but within this group also the bi-conical or delicately rounded urn with funnel-shaped neck and the handles at the equator (Types 1 A and 1 B) is the most abundantly represented form of vessel. It is found here in far greater variations than in the preceding group. To judge from the size of the mouth and the bottoms, these urns appear in some cases to have been of quite considerable dimensions. The mouth is generally very wide. The diameter is on an average about 15 cm., but in one case a cross section measured over 23 cm. The neck is as a rule 7—8 cm. high, though both higher and lower necks occur. It widens upwards into a funnel shape, sometimes so strongly pronounced at the mouth that the profile is broken. The rim of the mouth may occasionally be profiled. The neck either passes imperceptibly into the body or else, as is generally the case, the transition is marked by a line (Pl. 3,2) or some other incised pattern, which may have the character of a belt of oblique scores. Another form of decoration occurring on several sherds is a row of incised crosses (Pl. 4,2) or oblique squares (Pl. 4,5) applied either at the actual transition to the body or immediately below it. Sometimes the squared pattern is bounded on either side by a deep furrow. Another ornamentation that is somewhat akin to the above-mentioned types is in Pl. 4,4. Here the upper part of the body is decorated with double rows of small triangles, their apices pointing downwards.

Only a few fragments of the upper part of the body are left, but it was apparently smooth throughout and shows concentric striations. The handles are attached at the equator, and vary in length and breadth in proportion to the size of the vessels.

The lower part of the body is usually covered with mat or basket impressions of varying character (see e. g. Pl. 3,3, Pl. 4,13—16, cf. the chapter on Mat and Basket impressions). In a couple of fragments the lower part of the body is covered with parallel furrows, which resemble, it is true, mat impressions, but which were probably stamped on to the ware with the idea of imitating mat impressions (Pl. 14,12).

As in the I a group, the bottoms are clearly demarcated, though they are executed with far less care. Joints and standing surface are not smoothed over (Pl. 4,18).

A couple of vessel forms that are absent from the I a group constitute a novelty here. In the first place, a couple of fragments appear representing a new type of bowl (Type 4). The specimen illustrated in Pl. 3,5, with its straight sides expanding uniformly towards the mouth and the pronounced thickening of the wall of the vessel towards the base, is typical of the group.

Two smallish fragments (one of them illustrated in Pl. 4,3) have been identified with the aid of a vessel bought in Lanchou (Pl. 23,1) and have proved to belong to a rare and peculiar type of jug with an overvaulted top forming a kind of roof (Type 5). The pieces that resemble one another represent fragments of the neck

392

and a part of the overvaulted top. Even a small piece of the spout is discernible on one of the fragments (cf. the reconstruction in our Fig. 3).

Pl. 4, 6 is remarkable as it illustrates a lid (in a fragmentary state) that is unique within this group. As the illustration shows, the preserved portion is provided with a flat knob.

Among the fragments of pots excavated from the cultural deposits there is a small amphora (Pl. 3, 1) with long discoid handles extending from the rim of the mouth to the upper part of the body (Type 6). The height of the vessel is 12.4 cm., and its breadth 8.3 cm. To judge from the close similarities between this and the small vessels bought in the district (see p. 426) we are probably justified in assuming that these belong to the Ch'i Chia culture, so that special importance is to be attached to this amphora.

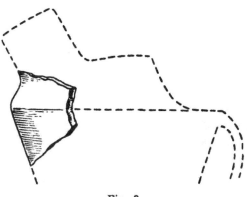

Fig. 3.

Sherds that are fragments of small vessels within this group practically all belong to the above-mentioned type of amphora (Pl. 4, 7—9). Otherwise they are related to some closely allied variant, which also occurs among the bought vessels (cf. Pl. 23). The thickness of the ware is in general directly proportional to the dimensions of the vessels and these smaller amphorae consequently have very much thinner walls than the vessels of larger size.

Décor. As has been mentioned above, only the large urns possess a décor (Types I A & B), whereas in all the other vessels any form of decorative or constructive pattern is entirely absent. On the other hand, on some of the smaller vessels (e. g. Pl. 3, 5) there are just discernible on the surface traces of deliberately effaced mat impressions, which are in curious contrast to the above-mentioned example of an imitation of a similar pattern (Pl. 4, 12) — assuming that the latter is actually not a genuine impression, a point that it is difficult to decide from the evidence.

CC: I c.

About 53 fragments.

This group shows a distinct affinity to the preceding group as far as regards certain vessel forms and decorative details, though it differs from it in that the quality of the ware is lower, the technical execution poorer, and some of the vessel forms are new. On the whole the group is a difficult one to keep quite distinct, as it is in part associated with group I b and in certain respects assumes an intermediate position between the latter and the following class (CC: II).

393

The Ware. The comparative lack of uniformity exhibited by this group is also noticeable in the character of the ware. One feature, however, that is common to the different sherds is that they have all been subject to a low firing temperature — considerably lower in fact than in group I b. The quantity and nature of the substance added to the clay to reduce its richness vary, but in the main the quantity forms a greater percentage than in group I b. The ware is of a strikingly dark colour compared with that of the preceding groups — usualy a dirty brown, though there also occur greyish and reddish-brown tints.

Slip. Only a couple of sherds show traces of any slip, which is here pale-yellow in tone.

Vessel forms. It has been possible to reconstruct only a very few forms out of the small number of extremely fragmentary sherds founds.

Three fragments of necks (Pl. 5,1—3) are reminiscent of the urn form (Type I) that is so common within the previous groups, although in view of their decoration and remarkable size the neck fragments in question belong to a somewhat divergent type, which occurs in Lo Han T'ang.[1]) Fig. 2 has a comparatively low neck (33 mm.), the rim of the mouth being bent slightly outwards. The transition between neck and body is marked by an imposed band with incised squares. Fig. 1 has a belt of incised crosses. Fig. 3 has a similar marking, but here the crosses, which are arranged in double rows, form a squared pattern demarcated on both sides by a shallow furrow. — Of the amphora type referred to above there remain only one or two fragments of a body and a base and a few lugs of the short and broad type that is characteristic of this form.

Further, there belong to this group some fragments of the form of bowl described above as Type 4.

Pl. 5,10 illustrates a fragment of the rim of a vessel the original size and appearance of which it is difficult to estimate. It may be presumed, however, that the vessel was fairly large and its shape straight and resembling a flowerpot, the rim of the mouth curving inwards. The exterior is covered with impressions of some kind of plaited work. If our reconstruction is correct, we have here a form that is new to the Ch'i Chia culture.

A number of small bowls standing on a foot (Type 7) are likewise new additions. The specimen illustrated in Pl. 5,4 is 5.5 cm. in height and both exterior and interior show slight traces of red colour. To judge from the shape it seems likely that the bowls were used as lamps, this supposition being supported by the fact that the bowl referred to above has on its inside a network of dark veins which might possibly be traces of oil.

A further feature characteristic of the group is a collection of lids (7) varying in type and size. The diameter ranges between 6 and 15 cm. Some are smooth (Pl. 5,5), but the upper side of the edge is occasionally ornamented. The vessel shown in Pl. 5,7 is decorated with crescent-shaped impressions facing one another

---

[1]) These fragments are closely akin to a very large urn from Lo Han T'ang, see Pl. 25,2.

394

in pairs, and the specimen in Pl. 5,6 is ornamented with simple slanting furrows. All the lids have had knobs, that shown in Pl. 6,8 being decorated with plait-like incisions. Pl. 15,6 illustrates a large knob with a similar ornamentation, and it is also, probably, a fragment of a lid belonging to this group.

Finally, we may refer to CC: I c three fragments of »ring-feet» (Pl. 15,7) and a hollow leg of a small tripod (Pl. 15,8).

Décor. The group possesses two kinds of décor: incised patterns and ornamentation in relief. As will be gathered from what has been said above, the incised patterns occur on the necks, where they mark the transition to the body (Pl. 5,1 and 5,3). Incisions appear on the lids as an edging. It should be observed that they are always placed on the upper side, indicating that the objects in question were actually lids and not, as might otherwise have been assumed, small bowls.

An incised ornamentation occurs in conjunction with relief in Pl. 5,2, in which a band running round the neck is decorated with incised squares.

Finally, among the vessels ornamented in relief must be placed the sherd Pl. 5,11, which forms an important link in our study of Ch'i Chia. Here we find on a lug of the short, broad type the remains of a snake coiling upwards and fashioned in relief. The direction taken by the snake is indicated by a contraction that marks the head on the surface of one of the broken edges. That this should be placed upwards is obvious from the appearance of the fragment. The lines of the animal's body are marked by deep impressions, arranged so is to indicate the sinuous movements of the reptile.

An impression of some indeterminable plaited work occurs on another handle of the same form as the preceding (Pl. 5,9). It is possible that this was permitted to remain for ornamental purposes.

Purely constructive impressions of mats and such-like are found on some bowl-fragments, but they are of very little significance in the material grouped under CC: I c.

In Pl. 5,13 is illustrated a fragment of a rim made of unusually thin, brown ware. The sherd appears to be part of a very high and quite straight neck. In the middle of the rim of the mouth the ware is pinched in, giving to the marginal edge the shape of a double arc.

The closest resemblance to this construction is found in a unique little jug from Ho Yin Hsien, Chih Kou Chai, see Andersson, RPC. pl. 35,1.[1]) This vessel, thin as an egg-shell, has a proportionally very high, straight neck with a spout formed by two pinches in the clay, similar to that referred to above. It is reasonable to assume that Pl. 5,13 illustrates a fragment of a similarly shaped vessel, though much larger than the jug we have just described.

The fragment in question differs from the Ch'i Chia material in its peculiar shape

---

[1]) J. G. Andersson, Researches into the Prehistory of the Chinese, BMFEA 15, 1943; henceforth quoted as RPC.

395

and its uncommonly thin ware, but the differences are not sufficiently great to warrant its rejection from the group without further evidence. The sherd has accordingly been dealt with in conjunction with CC: I c, the group in which it fits best.

Supplement to CC: I.

In this class may also be grouped a number of objects that are not remnants of vessels. There is consequently some difficulty in placing them in the respective sub-divisions of the potsherds, and they will therefore be discussed here separately.

Pl. 15,2 shows a rather badly damaged piece of animal sculpture, of which have been preserved, besides the body, remains of the neck and legs.

There are furthermore six balls of burnt clay (Pl. 15,3). Their purpose is not known, but they may possibly have been used for grinding colours or some similar purpose.

Pl. 15,1 shows a lump with a hole in it, which however does not go right through the centre, so that it is unlikely that the object was used as a spinning-whorl, which otherwise might have been surmised. On the other hand, the one half of a spinning-whorl is reproduced in Pl. 15,9, as also in Pl. 15,10. The former shows traces of mat impressions. The latter, although mentioned here, belongs to CC: II on account of its coarser ware.

CC: II.

266 fragments.

A very uniform class, within which, however, there is some justification for distinguishing two groups: one, here called II a, comprising some sherds which, owing to their décor or the higher quality of their ware or, usually, to both, are manifestly to be differentiated from the main bulk of the sherds falling within this class. These last have here been brought together to form group II b, which thus happens to comprise the great majority of the low household utensils belonging to the Ch'i Chia P'ing culture.

CC: II a.

About 65 fragments.

The ware. Compared with group II b, the sherds contain relatively little reducing substance. The colour is fairly light, usually yellowish, though pale brick-red or brown tints also occur. The colour of the exterior is generally uniform, but occasionally there is a red flaminess such as we find in CC: I. In contrast to the succeeding group, the fractures are fairly smooth in spite of the porosity of the ware. The temperature at which it was fired was probably comparatively low. In the case of a couple of sherds, however, it must have been as much as about

396

900° C. In these cases the fragments show close similarity to CCI : a, b, though they differ in the unusual size of the particles of lime.

Slip. One or two sherds are covered with a pale-yellow slip, applied either on the exterior only or else on both sides.

Vessel forms. The normal form both for this and for the succeeding group is that of an urn with gently rounded profile and fairly low neck expanded slightly upwards (Type 8). The body is covered with cord or mat impressions (cf. p. 412). It is difficult to gain any exact idea of the size of these vessels owing to their fragmentary state, but they appear to have been smaller than the urns classified under CC: I (Types 1 A and 1 B), from which they also differ in their having a lower neck and the *whole* of the body covered with mat or cord impressions.

The height of the neck varies, the average being about 3 cm. It is usually smooth, but there are also forms with ornamental patterns.

Only in exceptional cases do handles occur on this type of vessel. Pl. 6,3 shows a unique rudimentary boss-handle, which could hardly have had any practical purpose.

Four fragments of mouths (Pl. 7,3—5) reveal a new type of vessel, but it is now difficult to gauge its appearance when complete. To judge from the profile of the fragments, it might be guessed that the vessel here concerned had straight sides and perhaps resembled a flower-pot. In all cases the rim of the mouth was much thickened (see (Pl. 7,3). In all, too, the actual rim of the mouth is ornamented.

Another new and complicated form of vessel is reproduced in Pl. 6,1. Inside the rim of the mouth runs a broad groove, into which a lid has probably fitted. The vessel has a spout, which partially intersects the circular line of the groove, so that, if there were a lid, it must have had a corresponding excision. Below the rim of the mouth projects a disc-like handle. The part nearest the rim of the mouth is smooth, and from here begin cord impressions bounded at the top by an ornamental edging of crescent-shaped ridges.

Finally, it has seemed expedient to place in this group *in toto* a collection of eleven fragments (Pl. 8,4—9), two of which, however, are on the border-line between this and Group II b. The vessels are here brought together to form a unit on account of the puzzling manner in which they have been treated.[1]) Prior to being fired they were, either wholly or in part, slit by means of a thin cutting implement. In the latter case the fracture shows a shiny cut, from which it can be clearly seen how the »knife» has passed through the wet clay (Pl. 8,5, 7). On one vessel one can observe, along the border between the wall and the base, how the point of the implement was stuck in diagonally time after time (Pl. 8,4), and was finally drawn through the interior layer of the base. The exterior layer, which was not penetrated, shows a rough fracture, from which it may be assumed that the vessels were subsequently broken in two. This rough fracture lies, in the case of

---

[1]) A similar fragment of a vessel of grey ware and provided with a handle is known from Yang Shao Tsun, Honan (K. 6446).

397

nine of the fragments, on the inside. In the case of one fragment of a mouth-rim the cut surface is on the outside (Pl. 8,6), and another fragment, that of a base, has been cut right through the wall of the vessel (Pl. 8,8). Still another base fragment, which exhibits the most common type of section, was originally wrongly cut, the mistake being subsequently corrected without any care being taken to smooth over the traces of the first cut (Pl. 8,9). With the exception of one fragment (Pl. 8,6), which shows a slight bulge, these fragments of vessels are straight in profile. Moreover, in every case the exterior wall is covered with cord impressions, which in some fragments continue up to and over the flattened rim of the mouth. In the fragment illustrated in Pl. 8,6 the rim has a profile resembling a *cavetto*.

The purpose of these vessels may always remain an insoluble problem, though one or two possible hypotheses will be suggested below. The straight form that characterizes these vessels has no doubt some connection with their function. Seeing that, as stated above, the vessels have been split into two parts, it is conceivable that the two halves could be fitted together and thus be used in combination as moulds; in that case they were covered inside with grass fibres or grass or straw mats more or less carelessly joined together, or else with cords or a rough sacking made of cord (cf. the chapter on Technical details). On the other hand, the possibility should not be excluded that the vessels might have an association with some ritual custom, e. g. a ceremonial crushing, which would be facilitated by the cross-cut. For my part, however, I consider that this explanation is not very plausible, since we are here concerned with a dwelling-site material, and the Ch'i Chia people's burial customs are unknown to us. Finally, it should be pointed out that we cannot possibly be dealing here with the remains of double vessels containing a dividing wall of wood or some such material, since the incision is not sufficiently broad to permit of the insertion of a partition. Besides, in one fragment the cut surface is on the outside.

Décor. The décor, which in this group is confined to the rim of the mouth and the neck, or the transition between the latter and the body, consists for the most part of incisions or patterns made with an engraving stick. Décor in relief does not occur very often as the sole motif. The engraved patterns occur partly as a belt of incised crosses (Pl. 7,1), partly as oblique furrows (Pl. 7,2). These patterns may also be combined with bands in relief (Pl. 7,7, 9). The decorative forms just mentioned are also found in CC: I, whereas the ornamentation of the mouth-rim shown in Pl. 7,4 is of a type that is peculiar to CC: II. Here indentations have been made in the edge of the vessel by means of an engraving stick, thus giving to the edge the character of a wavy line. A similar motif recurs in Pl. 7,3, 5.

Ornamentation in relief occurs in the form of a dentated edging. A sherd shows such ornamentation applied to the rim of the mouth, while that shown in Pl. 7,10 has been placed lower down on the neck. A fine ornamental relief with a succession of rhombi is observed immediately below the rim of the mouth in Pl. 7,1.

398

In one or two cases within this group the constructive pattern has been made to serve an ornamental purpose. This has been done in its simplest form in Pl. 7,4, where it has been deliberately smoothed over by means of a fillet just below the mouth. The same idea has been further developed in Pl. 7,2,5 in which the cord impressions have been curtailed by furrows or lines, between which the constructive pattern has been allowed to remain as ornamental ridges.

CC: II b.

About 201 fragments.

This group embraces the main bulk of the coarsest ceramic material of the Ch'i Chia P'ing culture.

The ware. The richness of the clay used for this ware has been heavily reduced by an admixture of sand, as is clearly seen from the inner side of the wall of the vessels, whereas only an occasional grain is observable on the outside. The fractures frequently have a flaky appearance, the stratification being in the vertical plane. Some fragments appear to have been made of several layers of different kinds of clay. The most common colour is a dirty brown or dirty grey tone; brick-red and yellow tints also occur though with less frequency. The temperature at which the vessels were fired must have been very low, probably between 500 and 600°.

Most of the sherds within this group show signs of soot. This occurs either in the form of spots or else as a real, sometimes very thick coating. The soot is usually found on the outside, but occasionally on both sides and now and then on the inside only. It sometimes occurs also on the actual fractures. The coating is so heavy that it must be assumed that the soot was produced during cooking or some such process. The abundant presence of sand in the clay mass may also conceivably have some connection with the use of the vessels for cooking, since the sand particles would prevent the ware from cracking when overheated.

Vessel forms. As has been mentioned above, in this group also the most common form of vessel is an urn with a gently rounded profile and a smooth, not very high, neck expanding slightly upwards. The entire body is covered on the outside with cord or mat impressions (Type 8). To this type belongs one of the two complete vessels excavated at Ch'i Chia P'ing (Pl. 6,6). It is of relatively small size (Type 8), but it is clear from the fragments that larger specimens of the same type occurred (Pl. 6,5).

A closely related form of vessel (Type 9) is provided with two short, broad handles, which project from the rim of the mouth to the upper part of the body. The body and the outside of the handle are covered with cord impressions. Of this type only fragments (Pl. 8,2) were found at Ch'i Chia P'ing, but a fairly complete specimen was discovered at the closely related dwelling-site, known as Hsin Tien C (see p. 419 below). This pot, illustrated in Pl. 20,5, shows that the vessels were of relatively small size.

399

Under this group must further be placed, owing to its thick ware, containing a strong admixture of gravel, a small bowl, which otherwise differs from the uniform bulk of thick domestic ware in its slender form. It is provided with a foot (Pl. 5,14), which is ornamented with oblique notches and thus differs from the type of small bowls (Type 4) classified under CC: I.

In Pl. 8,3 a fragment of a rim is illustrated with a thick edge round the mouth. This is probably derived from a type of vessel that is found in Hsin Tien C, cf. p. 419 and Pl. 20,1. The vessel must have been fairly large and have had straight walls, possibly expanding upwards (reconstruction in fig. 4).

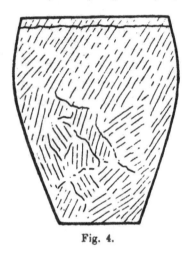

Fig. 4.

The group also contains three fragments of tripods. A solid leg is illustrated in Pl. 7,16. It consists of an inner core around which an outer coating of clay has been smeared. The exterior shows traces of mat impressions. The other fragment of a tripod illustrated here (Pl. 7,14) is a piece of the part where one of the legs is attached to the body. The outside shows basket impressions, representing the wicker-work technique.

In regard to the basket impressions and the ware, the fragment of a mouth illustrated in Pl. 7,13 is very closely related to the tripod fragment described above, but the points of resemblance are not so close as to justify the assumption that they belong to the same vessel.

Finally, mention should be made of two fragments of perforated bases. (Pl. 7,18). The inner uneven edge of the holes proves that they were made with an instrument that had pierced the bottom of the vessel from the outside. These vessels had cordimpressions on the body. Professor Andersson in An Early Chinese Culture (p. 61) explains the purpose of these vessels by assuming that they were used in conjunction with tripods for steaming food. Another possibility might be that they were used as braziers.

In this chapter we shall also deal with two fragments of the bodies of large vessels with strong handles (Pl. 7,6). The ware is very similar in the two fragments, and it is therefore not out of the question that they belong to one and the same vessel. We do not know what this vessel looked like originally when complete, except that the profile of the body at the points where the handles were attached was broken, and that the upper part was probably smooth while the lower part had on it quite fine mat impressions. Fragments of exactly the same type are met with in large numbers at the dwelling site of Hui Tsui. They resemble one another not only in shape but also in the ware and in the mat impressions. On the other hand, they do not differ so widely from the rest of the material as to warrant their being

400

classified apart, seeing that the stratigraphy lends no support to the argument either way.

CC: III.
About 93 fragments.

A scanty but strongly uniform group which is clearly differentiated from the preceding one in its décor, formal design, technical quality and ware.

The Ware. The clay mass contains, according to the microscopical slides, varying quantities of loess and mica and is characterized by a fairly uniform mixture of sand rich in felspar. The petrographical character of the sand entirely distinguishes the ware within this class from that of the preceding group. The ware is porous and appears to have been fired at a fairly low temperature. The colour varies between dirty brown and brick-red or pale-yellow and grayish-yellow tones. The pale-coloured ware is often flamy on the surface and sometimes has brick-red spots. Several sherds show a coating of soot, some of them both on the walls of the vessels and on the fractures.

The walls of the vessels are remarkably thin, their thickness being only a couple of mm. The necks exhibit no traces of being turned by hand, and in spite of their tasteful appearance the vessels give a general impression of a not very perfected technique, although the best specimens have obviously been executed with some care.

Vessel forms. In regard to form this group offers but few variations. The form of vessel that with one single exception predominates is a 30—40 cm. high pot with a low neck (Type 10). Occasionally it is provided with short, broad handles which extend from the mouth to the upper part of the body (breadth in the middle about 3 cm., distance between the points of attachment about 4 cm.). The bases comprise: 1) a type with a separate standing surface (Pl. 12,6, 8), although of a kind other than that occurring in the rest of the Ch'i Chia material; 2) a type in which the base is formed by compressing the lowest part of the vessel wall (Pl. 14,11). (The same method of making the base was employed in the Hsin Tien and the Sha Ching periods.)

The only divergent form of vessel is illustrated in Pl. 14,1 and differs, partly in its smaller proportions and partly in the neck's having a vaguer profile, from the type of vessel that is most common in this class. On the other hand it exhibits a certain association with a form (Type 9) occurring in CC: II b. Cf. also Pl. 8,2 and 20,5.

Décor. Most of the vessels have some kind of ornamentation. Only a couple of fragments indicate that entirely undecorated vessels also occurred (Pl. 13,6 and 14,2). The ornamented vessels may be divided into two groups. The one is characterized by a highly developed »Kamm» and stamp ornamentation combined with relief and incised lines, while the other has a simple décor in relief at the rim of the mouth. All ornamentation shows up against impressions, covering the

401

entire surface, of grass or vegetable fibres (which were possibly knit into rough mats). This mat pattern is constructive in character and if it possesses any ornamental significance that is purely secondary.

In the Kamm group all the patterns were applied according to a special ornamental system consisting of a horizontal division of the neck-part and the upper part of the body into zones. In those cases in which the lower part of the body is ornamented the grouping is vertical.

Kamm ornamentation. This occurs probably only on the upper part of the vessels, either alone or combined with other decorations. Alone it has been found only on a couple of fragments (Pl. 13,1 and 13,8—10), where it is applied to an attached band which either runs round the neck (13,1), in which case it is of considerable breadth and marks the transition between neck and belly, or else it decorates the belly as a horizontal band (13,8). In 13,9 the band in relief, which is only faintly discernible, shows horizontal Kamm impressions of an uncommon type.

Kamm impressions are combined in various ways with all the other types of pattern, one or several at the same time, that occur within the group. The Kamm impression itself may have a varying character; thus, we find horizontal (e. g. Pl. 13,4) or oblique lines (e. g. Pl. 13,2, 4), bands of consecutive triangles (Pl. 12,12), and squared patterns with a filling of incised cowrie shells (Pl. 13,5). The bands with Kamm pattern occur either accompanied by other patterns or else combined with one another, thus producing horizontal division of the upper part of the body into zones (e. g. Pl. 13,5). Finally we find narrow lines of Kamm pattern impressed on a relief band, such as that illustrated in Pl. 12,1—3.

Ornamentation in relief. Lines in relief occur also without Kamm impressions. These, which themselves have a decorative function, are of a different character from those previously mentioned. Generally, as e. g. in Pl. 12,2, 3, they run vertically in sharply defined ridges down over the belly. They are combined into groups, thus producing a rhythmical division of the belly. On the middle of the vessel there are occasionally formed, out of the lines in relief, meanders having right angles (Pl. 12,5, 8) or acute angles (Pl. 12,4). The intermediate spaces are sometimes filled with a zig-zag line in relief (Pl. 12,2).

The relief ornamentation may also assume the curious form of knobs, which occur in pairs on the handles and round the neck (Pl. 13,3). They are generally provided with a central knob and a circular incision forming a boundary (Pl. 13,3, 4). In Pl. 13,5 the décor on the knob consists of crescent-shaped impressions in imitation of cowrie shells. Pl. 14,1 illustrates a unique form in which the knob in the middle has an indentation.

On a separate group of simpler vessels the ornamentation occurs only round the mouth in the form of bands in relief. These are either in the shape of knob-like handles with a dentated ornamentation (Pl. 14,3—5), or they may develop into a dentated border running all the way round (Pl. 14,8), or a wavy or twisted band (Pl. 14,6, 7).

402

Incised ornamentation. Incised patterns are carried out either as simple straight lines (12,13 and 13,11), wedges (Pl. 13,2) or angle-lines (Pl. 13,11). These may be combined to form an ornamental system such as that shown on the handle in Pl. 13,11. Incised ornaments are also executed in the form of double halfmoons facing one another, probably imitating cowrie shells and sometimes in combination with Kamm lines to form a surface pattern (Pl. 13,5).

Stamp ornamentation. This occurs in the form of drops or grains of corn, invariably with the points facing one another (Pl. 12,1). Stamped rhombi and angles also occur (Pl. 12,10).

Painting. On a couple of neck fragments we find an entirely different type of décor. These have on their inner sides ornamental painting in reddish or brownish violet tones. Pl. 13,5 b illustrates broad vertical lines on the inside of a neck. On the exterior of this vessel are traces of the same reddish violet colour at the rim of the mouth and on the upper part of the handle. For the rest, the outside is covered with a heavy coating of soot. On the fragments reproduced in Pl. 13,7 b and in Fig. 5 the décor consists of triangles with the points downwards. The colour is the same as in the preceding case.

Fig. 5.

In one or two fragments this reddish-violet colour has been applied as a coating of paint covering the entire surface. In Pl. 12,1 it is confined to the inner side of the neck, whereas in Pl. 13,3 there are also traces of it on the outside.

Technical details of manufacture.

In treatises on ceramics, the method of manufacture is often entirely neglected as being too difficult or unprofitable a field of enquiry or else the subject is merely dismissed in a few brief words. Though fully realizing the risks involved in entering upon this subject, to which all too little attention has been given and in which any conclusions drawn must be more or less hypothetical, I shall nevertheless venture a few remarks on the Ch'i Chia P'ing pottery from the technical point of view.

All the numerical data regarding the firing temperature and such-like are v e r y a p p r o x i m a t i v e as I have not had an opportunity of having any chemical analysis made. I have however, obtained much valuable information from consulting experts, artisans and others engaged in the manufacture of modern pottery. My investigations have proved fruitful insofar that the divergences that exist in regard to the different ceramic classes become especially conspicuous when we examine the technical processes employed in the manufacture of the pottery.

403

CC: I.

The clay mass is extremely fine and well elutriated. Substances for reducing the richness of the clay are found in all groups, although in extremely small quantities in group I a. Regarded as a whole, however, the clay in CC: I contains, compared with the other classes, only small quantities of a »degraissant».

The technical method employed in the manufacture has naturally depended to a certain extent upon the form and size of the vessel to be produced, and the ambition to construct new and complicated vessel forms has probably been a powerful stimulus to the attainment of increased technical skill.

The process which, so far as one can judge from the few traces of manufacturing technique that are still preserved, was employed in making most of these vessels differs from the constructive method commonly used in making Stone Age pottery: the method of a band wound round upon itself spirally. In Ch'i Chia, we find in the very smallest vessels another technique common in neolithic pottery, viz. the vessel fashioned out of a single lump of clay, e. g. Pl. 5,4. It is possible that some of the bowls were made on this principle. Pl. 2,4 has been fashioned with the thumbs against basket work which has left traces on the outside beneath the turned-over edge. It is impossible, however, to determine whether the clay was smeared on directly or whether it was first formed into layers. The body of the small vessels was also probably hollowed out of one piece, though no definite conclusions can be drawn from the small fragments available.

In the case of other vessels, however, another kind of technique was employed. The first thing the potter did was to roll out strips of clay the width of which was made proportionate to the size of the intended vessel. Then on the inside of a mould or a supporting form (a basket, mat or other plaited material) these strips have been placed one on top of the other and the joints closed up with the thumbs, after which the joints have been carefully smoothed over either with the fingers or with some kind of spatula.

It is also conceivable of course that, at least in the case of some of the smaller vessels, the under part may have been made out of a single broad strip, though to judge from marks, impressions and cracks, the vessels were as a rule produced in several layers. It is difficult to gain any exact idea of the nature of the form or mould used in the manufacture of the vessels, but the impressions that are left on them and which pass more or less uninterruptedly across the under side of the body are evidence that some such form or supporting framework was actually in use. Had these impressions arisen when the layers of clay were being rolled out, on a mat or such-like, the joints would have been discernible. It has already been pointed out that in all probability the vessels were built up of a number of layers superimposed upon one another.

Nothing definite can be said as to the nature of the material of which this form was made. Moreover, it is very probable that in the group CC: I only the under part of the body was fashioned in the mould and that the upper part was then

404

built up on it. Some traces of partially smoothed-over impressions on the upper part of the body may be explained by their being derived from some mat or similar material used for pressing down the layers of clay.

The mould was probably fairly straight in profile in order to enable the potter to press the layers of clay against its wall. The mould may have been made of unfired clay, in which case it could easily be broken to pieces. But a vessel may also have served this purpose. It is possible that the split vessels mentioned above (p. 397) were actually moulds. This would naturally explain their straight profile and the peculiar character of the sherds.

Nevertheless, whether the mould was fired or unfired it must have been covered with some material in order to make the clay adhere to its wall. Vegetable fibres or some simple basket work have been used in CC: I and CC: III (cf. the chapter on Impressions), whereas in CC: II cords were pressed against the wall of the mould so that they adhered to it.

Still another type of mould, however, is conceivable. These plaited materials, or in isolated cases these baskets, may themselves have served the purpose of moulds, but if so we have to explain how they acquired the necessary rigidity. It is conceivable that clay was smeared over the exterior of the framework, but it is doubtful whether that would have been sufficient to give it the required strength. The theory that real moulds were used seems therefore to be the more plausible one.

In Pl. 5,12 there is seen on the inside near the base a row of triangular depressions, which may possibly be marks left by a tool used for pressing the clay against the plaited work. In this process the vessel was allowed to rotate, the impressions thus being given an oblique direction. When the body of the vessel produced by this means was sufficiently dry, that is to say had acquired the necessary degree of rigidity, and besides had contracted sufficiently to detach the vessel wall from the mat-covering, then this latter and the mould were removed.[1]

---

[1] A similar method of manufacturing clay vessels occurs amongst the Zuñi Indians and is described by Cushing in: A study of Pueblo pottery as illustrative of Zuñi culture growth (4th Annual Report of the Bureau of American Ethnology), Washington 1886 pp. 497 seq.: »The bottom part of the vessel was shaped in a basket, the inside of which had been bespread with sand, after which the rest of the vessel was built up with clay rolls until it eventually projected above the rim of the basket-mould. Through shrinking in the course of its drying the vessel loosened itself from the basket, this being facilitated by the sand's having prevented the clay from forming too intimate a contact with the basket work». See also Gustaf Nordenskiöld: The Cliff-dwellers of the Mesa Verde, Stockholm 1893; Holmes' Aboriginal Pottery of the Eastern United States (20th Annual Report of the Bureau of American Ethnology, Washington 1903 (pp. 58—59); Hunter: Manners and Customs of several Indian tribes located west of the Mississippi, Philadelphia 1823; Joyce, Th. A. Mexican Archaeology. An introduction to the archaeology of the Mexican and Mayan civilizations of pre-Spanish America. New York and London 1914, p. 185; Linné: The technique of South American ceramics (Göteborgs Kungl. Vetenskaps och Vitterhetssamhälles handlingar. Fourth Series. Vol 29 No. 5. Gothenburg 1925 (p. 93). Thus we can trace evidences of clay vessels made on this principle (basket-moulded clay vessels) from North America, Mexico and the region of the Andes right down to Brazil.

405

It is noteworthy that the bottom of the vessel was not fashioned in the mould but separately and was attached to the body from outside after the latter had been detached from the mould. The marks left by the body's attachment are clearly visible on the lowest part of the vessel (e. g. Pl. 2,10 and Pl. 4,18), and only in exceptional cases has care been taken to smooth over the joint. This is the case in some vessels with a smooth body, concerning which it is impossible to say whether they originally bore impressions of any mould; if they did, these marks have been removed in order to give the vessel a more attractive appearance.

Like the bottom, the neck was made separately and then joined to the body of the vessel. In group I a in particular the shape of the neck is extremely regular and almost circular. It is probable that at any rate the best types of necks were produced by means of a profiling or other shaping tool. Some fragments in I a show, on the inside, at the rim of the mouth a triple profile (Pl. 2,1), so far similar in the different specimen that it may be assumed that the same implement was used for them all. Most of the neck fragments and the best sherds from the upper part of the body have concentric striations; at first glance these appear to be marks left by the process of throwing, but on closer examination it is found that the concentricity is not complete and that frequently the striations, so to speak, lose direction. Consequently these striations cannot have arisen through a rapid rotary movement such as is given by throwing in the true sense of the word, seeing that that process leaves absolutely regular concentric marks. It will be seen from what has been said above about the construction of the vessels that a throwing process on modern lines out of a single lump of clay is *a priori* out of the question. Probably, however, we are confronted here with an early stage in the process of throwing, most closely comparable with what C. L. Wooley[1] calls »hand-turned ware», i. e. the vessels is built up on a more or less circular substructure, which is rotated in the course of manufacture. A similar process is known, e. g. from Phylakopi,[2] in which round plaited mats serve as a rotary base which has left impressions on the bottom surface of the vessels.[3]

At Ch'i Chia P'ing the potter probably used a wooden block, the base of a broken pot or something similar, for a clear impression of matting on the exterior of the base occurs in one case only (Pl. 2,12), and then in the form of clearly defined twill-

---

[1] Frankfort, Studies in Early Pottery of the Near East London 1924, p. 8.

[2] Excavations at Phylakopi by the British School at Athens. London 1904.

[3] Similar primitive substitutes for the potter's wheel are known from America. Cushing (Loc. cit. p. 504) mentions that during the process of manufacture the vessel was placed on the bottom portions of a broken clay vessel (cf. Torii: Les aborigines de Formose. Journal of the College of Science, Tokyo Imperial University, Vol. XVIII art. 6. Pl. LXIII B) or as found amongst the Zuñi Indians (Handbook of American Indians Vol. II p. 295) on a block made for the purpose. In North Yucatan a wooden block was used which was rotated with the foot (Mercer, H. C.: The hill-caves of Yucatan, Philadelphia 1896). Similar methods of procedure occur in our own day amongst the South American Indians (Linné, loc. cit. p. 947).

406

plaiting — curiously enough there occurs in one case on the interior of the base an impression of some sort of plaited work, but it is so incomplete that it is impossible to draw any definite conclusions from it (Pl. 2,9).   During this process of levelling and smoothing over the surface, the vessel was treated with some kind of tool suitable for the purpose.   At Ch'i Chia P'ing no instrument has come to light that would appear to be specially suited for the purpose, although objects such as those reproduced in Pl. 15,5 may conceivably have been used. There are preserved in the MFEA crescent-shaped mussel-knives and rectangular knives made of pot sherds, collected from other prehistoric dwelling-sites in China. These two types might very well have been used in the manufacture of pottery, seeing that they are far too fragile to be employed as ordinary knives. Of course, simple instruments of wood or bamboo might also have been used.

As regards the smaller vessels, it should be mentioned that these underwent a finishing process of being scraped, which usually left vertical marks over the entire vessel except on the middle part of the body, where the marks run in horizontal lines.

One or two sherds have a shiny surface, indicating that they were subjected to some actual polishing process.

The handles are all affixed in a simple manner.   They have been stuck on the outside of the vessel by smearing, the one hand being kept pressed against the inside, where finger prints are often observable in conjunction with a slight buckling of the vessel-wall.   The handles must in such cases have been attached while the wall was still in a comparatively plastic condition.

The décor, in so far as it is found in this class, in the form either of applied bands in relief or of incised patterns, was executed before the vessel had had time to become too dry.

Prior to firing, some of the vessels were covered with a thin coating of slip. Some of them are completely covered with it both inside and out, after being dipped in a slip-bath, whereas on others the slip was merely applied with the hand or with some implement over the outside of the vessel and the inside of the neck. The colour is usually yellowish-brown, but some sherds in group I a are distinguished by a characteristic whitish-yellow tone (cf. p. 390) which is not derived from lime but possibly from pipe-clay. Occasionally the tone of the slip coincides with that of the ware, in which case it is very difficult to decide whether there really is a coating of slip. It should be noted that the existence of a coating of slip on a sherd does not necessarily imply that it has been deliberately applied, for when a wet hand or a moist object is rubbed against an unfired vessel a kind of slip forms on it. Whether the slip was of a functional or of a decorative nature it is difficult to decide.   At any rate in those cases in which its colour does not differ appreciably from that of the ware, it is most natural to regard it as functional, whereas the white slip may have had an ornamental value.   It may possibly have been used in order to give the vessels the appearance of being made all of the same material

407

as the vessels illustrated in Pl. 11,13 (probably pipe-clay, which appears to have been rare at the place).[1])

To judge from the often strong brick-red colour and hard quality of the ware, it was no doubt fired at a high temperature in a closed heating chamber regulated by a draught, as a result of which oxidization took place. In the case of the hardest baked vessels the temperature probably ranged between 900 and 1.000°; at any rate it did not exceed the latter figure. Of course the temperature varied somewhat in the firing of the different vessels, but the mean temperature was no doubt round or slightly below 900°. Owing to irregularities in the supply of air the oxidizing process was occasionally not uniform or sometimes ceased altogether, so that deoxidization may have set in. These variations are discernible in the zonal striation noticed in some fragments, to which reference has already been made above (p. 388). Flaminess in the surface layer of the ware has also been caused by lack of continuity in the supply of air, ascribable, of course, to imperfections in the construction of the kiln. We are still ignorant on this latter point, but it may be assumed that the kiln was of quite a primitive type — constructed for instance somewhat after the fashion of a charcoal stack (cf. L. Franchet: Céramique primitive, Paris 1911).

CC: II.

The technical process employed in this class does not seem to differ essentially from that of CC: I. The fundamental principle governing the construction of the vessels is the same. The clay, which in this class usually contains a rich mixture of particles of gravel, is so porous, especially in II b, that the fracture has a slaty appearance.

Although here, as in the preceding class, the vessels have been built up on the inside of a mould or supporting basket-work, contrary to what was the case in CC: I, the latter has left impressions over the entire exterior of the vessel. These impressions, which will be discussed in the next chapter, are of an entirely different kind from those in CC: I.

The class under discussion provides the most definite evidence that the vessels were built up in layers. Pl. 6,4 reproduces a vessel that typologically is a transitional form between CC: I and CC: II. This fragment shows on its inside a horizontal crack 35 mm. in length representing the fracture between two layers. In the present case these layers do not appear to have been higher than 25—30 mm. The crack does not apparently run horizontally through the wall of the vessel but obliquely downwards when viewed from the inside. This isolated case offers, however, evidence far too slight to justify the assertion that the surfaces where the layers join one another were in any way faced, although it is probable that this was often done, seeing that it facilitated the joining of the layers. In any

---

[1]) A similar imitation is pointed out by T. Arne on painted pottery found in Honan. Arne: Painted Stone Age Pottery from Honan. Paleontologica Sinica, Vol. I Fasc. 2. Peking 1925, p. 15.

408

case, the adjacent layers must have been thumbed over one another, and this may have given rise to the formation of a crack such as that referred to. One of the cleft vessels likewise exhibits a crack between two strips (Pl. 8,7), but in this case it runs horizontally through the wall of the vessel. Among the materials collected at Hsin Tien C, those which are related to CC: II afford still further evidence of this method of construction. Here we find on the inside of a vessel (illustrated in Pl. 20,1) a straight crack about 130 mm. long. This unusually large vessel seems to have been built up of layers about 60 mm. high, thus still further confirming the theory that the height of the layers is in direct proportion to the size of the vessel.

In CC: II, unlike what we find in the preceding class, the neck is sometimes attached from the outside as well. This is clearly seen in Pl. 8,1, in which no care has been taken to thumb over the joint properly. The fragments reproduced in Pl. 10,1 and 9,2 reveal the fact that the neck was in this case shaped while the vessel was still in its mould. No joint is observable between the neck and body in these and similar sherds, and the impressions on the belly of the vessel continue uninterruptedly up to the neck. On the first-mentioned fragment, however, a separate band has been attached to the mouth, and the joint, ornamented with a dentated border in relief, is clearly visible through a deep crack. When the neck is made separately, which is usually the case, it has some-times — probably after being attached to the body — been levelled and smoothed over, besides which the rim of the mouth has often been given a slight profile (e. g. Pl. 6,5). Marks resulting from this finishing process are often observable in the form of a slight concentric striation.

In the few cases in which handles occur, they have been attached in the same way as in CC: I. This applies also to the specimen illustrated in Pl. 7,6, in spite of its unusual size. Moreover, on the surface where the layers join there are the same mat impressions as on the body, this being noticeable as a piece of the wall of the vessel has been broken off. These impressions may be due either to the fact that the potter desired to enlarge the connecting surface or that the handle was fashioned on a foundation of matting. It may be mentioned in passing that on a couple of the bought vessels there is a similar mat impression on the under-side of the long disc-like handles, and in one case the impression apparently came from a raw hide. Within this class we also have bottoms of vessels attached both from inside and from outside (cf. Pl. 7,15 and 7,17). In the former case the lower edge of the vessel-wall has been folded round the bottom, as can be seen from the fact that a ring has been left on the under-side, in which case the mat or cord impressions on the body extend right down below the edge. When the bottom is attached from the outside, the process is the same as in CC: I, but here the joint is usually far more clumsy. To judge from the fragments, both methods of attachment were equally common.

Slip occurs sometimes in this class as well. Its generally somewhat inconspicuous colour and its often considerable thickness, notably on the inside, afford evidence

409

that its function was purely practical, namely to prevent the exceedingly porous ware from absorbing too much moisture.

As has been mentioned before, a coating of soot is extremely common in CC: II. It is generally found on the outside, though sometimes also in patches on the inside or on the fractures. When the soot occurs in large quantities and adheres firmly to the wall of the vessel, it is probably the result of the vessel's being used for cooking purposes. The coating on the fractures can be explained by the fact that the vessel has cracked when in use. The vessels' firing temperature appears generally to have been decidedly lower than in the case of CC: I. Sherds of group II a show pale-yellow and occasionally brick-red tints, and we may therefore assume that they were fired in a kiln. The dirty brown and grayish, very uncompact ware of group II b indicates that it was baked at an open fire, the temperature hardly exceeding 600°.

CC: III.

In this class it is very difficult to arrive at any definite result as regards the technical process of manufacture, and most of our conclusions must be regarded as hypothetical.

No distinct joints or marks left by the process of thumbing over the layers of clay are discernible except in the case of Pl. 14,1.

The other fragments of vessels show indications of another method of construction. The wall is only a couple of mm. thick and the inside is smooth and even without any marks left by joints or fingerprints. It is probable therefore that in regard to these singularly thin-walled vessels we are confronted with some kind of casting technique. The clay has been smeared direct against a mould or supporting basket work without being first rolled out into layers. Slight impressions of the same kind as appear on the outside of the body are occasionally found on the inside of the vessel-wall. The explanation may be that in order to get the clay to adhere to the mould a piece of the same material was pressed with the hand against the vessel-wall. The neck was made separately, but sometimes it consists merely of a low strip round the mouth. The actual rim of the mouth was flattened and, like the other details, was frequently not fashioned with very much precision. On the inside of the neck the surface has been smoothed over, but this manipulation · has not left the regular concentric marks that are found in the preceding classes. The exterior of the neck is, like the body, covered with mat impressions.

As to the four fragments of bottoms, the basal surface of two of them is clearly differentiated (Pl. 12,6, 8). In these cases the loose bottom plate has been attached from inside. The two other fragments of bottom (Pl. 14,11) are in appearance reminiscent of vessels from the Hsin Tien period. Here vessel-wall and bottom seem to be all in one piece. The convex basal surface has the appearance of having been clamped together, owing presumably to the mould's having been made of a soft material which lay folded under the bottom of the vessel. Further evidence

410

that the vessel was made in one piece is offered by the fact that the mat impression continues over the basal surface. The handles, which have been fashioned with great care, are attached in the ordinary way to neck and body, but all traces of joints have been smoothed over. They show the same impressions on the outside, and sometimes also on the under-side, as are found on the body.

The vessels were decorated after the clay had become so firm that the supporting material could be removed, leaving a distinct impression covering the entire exterior. The whole decorative design has been superimposed on these impressions (see Pl. 14,9). In some cases, where the wall of the neck has tended to become too thin, after the removal of the support the surface has been coated over with a thin layer of clay-wash, which sometimes also forms a ground on which relief-work and Kamm décor have been applied, though the background for such designs is generally the constructive mat impressions. The relief bands are made up of applied strips and ovals of varying thickness and are frequently bordered by an incised line. Amongst the dwelling-site material no object has come to light that might conceivably have been used for producing the Kamm pattern.

The painted décor on the inside of two fragments of a neck (Pl. 13,5 b and 13,7 b) was done prior to firing, and the reddish-violet colour was probably made of manganese dioxide. On the exterior of the upper part of the body of some vessels (Pl. 13,3) and also on the inside of the neck, there is a reddish colour. This colour, apparently oxide of iron, was likewise applied before the vessel was fired.

The vessels appear to have been fired in a kiln, and, to judge from the colour, at about the same temperature as CC: I. The exterior of some vessels is covered with a thick coating of soot.

Mat and basket impressions.

The supporting material that enclosed the vessels or covered the mould during certain phases of their manufacture has left impressions the appearance of which depends on the method by which it was plaited or »sewn». On the whole the different classes are distinguished by their own particular impressions. In order to have a technical term applicable to them all we have given these different impressions the common term »mat impressions», though the »mat» is not of course to be conceived of as a real textile fabric consisting of threads running lengthwise and regularly crossed by woof, but rather as warp-threads sparsely joined together.

CC: I.

In CC: I the most common impression has been made by plait-work in which the warp has consisted of relatively broad, smooth vegetable fibres laid without any particular regard to orderly arrangement and held together by binding-thread or tape, which has been twined round the warp at irregular intervals. The binding

411

technique may best be compared with what Mason[1]) calls »wrapped work», but in actual fact it is done in such a manner that the woof forms a straight line.[2]) The carelessness with which the warp was sometimes laid will be seen, for instance, in Pl. 2,7—8. In order to enable the binding or wrapping to show up conspicuously in the impression it is necessary that the woof or binding-thread must be drawn so taut as to make a slight depression in the fibres of the warp. The absence in most impressions of any marks left by the stitching together of the fibres may be due partly to the fact that it was done somewhat loosely and partly to the thread itself having been thin or at any rate flat, like bast or some such material.

Professor J. G. Andersson reproduces in An Early Chinese Culture Pl. 16,1, a vessel from Yang Shao Tsun which shows impressions made by these bindings on the upper and under side of the body. Whether this indicates a thick woof-thread or whether the impressions were made by some implement for ornamental purposes it is impossible to say. Nor can we decide the question whether the fabric was in the form of a basket, with or without a bottom, or of a mat, possibly stitched together into the shape of a bag or muff. The latter assumption is however discounted by the fact that no marks left by any joint or stitching are definitely discernible on any of the whole vessels, although from one's general impressions this would appear to be the most obvious theory. A variant occurs (Pl. 3,3, Pl. 4,14—16) in the form of a fabric the impression of which leaves close transverse lines, though it is impossible to observe from their appearance the nature of the woof-threads. This latter type is not found in Hsin Tien C or on the bought vessels.

Evidence that woven mats in the ordinary sense of the term also occurred in the Ch'i Chia culture is offered by the impression left on the underside of the bottom of a vessel (Pl. 2,12), which reproduces a typical twill weave with a warp of narrow fibres and a broad bast-like woof.

CC: II.

The vessel mentioned below (p. 420) as being a transitional form between CC: I and CC: II carries an impression which, although coarser in character and covering the entire body, is nevertheless closely akin to that which is apparently most typical for CC: I (Pl. 6,4). We find a similar impression, though still coarser and likewise covering the entire body, on a vessel from Hsin Tien C (Pl. 20,4), which must be classed under CC: II on account of its shape and the quality of its ware.

The most common impression occurring in CC: II is seen on the vessels (see Pl. 7) as a quantity of cord impressions lying close together in the vessels' longitudinal direction and covering the body right up to where the neck begins, disap-

---

[1]) Mason, Aboriginal American Basketry. Annual Report of the Smithsonian Institution, 1902. Part II, p. 230.

[2]) Copies have been taken of a number of the most typical impressions by means of »negocoll» composition, which produced a positive picture of the fabric that was originally impressed on the clay vessel.

412

pearing into the clay that has been smeared over the neck (Pl. 6,3, 5, 6, 8,1). The same thing recurs at the base in cases in which the bottom has been attached from outside (Pl. 6,2, 6; 7,17). These are possibly cord impressions. As the impressions are very regular it is possible that cords were joined together to form a kind of muff or sack. Torii[1]) illustrates from Korea a cord sack of a type that still survives there. The cord sack was made of a long warp crossed by relatively sparse stitching threads — the same principle in fact as in primitive rush-mats. We are thus not concerned here with a real textile fabric consisting of warp and woof. The Korean sack was sewn together in such a way that the warp threads run horizontally, whereas in Ch'i Chia P'ing they run vertically. Further, as regards the latter it should be observed that, to judge from the impressions, the stitches were very far apart and often irregular (Cf. Pl. 6,3, 5—6; 7,4; 9,3). The impression shown in Pl. 11,1 a, b is derived from a similar material, though the cord was more tightly twisted. Another interpretation of these cord-like impressions is not quite excluded: they may have been caused by baskets executed in the technique known as »sewn basketry» (see Mason, Aboriginal American Basketry); but our cord-like impressions run in straighter lines than is usual in that technique.

In CC: II there are several examples of basketry. For instance, there are two cases of wicker-work (see Mason l. c., p. 228); they are reproduced here in Pl. 9,7.

We also find coiled basketry represented in the material. The most distinctly impressed specimens come from Hsin Tien C and are illustrated in Pl. 10,3 a, b, also in Pl. 20,2 (see Mason l. c. p. 244). These two impressions might also conceivably have been derived from a simple linen fabric, but to judge from the clear depressions left by the supporting material on the wall of the vessel they appear to have been made by some comparatively hard, firm stuff, so that it is not very likely that they are the impressions made by real cloth material. Ch'i Chia also provides a number of more or less typical specimens of this basket technique (Pl. 9,2 a, b; Pl. 10,2 a, b). It is often quite difficult to decide whether the impressions are derived from cord impressions or from coiled basketry (e. g. Pl. 10,2 a, b).

The origin of one or two impressions cannot be determined with any certainty. Pl. 9,4 shows a specimen of net-like and somewhat irregular plaited work as to the material and construction of which it is impossible to form an opinion. Pl. 11,3 likewise illustrates an impression the nature of which is indeterminable. It may possibly be derived from basketry, the technique of which in that case most closely resembles some kind of coiled basket-work, though another possibility is worth considering. The sherd might also be regarded as representing a specimen of »Treibkeramik», in which case the impression would be the marks made by a corrugated implement with which the surface of the wet clay was worked over.

---

[1]) R. Torii et Kimiko Torii: Populations primitives de la Mongolie Orientale. Journal of the College of Science, Imperial University of Tokyo, vol. XXXVI. Article 4, p. 60.

413

CC: III.

As in all other respects, this class is singularly uniform in regard to the impressions. One vessel only (Pl. 14,1) diverges somewhat in this respect, as also in its method of production, from CC: III and shows some association with other periods (Hsin Tien and Sha Ching).

Apart from the impression just mentioned, there is in this class only one type of impression and it has no appreciable variations. Its appearance will best be seen in its entirety in a vessel illustrated in Pl. 14,12. In view of the uniformity of the pattern only one negocoll impression of this type is reproduced (Pl. 9,5 a, b). As the illustration shows, the impressions on the sherd consist of a quantity of fine, closely aligned furrows, which on the negocoll positive resemble fibres or straw. If, as might conceivably have been the case, these latter had been combined to form a mat, the woof threads must have been concealed or else laid at considerable intervals. It is impossible to say what this construction was like, but being aware of the important part played by mats in the making of pottery by the Ch'i Chia people, we cannot entirely reject the idea that a mat alone formed the supporting material in the process of manufacturing these vessels. Possibly, however, there may be another explanation. As mentioned above, these vessels have extremely thin walls and appear to have been produced by means of some kind of casting technique. It is conceivable, then, that, in order to facilitate for the clay to adhere to its walls, a mould was covered on its inside with a matting of fine fibres or grass. In that case the absence of connecting threads can easily be explained by the fact that the straw was baked in or loosely applied.

Since it is beyond all dispute that the clay vessels were made in moulds, the question arises how the mould was removed when the vessel had become sufficiently firm to stand alone. The explanation that the supporting material was destroyed in the firing is untenable owing to the fact that not only the handles and bottoms but also the relief décor were attached and applied after the removal of the support but prior to firing. If the support were of soft material such as matting, cord-sacking or such-like, the explanation would be obvious, for in that case one could simply have severed the connecting threads nearest to the neck, and then removed the vessel. On the other hand, if the support consisted of firm, hard basketry, or of a baked clay mould, the only possible explanation is that the vessels must have shrunk in drying (cf. p. 405).

II. STONE IMPLEMENTS.

On the whole the stone material does not yield anything of peculiar interest. It does not differ appreciably from the stone artifacts that are generally found in other Chinese dwelling-sites, and several of them are of so stereotyped a character

414

that one might come across similar specimens in practically any Stone-Age dwelling-site.

The main bulk of the material consists of roughly made axes and rectangular stone knives. The axes are 32 in number, most of them being in a more or less fragmentary state, so that it is sometimes difficult to form any idea of what they originally looked like. Very little care seems to have been taken in making them and the majority appear to have been used as simple hewing axes. The material consists for the most part of greenstone. The method employed in their production was that of hammering the stone into shape. The axe was then usually polished, either wholly or in part. The process of grinding was generally confined to the edge, although the appearance of some fragments seems to indicate that sometimes the entire surface was polished. The size of the axes varies considerably. The largest entire specimen (Pl. 17,1) measures 180 mm. in length and 57 mm. in breadth (at the edge). The smallest (Pl. 18,5), on the other hand, is not more than 84 mm. long and 35 mm. broad. The type is, generally speaking, more or less markedly thin-butted. The edge takes up the maximum breadth of the axe. In a curious variant the upper part of the axe narrows considerably, the result being a handle-like shape (Pl. 17,2). Axes of this type were apparently fixed in a drilled haft which in hewing was supported by the shoulder formed by the narrowing-down of the upper half. The possibility of the axe's having been wielded with the hand direct must not, however, be overlooked. This fragment of a neck, the sole representative of this type, bears some resemblance to an axe from Somrong Sen in Cambodia, reproduced by Mansuy.[1]) This latter is the prototype of the shouldered celt that is so characteristic of the Neolithic age in India.   The specimen found at Ch'i Chia P'ing is, however, far too fragmentary and indistinct a type to be regarded as a representative of the shouldered celt. Nevertheless there is another axe that gives some indication of belonging to this type (Pl. 18,8) being thinned-out at the neck. It is made of polished argillite (clay-slate) and its narrowed-down neck part resembles somewhat the neck of a shouldered celt (cf. Mansuy, op. cit. Pl. II,13).

Another curious form of helve attachement is seen in Pl. 18,3. The axe has a hole for the helve, probably oval originally though its fragmentary state prevents our drawing any definite conclusion on this point.

A small number of chisels have been found (Pl. 18,6, 7). Some have an edge faced from both sides, while the other type is faced on one side only (cross-edged).

Pl. 18,9 illustrates an artifact of quartz, the edge of which is formed by polishing a surface that was already naturally smoothed. The implement was probably used as a scraper.

There are no arrow-heads but there are two specimens of dagger- or spear-heads made of slate. (Pl. 18,1, 2). 18,2 has the form of an isosceles triangle, the sides of

---

[1]) H. Mansuy. Contribution à l'étude de la préhistoire de l'Indochine III. Mémoires du Service géologique de l'Indochine Volume X. Fasc. I Pl. II: 12·a and b.

415

which constitute the sharpened edges. 18,1 has broader edges than the preceding one, and there is affixed a broad and somewhat irregular helve-tang. Just above the middle of the point can be seen the beginning of a bi-conical hole, which might indicate that the implement was intended for use as a harpoon. The type has hitherto been unknown in China, but similar specimens occur in Formosa (see BMFEA 4 pag. 105 seq.) and in Indo-China.[1]

The site of Ch'i Chia P'ing has further yielded about 30 specimens of rectangular stone-knives, 8 of which are provided with holes. The knives without holes frequently have corresponding recesses on the short sides, which appear to have served as grooves used for fastening (Pl. 19,2). The long sides are fashioned into edges. Some of those which have no recesses might be interpreted as unfinished specimens (9,1).

In those knives that are provided with a hole the latter is placed on the knife's vertical median line. Probably the holes were originally drilled in the true centre, but owing to wear and tear and to sharpening, the cutting edge has in many cases come nearer and nearer to the hole (Pl. 19,6).

As has been pointed out by Professor J. G. Andersson (An early Chinese Culture, pp. 4 and 5), the type still survives in the »kaoliang region» of North China in the form of iron knives (cf. Andersson, RPC p. 223 seq.).

The area of distribution of the rectangular and the closely allied crescent-shaped knife goes far beyond the boundaries of China. (See Torii op. cit. p. 41).

Pl. 19,8 reproduces an oval stone object provided with two grooves crossing one another in the middle, probably used for fastening purposes. The use of the implement is uncertain.

Another object, the function of which it is difficult to guess, consists of an irregularly shaped pinion made of porous sandstone and provided with a hole running obliquely through the middle, its direction refuting the otherwise possible assumption that the object is a spinning-whorl.

On the other hand, a fragment of a spinning-whorl is reproduced in Pl. 18,10. It is made of beautiful white marble and is singularly regular in shape.

Finally, the Ch'i Chia P'ing material contains a pestle.

III. BONE IMPLEMENTS.

The Ch'i Chia P'ing material contains (Pl. 16) 31 artifacts of bone of which there are:

13 needles of various size. Four of them are provided with an extraordinarily fine eye (16,10—12). The remaining needles have no eyes but are remarkable for the same elegant shape. (16,1—7, 9).

---

[1] M. Bylin, Notes sur quelques objets néolitiques, trouvés à Formose BMFEA 4; H. Mansuy, Contribution a l'étude de la préhistoire de l'Indochine II; Bulletin du service géologique de l'Indochine. Volume VII. Fasc. II. Pl. IV: 4—6.

416

8 bodkins (16,13—20). 16,13 has a groove for fastening purposes near the base and originally had a slanting point, which, however, was subsequently broken off so that a new point had to be made. The shininess caused by wear indicates that the second point was actually used. The original point is preserved in the other bodkins.

5 bone implements (16,22, 24—26) which may conceivably have been used in weaving or plaiting as weaving sticks (16,24—26), beaters (16,22) or such-like.

The chisel-like implements (16,21, 23) may have had a similar purpose though it is not impossible that they were used as bone chisels.

A small cylindrical bead of bone, the only definitely demonstrable ornament found at Ch'i Chia P'ing, is reproduced in 16,27, unless an irregularly shaped bone-disc with a hole in the centre is likewise to be regarded as an ornamental object.

The exquisitely fine bone needles and the weaving implements mentioned above are evidence of a comparatively high standard of culture possessing a highly developed textile art, but the scanty bone material is of too general a character to permit of our drawing from it any conclusions regarding the chronological position of Ch'i Chia P'ing and its cultural relations, although similar implements have been found both in China and in the bordering territories.

IV. VARIA.

In the first place, we have to record 17 sherds of a grey ware. In view of their paucity, they could not very well be made to constitute a separate class in the Ch'i Chia P'ing material. Since they differ in their firing process (reducing flame) from the rest of the pottery discussed above, I have not attributed them to any of the classes described there, although they show a considerable affinity with class CC: I.

Among these sherds we observe a fragment which probably formed part of the bottom of a vessel (Pl. 24,1). The characteristic feature of this fragment is the remains of holes, an inch in diameter, probably made with a stick with which the wet clay was pierced and which was then moved from side to side, thus giving the walls of the holes a convex rounded shape and causing small portions of the pressed-out clay to project all round the edges. The remains of two such holes. appear on this fragment, but it is impossible to determine how many the original bottom contained.[1]

In Pl. 24,2 we have another fragment provided with a hole and made of grey, well smoothed ware. This piece is pierced with comparatively small holes (6—7 mm. in diam.) made after firing.

---

[1] Cf. MFEA, K. 6549: a vessel from Yang Shao Tsun, a high bowl of reddish ware with the edge of the mouth profiled and with knob-like handles. In the bottom are 6 holes an inch in diameter, one in the centre and the rest in a circle round about it.

417

Pl. 24,3 reproduces what is probably a fragment of the neck of a small vessel. Thin, grey ware. The exterior decorated with an incised pattern of squares bordered on both sides by parallel lines. The decorative method is reminiscent of the dwelling-site pottery of the Hsin Tien period. Pl. 24,4 shows another fragment of the neck of a small vessel of grey ware. Mat impressions are visible on the outside. (Cf. Hsin Tien C, p. 419).

Further, there should be mentioned here 5 fragmentary rings of greyish ware. (Pl. 15,11—15). The diameter of none of them is large enough to permit of the rings being passed over the hand of a grown person. If they were used as armlets, they must already have been passed over the hand of the bearer in childhood. In four of these specimens the section is triangular (Pl. 15,11—14), in one it is rounded (15,15).

Finally, the excavations at Ch'i Chia P'ing also yielded 20 sherds with a painted décor. Four of these (Pl. 24,6, 13, 23, 24) were gathered on the surface of the soil or purchased in the neighbourhood. The painted sherds shall be discussed below. In the dwelling-site were furthermore excavated fragments of a lid (Pl. 24,27) and a foot (Pl. 24,6) belonging to a vessel of the Han era. The latter is stated to have been discovered near the surface.

V. FINDS FROM HSIN TIEN C.

In the dwelling-site known as Hsin Tien C in T'ao Sha Hsien a body of material was excavated similar to that of Ch'i Chia P'ing. These finds were all (acc. to Professor Andersson's report) »collected by Chuang in a small pocket with charcoal earth».

The material consists of 6 more or less incomplete vessels and 15 potsherds. The find further comprises a mushroom-like smoothing implement made of burnt clay (Pl. 15,5).

Curiously enough, the material permits of incorporation in the same system as the Ch'i Chia P'ing finds, though with the noteworthy and significant difference that there is not one single specimen of type CC: III.

Thus CC: I is represented by 2 fragmentary vessels and 12 sherds. One of the vessels is a distinctly bi-conical urn (Pl. 22,1). The upper part is smoothed, the under-part covered with sparse mat impressions.

Pl. 3,4 shows an amphora with a smoothed body, its ceramic quality being related to CC: I.

The sherds consist of fragments of necks and bodies, some of which must have belonged to remarkably large vessels with a distinctly bi-conical body. Fragments of the under-part of the body bear the same mat impressions as in CC: I. (Cf. Pl. 1,5 and 1,9 with Pl. 22,1).

418

Three fragments show the same characteristic whitish slip as that observed in CC: I a. All the sherds just mentioned are remarkable for their extremely fine ware with brick-red or pale-yellow tints, and for their very high technical quality, so that they may be directly associated with CC: I a.

CC: II is represented by four fragmentary vessels and three sherds. All types of vessels in CC: II b have their counterparts here. There are some specimens of the urn of type 8 (Pl. 20, 2—4). In 20, 3 the body is covered with cord impressions, whereas 20, 2 which has already been discussed in connection with Ch'i Chia P'ing (see above page 413) shows impressions of coiled basketry. It might also be derived from some simple textile but, since to judge from the depth and distinctness of the holes the impressions may perhaps have been made by some harder material, the former interpretation is more probably correct. — A variant of the above-mentioned type of urn is also reproduced in Pl. 20, 4. The neck is ornamented just below the rim of the mouth by a dentated band. The body is curiously enough covered with a sparse impression akin to that of CC: I, although both ware and form refer the vessel to CC: II. It might best be compared with the transitional form between CC: I and CC: II which is illustrated in Pl. 6, 4.

Type 9, which belongs to CC: II, is also represented by a relatively undamaged specimen (Pl. 20, 5). Pl. 20, 1 reproduces the upper portion of a large vessel, the walls of which probably narrowed down somewhat towards the base. Below the broad flattened rim of the mouth runs a band, now partially disappeared, which had been firmly pressed against the wall of the vessel. The body is covered with cord impression.[1])

CC: II also includes, as mentioned above, three sherds, from among which one fragment represents the transitional part between the body and leg of a tripod. All the sherds have cord impressions.

Finally, a small fragment of grey ware belongs to this material. The sherd agrees in every respect with the fragment illustrated in Pl. 24, 4 which forms part of the finds from Ch'i Chia P'ing.

The Hsin Tien C finds are in very close agreement with the Ch'i Chia P'ing material, although they contain no pottery of type CC: III. It may be pointed out *en passant* that a coating of soot occurs on vessels and fragments that are in accord with CC: II but not on such of type CC: I — this fact still further confirms the resemblances between the two sites. It is further to be observed that the frequency with which the two classes are represented is about the same as in Ch'i Chia P'ing. This fact must not however be too strongly emphasized on account of the paucity of the materials, due to the fact that the Hsin Tien C site has not yet been exhaustively examined.

---

[1]) We probably find a form corresponding to that of this vessel in a vessel from Shansi, Yang Chü Hsien, Yang Chü Chen B (K. 5932), and with the aid of this the vessel might be reconstructed.

419

VI. THE INTERRELATION BETWEEN THE CLASSES OF POTTERY IN THE SITE OF CH'I CHIA P'ING.

A decisive answer to the question whether the different ceramic classes established above represent different chronological periods or simply different modes of employment (vessels produced for different purposes), cannot be given since there are no stratigraphical data whatsoever which could furnish us with some *points d'appui*.

The classes CC: I and CC: II are found to differ in ware, form and mat impressions. The vessel in Pl. 6,4, however, is a transitional form between the two classes, and in spite of their dissimilarities CC: I and CC: II must be considered as one chronological group. This is emphasized by the fact that the dwelling-site material of Hsin Tien C, which forms a distinct unity (all found in one small »pocket», see p. 418) contains sherds and vessels proportionally divided between the two classes.

The dissimilarities between them may be due to the vessel's having been made for different purposes, those of CC: I perhaps being preserving and drinking vessels, whereas the coarse, thick-wared specimens of CC: II would undoubtedly be most suitable as cooking utensils. This assumption is supported by the abundant presence of soot on sherds of the latter group.

If any of the three classes differed from the rest chronologically, that would certainly be CC: III, which diverges from the other groups in its peculiar décor, its fine mat impressions and its unusually thin ware. It is true that the vessel in Pl. 14,1 has a certain affinity with CC: II (cf. Pl. 8,2 and 20,5); but this specimen is in fact unique within group CC: III both in form and in the mat impressions. The other vessels in CC: III exhibit no real affinity with those of the other classes either in their general character or in any peculiar features. It should be remembered that CC: III has a comparatively low technical standard, although its décor is of an advanced character. Here again the testimony of the material in Hsin Tien C — all of it forming a »unity», since it was all found in one »pocket» — is very significant, since this material does not contain a single representative of group CC: III but exclusively such as correspond to groups CC: I and CC: II.

Certain associations with other prehistoric Chinese periods can be demonstrated, though they are few and slight.[1]

In the first place the technical execution and the quality of the ware show a striking resemblance to a large portion of the materials from the Hsin Tien stage (Andersson's »4th period») and the Sha Ching stage (Andersson's »6th period»), which, on the whole, exhibit a lower standard of quality than the other periods.

---

[1] To the Kamm décor there are no Chinese parallels whatever, it is entirely limited to Ch'i Chia P'ing.

420

On the other hand, in regard to the forms of vessels there is no apparent connection between our materials here and that of the 4th or 6th periods.[1])

Secondly, in regard to the décor, the Hui Tsui dwelling-site material (Andersson's period 4) has as one of its most conspicuous features the same kind of band in relief as that which characterizes a part of the CC: III specimens. In this respect the similarity is so great that certain sherds of the two sites may be said to be identical in type, and cannot be distinguished. Period 4, however, has no other parallels to the décor of our gr. CC: III, with one exception: the knob-like ornaments. A fragment of a Hui Tsui vessel (K. 11240: 23) has knobs with a depression in the centre (cf. our Pl. 14,1) close to the mouth; this sherd also shows the same mat impressions as are found in CC: III (knob-like ornaments without depressions or incisions occur on small tripods in Hui Tsui). For the rest, the unpainted pottery of Hui Tsui offers no parallels to the materials of Ch'i Chia P'ing.

The finds from period 6 (Sha Ching) likewise offer some further points of contact, besides the mat impressions already adduced. A sherd found at Sha Ching shows close affinity to the fine relief décor of CC: III (though the typical Kamm impressions are lacking); the ware of this sherd resembles that of CC: III, though it is fairly thick; the exterior is covered with the usual ground pattern of mat impressions, against which the relief décor (now in part obliterated) stands out, the arrangement being the same as in CC: III (Pl. 12,2, 3, 5). The coating of paint described p. 403 above recurs as a characteristic feature in period 6, and the painted triangles found on a couple of vessels in CC: III recall the simple geometrical décor of period 6, which also occurs on the inside of the neck. The patterns, however, are too simple and elementary to allow of any definite conclusions as to an historical connection, all the more since both the ware and the pigment are different in CC: III and period 6.

Against a theory that would assume some connection between the dwelling-site of Ch'i Chia P'ing and those of Hui Tsui (period 4) and Sha Ching (period 6) — both bronze-age cultures — could be adduced an apparently very strong argument: no metal whatever was found in Ch'i Chia P'ing, and this site should consequently be defined as frankly neolithic. But this argument may not be absolutely conclusive, seeing that only a very small part of the site has been investigated — the entire culture deposit extending over more than five hundred metres; the absence of metal in the present finds may thus be due to mere chance.

It has sometimes been assumed that the Kamm ornamentation in CC: III had some association with the Russo-Baltic pottery with a Kamm décor. This theory was enounced by Professor Andersson.[2]) He finds that there is a striking

---

[1]) A future detailed examination of the materials of these stages may modify this statement. We might point out that two of the CC: III fragments of bottoms exhibit the same concave, undemarcated type that occurs in periods 4 and 6. The other bottoms of CC: III, which have a more pronounced standing surface, likewise differ entirely in construction from the bottoms of CC: I and II.

[2]) Preliminary Report, p. 12; RPC. p. 80.

421

resemblance between the vessels with a Kamm ornamentation found at Ch'i Chia P'ing and similar vessels from northern Europe.[1])

⌄ For my part, however, I cannot find the similarity convincing. The feature they have in common is confined in my opinion to the technical method employed in producing the ornamentation, viz. the use of Kamm impressions. In its very nature the delicate Chinese material is essentially different from the Russo-Baltic Kamm pottery with its off-shoots in Siberia. In the first place the vessel forms have no features whatsoever in common. In the second place the Chinese ware is both thinner and of higher quality. In the third place we find in our Chinese pottery no coarse hole-ornamentation, which commonly occurs in connection with the Russo-Baltic Kamm décor. Finally there are no essential similarities in the design and general composition of the patterns. Nor, indeed, do the artifacts in general exhibit any common characteristics. All this, however, does not exclude the possibility that the Baltic-Siberian and the Chinese Kamm pottery — without having any direct cultural interconnection — may represent different branches of one and the same tree or emanate from the same ideology.

I venture to offer the same objections to Menghin's views. He considers[2]) that »die Ergologie der Hoang-ho-kulturen erinnert sonst vielfach an den früharktischen und kammkeramischen Kreis».

He finds it significative, *inter alia*, that the stone implements are for the most part made of slate. As, however, will be seen from the chapter on stone implements, this is not the case, at any rate as far as regards Ch'i Chia P'ing, for here specimens of green-stone predominate and only a few chisels and spear-heads are made of slate.

Ailio[3]) was of the opion that the influence derived from the Kamm décor »finds itself up against a Chinese wall at Ulan-Chada». However, Professor Andersson's excavations had not yet been carried out at the time of the publication of Ailio's work, so that the peculiar Kamm pottery of Ch'i Chia P'ing could not be taken into account in his book. Nevertheless, Ailio would appear to be right in so far as the Ch'i Chia P'ing Kamm pottery has no direct associations with the true Russo-Baltic Kamm décor.[4])

---

[1]) He quotes as comparative material figs. 14 and 15 in Ailio, Fragen der russischen Steinzeit, Zeitschrift der Finnischen Altertumsgesellschaft XXIX: 1, figs. 14—15.

[2]) A. Menghin: Weltgeschichte der Steinzeit p. 290 et seq.

[3]) Ailio, Fragen der Russischen Steinzeit. Zeitschrift der Finnischen Altertumsgesellschaft XXIX: 1 p. 68.

[4]) It is just possible, on the other hand, that a parallel can be drawn with a special type of Siberian Kamm pottery. This is mentioned by Ailio in his above-cited work (pp 66—67). On the subject of Kamm pottery in Siberia he says, *inter alia:* »In derselben Weise kanellierte, von der Kammkeramik abweichende Gefässtücke sind beispielsweise in der Umgebung von Irkutsk angetroffen worden (Zap. Arch. Ges. XI, Bortwin T XIV: 1). — In demselben Zusammenhang sind die in Cuwaskij Mys unweit Tobolsk gefundenen schönen kragförmigen mit einer Standfläche versehenen aus feinkörnigen graugelblichen Ton gefertigten Gefässe zu erwähnen, die in ihrem oberen Teil regelmässig und sogar schön mit

422

It should be pointed out in this connection that there is some slight resemblance between the Ch'i Chia P'ing Kamm pottery and one or two fragments of vessels belonging to the Tripolje culture. These fragments may be referred to Ailio's »mixed style», i. e. Chwoika's style I. They are decorated round the rim of the mouth with a delicate band of dentations or pearls.[1]) Below the neck are seen dot-like impressions arranged in rows, and these may have been done with a Kamm-like implement.[2]) So far as one can judge from the illustrations, which do not throw much light on this point, the vessels exhibit some features in common with the Kamm pottery of type CC: III, the resemblance showing itself primarily in the form and in the impressions. Perhaps, however, it is merely a chance resemblance without any deeper significance.[3])

VII. THE ORNAMENTATION AND ITS SYMBOLICAL SIGNIFICANCE.

In scrutinizing the ornamentation in the material here under discussion we find that it is of two kinds. In the first place we have the ornamentation that occurs in CC: I and CC: II and which, with a few exceptions, may be said to have a purely decorative function; in the second place we have the ornamentation to be found in CC: III, the spirit of which appears, on the whole, to be symbolical. The essential difference outlined here in the ornamentation of the different classes of pottery still further emphasizes the divergence which we have already stressed between CC: I and CC: II on the one hand and CC: III on the other.

The neck ornamentation found in CC: I and CC: II — if not merely decorative — may be explained as a relic of a primitive method of manufacture dating back to a time when the material of which the neck was made differed from that of the body. In that process it had by some means or other been affixed to the body. The marks left by this method have since been allowed to survive, thus giving

---

Kammotiven und teilweise nach den Traditionen des Kammstiles verziert sind. Ähnliche Gefässe sind am Ural im Gouvernement Kasan und in Südrussland angetroffen, aber nie im Kammkeramischen Kulturgebiet sondern sie müssen einem südlicheren Kulturkreis angehören. In Karadzar, im Gebiete Semipalatinsk, sind aus feinkörnigem Ton bestehende, mit Kamm- und breiten Kanelürornamenten verzierte Tongefässfragmente angetroffen worden, die auf die tief ornamentierte Gefässe der Tripolje-kultur hinweisen; aus demselben Gebiete liegen auch Gefässfunde vor, die an die Kammkeramik erin-nern, deren Ton aber rötlich gebrannt ist und deren Gefässform einen platten Boden und die nicht der Kammkeramik zuzuzählen sind.» As I have unfortunately not had an opportunity of seeing these finds, no account of which, so far as I am aware, has been published, I cannot venture to do more than point out that there may exist here a material reminiscent of Ch'i Chia P'ing (CC: III).

[1]) T. Passek, La céramique tripolienne, Moscow 1935, Pl. X: 12—13.

[2]) Cf. Ailio, op. cit. fig. 31.

[3]) Professor T. Arne has kindly brought to my notice the fact that there is preserved in the Sevenko Museum in Kiev (Cat. 16506) a sherd of Tripolje pottery from Iljintsy, district of Lipovets, Govt. of Kiev, on which are genuine Kamm-impressions, although, to judge from a sketch I have seen, the way in which these impressions are arranged is quite different from the Ch'i Chia P'ing designs.

rise to a development parallel to that of the Nordic »collared» bottle (Kragen-Flasche).[1])

Another possible explanation would be that ornaments such as the plaited pattern applied to a band in relief (Pl. 5,2) represent the last traces of a plaited leather strap or such-like, which at an earlier evolutional stage had been tied round the neck of vessels of this type.

Other simple incised patterns have been regarded by me either as a degeneration of the decorative types just referred to, e. g. Pl. 4,2, or as serving a purely ornamental purpose (e. g. Pl. 1,12 or Pl. 4,10).

When studying the constructive patterns described above, one is inclined to ask why in type CC: I these patterns occur only on the lower part of the vessels.[2])

There may perhaps be a simple explanation of this of a practical order. Amongst the Chinese collections in the Ethnographical Museum in Stockholm there are some baskets which are covered, on the inside entirely and on the outside to the extent of the upper half, with pitch, the actual basket-work thus being visible on the lower part of the body only. If we conceive the possibility of clay vessels of type CC: I having originally evolved out of vessels made of basketry, we can imagine the constructive pattern surviving on the lower part only as an ornamental reminiscence of an earlier method of production.

Another possibility would be that the pattern on the lower part of the vessel was deliberately not made smooth, the corrugated surface affording a better grip for the hands.

It is difficult to explain why the pattern has been eliminated from the upper part of the vessel in this class but not in CC: II. This circumstance indeed still further emphasizes the difference between the classes.

As indicated above, it is evident that some ornaments in Ch'i Chia P'ing are essentially symbolical of certain vital aspects of primitive life.

This applies almost entirely to CC: III. There is, however, one single instance in the first two classes of an ornament that may possibly be traced back to some kind of symbolism. The snake illustrated in Pl. 5,11 (cf. p. 395) might have some connection with a primitive fertility cult. This snake shows a striking resemblance to several representations of snakes from Susa II (Observe particularly figs. 415 and 416 in Toscanne, Etudes sur le serpent figure et symbole dans

---

[1]) Cf. also M. Schuchardt, Das technische Ornament in den Anfängen der Kunst. Praehistorische Zeitschrift 1909.

[2]) In this connection it may be pointed out that in the painted pottery found in other sites in China the decoration is generally confined to the upper part of vessels of urn type. It is also worth noting that in a few cases (Lo Han T'ang) the lower part has been made of thick ware mixed with gravel and this part of the body has a constructive pattern, whereas the upper part is made of fine clay and has a painted decoration. The quality of and impressions on the under part, however, most closely recall CC: II.

424

l'antiquité Elamite, Mémoires de la Délégation en Perse, Tome XII). Snakes executed in relief are likewise known from the G temple in Assur,[1] where they occur on models of houses[2] made of fired clay.

It should be pointed out that the Ch'i Chia P'ing snake is not the only representation of this animal in relief occurring in prehistoric China. The MFEA owns a lid with a representation of a human head, on the back of which is a snake. See Palmgren, Kansu Mortuary Urns of the Pan Shan and Ma Chang Groups, Pl. XIX: 9. Cf. also A. Salmony, Eine neolitische Menschendarstellung in China, Ipek. V 1929, who finds a connection between this representation and the Indian culture.

In contrast to the décor of CC: I and II, that of CC: III may be assumed to be of a symbolical nature, the ornaments in question being either in relief (lines and nipple-like knobs) or Kamm impressions or other impressed patterns. The ideas symbolized seem to refer to fecundity and fertility. In Pl. 13,5 a we find a handle covered with symbols which might have such a significance: triangles (made by Kamm impressions) antithetically placed combined with representations of cowries, have often been interpreted as sexual symbols. This explanation seems to be confirmed by their combination, in this case, with pairs of nipples which might represent the female breasts. For that same combination of triangles and »breasts» see also Pl. 12,14.

Sometimes triangles combine with patterns which appear to symbolize fertility in a wider sense; thus, in Pl. 13,2 we find them in conjunction with lightning and fertilizing rain.[3]

VIII. BOUGHT VESSELS.

As mentioned before, there were bought or excavated, in the city of Lanchou and in the neighbouring district, twenty vessels, whose exact provenience, and the conditions under which they were found, are not known.

Their chief significance as far as the Ch'i Chia P'ing material is concerned, is the assistance they afford in reconstructing the types of vessels occurring in this culture. Through comparisons with the ware, technique and form of the sherds it has been possible to fit the bought vessels into the class CC: I. It is a curious fact that only this group can come into question for their classification.

---

[1] W. André, Die archaischen Ishtar Tempel in Assur.

[2] Contenau, Manuel d'archéologie orientale I, fig. 159.

[3] The meander patterns of our class CC: III (differing from those of other Chinese periods) may be interpreted as depicting down-pouring rain; observe that the meanders run vertically across the belly of the vessel, and that they do not form a continuous pattern. — There are further (Pl. 13,2) a zigzag line probably depicting lightning, and a wavy line designating either water or a snake. For the same combination in the Hsin Tien period (per. 4), see Andersson, RPC. Pl. 137. The polychrome pottery of Susa has zigzag lines symbolizing water.

425

The above-mentioned vessels are urns, appearing in several variants. Just as in Ch'i Chia P'ing proper, there occur two types of this vessel (type I A and B). In the one case the vertical profile is more or less distinctly broken, and the vessel has handles attached to the broadest part of the body (Pl. 21,1). These handles appear to be rudimentary, and on the under-side of the body there are mat impressions which are more or less completely erased. The second urn, which has a gently rounded profile and handles at the equator, is illustrated in 22,2 (type I B), there being several specimens of this type. Pl. 21,2, 4 show a broad-bellied urn, on which the mat impression does not reach to the middle of the body. One of the two specimens has no handles, while the other has well-advanced handles attached to the neck.

In regard to the nine small vessels, of which eight are reproduced here (Pl. 23,2 —9), it might be possible with a greater degree of certainty to arrange them according to types. Making 23,2 our point of departure, we may draw two lines of evolution. In the one series we observe how the neck grows at the expense of the body, which thus becomes increasingly rudimentary; moreover, the handles follow the course of development of the neck (23,2—23,5). The second line of development proceeds via a more and more rounded belly (23,6—8) to the vessel illustrated in 23,9, whose shape has become emaciated, and in which the pear-shaped body entirely predominates, so that the neck has practically disappeared, while the ears have survived throughout the process of development.

It should be observed that, as in CC: I, the small vessels lack mat or basket impressions. There is ornamentation on vessel 22,7, which has a painted pattern in violet, consisting of groups of angles pointing downwards, starting from the boundary line between neck and body. In another case an incision gives this line an ornamental function (22,8).

The handles are also provided with an ornamental motif on two vessels. On 22,5 this décor consists of an impressed hour-glass-like ornament surrounded by four dots. On the other vessel (22,2) it consists of two groups of incised lines between which have been placed three ornamental strokes.

There is still one other form among the bought vessels (type 5) which is represented in CC: I by two fragments (cf. Pl. 4,3 and p. 392). This consists of a jug with a gently rounded body and funnel-shaped neck which continues over the mouth of the vessel, covering it to the extent of two thirds. From the mouth a spout projects obliquely upwards. In the profile of the neck and the body and in its technical execution this jug, which is provided with one broad, disc-like handle, is very closely reminiscent of the small vessels described above.

In their design all the vessels just referred to appear to be traceable to metal prototypes, although otherwise no traces of any metal culture have been found in Ch'i Chia Ping.

Akin to this jug mentioned above, although typologically of later date, is the vessel in Pl. 22,5. Moreover, the ware differs from that of the other vessels

426

in its grey tone and its well-smoothed surface, which strongly recalls the fragments described on page 417 above. There are slight traces of red on the entire exterior of the vessel. Compared with the jug described above (type 5) the shape exhibits mannered forms. Thus, the extension of the rim over part of the mouth covers so much of it as to leave only a small kidney-shaped opening, in front of which, close to the edge, there projects obliquely upwards a spout ornamented with rivet-like knobs. Just as the body which became compressed through the extension of the neck, makes a bulbous and inflated inpression, so this cover appears bulbous and »swollen». When the body acquired its swollen form the under-part of the belly did not follow suit but formed a foot-like base. On the other hand, as the neck became extended downwards, the broad disc-like handle did the same. The fact that the handle is attached to a portion projecting from the over-vaulted rim, this part being decorated with two knobs resembling rivet-heads, lends force to the general characterization of the vessel as a direct imitation of metal ware.

Finally, among the bought vessels are two specimens (22,3, 4) which cannot be classified with reference to our sherd material. Even the very porous, strongly yellowish-brown and brick-red ware differs somewhat from that of Ch'i Chia P'ing. The form is that of a big-bellied vessel with a wide mouth and four handles at the rim standing on a circular foot pierced with four holes. Typologically, I am inclined to place 22,3 before 22,4 owing to its markedly broken profile.

IX. ANALYSIS OF MICROSCOPICAL SLIDES.

(by Dr. Gunnar Beskow)

The following features are the most important characteristics:
I. The admixture of sand:
   a) Quantity, b) Coarseness, c) Shape of grains, d) Mineral composition.
II. The clay mass:
   a) Natural admixture: Particles of loess, organic material.
   b) Structure and optical characteristics (especially mica content).
In the material under analysis organic matter is entirely absent.

CC: I a.

Nos. K. 11242: 90, 285, 101, with addition of No. 232 from group I b.
An exceedingly uniform group (in particular 90 and 285 are very similar).

Characteristic features:

a) *Intermixed material:* Extremely little. All the microscopical slides are a l m o s t e n t i r e l y   l a c k i n g   i n   m i n e r a l   s a n d. No. 101 contains a considerable quantity of brown, amorphous, dense lumps about one mm. in size, of which the others show only a very sparse admixture.

427

b) *The clay mass.* Rich in grains of quartz of sizes between 0.05—0.04 and 0.02—0.01 mm., most frequently about 0.02 mm. This size of grain is the most frequently occurring one in the loess soils; the quartz grains in question are thus to be regarded as loess material (wind sediment) which was embedded in the course of the precipitation of the clay.

In Nos. 90 and 285 the clay substance possesses a finely agglomerated structure with a rich content of mica or micaceous mineral scales: the amount of loess is considerable, being greatest in No. 285.

No. 101, on the other hand, shows an almost entirely opaque, »structureless» clay mass, with only isolated scales of mica; the loess content is likewise lower.

One sample from group I b is entirely associated with group I a, viz. 232. This sherd likewise contains no admixture of sand, but the clay mass has an abundant loess content. The structure of the actual clay substance and the abundance of mica are in full conformity with those of Nos. 90 and 285.

The extended group I a is thus a relatively uniform group, characterized by an extremely small content or else an entire absence of admixed sand, and also by a relatively large content of loess material in the clay. Nos. 90, 285 and 232 are extremely alike in every respect, notably in their high loess content and the fineness of the microscopical structure of the clay, which is rich in mica. No. 101 differs from the above-mentioned in having a lower loess content and in the clay substance being dense and practically structureless.

CC: I b. (two specimens).

A very uniform group, characterized by an extremely high sand content. The sand consists chiefly of quartz but also contains a fair amount of alkaline feldspar. Strikingly fresh appearance; the grains angular and only slightly rounded.

The clay mass of both specimens is rich in loess particles, the clay substance showing a light structure as having a moderate content of quite small scales of mica. It is striking to note the high calc-spar content, appearing in the form of rounded grains, the size of which is the same as that of the loess (mostly about 0.05—0.02 mm).

CC: I c. (214, 265, 84).

A not very uniform group.

The most characteristic feature is a high content of coarse sand, the grains of which are considerably more rounded than I b. Moreover, the composition also differs from that in I b, since from a petrographical point of view the sand is a far more heterogeneous mixture. A characteristic feature of all three microscopical slides is also the presence of *grains of sandstone.*

As regards the composition and distribution of the sand, 214 and 265 are very similar. 84 differs from the others in that the composition of the sand varies very considerably, there being only quite a low content of quartz and feldspar grains and a high content of small lumps of different kinds of sedimentary rock species.

In all three samples within this group the composition of the clay varies considerably.

In 214 and 84 there is present a rather high percentage of quartz-loess particles, although in 84 they are smaller than usual (0.02—0.015 mm. being the predominant size; particles larger than 0.025 occur extremely seldom). The quartz-loess content in 265 is very small, while that sample is particularly rich in rounded limedust of the size of fine loess.

Also the content of mica scales, as also the structure of the clay substance, is different.

428

CC: II a. (642 and 503).

A very uniform type, characterized by its admixture of sand, which is very coarse (2—3 to 4 mm.), its grains being exceedingly rounded (river sand — river gravel). Its petrographical composition is also similar: sandstone, quartz and lime (more or less fine-grained and coloured calc-spar).

The clay mass is not quite uniform, though fairly homogeneous. The loess particles are of normal size, fairly abundant in 642, sparser in 503. The clay substance in ordinary light is very similar; between crossed nicols, on the other hand, 642 proves to be practically black, the mica content being extremely scanty; 503 is fairly dark, but its structure is clearly visible (a considerable content of mica scales).

CC: II b. (591).

This group differs entirely from II a in its sand. The abundant admixture of sand consists of strikingly fine grains (maximum size 0.5 mm.) chiefly of not very rounded quartz.

In the clay mass there is an abundance of loess particles, also a good deal of fine loess about 0.01 mm. in size, and a very considerable proportion lime-dust. The clay substance appears to consist almost entirely of micaceous substance.

CC: III. (729 and 738).

Fairly uniform as far as regards the admixture of sand, consisting in both slides of coarse (> 1 mm). angular (not rounded) sand, rich in quite fresh-looking feldspar. One dissimilarity however, is that 729 has — besides the coarse sand — an abundance of sand ranging from middling coarse to fine (down to one or two 1/10 mm.), which is almost entirely lacking in 738.

The clay mass is also somewhat different, 738 having a high and 729 a low content of loess particles. The clay substance, on the other hand, is quite similar, although the mica content is larger in 738.

But the one feature that absolutely and definitely characterizes the group and differentiates it qualitatively from all the others is the petrographical nature of the sand. In both these samples it contains — besides the not very weathered feldspar — a very typical iron-rich pyroxene, pleochromatic in pale green and brown, partially converted into an intensely dark-brown biotite; in addition there are small grains of epidote.

The nature of the ware, as ascertained from the microscopical examination, permits of the division of the material under investigation into a number of natural groups, each of which, although of different degrees of uniformity, differs from all the others in the existence as a distinct gap in the multi-dimensional variable system.

LO HAN T'ANG WEST SITE, KUEI TE HSIEN, KANSU.

Professor Andersson describes the site of Lo Han T'ang thus:[1]

»This site is located 240 km W. from Lanchow, the capital of Kansu, in the section of the Huang Ho where that river descends from the Tibetan highland into the Kansu plain. Because of its steep fall the river has here cut down a canyon some

---

[1] J. G. Andersson, RPC. p. 84.

800 m. deep through »horsts» of old crystalline rocks and through sunken blocks of the soft Pliocene Kuei Te beds.

The exact position of the site is about 20 km W of the small town of Kuei Te in a side valley on the north side of the Huang Ho.»

A picture of the site and its surroundings were published by Professor Andersson.[1]) The site is on the top of the vertically sculptural cliff behind the two white tents of the explorer.

The site was examined by Professor Andersson and his Chinese boys during the late summer of 1923. The explorer writes about his field work in a still unprinted manuscript:

»On the 16th August 1923, when we were encamped at Lo Han T'ang village, Chen[2]) heard from a Tibetan of the existence, only a couple of li from our camp in a NNW direction on the other side of the valley, of a place where good prehistoric pottery was to be found. He visited the place on the following day and found it very promising. On the 18th we all worked there and found that the yield from this site would be far beyond our highest expectations. Above all, there occurred here painted pottery of Yang Shao type in larger numbers and better quality than anything we had so far encountered in NW China. This place, which is located 3 li N 35° W from our camp at Lo Han T'ang village, I have named Lo Han T'ang West. The surroundings of the site are shown in the map BMFEA 15, p. 83, surveyed on the scale of 1: 5,000 with 10-metre equidistant contour-lines.

We worked at the excavation of this deposit during two different periods, August 18 —19 and August 29—September 10.

In the eastern part of the map we see a narrow triangular spur separating the main valley through which we came down from the Tibetan grassland, from a side valley on the western side of which the site is located. The village of Lo Han T'ang is situated on the eastern side of the main valley, SE of the area shown on the map. The terrace upon which the village lies once formed together with the said spur the Malan river-plain of the main valley.

During our second and longer stay we settled down nearer to the site at the spot marked »Camp» on the map. This camp I selected as the zero point of the survey.

The surroundings of the site consist of these four physiographical elements:

1: The modern river-plain, relatively flat, gravel-strewn, sloping downstream at a gradient of about 1: 30.

2: The precipitous cliffs of the Malan terrace with a height of 20—30 m. In many cases, as for instance the eastern side of the big spur, this cliff is nearly perpendicular. Its lower part everywhere consists of the Kuei Te beds, the upper of gravel and loess-like material. Thus below the site here in question the lower two-thirds of the cliff are formed of the clays of the Kuei Te series, whereas the upper one-third is gravel with a cap of about six metres of loess-like material, possibly a redeposition of the Kuei Te beds.

3: The Malan terrace plain, best shown upon the eastern spur of the map. The site itself is also part of this old river-plain.

4: The steep, richly dissected hill-slopes rising above the Malan terrace plain. Only some of the adjacent hill-slopes, rising on one side above the Malan terrace spur, on

---

[1]) J. G. Andersson, o. c. Pl. 1.

[2]) One of Professor Andersson's collaborators.

430

the other above the prehistoric site, are indicated on the map up to heights of 100 —150 metres, but these dissected hills, which are throughout built up of the Kuei Te clays, rise in many places to much greater heights.

As already stated above, the place where the people of the Yang Shao time once lived is part of the old Malan surface. In fact, the narrow space occupied by the site forms an island of Malan ground surrounded everywhere by precipitous cliffs or steep slopes. As stated above, the cliff facing the modern river-plain is 31 m. high and nearly perpendicular. To the south and southwest the slope is also very steep. The site is most easily accessible from the northwest, but even here the slope served as a kind of natural fortification. Every indication goes to show that the topography 4—5000 years ago, when the place was inhabited by the Yang Shao people, was much the same as it is today and that this spot of the old Malan surface was deliberately chosen on account of its difficult approach.

The area of the site is located as shown on the map. Its length is 90 m. in a NE—SW direction and 55 m. in NW—SE. The level containing artifacts belongs to the uppermost loess-like stratum mentioned above. It contains very few pebbles. Its thickness and stratification can be judged from the following sections:

Section 1:

a. (uppermost) Yellowish-grey, homogeneous, unstratified, loess-like sediment with numerous grass-roots. No artifacts.   0.36 m.

b. Yellowish-grey sediment, like a, but containing numerous pieces of charcoal and patches of a white substance. This is the stratum that is rich in artifacts. At top and bottom there is a thin zone where the earth is chocolate-brown, as if burnt.
                                                                                0.25 m.

c. Yellowish-grey loess-like sediment. In the uppermost part the sediment in numerous small spots is coarser, like fine sand. No artifacts anywhere in this layer, but even at this depth numerous grass-roots.   0.42 m.

Section 2, in the western corner of the site:

1. (uppermost) — (a of section 1). Yellowish-grey, homogeneous, unstratified loess-like sediment, in the lower part some few white spots and artifacts.   0.66 m.

2. Same kind of sediment as bed 1 but containing numerous pieces of charcoal, white spots and splendid artifacts.   0.72 m.
Below this level no artifacts.

In the course of this excavation we came across a feature which we never met with in any other prehistoric site: apparently the bases of two kilns, probably for the firing of pottery. (One is shown in fig. 6.) One diameter is 1.05 m. Of the other one, at right angles to the first, only 0.61 m was still preserved. The bottom and what remains of the sides (13—22 cm. in height) are smooth and hard packed on the inside, with some scratches on the surface. Both the bottom and the sides consisted of several layers, apparently formed in such a way that a new layer was smeared on over the inside from time to time as required. The bottom was black from charcoal soot, the sides grey. Beneath the grey surface the wall was burnt a reddish brown to a depth of 7—8 cm. Under the bottom the burning had penetrated to a depth of 11 cm., and here was a regular layer of flat pebbles, 10—20 cm. long.

The second kiln base was smaller. For the rest, it was similar in every feature to the big one, with the single difference that in this case the basal flat pebbles were only 7—10 cm. in length.

431

This is beyond comparison the richest prehistoric site that has come to our knowledge in the Kuei Te valley. It yielded large fragments of vessels painted in beautiful and varied patterns. Specially characteristic features are winged stone knives and roughly hewn discus-like stone objects, 10—14 cm. in diameter.*

As professor Andersson has mentioned above, the site has not been systematically excavated all over the cultural deposit, so that we have no regular account of the different strata or other data of importance for the classification of the artifacts, except professor Andersson's description quoted above. The conclusions we might draw from examining the artifacts must therefore be very uncertain, although the cultural deposit of Lo Han T'ang, situated in the pasture district of the Sino-Mongolian borderland, is intact and undisturbed by farming, while the locality of Ch'i Chia P'ing has probably been disturbed by the Chinese agricultural system.

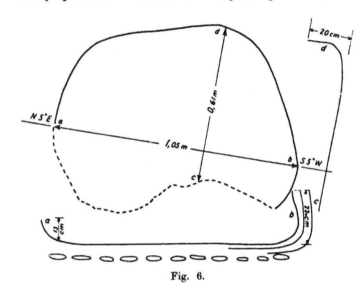

Fig. 6.

The furniture from the dwelling site of Lo Han T'ang contains about 1500[1]) pottery fragments of varying size, among which have been excavated only a couple of entirely or partly intact vessels. Further, 108 stone objects belong to the material, such as rectangular or crescent-shaped stone knives, axes and pebbles. There are 90 fragments of fine bone implements, such as knives with flint flakes, awls and sewing needles. Finally, it should be mentioned that the cultural deposit has yielded an abundant material of animal bones which will be examined in a special chapter.

X. POTTERY.

When we consider the above-mentioned lack of scientifically examined strata in the excavation it is manifestly very difficult to draw any definite chronological conclusions about the pottery. If we examine the pottery, three main groups may be noted:

1. Unpainted pottery, of high quality in regard to ware and shape. The outside is sometimes covered with mat or basket impressions.

---

[1]) Some bigger fragments, reconstructed out of several small sherds have only a single diary number so it is difficult to give exact statistics about the whole record.

432

2. Unpainted pottery of coarse ware. The outside is covered with cord impressions.
3. Painted pottery of high quality.

LHT: I. Unpainted pottery of high quality.

About 178 fragments.

The ware. The pottery is made of well-purified clay, free from any admixture[1]) of »dégraissant» in large quantities. An admixture of lime or quartz in small quantities could be noticed on most sherds. Only a few sherds, for several reasons attributed to this group, are made of porous ware mixed with mica or quartz gravel in large quantities. Some of these fragments might also be attributed to group II, since it is sometimes very difficult to classify small, undecorated fragments.

Colour. The colour varies from pale yellowish brown to brick-red and various shades of grey. About one third of the sherds referred to this group have a more or less pronounced grey colour.

It should be noted in this connection how difficult it is to draw any definite conclusions about the colour of the ware as Dr. Wu[2]) for instance has frequently done in his book on prehistoric pottery in China. The pottery might through its thousands of years of conservation have absorbed materials in the earth capable of discolouring the pottery in a remarkable way. Thus there belongs to the furniture from Lo Han T'ang part of a bowl, reconstructed from several small sherds (Pl. 27,2). Most of the sherds have a bright yellowish-red colour, whereas one of the fragments is brown. Another bowl (Pl. 28,1) reconstructed from three pieces shows the same subsequent discolouring, which is unfortunately not clearly visible in reproduction. Other examples of discoloured sherds are seen in Pl. 28,2 and Pl. 29,6 (N. B. three pieces). In all the cases mentioned not only has the surface changed colour, but the discolouring process has penetrated to the core of the fragment. Consequently if we are to draw any conclusions from the colour, we have to proceed very warily. It might happen that under certain conditions the whole of the material has become discoloured during its long rest in the deposit.

The colour of the ware is often homogeneous. Some sherds, however, have a darker, grey core surrounded by brighter outer layers. The greyness of the core is caused by irregularities in the process of oxidation during the firing (cf. p. 408).

Technique. The method of manufacture seems to have varied with the form of vessel required. Small vessels were obviously shaped from a single lump of clay, which was treated with the hands until the desired form was obtained.

The bowls and basins that frequently appear in the material are probably shaped

---

[1]) Frankfort points out the difficulty to determine if well purified clay in a certain case depends on the occurrence of naturally purified clay or if the high quality of the clay is due to an intentional purifying process. See H. Frankfort, Studies in early pottery of the Near East I, London 1924, p. 5 seq.

[2]) G. D. Wu, Prehistoric pottery in China. London 1938.

on a mould, although no marks from the mould are discernible. In fig. 7 is reproduced a bowl fragment of decorated ware on which may be observed cord impressions partly smoothed away. I interpret the cord impressions as being marks from the mould, which might have been covered with cords in order to facilitate for the clay to stick to the mould. It is scarcely credible that the elegantly shaped bowls could have been made from a single lump of clay without the aid of a mould. The objects would in that case have been thick and clumsy and without homogeneous walls. There remains the possibility of the bowls having been constructed by the thumbing method e. o. by adding layer to layer and thumbing together the joints. But if this method had been used, we should have been able to discern here and there the junction between two layers.

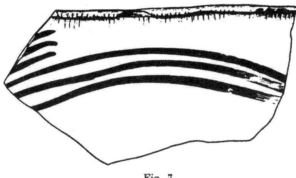

Fig. 7.

When the bowl has a biconical profile, the upper part must have been added after the bottom portion had been removed from the mould.

I would suggest that the small amphora reproduced in Pl. 25,1 has been constructed in the following way. The belly was made of two different pieces joined together. The joint between the two parts is clearly visible. The collar is made separately and joined to the inside of the body by thumbing. On the outside of the collar vertical scratches are clearly visible. On the inside of the collar appear concentric striations after a template which has rotated in order to smooth the surface and correct the profile. The length of the tool must have been 15 cm., while the marks left by its edge are clearly discernible. The long handles have been attached to the body after the vessel was completed. It seems likely that the larger amphorae (for instance Pl. 25,2) have been constructed in the same way, layer upon layer, by the thumbing method, whereas the base may have been built up in a mould (cf. p. 404). The lower portion of the amphorae have the same impressions as those familiar to us in Ch'i Chia P'ing.

After manufacture, the surface was carefully smoothed and sometimes polished. Only the impressions on the base are left intact. It is difficult to know whether they are left on for ornamental purposes or for some practical use, for instance to facilitate handling.

As already mentioned, the necks of the amphorae and sometimes also the bowls have been smoothed over with a tool. The vessel was evidently kept in rotation during this finishing process.

The concentric striation visible on the neck of the amphorae and on the bowls from different Chinese localities have been interpreted by some archaeologists as

434

marks from the potter's wheel. Professor Andersson[1]) is of the opinion that the bulk of the painted vessels from Yang Shao Tsun were turned on the potter's wheel. He likewise suggests that a vessel from Chih Kou Chai was made[2]) on the wheel. Professor Arne, moreover, believes that the Honan pottery was thrown.[3]) I doubt, however, whether the inhabitants of the prehistoric sites in China were familiar with the potter's wheel; in any case, there is no real evidence that the throwing method was used at Lo Han T'ang, although the ware as seen in a cross-section of some of the finest specimens is so homogeneous that it might be queried whether they were not made on the potter's wheel. It seems to me highly unprobable that if the throwing method was known, the potters did not employ it for every vessel. There is, however, no doubt that the bulk of the pottery is built up, layer upon layer, by the thumbing method, which is a technique quite different from throwing. It seems to me that archaeologists dealing with the matter of technique have often failed to realize that concentric striation does not always indicate that a vessel has been made on the potter's wheel. There is a considerable difference in construction between a vessel built up layer upon layer by thumbing and a thrown vessel, even if the former was smoothed over with a tool during rotation and in the course of this process has obtained striated zones on the surface. A thrown vessel is shaped directly from a single lump of clay by centrifugal force and shows traces of the process of manufacture in form of regular striae all over the inside. Sometimes the wall of thrown vessels is divided into sections.

Dr. G. D. Wu,[4]) who has closely studied the technique of the pottery from the prehistoric sites of China, suggests that the striation has arisen during the shaping process, while the vessels have been rotating on a turn-table. However, Dr. Wu apparently is of the opinion that prehistoric pottery has been built up layer upon layer, by the coiling method or with the aid of a mould, wherefore the »turn-table« in Dr. Wu's sense only implies a means of smoothing the vessel and removing the joints. In this case the turn-table does not signify a method of construction and it is therefore unimportant whether the vessel itself has been turned by hand or whether it has been put into rotation on a special turntable.

Firing. It is very difficult to draw any definite conclusions about the firing temperature. We can only operate with approximate calculations and theories of probability based on comparisons with modern ceramics. I estimate the firing temperature of this group to be about 900°, at any rate not higher than 1000°[5]). In

---

[1]) J. G. Andersson, An Early Chinese Culture. Bulletin of the Geological Survey of China, N:r 5, Peking 1923, p. 53.

[2]) RPC. p. 78, Pl. 35,1.

[3]) T. J. Arne, Painted stone age pottery from the province of Honan, China. Palaeontologica Sinica, Vol. 1, Fasc. 2, Peking 1925, p. 11.

[4]) G. D. Wu, o. c. p. 28, 47, 91.

[5]) Dr. Nils Palmgren considers the firing temperature of the Pan Shan urns to have been about 900°—1000° C. See Nils Palmgren, Kansu mortuary urns of the Pan Shan and Ma Chang groups. Palaeontologica Sinica, Series D. Vol. III. Fasc. 1. Peiping 1934. p. 5. — The prehistoric pottery from

435

any case the pottery is well baked and often has a reddish shade which indicates that the clay contains iron and that the firing temperature must have been quite high. A very high temperature could only be produced in a kiln with a powerful draught. In the digging report it is stated that the inhabitants of Lo Han T'ang evidently used kilns for pottery baking. During the excavations the diggers came across the base of two kilns. Professor Andersson describes them in his introduction on page 431.

Vessel forms. Within this group appear the following vessel forms:

a) *Small amphorae* with long handles, well known from Ch'i Chia P'ing. Only one intact vessel of this type has been found. This vessel, already examined on p. 434, is reproduced in Pl. 25,1. A few sherds are obviously remnants of the same type, although this vessel form does not seem to have been very common.

b) Large *urns* with gently curved profile and lugs attached at the equatorial line. Some specimens may also have had a bi-conical body of the same type as that we know from Ch'i Chia P'ing, but owing to the fragmentary state of the artifacts it is impossible to draw any definite conclusions. We have been able to reconstruct only one vessel of this type.

The big urn already published by Professor Andersson is reproduced in Pl. 25,2. This vessel, reconstructed from many sherds, in part secondarily discoloured, has a brown shade with light brown and reddish spots. The collar is slightly flaring and the transition to the body is marked by a superimposed band, which is divided by diagonal incisions into small raised rhombs. Below the equatorial line two lugs are attached (partly reconstructed). The upper part of the body is smooth. The lower portion is covered with mat impressions. The impressions must originate from a mould or some fabric which has covered the mould. This vessel gives clear indications of its lower part having been built up in a mould. On that part of the belly where the impressions begin, a border or fold is visible, which obviously must emanate from the mould. Owing to the pressure from the upper part of the body its lower part has settled a little after the upper section had been joined to the base. This has resulted in the edge of the base portion bending slightly outwards.

This type of urn is represented by several fragments from bellies (about 10 large sherds), collars and bases (Pl. 26,1—4, 29,10). The size of the urns may have varied from very large specimens, such as the urn mentioned above, to medium-sized vessels such as the urns from Ch'i Chia P'ing. The lower portion of the body generally has mat or basket impressions of the same type as is well known from Ch'i Chia P'ing (about 10 belly fragments with this type of impressions) but even smooth bellies appear, e. g. the fragment reproduced in Pl. 29,6 and 28,5. If we were to judge entirely from the base fragments, most of the urns would be assumed

---

Honan has been subjected to chemical analysis by Dr. Paul Meyersberg, who assumes a temperature of 1300°—1400° C for this pottery. These figures seem to me to be surprisingly high. See T. J. Arne, o. c. p. 38.

436

Fig. 8.

to have had a smooth belly without impressions on the lower part but we must not forget that the bottoms might be remnants of painted urns. Anyhow, the bottoms are always clearly defined, e. g. the specimen reproduced in Pl. 29,10.

Only a few collars occur in this material. The shape varies, but the rim is generally flaring and sometimes annular (Pl. 29,5). The big collar-fragment reproduced in Pl. 29,1 might belong to a large urn. Other big collar fragments are reproduced in text figures 8 and 9. Two collar-fragments reproduced in Pl. 29,2, 3 are interesting on account of their flattened, outward-curving rim. This type of collar is quite unknown amongst the Ch'i Chia P'ing material but occurs in Ma Chia Yao.[1])

To judge from the reconstructed specimen (Pl. 25,2), the urns have been provided with lugs. A lug-fragment reproduced in Pl. 29,4 is ornamented with a superimposed wavy band. Another handle to a vessel of unknown shape, reproduced in Pl. 29,7, is shaped like a wavy ridge, but generally the lugs seem to have been undecorated.

c) *Bowls* and *basins* of varying size and shape. Not a single specimen of this type is intact. The ware of these vessels is generally of the highest quality, pure and well baked.

Some sherds have a dark interior core. On a few sherds, probably fragments of the same vessel, the ware as seen in a cross-section of the wall is so homogeneous that the vessel might have been conceivably made on the potter's wheel, but as I have already pointed out, it seems very unlikely that the wheel was used for making a few vessels only.

Some of the best specimens of bowls are reproduced in Pl. 27,2, 4, 28,1—4 and 30,3—6. There are many variations in profile and margin. Some bowls expand towards the mouth; in other cases the wall of the bowl contracts towards the mouth. The profile of the body is often gently curved. The rim may be annular (Pl. 27,3), simple (Pl. 30,3) or flattened and curved

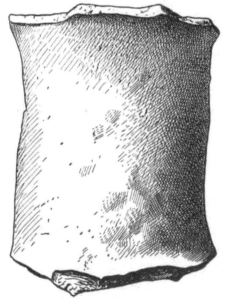

Fig. 9.

---

[1]) Cf. J. G. Andersson, RPC. Pl. 56,1—2, 62,1.

437

outwards (Pl. 30,4—6); only one single fragment has a piece of the bottom left (Pl. 27,4). The bottoms have evidently been clearly defined.

Some bowls (e. g. Pl. 27,3, 30,1) are shaped with less care and skill than the majority of the bowl-fragments. No striation is discernible. The surface is not smoothed, so that scratches and scores are clearly visible. The small bowl reproduced in Pl. 30,1 has the shape of a flower pot and is the only fragment of that type attributed to this group, but in regard to vessel form it is closely related to the coarse specimen in Pl. 31,1.

The fragment in Pl. 30,7 is a transitional form between bowl and urn. The vessel has a bi-conical shape and wide mouth but no collar. Unfortunately there is no piece of the base portion left, wherefore it is impossible to reconstruct it in its entirety. This vessel may be compared with a neck fragment of a very large vessel with rudimentary collar and wide mouth (Pl. 27,1), the latter also being a hybrid.

The fragment of a small bowl in Pl. 30,2 has, on the inside, two stripes of a reddish-brown colour, probably applied for testing purposes. I do not interpret them as constituting a decoration.

In Pl. 26,5, 6 are reproduced two unique fragments. 26,5 might be a piece of a small amphora or urn with very prominent belly and narrow collar. The ware is well-baked and of high quality. Colour brown. 26,6 is made of comparatively pure clay but not very well fired. The shape of the vessel is unknown, but the profile of the wall is straight. The outside is ornamented with a superimposed wavy clay band.

Finally, mention must be made of about fifty sherds of dark grey or greyish ware. Most of them are fragments of bowls or pieces impossible to classify. The rest of the sherds which have a brown or reddish-brown shade are, for the most part, only small pieces without character, so that it is difficult to draw any conclusions as to the size and shape of the vessels.

2. LHT: II. Coarse unpainted pottery.
About 632 fragments.

This group is uniform in vessel forms, quality of the ware and décor. Most of the fragments consist of coarse yellowish-brown, yellow or red ware. Sometimes the colour is grey or dark brown. Many of the fragments are covered with soot, probably not emanating from cooking. It may be a later infection from the earth, or perhaps we have here traces left by a contemporaneous conflagration, because it is often only the margin or the upper part of the body that are sooty (K. 12003: 962, K. 12003: 934). The bottom pieces belonging to this group show no traces of soot on the outside, but one specimen (K. 12003: 1120) has, on the inside, a sooty belt near the bottom, a fact which proves that the soot did not result from cooking.

438

The ware. Generally the quality of the ware is inferior to that of the preceding group, consisting of unpurified clay rich in mica or quartz.

Burning. The ware is uniformly baked at a temperature which, to judge from the porosity of the ware, must have been very low, probably about 600° C.

To this group belongs a broken urn, which we have been able to reconstruct (Pl. 31,4). It seems that this vessel represents the most common form of vessel in this group. It is therefore of interest to examine the technique of that specimen.

Technique. This vessel has been built up in a mould. The bottom part has been made separately in one mould, the upper part in another mould. Afterwards the two separate parts have been joined together and the junction smeared over with clay. The joint is now clearly visible, since the vessel has cracked just at the delicate point of junction. The joint is accentuated on the vessel by a wavy clay string probably applied for the purpose of covering the junction. In order to give the surface a symmetrical appearance, wavy bands decorate the body at regular intervals. In order to obtain a collar, the mouth of the vessel has been bent outwards, before the clay was dry. The outside of the body shows impressions of twisted cord. The cords may have covered the mould in order to facilitate the clay's adhering to the mould, or they may have been applied for the purpose of preventing the vessel form cracking, after manufacture but before the vessel became dry. In any case the vessel was not decorated with the above-mentioned wavy bands until after the cords had been removed. On one of the vessels belonging to this material the cord marks are visible even on the outside of the bottom.

On the specimen in Pl. 32,2, marks of the manufacturing process are clearly visible in the form of cracks between the different clay strings. From this we may conclude that the upper part of very large vessels has been built up by the coiling method. The fragment shown above is certainly not moulded. It seems probable that other big vessels have also been made in the same way.

Vessel forms. As mentioned above, we have been able to reconstruct only one complete specimen which represents the most common vessel form within this group of the material, although the profile may differ slightly from one vessel to another. The reconstructed vessel (Pl. 31,4) consists of an urn 235 mm. high with slightly curved profile and a low collar with a slightly flaring rim. Max. diam. of the vessel 258 mm. Diam. of mouth 160 mm. The surface is smooth below the mouth, the rest of the vessel is covered with regular cord impressions. At equal intervals wavy clay bands are attached to the body.

Vessels far larger than the urn now described also belong to the material. We have been able to reconstruct part of a large vessel, urn or amphora of an unusual size. The upper part of the body is smooth, the lower part has been covered with

439

vertical impressions of crossed cords. The ware is hard but to some extent mixed with mica and quartz. The colour is brownish-red. It is doubtful whether this vessel should be attributed to this group or to the first one. In Pl. 33 and 35,4 are reproduced other specimens of large vessels probably of an urn type.

Two collar fragments (Pl. 35: 1—2) also represent large vessels, but in this case it is impossible to draw any definite conclusions about the shape of the body.

12 marginal sherds of varying colour — grey, brown, yellow — are fragments of bowls having a simple margin and a slightly curved upper part with contracted mouth. On most of the fragments the zone below the margin is smooth and bordered with a deep furrow. The rest of the body is covered with diagonal cord impressions (Pl. 34,1—2, 4 and 6). The bowl reproduced in Pl. 34.4 has on the inside a coat of red colour (not slip). These sherds may be fragments of bowls of the same Honan type as Professor Andersson reproduces in An Early Chinese Culture Pl. XIV: 3 and 4, although the Lo Han T'ang bowls have no painted décor and the mouth may be wider. 7 marginal fragments of varying colour have less curved profiles than the sherds mentioned above (Pl. 34,3, 5—8). They seem to represent vessels of medium size except the specimen reproduced in Pl. 34,8, which must be a fragment of a very large vessel of coarse grey ware. The thickness of the wall is 14 mm. The flattened margin and the outside of the body are covered with diagonal cord impressions. 15 mm. below the margin is a fragmentary lug or knob. Pl. 34,5 has a wavy ridge below the rim. The profile is slightly curved and the outside of the body below the ridge is covered with diagonal cord impressions. Pl. 34,3 is closely related to Pl. 34,5. The ridge is ornamented with oblique fossae. The fragment reproduced in Pl. 34,7 has a knob forming a handle.[1]

Many fragments attributed to this group represent a type very common within this material, an urn resembling the reconstructed pot reproduced in Pl. 31,4, although the profile of the fragments is weaker and the brick-red ware is of a higher quality. Nevertheless mica and quartz grains are clearly visible. The collar curves slightly outwards. The neck and the outside of the body are covered with cord impressions in two directions (Pl. 36,1—3, Pl. 38,11). Some fragments are remnants of small urns (for instance Pl. 38,1) of thin ware. The outside is often decorated with horizontal clay bands below the neck and the belly. Between them are portions of small diagonal clay bands (Pl. 37,1).

Though our class LHT: II is defined above as »coarse unpainted pottery», we have to include in it a few specimens which are, after all, not quite »unpainted» but have a few ornaments in colour.

Some marginal sherds (Pl. 37) are fragments of delicate vessels decorated with bands in relief, with designs painted in violet or incised lines. They are

---

[1] The same kind of handle has been found on the site of Chu Chia Chai. BMFEA 17, Pl. 12,18.

440

undoubtedly all fragments of urns with wide mouth and slightly curved profile. Some of the specimens are provided with lugs of varying size (Pl. 37,2—5). The fragmentary urn in Pl. 38,1 gives some idea of the form of the vessels. I refer to the Kamm-decorated vessels from Ch'i Chia P'ing, to which they are related both in form and in size. The same kind of violet painting also occurs on the neck of specimens from both groups (cf. 403).

The vessel in Pl. 37,3 has at one side a lug attached to the outward curving rim. The body is covered with diagonal cord impressions. Below the neck a wavy clay band. The thin ware is mixed with mica and quartz but is hard and well baked. The thickness is about 4 mm.

Fig. 10.

The specimen in Pl. 38,8 is made of grey ware, hard and mixed with a remarkably high percentage of quartz. Thickness 5 mm. On the outside diagonal cord impressions. The outward-curving rim has on the inside a décor of oblique violet-painted triangles (text fig. 10). The outside is decorated with a small wavy band in relief and below it, at equal intervals, groups of small strings in relief. All painted in the same violet tone as the triangles.

The marginal sherd in Pl. 37,7 has the same groups of strings in relief as the neck fragment referred to above, but no painting is discernible. The fragment in Pl. 37,5 has a distinctly profiled rim provided with a small lug on the outside. The inside of the rim being provided with a ridge, I suggest that the mouth was covered with a lid. Below the rim and on the upper part of the body are two zones of incised horizontal lines. The area between them is decorated with a wedge in relief. The decorative system is cognate to the Kamm and relief ceramics of Ch'i Chia P'ing, although there are no Kamm impressions.

The marginal fragment in Pl. 37,9 is made of brown hard-baked ware, the surface of which is grey. The rim is flaring, curving outwards. Immediately below the margin a decoration of horizontal and vertical zones containing incised lines. In the centre of the horizontal zone a knob.

This kind of incised decoration is known from Wu lan Kou, Fu Ku Hsien, Shensi[1]) and Tsao Chiao Tsun, Chao Hsien, Shansi.

In Pl. 37,2 we see the upper part of a vessel, probably a small amphora. The colour is yellow. Below the lug a white spot. Grains of mica and quartz are discernible even on the surface. Inside, the vessel has a peculiar bi-conical shape which does not correspond to the soft curvature of the outside. On the outside indistinct cord impressions. The lug is decorated with numerous small wavy clay bands. Round the neck and belly the same sort of wavy band. On the inside are traces of violet colour. Since the vessel probably had a narrow rim, I cannot explain the spots of colour on the inside as a kind of decoration. I suggest that a liquid paint has been preserved in the vessel.

---

[1]) J. G. Andersson, RPC. pl. 94,6, 98,5.

441

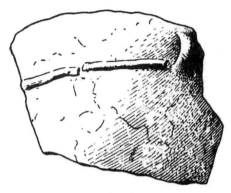

Fig. 11.

Before ending this description of the small vessels decorated in relief I have to point out a single fragment of dark grey ware (text fig. 11). The outside is polished, provided with a rudimentary lug and ornamented with a small horizontal ridge—a kind of decoration which recalls the ornamental style of some Ordos bronze vessels exhibited in the MFEA.

Two neck fragments (Pl. 35,1—2) 413 ornamented with oblique fossal below the rim are closely related to those Pl. 9,1—2, Pl. 10,1 and are obviously fragments of the same type of vessel. Another marginal fragment has a decorative clay band with crescent-shaped incisions below the rim (Pl. 35,3).

To this group belong about 70 different body fragments, probably remnants of urns (cf. p. 440). All are covered on the outside with traces of cords or similar impressions. Many of them are decorated with clay bands (Pl. 36,1, 3; Pl. 38,4, 9, 11) or broad flat ribbons (Pl. 40,2). Some specimens are provided with a small lug (Pl. 35,5, 7). Sometimes a wavy ridge forms a kind of lug (Pl. 35,6). Even the lugs are ornamented with wavy bands in relief.

One sherd should be mentioned for its extremely interesting ornamentation. The sherd (Pl. 36,4) is made of brick-red ware, has indistinct surface-impressions, the direction of which is, I presume, horizontal and is decorated with a snake (unfortunately fragmentary) in relief. The dark spots on the animal are marked by incisions (Cf. p. 424). Another body fragment, fig. 12, has also probably snake ornaments.

The bottoms of the vessels belonging to this group are well set off. (Pl. 38,1, 4, 11; Pl. 39,1, 4). Cord impressions often occur even on the bottom or, as in Pl. 41,4, marks of real plaiting are discernible on the outside of the bottom surface.

It should be pointed out that even on the small vessels belonging to specimens vaguely resembling the Kamm ceramics of Ch'i Chia P'ing as, for instance, the small vessel with saddle-shaped mouth reproduced in Pl. 38,1, the bottom is always clearly set off, whereas the corresponding vessels from Ch'i Chia P'ing often have a carelessly executed and undefined bottom.

Further, we have to note two neck fragments reproduced in Pl. 31,2—3. The

Fig. 12.

442

first one must be classified as an oblique spout, the kind of which Dr. Palmgren in his work on Pan Shan urns (Pl. 20) describes as »chamber-pot for men». The second fragment quoted seems to be a neck of a medium-sized vessel reminding of some urns from the burial site of Chu Chia Chai.[1]) I have examined both the vessels published by Professor Andersson and compared with them the neck fragment from Lo Han T'ang. In regard to ware, technical treatment and profile this collar is obviously closely connected with the urns from Chu Chia Chai.

Finally should be mentioned 5 fragments of legs of Li tripods (Pl. 38,3, 5, 8, 10). All of them are fragments of the very base of the leg. No fragment of the bulbous part of the legs has been preserved.

3. LHT: III. Painted pottery.
About 630 fragments.

The painted pottery forms a very uniform group as regards technical quality, vessel forms and décor.

The ware. All vessels belonging to this group are made of well purified clay offering a superior material for forming the beautiful urns and the fragile bowls which we are able to reconstruct from the fragments and small sherds of the Lo Han T'ang deposit.

Some fragments (8 pieces) are from the technical point of view quite unique (Pl. 43,4—5, Pl. 44,1—2). They are all fragments of large vessels, the upper part of which is made of fine purified clay, whereas the lower part is constructed of coarse clay mixed with quartz. All the fragments have a painted décor on the smooth upper part, while the bottom portion shows impressions of cord or plait-work. The sherd reproduced in Pl. 43,3 differs from the other fragments in being made throughout of coarse ware. There is black painting below the relief ridge, whereas we should expect to find the painting above the ridge-shaped handle. As far as I can judge from the direction of the furrows on the ridge, the painting must have been applied to the lower part of the vessel, but I interpret this as an exception, suggesting that the unknown part above the handle was made of fine clay and painted. The painting below the ridge might thus have belonged to the decorative system of the upper part although placed below the equatorial line.

I would suggest that this curious way of constructing a vessel of two different clays is uniquely a matter of technique. All the fragments seem to be parts of large vessels, and I believe that a bottom portion built up of coarse clay is better adapted for carrying a heavy upper part than a vessel constructed throughout of the same fine clay.

---

[1]) J. G. Andersson, The site of Chu Chia Chai. BMFEA N:r 17, Pl. 7,7 and 8,11.

443

Some very big undecorated fragments of large vessels are made of the same type of ware and bear the same impressions as the lower part of the fragments dealt with above, wherefore I suppose they are remnants of this kind of vessels consisting partly of fine and partly of coarse ware. The profile of the lower part of these vessels seems to have been almost straight, although to some extent expanding from the bottom towards the upper part. The bottom portion reproduced in Pl. 39,1 might, in spite of its grey colour, be attributed to this type. The shape of the upper part of these vessels is unknown, but I suppose we are here concerned with very large urns.

Technique. Both the urns and the bowls forming the main types of this group seem to have been built up in the same way as the vessels described in the preceding groups. I have not observed any evident trace of the potter's wheel when examining the bowls of the painted pottery. Some of them are shaped with very little care, for instance the specimen reproduced in Pl. 46,2.

On a bowl fragment (text fig. 7) are traces of half obliterated cord impressions visible below the outside of the rim, which proves that the bowls have been formed with the aid of a mould or muffle. In any case, the cord impressions are of a constructive character.

The visible surfaces of the vessels are polished. In some cases the state of the fragment is badly corroded, so that it is impossible to draw any conclusions about the original character of the surface.

Colour. The ware seems to have been fired at a comparatively high temperature, perhaps about 900° C. Most of the fragments have a pale-brown or yellow colour. Some sherds are brick-red and a few pieces have a dusty brown or grey colour. In some cases brick-red or grey spots are visible on the otherwise homogeneously coloured surface, due possibly to irregularities in the firing process or the composition of the clay.

The colour of the painted décor is entirely black or, in a few cases, violet or brown. In one case the black pattern is combined with a heavy white colour, but a combination of black and violet never occurs in the painted décors such as is found in the material from the Pan Shan graves.

Vessel forms. The bulk of the painted sherds are fragments of big urns (Pl. 42,1, 3, 4) or bowls with wide mouth. The urns have been of varying size, most of them large, though small specimens also occur (Pl. 44,8). Unfortunately no urn is intact and we have not been able to reconstruct a single vessel from the small fragments at our disposal. But if we look at the painted pottery from the site of Ma Chia Yao, we get a good idea[1]) of the shape of the Lo Han T'ang urns. The neck seems to have been high in most cases and the rim curving outwards (Pl. 44,5, 6, 11), but specimens with low collar also occur (Pl. 43,1). Some of the vessels, obviously the urns as well, have been provided with lugs (Pl. 45,1—4).

The size of the urns may have varied from large specimens such as the fragments

---

[1]) J. G. Andersson, RPC. Pl. 56,2, 57,1 5.

444

reproduced in Pl. 42 to very small vessels from among which two neck fragments are illustrated in Pl. 44,7—8.

The profile of the body seems in most cases to have been gently rounded. The profile of the big fragment in Pl. 42,4 is sharply broken where the horizontal zone of the painted design begins. Comparing the pattern of the painted décor and the relief band on this fragment with the decorative elements on the fragments

Fig. 13.

constructed of two different clays (Pl. 43,4, 5 Pl. 44,1), I suggest that we here have the upper part of an urn built up of two different qualities of material.

Beside the fragmentary urns, some sherds of *bowls* and *basins* (Pl. 45—48, Pl. 50—51) are found. Owing to the fragmentary state of the majority of the material it is often difficult to decide whether a sherd is a remnant of a bowl or a basin. The profile of the vessels varies from widely expanding walls to specimens contracting towards the mouth. The mouth is often provided with a rim (Pl. 48,3, 6). On many fragments the rim curves outward and is decorated (Pl. 50,7, 11, 13, 14, 15, 17, 18, 20, 21).

On the bowl fragment reproduced in Pl. 44,9 the wall of the vessel contracts towards the narrow mouth, which has no rim. This is a unique variation among the bowls that ordinarily have a more or less wide-open mouth. Another fragment of a rim (text fig. 13) has a narrow mouth, but it is also provided with a rudimentary collar. They are closely related, both being fragments of vessels with narrow mouths, and I suggest that we here have a transition form between the urns and the bowls.

About 15 *bottom pieces* were found among the sherds. Some of them are reproduced in Pl. 51,10—13. The bottom surface is always clearly demarcated (fig. 14) and of the same type as that of the bowls from Ma Chia Yao.

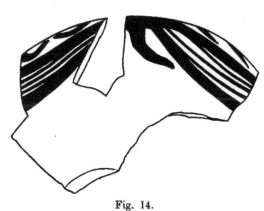

Fig. 14.

As has already been mentioned, some of the urns and, in a few cases, even the bowls have been provided with *lugs*. On the large urns the lugs are short and broad (Pl. 45,1, 4), on the smaller specimens they are diminutive (Pl. 45,2, 3). The bowl fragment reproduced in Pl. 48,4 has a fragmentary lug, which is placed horizontally. Another bowl fragment has a wavy ridge forming a kind of fragmentary handle (text fig. 15). The same

445

type of handle is known from Chin Wang Chai. Some of them have been published by Professor Arne.[1])

A quite different type of handle is represented by 6 fragments (cf. p. 457). They are all long, flat and slightly curved. The breadth varies from about 1.5 to 3 cm. The outside is decorated with horizontal lines (Pl. 51,15, 16) or crossed lines (Pl. 51,14). I suggest that they are remnants of small amphorae with long handles. Professor Andersson[2]) has published a handle from Ma Chia Yao which seems to be connected with this type.

Before ending this description of the vessels I should like to point out a very peculiar ceramic object reproduced in Pl. 51,18. It is probably the handle of a bowl. It is decorated on both sides with black lines on the inside combined with an oblong spot. As far as we can judge from the fragmentary state of the object, the handle is in shape closely related to that of a bowl published by Professor Andersson.[3])

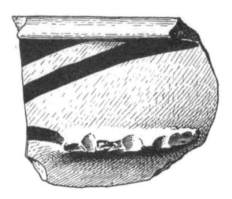

Fig. 15.

Designs. Both the urns and the bowls have a rich black décor of varying character. The colour is, with a few exceptions which will be described later, entirely black. The pigment is applied to a carefully smoothed and polished surface. Only in a few cases is painting found on a rough surface (Pl. 43,3). On a body fragment not reproduced (K. 12003: 1384) is a broad band of violet paint applied to the rough surface which is covered with intersecting cord impressions and decorated with a superimposed wavy clay band. This kind of painting is quite unique but may have some connection with certain vessels having been composed of two different kinds of clay (cf. 443).

As we have no complete urn extant, it is difficult to get any idea of the entire decorative system on these vessels. The belly fragment reproduced in Pl. 42.1 has no collar left, but we may presume that the neck was decorated with horizontal rings or zones as is the case in Pl. 44,6, 7, 10. Other collar fragments have the horizontal lines combined with circular dots (Pl. 44,4), oblong dots (Pl. 44,5) or circle a segments (Pl. 44,11). One single neck fragment of coarse ware is decorated with horizontal lines, between which is a zone with vertical lines (Pl. 44,3). The small neck fragment reproduced in Pl. 44,7 has on the flaring rim a very attractive décor of garland-shaped lines and tendril figures. The outside of the neck is ornamented with parallel horizontal lines. To revert to the urn reproduced in Pl. 42,1, the design of the belly shows the most frequently occurring

---

[1]) T. J. Arne, Painted Stone-Age Pottery from Honan, Pl. VII: 20 and IX: 30.

[2]) J. G. Andersson, RPC. Pl. 52,5.

[3]) J. G. Andersson, RPC. Pl. 182,2.

446

component of the decorative patterns from Lo Han T'ang, the horizonally grouped, parallel lines. Here they alternate with black bands and at equal distances are interrupted and bordered by oblong spots. The centre of the lineal zone is ornamented with two diagonal lines. The lower part of this urn is undecorated.

This combination of groups of parallel lines interrupted by *oblong dots* appears on some fragments (Pl. 50,16 and 23, 51,3, 18) which are remnants of both urns and bowls. Sometimes parallel lines, bands or circles are combined with circular dots (Pl. 49,6, 7, 9). On a few sherds the zone of horizontally grouped lines is bordered by dots, combined with trellis work (Pl. 49,1; compare Pl. 42,1).

On the belly fragment in Pl. 42,4 the central zone of the parallel lines is replaced by groups of diagonal circle segments and a triangle with elongated apices. These two elements, *diagonal circle segments* and *triangle-shaped figures*, sometimes combined with inscribed dots (Pl. 43,1) are very common elements in the designs both of the urns and of the bowls and appear combined with zones of parallel lines. (Pl. 49,10, 14). A belly fragment reproduced in Pl. 42,5 shows what appears to be a big circle, crossed by a horizontal line and combined with a group of circle segments. Another belly fragment in 42,2 has a simple décor consisting of a zone of broad vertical lines on the lower part of the body succeeded by horizontal lines (2 sherds of this kind). Sometimes on the urns the lowest part of the zone with horizontal lines is bordered by a *garland* (Pl. 42,4).

On some sherds there is a simple décor formed of *alternating horizontal lines and bands* (Pl. 49,15, 16). Pl. 49,15 seems to be closely related to a sherd from Chu Chia Chai.[1] On other belly fragments there are groups of lines combined with bands or triangle-shaped figures (Pl. 49,8, 14).

Before ending the description of the urn fragments we have to examine some very important belly fragments reproduced in Pl. 49,2, 11—13. They all have a dentated band, in 49,2 combined with vertically radiating groups of lines and big dots, on the other sherds combined with circle segments. The dentated band is kindred to the well-known »death-pattern» but is here entirely executed in black.

As I have already mentioned, the ceramic material is very fragmentary, wherefore it is sometimes difficult to know whether a sherd is a remnant of a bowl or an urn. Nevertheless there is little doubt that most of the sherds now examined are fragments of urns.

As to the decoration on the *bowls*, some specimens have a very poor ornamentation, combined with black painting on the rim (Pl. 46,2). Other bowls have a simple décor of parallel lines (Pl. 51,1) sometimes concentrated within the upper part of the body (Pl. 46,1). Often the lines form garlands on the outside (Pl. 45,5, 46,3—5, 50,3). Sometimes the garlands consist of heavy lines, the spaces between which are filled with finer lines (Pl. 50,3, 6) in the same manner as on the Ma Chia Yao bowls. The points of junction between two festoons sometimes have a hook

---

[1] J. G. Andersson, The site of Chu Chia Chai, BMFEA N:r 15, Pl. 101,7.

447

(Pl. 50,3), a ring (Pl. 46,4 b) or, as in Pl. 50,6, a more complicated ornament. The slender tendrils well known from Ma Chia Yao occur on several bowl fragments (Pl. 47,1 a, 2 a).

On the fragment reproduced in Pl. 50,2, diagonal lines form a border below the rim. A more elaborate system of line ornamentation occurs on the unique and elegant bowl fragment reproduced in Pl. 50,1. The vessel is markedly bi-conical and has a low, wide collar with flattened rim. The black design consists of horizontal bands combined with finer horizontal or vertical lines, a big circular dot and above the equatorial line a triangle, the extended sides of which border a knob in relief. Besides the black painting just described there are circular dots and a line executed in white. This bowl has no interior décor.

Bowls or basins with flattened rim generally have decorative painting on the margin. The most frequent marginal patterns are shown in Pl. 50. The elements appearing in varying combinations are oblique or straight lines, sometimes wavy lines, trellis works, dots, circles, circle segments, and triangle-shaped lines.

Bowls or basins with a wide mouth generally have an interior decoration, sometimes only a few lines (Pl. 45,6 a); in other cases a rich system of parallel lines (Pl. 47,1 b—3 b), on many sherds combined with trellis work (Pl. 47,1 b, 4) or dots (Pl. 50,19, 22).

On several insides occur triangles, separate (Pl. 46,5 a) or together with a linear system (Pl. 46,4 a, 50,19, 22). Some sherds are decorated with peculiar triangle-shaped figures (Pl. 50,4, 8, 12). They are all applied near the margin. Their points are elongated and end in dots. Other dots flank the points.

Some bowl fragments reproduced in Pl. 48 illustrate the most highly developed designs from Lo Han T'ang. 48,1 has the outside ornamented with thickly painted horizontal lines, below which appear the ends of vertically placed lines. The inside is undecorated. The rim is painted black and is undecorated. 48,2 has on the flaring, slightly curved rim a belt of triangles. The body has the slender tendril pattern already mentioned. The pattern of 48,3 is not very carefully drawn. It consists of a heavy dot inscribed in a circle surrounded by circle segments which are flanked by triangle-shaped figures. The margin has black painting. The inside is ornamented with two roughly drawn parallel lines. 48,4 has on the outside a knob in relief placed in the centre of a border filled with vertical circle segments. The brick-red inside has a rare hour-glass-shaped ornament which is obviously the black-painted space between two circles in which are inscribed pairs of dots (cf. 48, 6 a). 48,5 has on the outside almost the same pattern of vertical circle segments as are seen in 48,4. Here they are combined with a triangle-shaped figure. The inside is decorated with groups of transverse lines forming a chessboard pattern. 48,6 has on the eroded outside a design consisting of a triangle-shaped figure, a group of diagonal lines and circle segments. The interior decoration consists of pairs of circles, in which are inscribed pairs of dots separated by three vertical lines. The groups of circles seem to have alternated with zones of horizontal lines combined with

448

belts of oblong dots. Similar belts of dots seem to appear on a small sherd reproduced in Pl. 51,4.

In Pl. 51,6 is reproduced a small bowl fragment of brick-red ware. The outside has a garland filled with fine horizontal lines. In the space between the garland and a lower horizontal band is the fragment of a knob. The inside has a single marginal belt of triangles. A small bowl fragment shown in Pl. 51,7 has obviously the same simple linear pattern on both sides.

There are furthermore some b o t t o m s   w i t h
i n t e r i o r   d e c o r a t i o n. The most important specimens are reproduced in Pl. 51,10—13. 5,10 has in

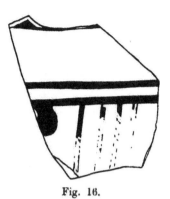

Fig. 16.

the centre the already described circle pattern (cf. p. 448) with inscribed dots. In this case the groups of lines inside the circle form a cross. In the centre and in the spaces between the cross-arms are dots. 51,13 has groups of trellis work on the bottom plate, while 51,11 and 12 are sparsely ornamented, the first with circles or wavy lines, the second with circle segments radiating from a ring in the centre of the bottom. Apparently many of the bottoms were decorated in the same way as the intact bowls from Ma Chia Yao with a dot in the centre or a pair of curved lines.[1])

Before ending the description of the ceramics I have to point out some fragments differing in colour from the rest. They are all painted with a reddish-violet or reddish-brown colour quite different from the black (or in a few cases dark brown) pigmentation of the preceding fragments. In Pl. 51,17 is reproduced a marginal sherd of a bowl made of yellowish-white ware. Both the outside and the inside are decorated with reddish-brown zig-zag lines. The fragment of a rim in Pl. 51,8 has violet paint forming a marginal band from which, on the inside, run vertical lines. A rim fragment not reproduced has on the inside two simple vertical lines in violet paint. The bowl fragment in Pl. 30,2 has on the inside two violet-brown strokes of a paint-brush, but they are too clumsy to be regarded with any certainty as a form of decoration. The violet-painted handles are already described on p. 446.

In Pl. 51,19 is reproduced a small sherd with pale reddish-brown painting on the pale yellow-outside. The pattern consists of a dot and traces of a band. The text fig. 16 shows a sherd of pale yellow-brown ware with brick-red spots on the

outside ornamented with horizontal lines. From the lowest one runs a group of four vertical lines, alongside which is a dot.

Finally, 5 very important fragments (text fig. 17—18) should be described. 4 are pale grey fragments with painted décor in dirty brown colour (fig. 17). Both ware and colour recall the famous bowls from Yang Shao Tsun and Chin

Fig. 17.

[1]) J. S. Andersson, RPC. Pl. 54,1 2 a.

449

Wang Chai.[1]) The last one is a bowl fragment with a reddish-brown exterior surface, ornamented with a grey pattern, from which a triangle with an elongated apex protrudes (fig. 18). The ware and the colour of the design is exactly the same as a type well known from the Yang Shao sites from Honan.[2])

An examination of the unfortunately too fragmentary pottery from Lo Han T'ang shows that the painted pottery is closely related to that of Ma Chia Yao. Once the materials from that site have been thoroughly examined, it will probably be found that all the painted designs occurring on Lo Han T'ang pottery will recur on such from Ma Chia Yao. A comparison with a few painted vessels and sherds published by Professor Andersson or exhibited in the Museum of Far Eastern Antiquities has convinced me that the connection between the two sites must be very close. I have not had an opportunity of examining in detail the coarser pottery of Ma Chia Yao, and I am therefore unable to state anything definite about correlations in regard to such wares; nor I am aware of any amphorae or large urns with mat impressions in the Ma Chia Yao material; professor Andersson's preliminary survey indicates no such specimens.

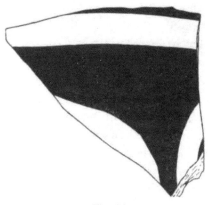

Fig. 18.

The Lo Han T'ang pottery also has some features in common with the Chu Chia Chai culture.[3]) If we first examine the painted pottery from the dwelling site of Chu Chia Chai, that category of the latter called by Andersson the class »of Ma Chia Yao type» (RPC. Pl. 100,1, 2, 4) has obvious affinities with wares from Lo Han T'ang; and even the sherds of what Professor Andersson calls »Late Yang Shao type» have features in common with the painted pottery from Lo Han T'ang (RPC. Pl. 100,9, 101,1, 5, 7, 8, 103,15, 17). The coarse pottery of Chu Chia Chai has also a certain resemblance to that of Lo Han T'ang.

It is a most astonishing fact that three fragments of Ch'i Chia P'ing type were found in Chu Chia Chai (Andersson BMFEA 17, Pl. 11,2, 8; 12,7), and equally remarkable that fragments of real Lo Han T'ang type were found in that site. There appear for instance fragments of bodies decorated with superimposed clay bands (Cf. Andersson loc. cit. Pl. 11,1, 5, 12,2). The fragment illustrated in Andersson's Pl. 11,1 is almost identical with the neck fragment from Lo Han T'ang reproduced in Pl. 57,2. Further should be mentioned the bowl fragment

---

[1]) T. J. Arne, Painted stone age pottery from Honan, Pl. II and III.

[2]) T. J. Arne, op. cit. Pl. IV: 8.

[3]) The materials from this site were published by Professor Andersson in BMFEA N:r 17. A summary review of the painted dwelling-site pottery from this culture was also published in Andersson, RPC. p. 152—159, Pl. 100—106.

450

with a knob-like handle illustrated in Pl. 34,7 (cf. p. 440). Finally we have to observe two fragments of black pottery published by Andersson, RPC. Pl. 11,4 and 12,4. The first one is a marginal sherd from a bowl of black pottery of a type that occurs in Lo Han T'ang. The second sherd is a neck fragment decorated with ridges of the same kind as those illustrated in fig. 11.

Even »winged stone knives» and bone knives with flint-flakes are known both from Chu Chia Chai and Lo Han T'ang, as pointed out by Professor Andersson.

The similarities just adduced are sufficient to prove certain connections of Lo Han T'ang on the one hand with Ma Chia Yao, on the other hand with Chu Chia Chai. As to the chronological conclusion to be drawn from these connections, it would be premature to make any more definite statements before the important Ma Chia Yao material has been thoroughly examined and published.

XI. STONE IMPLEMENTS.

The stone implements from the dwelling-sites do not yield anything of any particular interest. The bulk of the stone artifacts are types well-known from other sites, such as axes, chisels, stone knives and discs. Some of the finest specimens have already been published by Professor Andersson[1]) in his elaborate study on the prehistory of the Chinese. In addition I will here only briefly mention that a fine chisel of silk-grey jade was found at Lo Han T'ang. This is the only specimen of a semi-precious stone from this site.

Among the most frequent artifacts (19 pieces) are big discs, crudely cut from diorite pebbles.[2]) Sometimes the rough surfaces are retained, while a kind of edge is shaped by means of some crude chipping. Other pebbles are carefully ground or polished until they have obtained an oblong form (Pl. 53,2).

Three big granite pebbles are carefully ground into flattened discs for unknown purpose.

In Pl. 52,1 is reproduced a mace head of crystalline rock having all around the body a deep groove at one side crossed by another broad groove evidently intended for fastening (cf. p. 416 and Pl. 19,8).

Many fragments of big stone axes are included in the material, but only one specimen, already published by Professor Andersson,[3]) is intact. He attributes this axe to what he calls »The Pan Shan type», occupying a position between his Honan axe and the Northern rounded axe.[4]) Our specimen has an oval cross-section and narrow neck. The material is black schistose rock.

Many blocks (Pl. 52,4) with a few cuts on them or broken axes of the same material are extant. A small carefully polished diorite axe is reproduced in Pl. 52,7. 52,5, 6, 9 are in all probability *Pen* axes of dark, hard rock. The neck is

---

[1]) J. G. Andersson, RPC. p. 85—86, 224—225, 262, 270, Pl. 40—41, 73,4, 164,1—3, 7—10.

[2]) J. G. Andersson, RPC. p. 85, Pl. 40,3.

[3]) RPC. p. 85, Pl. 40,1.

[4]) RPC. p. 48.

broken in all these specimens. The fragment in Pl. 52,8 is reproduced in order to show the beautiful structure of the material.

Some schist chisels have been found. Two of them were reproduced by Professor Andersson.[1]) Most of the chisels are asymmetrical in cross-section (Pl. 52,16—18). The chisel-like implement in Pl. 52,19 has the same edge on both sides.

An axe-neck of schistose rock is considered by Professor Andersson to be a fragment of the type he calls »Broad axes with square neck».[2]) Unfortunately the specimen in the plate lies horizontally, so that it gives the impression of being a stone knife with two holes. Although there is no edge and the sides are contracting, we have here obviously a neck fragment of an axe. This specimen, as a type, was a unique find at Lo Han T'ang.

26 fragments of stone knives are found among the artifacts. The most beautiful specimens have already been published by Professor Andersson.[3]) All forms are represented, from crude blocks without holes (Pl. 52,15) to the finest specimen reproduced by the author.

Some knives without holes have corresponding recesses on the short sides (Pl. 52,11), which seem to have served as grooves for attachment. This simple type occurs also in Ch'i Chia P'ing (cf. p. 416) and other Chinese sites. Other specimens are provided with one or two holes (Pl. 52,12—14). In 52,12 the hole is very elongated. Sometimes the hole is placed near the edge, in other cases in the centre or the neck. On most specimens the short sides expand, which gives the knives a »winged» shape. Professor Andersson has given to these knives the name *winged stone knives*. Some of the knives published by Professor Andersson have indentations on both short sides. I presume that these indentations enabled the knives to serve also as saws, obviously a very practical invention. The indentations however, are not very sharp. If they have served a practical purpose, they must have been used on soft material. They might therefore possibly be interpreted as notches for facilitating tying or as serving an ornamental purpose.

As far as I am aware these winged and dentated stone knives are so far only known from Lo Han T'ang.

An asymmetrically semi-lunar stone knife is reproduced in Pl. 52,15. The edge is sharpened. Only one side is smooth. The back is very thick. In his RPC. p. 223. Professor Andersson has pointed out the great importance and wide distribution of the rectangular and semi-lunar knives.

In Pl. 53,1 is reproduced a big specimen which is unique. It seems to be a hoe with two opposed recesses probably made for fastening purposes. This hoe seems to be related to what Professor Andersson calls »the broad northern typ» from the Sino-Mongolian border land.[4])

---

[1]) RPC. p. 85, Pl. 40,10—11.

[2]) RPC. p. 85, Pl. 40,13.

[3]) RPC. p. 224—225, Pl. 40,12, 164,1—3, 7—10.

[4]) RPC. p. 58, Pl. 25,1—4.

452

Pl. 52,10 shows a semi-circular fragment of crystalline rock. It might have been an axe with shaft-hole, but the artifact is too fragmentary to make any definite conclusions possible.

Another stone fragment of unknown use is shown in Pl. 52,3. It has a deep furrow in the centre. Probably we have here a fragment of a grindstone. Another grindstone in the shape of a block also was found on our site, and some pieces of round sand stone may also have been used for grinding purposes.

Two *pendants* of slate should also be noticed. One has been reproduced by Professor Andersson,[1] the other one is shown in Pl. 54,14. The latter has a furrow for tying with string. The furrow does not continue round the back. One short side has the same kind of furrow at the other end. For a small disc-like pendant made of white marble see Pl. 52,2.

7 fragments, also made of marble, should next be recorded. The most beautiful specimens are reproduced in Pl. 53,3—5. Probably these objects are fragments of armlets. The elegant fragment in 53,3 is made of fine white marble with a tinge of warm yellowish rose. The ring is regularly cut with almost the same thickness throughout, slightly tapering towards one of the margins. The outside is polished; on the inside traces of red pigment. On both margins there are groups of small incised lines. At one side, near the margin, there is a hole drilled from the outside. The specimen in 53,5 is cut of shiny white-grained marble. The sides expand towards the margins. The cross-section is consequently concave on the outside and correspondingly convex on the inside. Both the outside and inside are polished. The other armlet fragments in Pl. 53,5 and 54,8 are cut out of white marble with innumerable small pores typical of weathered stone.

A small, beautifully shaped slate ring has also probably been used as an armlet (Pl. 54,6). Finally we may note a small cylindrical marble bead in Pl. 53,28.

Before we conclude the description of the stone objects it should be mentioned that Professor Andersson[2] has published a unique stone specimen, the upper part of which is shaped like a shoulder-blade. This peculiar implement was excavated in a locality close to the village of Lo Han T'ang, but no object of a similar shape has been found on its prehistoric site.

XII. BONE IMPLEMENTS.
About 90 fragments.

The most important objects have already been published by Professor Andersson.[3] In order to give a selection of the best bone implements, some of the specimens are here republished in Pl. 54.

The most characteristic implements are *bone knives* with a deep furrow for

---

[1] RPC. p. 85, Pl. 41,6.

[2] RPC. p. 56, Pl. 22,5.

[3] RPC. p. 86—87, Pl. 41,1—4, 7—9.

453

fastening flint flakes (6 fragments). The most intact specimens are found in Pl. 54,12, 13. Other knife fragments are reproduced in Pl. 53,16, 25—27. They all have at one side a deep furrow, where flint flakes have been attached. In all specimens the furrow extends to the point. The upper part of the knives is unfurrowed and serves as a handle. In some specimens the knife-blade is curved. A number of more or less fragmentary *awls* have been excavated. Some of them are illustrated in Pl. 53,18—25.

Furthermore, 29 *sewing needles* belong to the material. They are of varying size and length. Some are extremely small and fine (Pl. 53,8—9, 11). Many of them have a skilfully executed eye.

In Pl. 54,10, 11 are reproduced two unique bone-implements. 54,10 shows a thin plate split from a big bone and provided with two holes at one end. Below and above these holes are two symmetrical identations. At the other end is another hole. The holes are bi-conical, bored from both sides. Between the lateral indentations marks of wear are clearly visible. The same kind of marks are also observable from the holes to the top-indentations and from the holes to the lateral indentations. It looks as if ribbons or strings were once wound round the specimen between these points. I suggest that we here have an implement for weaving or basket-making.

Pl. 54,11 shows a flat bone object with a peculiar hole at the top. The pointed part is decorated with five small pits. The back has a similar pit slightly higher up than those on the front side. This implement also and the fragment in Pl. 53,25 might have been used for weaving. The latter object is closely related to some bone implements from Ch'i Chia P'ing (cf. Pl. 16,24—26), probably used for weaving or plaiting work.

A remarkable bone implement is a hoe or axe made of a split from a big bone (Pl. 53,6). The upper side is convex, the back concave. The edge is sharpened.

We might conclude from the fine bone needles and other implements obviously adapted for weaving or plaiting that the inhabitants of the site were skilful in cloth-making, mat-making and other domestic handiwork.

XIII. BASKET AND CORD IMPRESSIONS.

As this subject has been closely studied in connection with the pottery from Ch'i Chia P'ing, I will here give only some short notes on the most remarkable differences between the impressions from the two sites. At the end of this paragraph I add a few remarks on the pottery furniture from certain sites of Ch'i Chia type in south Kansu (cf. p. 456).

In the first group from Lo Han T'ang (LHT: I), to which are attributed the amphorae, the big urns and undecorated bowls of fine ware, identically the same impressions occur as in CC: I (cf. p. 411). I have accepted the term »mat or basket impression» for them, according to Professor Anderssons terminology, although I am not convinced that the impressions are derived from real baskets. I am more

454

inclined to consider them as emanating from a softer kind of plait-work, perhaps rough matting, which has covered the mould in which the vessels were shaped. As I have already pointed out in the description of the Ch'i Chia P'ing impressions, the plaiting does not imply a very regular or complicated design. It may be that the textile fibres have merely been smeared on to the wall of the mould without any »binding threads«, or else the vegetable bundles were held in position by loose strands of the same material. This kind of simple plait-work or matting is well-known from many savage tribes.[1]) Some examples of the impressions from Lo Han T'ang I corresponding to CC: I are shown in Pl. 26,1—4.

As in Ch'i Chia P'ing, the simple mat-impression described above occurs only on vessels or fragments of vessels belonging to the first group. One exception is a large fragment of an urn (K. 12003: 1127) resembling the vessel in Pl. 25,2. The upper part of this vessel is smooth, the lower part is covered with cord impressions. The urn fragment in Pl. 28,5 shows traces of impressions (cord or basket?) on the space where a now lost lug had been attached. This proves that the impressions must have had a constructive purpose.

The coarse pottery attributed to the second group (LHT: II) has always the whole body covered with impressions, not only the lower portion, as in the first group. This is the same system of arranging the impressions as in Ch'i Chia P'ing, although the impressions themselves are mostly of quite a different character.

A few fragments have vertical or diagonal cord impressions (Pl. 31,4, 33,1) of exactly the same type as the majority of the pottery attributed to CC: II (cf. p. 412), and some other sherds have the same fine impressions that characterize CC: III (Pl. 32,1, 35,1—2), but most of the fragments have the whole exterior covered with impressions of the same kind as those shown in Pl. 36,1—3, and 38,11. They are obviously marks of twisted cords, running diagonally and intersecting one another in two directions. In Pl. 40,1 b—3 b are modelling clay casts (positive) of impressions of the same type as that reproduced. I suggest that this type of impressions emanated from some kind of not very carefully executed and irregular plait-work, the material of which consisted of twisted cord. »Net-work« might perhaps be the best expression.

Another type of impression, superficially related to this »net-work«, occurs on many sherds and is shown on three base fragments in Pl. 39,1—3 and two sherds reproduced in Pl. 41,2—3. They might be of the same kind as the »net-work«, but the impressions are grouped in small clearly discernible patches, wherefore I am inclined to explain them as marks of a beater, wrapped in cords, although they might be interpreted as very irregular net-work. Some sherds belonging to the group of painted vessels that were constructed of two different clays might like-wise have been treated with a beater (Pl. 43,4, 44,1). The fragment shown in Pl.

---

[1]) See, for instance, Jesse L. Nussbaum, A basket-maker cave in Kane county, Utah. Indian notes and monographs. Museum of the American Indians, Heye foundation New York 1922, p. 18 ff. Pl. L and LI.

455

41,1 has on the upper part simple diagonal impressions and on the lower part the same impressions crossing each other in two directions. In any case the problem of the cord impressions is very difficult and I am not convinced that all somewhat irregular cord impressions could be interpreted as marks from a beater.[1])

A few sherds have horizontal cord impressions (Pl. 31,1, 39,4, 36,4), and some sherds have impressions of the same type as the Kamm pottery from Ch'i Chia P'ing. The urn in Pl. 31, the base of which is shown in Pl. 41,4, has real basket or textile impressions on the bottom.

The few sherds from Ch'i Li Tun and Hsiao Shih Hsia (cf. p. 459) have yielded some examples of real basket or textile impressions. From Ch'i Li Tun emanate two fragments with impressions of a real textile character (Pl. 55,10, 12). It might be the impression left by a coiled basket or, if the material was soft, a coarse canvas cloth. From Hsiao Shih Hsia comes a small fragment of regularly plaited basket-work shown in Pl. 56,10.

As a result of our investigations we find that the inhabitants of the Kansu sites here referred to were skilful in spinning cord and knew how to make sacks and nets of this cord. Obviously they produced rough mats, baskets and probably also cloth. The fine bone needles afford evidence that they could do needle-work, probably even in very soft material. The finest sewing needles could scarcely be used for skins or other rough material without breaking.

XIV. VARIA.

Some clay objects which it is impossible to attribute to any of the groups examined above are described in the following paragraph.

A very peculiar object was excavated in L. H. T. and is reproduced in Pl. 25,4. The body is laterally expanding from the flattened base. Each side has at the top two fragmentary tips. The interior is hollow and filled with small objects, which rattle when the object is shaken. Probably it has been used as a child's *rattle* or has served some now unknown ceremonial purpose.

In this connection should also be mentioned three diminutive vessels, one of which is illustrated in Pl. 54,7. Two of them have the shape of an urn, and the third one has straight walls; all are extremely small. They might have been children's toys or used for preserving some very precious liquid.

In Pl. 25,3 is reproduced another unique object of greyish-brown clay. The shape is cylindrical, though slightly tapering towards one end. I suggest that this cuff-like object was used as an armlet, but it could also be interpreted as some kind of support.

Further some eighty fragments of small clay rings should be mentioned. A few specimens are reproduced in Pl. 54,2—5. Most of them are grey, but there are also

---

[1]) G. D. Wu, op. cit. p. 139.

456

brown shades among them.   The cross-section varies from rectangular to triangular. About 30 fragments might have been used as armlets, although the diameter of some specimens is not very large.   The rest of these fragments being of a flattened shape are obviously remnants of handles of small vessels.

A few clay-balls of varying size belong to our material here.   Two of them are reproduced in Pl. 25,5—6.   Probably they have been used for grinding purposes.

Finally there is a disc-like object of brown clay (Pl. 26,7). The edge is irregular. In the centre is an incomplete hole. The disc was probably intended to be used as a spinning-whorl.

XV. MAMMAL REMAINS FROM CH'I CHIA P'ING AND LO HAN T'ANG.

These bone-collections have been examined by Doctor Elias Dahr, who has written preliminary reports, now in the archives of MFEA, about his investigations. Dr. Dahr has kindly permitted me to base my remarks below on his investigations.

The material from Ch'i Chia P'ing was excavated partly from the steep river bank of the T'ao river and partly from the ravine through which the road runs. At this latter place the stratigraphical conditions are very uncertain, while the carving-in of the ground might have mixed different strata; hence it is quite possible that remnants differing in age may have been found together. Thus among the other bones several specimens have been found which might be of very recent age — for instance some mandibles of goats and sheep which still possess a distinct smell of fat.

However, after the elimination of some specimens, the material from Ch'i Chia P'ing shows the same state of conservation as collections from other prehistoric sites.

The colour of the bones is generally pale, sometimes with a beautiful yellowish, sometimes a greyish, shade. The surface is in several cases covered with firmly adhering concretions and is often sculptured with fine furrows caused by vegetable roots.

The bulk of the material consists of the remains of domesticated mammals, such as dogs, pigs, cattle, goats and sheep. Wild animals are represented only by some specimens of deer and skulls of rodents (Siphneus). The latter might be recent remnants of animals which have burrowed down, having thus been mixed with those of the deposit.

The dog remnants, 40 in number, indicate that the animals were small, probably comparable in size with modern fox-terriers. A well-preserved cranium belongs to the European Neolithic Canis fam. Palustris).

The pig remnants show interesting features. One facial fragment with well-preserved os lachrymosum is of a real Vitalis type. The bulk of the pig remnants are parts of mandibles, the low and weak ramus of which, together

457

with the insignificant (not fang-shaped) teeth, clearly indicate that the pigs were domesticated. The fragments are about 30 in number.

The remnants of cattle indicate that the animals were of large size. Many of the fragments show signs of having been worked by human hand. Some mandibles are shaped into cutting implements, the ramus being separated from the other part of the mandible and sharpened to form an edge. Hoes, or perhaps more correctly axes, have been made from the scapulae.

It is remarkable that implements should have been shaped from cattle bones, bones of this kind, owing to their weakness, not being very well adapted to such a purpose. In the European Stone-Age cultures it was chiefly the wild fauna, especially deer, that yielded the material for bone implements. Dr. Dahr consequently suggests, that at least a portion of the bone fragments might have belonged to wild oxen.

In Lo Han T'ang the same species of animals occur as in Ch'i Chia P'ing, but their frequency is quite different. In Lo Han T'ang wild animals such as gazelle and deer abound. Another feature characterizing Lo Han T'ang is the low frequency of pigs, which are represented by only two fragments, whereas more than 300 bone fragments might be indentified as belonging to small ruminants and about 40 to cattle. The latter were probably domesticated, as were also goats and sheep.

The numerous fragments of antelope, deer, hare, and marmot (Arctomys Robusta) indicate that the inhabitants of the dwelling-site were great hunters, able to pursue even very swift animals. It is probable, therefore, that the fragments of dogs (about 20) are derived from animals which assisted the hunters. The fact that the dogs are few in number might be explained by assuming that they did not serve as food.

A striking feature of the mammal remnants from Lo Han T'ang is their split state. This remark has especially reference to long legs of the Ungulata. The ends of these legs have generally been separated from the tubular centre, which has been crushed in order to get at the marrow. Moreover the pelvic bones have regular fractures, which might be explained as being the marks left by a special kind of slaughtering or dismembering implement. The fractures are always very rough and indicate that the bones have been crushed with a primitive and not very sharp implement.

The fact that the pig fragments are few in number while the fragments of wild animals are abundant indicates that the inhabitants of Lo Han T'ang lived by hunting or were cattle-breeding nomads. Undoubtedly did they not have any advanced agricultural system; otherwise the pig — an animal characteristic of a population living by farming — would have been far more abundant. Finally it should be mentioned that the two remnants of pig's bones described above might also be explained as beeing the remains of wild animals occasionally caught by hunters.

458

XVI. TIEN SHUEI HSIEN, E 7 LI, CH'I LI TUN (C. L. T.)

This site, situated in southern Kansu, belongs to a group of sites briefly examined by Professor Andersson's Chinese collector Pai.[1])

The collection from this deposit contains only 49 artifacts (N:ris K. 2353: 1—49). The majority consists of pot-sherds, but there are also among the collection 6 clay-rings, 7 bone implements, 5 (mussel?) shells, 1 flint artifact, the half of a stone-ring and two other stone implements.

Most of the pot-sherds might be attributed to types comparable with Ch'i Chia P'ing I. The quality of the ware is generally high, wherefore the majority correspond to group CC: I a.

The small amphora of Ch'i Chia P'ing type is represented by 5 fragments of small specimens (Pl. 57,8). A neck fragment probably belongs to an urn of very large size (Pl. 56,4).

A fragment of a handle Pl. 55,9 probably emanating from a small amphora is specially interesting, the upper part being ornamented with a cruciform figure, which is undoubtedly related to one of the bought vessels of Ch'i Chia P'ing type (cf. Pl. 23). Another handle of a fragmentary amphora has a long and narrow recess on the upper part, obviously for ornamental purposes.

The bowls the type of which is well known from Ch'i Chia P'ing, are represented by five rim fragments, four of them being annular.

A base portion with mat impressions may be correlated with CC: I a (Pl. 55,14).

A fragment of a big handle of yellow ware (Pl. 55,13) is of exactly the same type as the handles from Ch'i Chia P'ing (cf. p. 391).

Two mouth fragments (Pl. 55,10, 12, 16) and two tripod-legs are made of dark porous ware and have impressions which might emanate from real textile fabric. The fragments now mentioned are of the same type as CC: II.

Further, there are seven clay-rings of grey colour. The cross-section is more or less triangular. The same type of rings was found at Ch'i Chia P'ing and Lo Han T'ang.

Some fragments have no connection with Ch'i Chia P'ing. One fragment (Pl. 55,3) is probably the mouth of a vessel with a pointed bottom (cf. J. G. Andersson, RPC, Pl. 49,1, where a similar fragment from Ma Chia Yao is reproduced).

Another sherd reproduced in Pl. 56,2, might be a fragment of a neck or foot. It is decorated with carelessly incised, horizontal lines, between which are oblique lines of varying size.

A third fragment has the surface covered with a net-work of fine, impressed lines of a type that in some cases appears on vessels with a pointed bottom.

Further, mention should be made of a fragment reproduced in Pl. 55,1, probably emanating from a funnel-shaped foot. The colour of the ware is grey and the surface is decorated with horizontal scratches.

---

[1]) J. G. Andersson, RPC. p. 99—102.

459

Finally, there are five sherds of painted pottery, four of which are indifferent. The fifth sherd (Pl. 56,1) is of the red type with brown painting that is well known from the Honan sites.

XVII. YÜ CHUNG HSIEN, HSIAO SHIH HSIA (H. S. S.).

This site belongs to those localities in southernmost Kansu which were briefly examined by Professor Andersson's collector Pai.

The material from this deposit consists of 33 fragments. Most of them are remnants of large urns (type CC: I) very similar to the specimens excavated at Hsin Tien C.

A small sherd reproduced in Pl. 56,10 has distinct impressions of a basket or a real textile fabric.

Some fragments of coarse ware and provided with cord impressions represent the type CC: II.

Five sherds with painted décor form part of this material. Two of them probably emanate from vessels of Pan Shan type. A small handle of red ware is decorated with oblique black lines, such as occur on the Ma Chang vessels.

Finally, we should mention the urn reproduced in Pl. 56,9. The colour is brown and the surface is carefully smoothed. Below the rim and on the handles there is an incised ornamentation. There is nothing to show that the vessel was not excavated from the deposit, but I wonder whether the vessel was not bought; it seems astonishing that this vessel should be intact while the collection otherwise consists of small sherds. In any case, as a type it is closely connected with two of the bought urns from Ch'i Chia P'ing, reproduced in Pl. 22,3—4.

According to a brief note made by Professor Andersson (RPC. p. 101) a small sherd of an amphora of Ch'i Chia P'ing type was found at Li Hsien, S 3 li, Hung T'ung P'u, one of the sites in south Kansu examined by professor Andersson's collector Pai.

Summing up the results of this brief examination of localities in southernmost Kansu, we find that both the types CC: I and CC: II are found in two of the deposits, whereas the Kamm pottery is not represented. While the collections are too small to enable us to draw more than a few conclusions, they nevertheless prove that the Ch'i Chia P'ing culture was not confined to the locality of Ch'i Chia P'ing. We might be justified in expecting that future explorations of new deposits all over Kansu will enable us definitively to establish the chronology of the Ch'i Chia P'ing era.

XVIII. THE CORRELATION BETWEEN CH'I CHIA P'ING AND LO HAN T'ANG.

Dealing with this intricate problem we first have to notice the different geographical positions of the two sites. The fact that Ch'i Chia P'ing is situated in the plain agricultural district of central Kansu, while Lo Han T'ang is located

460

in the rocky mountains of the Sino-Tibetan borderland, might give the key to many of the problems connected with the question of the correlation between the two sites.

Summing up the results of the examination of the furniture from the two sites we find the following features in common.

In both cultures occur small amphorae with high collar and long handles, although this type is more frequent in Ch'i Chia P'ing than in Lo Han T'ang. Likewise, urns with a funnel-shaped collar and bi-conical or gently rounded profile are known from both sites, although the urns seem to have been much more abundant at Ch'i Chia P'ing. Only a few body fragments of this type have been identified in Lo Han T'ang, the large reconstructed urn not being included in the account. From both sites, moreover, several fragments of medium-sized bowls have been excavated, although this type seems to have been more common in Lo Han T'ang than in Ch'i Chia P'ing.

The types of vessel now described are all attributable, in regard to both sites, to what we call the first class (CC: I resp. LHT: I). Consequently there appears on vessels of the urn type from both sites the same kind of characteristic basket or mat impression that is well known from the large urn found at Lo Han T'ang (Pl. 25,2).

Pursuing our comparison, we further find on both sites a coarser group of ware (CC: II and LHT: II), although the differences in the form, decoration and »constructive impressions» of the vessels are remarkable. Generally the coarse pottery from Lo Han T'ang (LHT: II) is more elegant and often decorated on the belly with superimposed wavy clay bands, an element that is not known from CC: II. A few specimens from LHT: II have almost the same vertical cord impressions as those which characterize CC: II (for instance Pl. 31,4 and Pl 33), but most of the fragments are covered with a net-work of diagonally intersecting cord impressions, which gives the outside a checkerboard pattern. While discussing the subject of coarse pottery, we may note the legs of Li tripods and perforated bottoms as a feature common to both localities; but these types are well known from all prehistoric sites in China, wherefore they afford no evidence of the correlation between Ch'i Chia P'ing and Lo Han T'ang.

If we extend our comparison to CC: III, distinguished by its exquisite Kamm pottery, we find no direct equivalent in Lo Han T'ang; nevertheless I consider that a group of delicate vessels with an exquitite décor in relief or stamped design reproduced in Pl. 37 (cf. p. 440), is related to the Kamm pottery, although they are not ornamented with Kamm impressions. The Lo Han T'ang vessels certainly possess the same delicacy as the Kamm pottery, being thin-walled and decorated with fine superimposed bands or incised ornamentation. One fragment has on the inside of the rim a belt of violet dentations (text fig. 10) which is related to the painted triangles from Ch'i Chia P'ing (Pl. 13,5 b, 7 b). I consider it to be a very important feature that this kind of marginal painting should appear on vessels of related types from both sites.

461

The bone implements and stone artifacts from both sites are similar in many respects, but the forms are of so common a character that they afford no evidence as to the relations between the two sites.

If we now try to determine the most striking difference between the sites, we find that in the Ch'i Chia P'ing furniture there is no counterpart to the abundant group of painted pottery in Lo Han T'ang. As has already been mentioned on page 418, the Ch'i Chia material contains a small collection of painted sherds, most of which might be identified as belonging to vessels of types known from the burial place or dwelling-site of Chu Chia Chai (cf. p. 463), and not as we might expect, to dwelling-site pottery of Ma Chia Yao type; there is not a single sherd of typical Ma Chia Yao pottery among the painted sherds from Ch'i Chia P'ing, while the painted pottery from Lo Han T'ang is closely related to that of Ma Chia Yao.

To sum up the principal facts in the complicated relationships between these sites: there is obviously, on the one hand, a connection between Ch'i Chia P'ing and Lo Han T'ang in the small amphorae and the urns with mat impressions; on the other hand, there is in Ch'i Chia P'ing no counterpart to the rich furniture of painted pottery from Lo Han T'ang, nor are the characteristic »winged» stone knives and the bone knives with flint flakes, so characteristic of Lo Han T'ang, found there.

In accordance with Professor Andersson's chronology, I have placed the description of Ch'i Chia P'ing first in this paper, but I am not convinced that Ch'i Chia P'ing really represents the earliest culture among the prehistoric stages discovered by Professor Andersson. A definite relative chronology cannot be established at present, before much more extensive excavations have been carried out. In the following notes I therefore limit myself to a few remarks bearing particularly on the two sites treated in this paper.

Professor Andersson says (RPC. p. 82): »On account of the very advanced »amphorae» we might feel inclined to assign a relatively recent date to this deposit. On the other hand, we have in Kansu such an unbroken chain of ceramic development from Yang Shao through Ma Chang, Hsin Tien and Ssu Wa far into the Bronze Age that we clearly realize that Ch'i Chia cannot be placed within this ceramic sequence, still less at the top of it. Ch'i Chia is undoubtedly a pre-metallic stage, and consequently we are forced to mark it down as pre-Yang Shao. »[1])

Undoubtedly there are no remnants of metal in the Ch'i Chia culture, but that

---

[1]) By »Yang Shao» in Kansu Professor Andersson means Ma Chia Yao and Pan Shan, which he correlates with Yang Shao Tsun in Honan. All the prehistoric sites, not only those of Kansu but also those of Honan, would thus be organically included in the great »unbroken chain» of development. This correlation of Ma Chia Yao and Pan Shan in Kansu on the one hand and Yang Shao Tsun i Honan on the other seems to me not to have been established beyond dispute. There is a remarkable difference between the Honan sites and the Kansu sites, if we compare, for instance, the dwelling sites of Ma Chia Yao with Yang Shao Tsun and other Honan sites, and, on the other hand the rich Pan Shan grave-field furniture with the meagre contents of the as yet published graves of Yang Shao Tsun.

462

is no reason for placing it first in time. The absence of metal in the finds might be due to a mere accident. I am convinced that the inhabitants of Ch'i Chia P'ing had been in contact with a metal-culture which has influenced the forms of the vessels, although they did not use precious objects of metal in daily life. Vessels and implements of metal may perhaps have served the Ch'i Chia people merely as models. I shall revert to this problem below.

Professor Andersson suggests (RPC. p. 82) that there is stratigraphical evidence in support of his interpretation of Ch'i Chia as being »pre-Yang Shao», since no Yang Shao sherds were ever found in the »undisturbed» Ch'i Chia culture. He further states that he found on the surface of the deposit, in the cultivated fields, quite a number of small Yang Shao sherds, a fact that he explains by the theory that when the Yang Shao people passed from time to time over the abandoned Ch'i Chia settlement they dropped some of their refuse over the area once inhabited by the makers of Kamm pottery and amphoræ.

I venture to suggest that Professor Andersson makes the problem of the age of Ch'i Chia P'ing simpler than it really is by explaining the painted sherds of what he calls Yang Shao type as objects casually dropped by the Yang Shao people.

First I would object to his interpretation on the following grounds: According to a written statement accompanying the collection there are some painted sherds »collected on the surface». These sherds are four in number and all marked with letters, in order to distinguish them from the excavated material. They are illustrated in Pl. 24,6, 13, 23, 24. Other sherds with a painted décor occur to a number of 16; since they are not marked with the letter indicating »surface find», we must reasonably conclude that they belong to the specimens excavated. In any case this is positively sure of at least one of them, the sherd with a chess-board pattern (Pl. 24,14), which is expressly stated to have been excavated by Li at a depth of 1.5 m. The importance of the »surface sherds» (out of which, besides, only 3 are of »Yang Shao» type) seems strongly reduced by these facts.[1])

Secondly I wish to emphasize that the painted sherds of Ch'i Chia P'ing need not necessarily correspond to »Middle Yang Shao» (in Andersson's terminology), they could equally well be styled »late Yang Shao». If we examine the designs of the sherds we find that most of them can be identified as recurring in the Chu Chia Chai culture. The sherds with dentated bands (Pl. 24,6—10, 20) might very well come from vessels of the type illustrated in BMFEA 17, Pl. 1. This urn is, according to Andersson's terminology, of »Middle Yang Shao type», although excavated from a Chu Chia Chai grave (RPC. p. 26). The neck fragment with trellis pattern (our Pl. 24,12) is of the same type as the collar of the urn reproduced in BMFEA 17, Pl. 1,4 or 2,1 (both Chu Chia Chai). The chess-board pattern in our Pl. 24,14

---

[1]) In fact it seems doubtful whether we can justifiably speak at all of an »undisturbed part» of the site, the whole deposit being situated in the farming district of Kansu, where any plot of fertile soil may have been disturbed one or several times during the last three thousand years.

463

might be compared with BMFEA 17, Pl. 1,4, 2,4, 4,4 or BMFEA 15, Pl. 103,18. (all Chu Chia Chai). The marginal sherd in our Pl. 24,15 has its counterpart in BMFEA 15, Pl. 103,21 or 101,8 (both Chu Chia Chai). The meander pattern in our Pl. 24,23 occurs also in the Chu Chia Chai culture (BMFEA 15, Pl. 103,5, 106,2, BMFEA 17, Pl. 3, the urn in the centre), although I doubt whether the colour of the specimen from Chu Chia Chai is the same as the brownish shade of the sherd from Ch'i Chia P'ing. The fuzzy design of the small sherd illustrated in our Pl. 24,11 might be compared to the fragment reproduced in BMFEA 15, Pl. 102,6 and the transverse fields of chess-board pattern illustrated in our Pl. 24,16 to BMFEA 15, Pl. 103,12 (both Chu Chia Chai). The sherds reproduced in Pl. 24,21, 22, 24 are obviously of the same type as a group of sherds from Chu Chia Chai, which Professor Andersson defines as Ma Chang type (BMFEA 15, p. 158—159). They all have a reddish-brown exterior, that in 24,24, however, being of a violet shade. The design is in dark blue-black or violet-brown.

After this detailed examination of the painted sherds we are able to draw the conclusion that although the sherds with dentated bands might be interpreted as belonging to urns of the Pan Shan type, they could equally well belong to vessels of Chu Chia Chai type. Furthermore, some sherds are obviously of another type, related to a group of sherds from Chu Chia Chai, which Professor Andersson defines as being of the »Ma Chang type».

If we extend our comparisons of the Ch'i Chia P'ing and the Chu Chia Chai cultures to the unpainted pottery, we find in the Chu Chia Chai dwelling-site pottery three fragments of a characteristic Ch'i Chia P'ing type (CC: I). These fragments are reproduced in BMFEA 17, Pl. 11,2, 8, 12,7. The most striking resemblance is found in the body fragment shown in 11,8. The two flat knobs are especially noteworthy. They are unknown from the urns belonging to CC: I, but they appear on one of the bought vessels (Pl. 22,5). Moreover, the fragment reproduced in BMFEA 17, Pl. 11,7 might be of the Ch'i Chia P'ing type — although this is not very important — and perhaps also the collar fragments in BMFEA 17, Pl. 10,1, 2, 4—6.

Finally, we should note the striking resemblance between »Chen's big urn» from the burial site (BMFEA 17, Pl. 1,3) and two of the bought Ch'i Chia P'ing vessels reproduced in our Pl. 22,3—4. These vessels are obviously related also to a vessel from Yü Chung Hsien, Hsiao Shih Hsia (Pl. 50). It is not stated whether this vessel was excavated or bought.

Professor Andersson says of the two Ch'i Chia P'ing sherds BMFEA 17, Pl. 11,8, 12,7: »I have no doubt that these two specimens are actually of Ch'i Chia age, which means that they were already old when the Chu Chia Chai people settled here, antique objects left on the spot by some Ch'i Chia emigrants» (BMFEA 17, p. 47 and 63). I doubt whether we can attribute the occurrence of Ch'i Chia P'ing sherds in Chu Chia Chai to mere chance. I am inclined to interpret this fact as an indication that Ch'i Chia P'ing is much more recent than Professor

464

Andersson maintains. This is supported by the obviously advanced character of the amphorae. As far as I can see, they are made in imitation of metallic models. Their often high necks and long handles are not features that are typical of pottery vessels. The imitation of metal is striking in the pot reproduced in Pl. 22,5. The long handle of this vessel has, on the upper part, a clearly visible joint, marked by an incision and two »rivet heads». The same »rivet heads» appear also on the spout.[1]) Even the kidney-shaped opening in the superstructure, the extremely high neck and the body with its bulbous belly and narrow foot part must have been influenced by metal models.

The vessel reproduced in Pl. 23,1 is closely related to the pot mentioned above, both having the collar »vaulted over» by a superstructure unknown in other periods of Chinese prehistoric pottery. Both vessels were bought in Lanchou, but there is no doubt that they represent a real Ch'i Chia P'ing type, since two fragments with the same kind of superstructure were found in the deposit, one of which is reproduced in Pl. 4,3 (cf. p. 392). If we look for the prototypes of the vessels with »over-vaulted» collars and examine the earliest bronzes from historic China, those of the Yin dynasty, we shall find a bronze vessel which has the same kind of superstructure provided with a spout and on the opposite side a hole. The handle is of the same shape as the vessels from the Ch'i Chia P'ing culture. This vessel belonging to the collection of the Museum in Berlin, is published by Kümmel.[2]) He considers this vessel to be of very early date. The resemblance between this bronze vessel and especially the pottery vessel reproduced in Pl. 22,5 is striking (although the bronze vessel has three bulbous legs). If we examine other bronze vessels of early date, we find that the bulbous curvature of the belly and the narrow foot part of the vessel reproduced in Pl. 22,5 are features appearing on many bronze vessels of early age,[3]) wherefore they might equally well appear on vessels of the »over-vaulted» type.

The pots reproduced in Pl. 22,3—4, which are bought vessels, and »Chen's big urn» from Chu Chia Chai likewise have a strongly curved belly and narrow foot part, both features characteristic of the bronze vessels. Since none of the vessels or fragments from the excavated deposit have this narrow foot part, the possibility is not excluded that the bought vessels are slightly more recent than the deposit, but obviously they are in any case closely related to those of the dwelling site. The affinities discussed above between Ch'i Chia P'ing specimens and bronzes of the Yin dynasty seem in fact to indicate that we have to assign a much more recent date to the Ch'i Chia P'ing culture than has hitherto been attributed to it

---

[1]) This pot is reproduced by Professor Andersson in BMFEA 15, Pl. 38, the »joint» on the handle being clearly visible in his reproduction.

[2]) Otto Kümmel, Chinesische Bronzen, Gesellschaft für ostasiatische Kunst. Berlin 1928. P. 9, Pl. 5 and 6.

[3]) Kümmel loc. cit. Pl. 2; Jung Keng, The bronzes of Shang and Chou, Yenching Journal of Chinese Studies, Monograph series no. 17, Vol. II, Peiping 1941, P. 323 and 335. Cf. the reproduction on p. 256 also with specimens illustrated on pp. 412—413.

465

(future excavations may possibly necessitate a dating in more recent times of other cultures as well, at present assigned to very early times). In any case I am convinced that the Ch'i Chia P'ing culture cannot be placed as the very earliest period of prehistoric pottery in China. If this culture is not contemporary with the Yin dynasty, Ch'i Chia P'ing and Yin must anyhow have some prototypes in common — a point that indicates that the Ch'i Chia P'ing culture is of a comparatively recent date. This conclusion cannot be invalidated by the absence of metal or the scarcity of painted pottery. The absence of metal in the excavated finds may, as stated p. 463 above, be due to mere chance: only a very few specimens of bronze have been found in Chinese deposits of the early bronze age.[1]) As to the painted pottery, I have already explained (p. 463) why a fair number of painted sherds can reasonably be considered as emanating from the deposit itself (not only being surface finds). Hence I do not agree with Professor Andersson's theory that the painted sherds were »dropped» specimens. I cannot explain why the painted sherds are so few in numbers; but I certainly cannot accept them, nor the painted triangles on the Kamm pottery vessels, nor the belt of triangles on the small amphorae among the bought vessels as representing the very earliest phase of painting on Far-Eastern pottery, which appears to be Professor Andersson's opinion.[2])

Finally, it should be mentioned that we have two Kansu bronze age sites, Ssu Wa and Ch'ia Yao and a Honan site of probably recent age, Pu Chao Chai, where not a single sherd of painted pottery has been found. Professor Andersson considers this last site to be slightly more recent than Yang Shao Tsun (BMFEA nr 15, p. 66). Furthermore, in the vicinity of Yang Shao Tsun there are two other sites, Hsi Chun Tsun and Yang Ho Tsun, in which elements of a late age occur but no painted pottery (op. cit. above p. 66); these facts support my opinion that the absence or scarcity of painted pottery is no evidence of early age. This is supported by the fact that at Hou Kang, in the vicinity of Anyang, where Chinese archaeologists have carried on scientific excavations, there was found in one section deepest down painted pottery over which was a layer of black pottery and in the top-stratum white pottery, which is thought to be related to the white ware of Yin time (D. G. Wu, op. cit. p. 21). Here again periods with unpainted pottery follow, as more recent stages, upon periods with painted ware.

Another feature that indicates that the Ch'i Chia culture is of more recent age is the advanced character of the mammal remains from the site (compare p. 457). Professor Andersson says in speaking of Dr. E. Dahr's investigation of the material:

---

[1]) Only 5 bronze objects were found on the site of Hui Tsui, and only 3 objects on the grave field of Hsin Tien (Andersson, RPC. p. 171 and 177).

[2]) Bachhofer does not consider Ch'i Chia to be the earliest period, connecting this site with the Hsin Tien stage. I cannot share his opinion, although I admit that there might be some very vague resemblance between CC: III and the Hui Tsui dwelling-site. This question cannot be discussed before the Hui Tsui furniture has been examined (See L. Bachhofer, Zur Frühgeschichte Chinas. Die Welt als Geschichte 1937, p. 270).

466

»Here the domestic animals are more fully represented than in any other site: dogs, pigs, cattle, goats and sheep are all identified from numerous bones. Of deer there are some few fragments.» (BMFEA 15, p. 43).

It is striking that at Lo Han T'ang the pig should be very poorly represented. Cattle are common and were probably domesticated; also the dog. The bulk of the material from this site consists of the bones of wild animals, a fact that indicates that the inhabitants of Lo Han T'ang were great hunters.

If we compare these two sites with Ma Chia Yao, we find that at the latter only the pig and the dog were domesticated.

The investigations just referred to indicate that Ch'i Chia P'ing represents the most advanced of these three cultures, a fact that affords clear evidence in support of my opinion regarding the recent age of the Ch'i Chia culture.

All the investigations so far carried out indicate that there is a certain connection between the Ch'i Chia P'ing culture and Lo Han T'ang manifested by the small amphorae, the urns with mat impressions and the undecorated bowls, although Ch'i Chia P'ing is probably of more recent date than Lo Han T'ang. Ch'i Chia must obviously have been inspired by an advanced metal culture, and, as I have mentioned above, it seems probable that the prototypes of some of the vessel-forms are somehow connected with the Yin bronzes, Ch'i Chia probably being a low culture which has been influenced by the art that flourished in the kingdom of Anyang or its predecessors. I suggest that the Lo Han T'ang culture is of earlier date than the Ch'i Chia culture, although the difference in time is perhaps not so very great. I have already pointed out that the difference might also be interpreted as being of geographical nature, or perhaps a question of tribes. Anyhow the Lo Han T'ang pottery does not show the same influence from metal-objects as is clearly discernible in Ch'i Chia. One LHT fragment of black pottery reproduced in text fig. 11 recalls, it is true, in shape and décor some bronze-vessels of Ordos type,[1]) but this fragment is unique and the conformity not absolute, hence its significance should not be overrated.

But even if we are not able to presume any influence exercised by the metal-working art on the pottery in Lo Han T'ang, it is not out of the question that the characteristic bone knives with flint flakes had metallic prototypes. It seems as if there were a certain resemblance in shape between them and some simple knives of Ordos type. Both types are provided with a handle and have a slightly curved blade.[2])

Professor Karlgren has pointed out that there are simple bronze-knives common to both the Siberian and Mongolian steppe-culture and the culture of earliest China

---

[1]) J. G. Andersson: Hunting Magic in the Animal Style, BMFEA 4, Pl. XIX: 2—5.

[2]) Compare the specimens reproduced in Pl. 53, 26, 27 with J. G. Andersson, Hunting Magic in the Animal Style, BMFEA 4, Pl. 1—4 and B. Karlgren, Some Weapons and Tools of the Yin Dynasty. BMFEA 17, Pl. 27,147, Pl. 29: 158 seq. Pl. 30.

467

(Yin dynasty) (BMFEA 17). These simple prototypes gave rise on the Chinese border to a long process of development ending in very elaborate »inward-curving» types with a ring- or animal's head. This long evolution must have been passed through at a very early date, since Professor Karlgren presumes that the animal-head knives existed already at the beginning of the Anyang era, i. e. in the 13th century B. C. Obviously the Lo Han T'ang knives are to be connected with the simple prototypes mentioned above, not with the advanced specimens with animal's head.

On the subject of tools I have, finally, to mention another fact, which indicates a comparatively recent date not only for Chi Chia P'ing but also for Lo Han T'ang. In Pl. 52,15 is reproduced an asymmetrical stone-knife, the type of which occurs not only in Pu Chao Chai but also in Anyang (J. G. Andersson, RPC. p. 228, Pl. 165,8—10).

DESCRIPTION OF PLATES

Plates 1—19 and 24 reproduce specimens from Ch'i Chia P'ing (with a few specially marked exceptions in Pls. 10, 15). Plate 20 are such from Hsin Tien C. Plates 21—23 are specimens from various places in Kansu. Plates 25—54 illustrate specimens from Lo Han T'ang. Plates 55 and 56 are such from Ch'i Li Tun and Hsiao Shih Hsia.

Plate 1.
Half natural size.

1. K. 11242: 105. Fragment of the rim of a bowl of pale-brown ware with a greyish core. On the interior concentric striations as a result of the clay being smoothed over. The exterior, with the exception of the part nearest the mouth, unsmoothed and covered with scratches. CC: I a.

2. K. 11242: 387. Fragment of neck of brownish ware with brick-red core. On both exterior and interior greyish-yellow slip applied so unevenly that the surface layer has a streaky appearance. CC: I a.

3. K. 11242: 41. Fragment of mouth of brick-red ware. On both exterior and interior a pale yellowish-brown slip. CC: I a.

4. K. 11242: D. Small fragment of a vessel of pale brick-red ware with greyish-white slip on both sides. CC: I a.

5. K. 11242: 23. Fragment of body of brick-red ware with whitish-yellow slip on the outside. The under part of the body covered with mat impressions. CC: I a.

6. K. 11242: 159. Fragment of a body of brownish ware with whitish-yellow slip on the outside. The body smooth, but on its lower part can be discerned faint traces of erased mat impressions. CC: I a.

7. K. 11242: 300. Fragment of body of brownish ware. Typical mat impressions on the outside. CC: I a.

8. K. 11242: 30. Fragment of body of brick-red ware with pale-brown slip. Mat impressions on the outside. CC: I a.

9. K. 11242: 281. Fragment of body of brick-red ware with pale-yellow slip. Mat impressions on the outside. CC: I a.

468

10. K. 11242: 298. Fragment of body of brownish ware with smoothed-over exterior, which also shows traces of partially erased mat impressions. CC: I a.

11. K. 11242: 282. Fragment of handle of whitish-yellow ware. The outside decorated with incised lines and dashes.

12. K. 11242: 24. Fragment of handle of pale-brown ware. The exterior decorated with incised lines. CC: I a.

13. K. 11242: 22. Fragment of handle of white ware with grey core. On the inside traces of mat impressions. Here are also remains of a supporting plug. The exterior decorated with incised crosses. At the join ornamental notches on the rim. CC: I a.

14. K. 11242: 60. Neck fragment with annular rim. The transition to the body marked by a superimposed band ornated with incised pattern of squares. CC: I a.

Plate 2.
Half natural size.

1. K. 11242: 73. Fragment of neck of brick-red ware. Triple profile on the inside of the mouth. CC: I a.

2. K. 11242: 120. Fragment of mouth of brick-red ware with surface layer and greyish-brown core. The rim of the mouth flattened. CC: I a.

3. K. 11242: 396. Fragment of mouth of brick-red ware. Brown slip on the exterior. The rim flattened. The transition to the body marked by an imposed band decorated with an incised pattern of squares. CC: I a.

4. K. 11242: 63. Fragment of rim of a bowl. Brick-red ware. The inside smooth. On the exterior at the mouth is a turned-over rim, below which is faintly seen an indistinct mat impression. CC: I a.

5. K. 11242: 315. Fragment of distinctly bi-conical bowl. Brick-red ware. The tone of the exterior partly brownish. The lower part of the body shows mat impressions. CC: I a.

6. K. 11242: 290. Small fragment of body of brick-red ware. On the exterior mat impressions. CC: I a.

7. 11242: 294. Fragment of body of brick-red ware. The exterior, the colour of which is brown, shows basket impressions. CC: I a.

8. K. 11242: 295. Fragment of body of brown ware. On the exterior impressions. CC: I a.

9. K. 11242: 356. Fragment of bottom of brick-red ware. On the exterior yellowish-white slip. On the outside of the bottom faint traces of fine mat impressions or something similar. On the inside coarser basket impressions. CC: I a.

10. K. 11242: 341. Fragment of a bottom of brick-red ware. On the exterior traces of coarse mat impressions. The bottom attached to the wall of the vessel on the inside, which can be plainly seen on the picture. CC: I a.

11. K. 11242: 370. Fragment of bottom with bi-conical holes. Pale-brown ware CC: I a.

12. K. 11242: 14. Fragment of bottom of brick-red ware. On the exterior mat impressions in twill-plaiting. CC: I a.

Plate 3.
Half natural size.

1. K. 11242: 818. Small amphora of pale-brown ware. One handle missing. The other bears mat impressions. The bottom not particularly clearly defined. CC: I b.

2. K. 11242: 107. Fragment of neck and body of a large vessel. Brick-red ware

469

with brownish surface layer and grey core. The transition of the neck to the body marked by an incised line. CC: I b.

3. K. 11242: 260. Large fragment of body of brick-red ware. The tone of the exterior pale-yellow with red spots. The greater part of the body covered with mat impressions. CC: I b.

4. K. 11269: 2. Small pot of brick-red ware. The tone of the exterior light brown with red spots. The vessel provided with only one handle. On the body is discernible a mat impression, which has been intentionally almost smoothed out. The same impression also on the outside of the bottom, where another impression, possibly of wood, can also be observed. CC: I b.

5. K. 11242: 144. Fragmentary bowl of brick-red ware. Both on the outside and the inside pale yellowish-grey slip. On the outside is faintly seen a mat impression, which is almost smoothed| out. The join between the bowl and the base which has been fastened on the inside is seen plainly. The quality of the ware high, but the production technique poor. CC: I b.

Plate 4.
Half natural size.

1. K. 11242: 166. Fragment of neck of pale-brown ware. CC: I b.

2. K. 11242: 37. Fragment of neck and body of brick-red ware with yellowish-white slip on both sides. The transition of the neck to the body marked by incised crosses. CC: I b.

3. K. 11242: 380. Fragment of jug of type 5. Pale-brown ware. CC: I b.

4. K. 11242: 283. Small fragment of the upper part of the body of a vessel. Brown ware with greyish core. Decoration of double rows of stamped triangles. Ware clean but loose. CC: I b.

5. K. 11242: 216. Fragment of vessel of brick-red ware with brown slip. The transition of the neck to the body marked by an incised pattern of squares. CC: I b.

6. K. 11242: 407. Fragment of lid with flat knob. Pale-brown ware. CC: I b.

7. K. 11242: 377. Fragment of small vessel. Pale-brown with darker core. CC: I b.

8. K. 11242: 381. Fragment of neck with a fragmentary handle. Pale-brown ware. CC: I b.

9. K. 11242: 431. Fragment of small vessel. Brick-red ware. Brown slip on the exterior. CC: I a.

10. K. 11242: 403. Fragment of rim of a bowl. Brick-red ware with pale yellowish-brown slip. The rim ornamented with oblique notches. CC: I a or b.

11. K. 11242: 398. Fragment of rim of a bowl. Brick-red ware with pale-brown core. Both on exterior and interior pale-yellow slip. The rim decorated with ornamental dentations. CC: I a or b.

12. K. 11242: 272. Fragment of body of brick-red ware with greyish layer farthest in. The exterior covered with dirty grey slip and partly coated with soot. The lower part of the body shows impressions. CC: I a or b.

13. K. 11242: 293. Fragment of body of pale-brown ware with greyish-brown core. On the exterior mat impressions. CC: I b.

14. K. 11242: 312. Small fragment of body of brick-red ware. On the exterior mat impressions. CC: I a (ware) or b (technique).

15. K. 11242: 278. Fragment of body of brownish-red ware with greyish core. On the exterior pale greyish-yellow slip. Mat impressions. CC: I a or b.

16. K. 11242: 197. Fragment of body of brown ware. On the exterior mat impressions. CC: I b (or c).

470

17. K. 11242: 297. Fragment of body of brown ware. On the exterior impressed pattern of squares. CC: I b (or c).

18. K. 11242: 334. Fragment of body with bottom. Brick-red ware. On the exterior pale yellowish-white slip. Mat impressions on the body. The bottom fastened from the outside. CC: I a or b.

Plate 5.
Half natural size.

1. K. 11242: B. Fragment of neck of thick brown ware. Transition to the body marked by an incised pattern of squares. CC: I a.

2. K. 11242: 57. Fragment of neck of thick brown ware. Transition of the neck to the body marked by an imposed band with pattern of squares. CC: I c.

3. K. 11242: 25. Fragment of neck and body of thick brown ware. Transition to the body marked by a belt with incised pattern of squares. CC: I c.

4. K. 11242: 859. Small bowl on foot, probably a lamp. Brownish-grey ware. Traces of red colour. CC: I c.

5. K. 11242: 268. Fragmentary lid of brick-red ware with grey surface layer. CC: I c.

6. K. 11242: 269. Fragment of lid with knob. The rim ornamented with oblique notches. Brown ware with grey surface layer. CC: I c.

7. K. 11242: 812. Fragmentary lid of pale-brown ware. The edge ornamented with half-moon shaped incisions. CC: I c.

8. K. 11242: 267. Fragment of a lid with knob, the edge of which is ornamented with a row of depressions. Brown ware with grey surface layer. Coated with soot. CC: I c.

9. K. 11242: 150. Fragment of body with handle. Greyish-brown ware with red-brown core. On the handle an impression in pattern of squares. CC: I c.

10. K. 11242: 103. Fragment of rim of bowl. Brownish-red ware. On the exterior basket impressions. CC: I c.

11. K. 11242: 774. Fragment of body with handle, which is decorated with a snake in relief. On the body mat impressions. Brownish-grey ware. CC: I c.

12. K. 11242: 336. Fragment of body and bottom. Brown ware. The body covered with mat impressions. At the base on the inside triangular impressions, marks left in the fabrication. CC: I b.

13. K. 11242: 99 and 29. Fragment of a rim of thin, brown ware. The edge kidney-shaped, inbent. CC: I c.

14. K. 11242: 145. Bowl on low foot ornamented with oblique notches. Brownish-yellow ware. CC: I b.

Plate 6.
Half natural size.

1. K. 11242: 10. Fragment of rim with spout. Inside the rim of the mouth a broad groove for a lid. Pale-brown ware. On the exterior soot spots. A little below the mouth mat impressions, which are also present on the handle. These are bordered by crescent-shaped ridges, after which follows a smooth part nearest to the mouth. CC: II b.

2. K. 11242: 335. Fragment of base of pale-brown ware. Mat impressions. CC: II a.

3. K. 11242: 436. Fragment of vessel of yellowish-brown ware. The exterior of the body covered with cord impressions and provided with a knob handle. CC: II a.

4. K. 11242: 33. Fragment of vessel of brown ware. Soot spots both on the exterior and the interior. The exterior of the body covered with basket impressions. CC: II b.

5. K. 11242: 815. Fragment of vessel of brown ware. The body covered with impressions. Strong soot coating over the whole exterior and in spots in the interior also. CC: II b.

471

6. K. 11242:816. Small pot of brown ware with soot coating on the exterior. On the body cord impressions. Interior thickening towards the bottom. CC: II b.

Plate 7.
Half natural size.

1. K. 11242:461. Fragment of vessel of brick-red ware with brown slip on both sides. The mouth decorated with incisions. Transition between the neck and body marked by a torus decorated with incised crosses. The body covered with cord impressions. CC: II a.

2. K. 11242:446. Fragment of a vessel of brown ware with slip of much the same colour. The mouth decorated with oblique notches. The body shows cord impressions. Nearest to the neck they are partially smoothed over but remain as ornamental ridges between the incised furrows. CC: II b.

3. K. 11242:36. Fragment of rim with greatly thickened mouth, the outer edge of which is ornamented with oblique notches. Brick-red ware with pale-yellow slip on both sides. Mat impressions on the exterior. CC: II b.

4. K. 11242:11. Fragment of rim with thickened mouth the outer edge of which is bent in waves. On the exterior mat impressions. Immediately below the mouth a smoothed-over portion. Brick-red ware with greyish core and pale-brown surface layer. CC: II a. Fig. b. negocoll positive.

5. K. 11242:462. Fragment of rim with thickened mouth, the outer edge of which is bent in waves. Below the mouth smooth furrows between which a part of the mat impressions, which for the rest cover the body, have been obliterated. CC: II b.

6. K. 11242:147. Fragment of body with large handle. Brick-red ware with pale-brown slip. The lower part of the body covered with mat impressions, which also occur on the under-side of the handle. CC: II b.

7. K. 11242:26. Fragment of neck of greyish-brown ware. Transition between neck and body marked with an imposed band ornamented with an incised pattern of squares. CC: II b.

9. K. 11242:53. Fragment of rim of brick-red ware with brownish tone on the exterior. Immediately below the mouth a border ornamented with oblique notches. CC: II b.

10. K. 11242:35. Fragment of rim of pale-brown ware with reddish core. 30 mm. below the mouth indented moulding. CC: II b.

11. K. 11242:574. Fragment of vessel of brown ware with pale greyish-yellow slip. Large patches of sooth both on the exterior and the interior. The body and the outer-side of the handle covered with cord impressions, which, although nearly erased, can be discerned also on the outside of the neck. CC: II b.

12. K. 11232:4. Fragment of vessel of yellowish-red ware. The exterior of the body covered with cord impressions. CC: II b.

13. K. 11242:52. Fragment of vessel of pale-brown ware. On the exterior and interior pale greyish-yellow slip. The exterior of the body covered with basket impressions. CC: II b.

14. K. 11242:249. Fragment of tripod of brick-red ware with brownish surface layer. The exterior covered with basket impressions. CC: II b or a.

15. K. 11242:718. Fragment of body and bottom of brown ware. The bottom attached from the interior and the edge of the wall of the vessel turned over. The body covered with cord impressions. On the under-side of the bottom an indistinct mat impression or something of the kind. CC: II b.

16. K. 11242:202. Tripod leg of brick-red ware. Cord impressions CC: II b.

472

17. K. 11242: 715. Fragment of bottom of brown ware. The bottom attached from the outside. The body has cord impressions. CC: II b.

18. K. 11242: 366. Fragment of bottom with hole. Brick-red ware. On the exterior brown slip and traces of soot. CC: II b.

Plate 8.
Half natural size.

1. K. 11242: 441. Fragment of neck of greyish-brown ware. The body covered with cord impressions. The join between the neck and body clearly apparent. CC: II b.

2. K. 11242: 573. Fragment of neck of brown ware. On the exterior soot spots. The body and handle covered with cord impressions. CC: II b.

3. K. 11242: 493. Fragment of rim, strengthened by a superimposed band. On the exterior impressions of a mat or something similar. CC: II a.

4. K. 11242: 705. Fragment of body and bottom of cloven vessel the cutting made from inside. Brown ware. Cord impressions on the body. CC: II a.

5. K. 11242: 576. Fragment of rim of cloven vessel. Cord impressions both on the exterior of the body and on the flat rim of the mouth. Pale brick-red ware. CC: II a.

6. K. 11242: 555. Fragment of rim and body of cloven vessel, with faint convex profile, cutting made from the outside. Pale brick-red ware. The exterior of the body covered with cord impressions. The rim of the mouth has a slightly hollowed profile. CC: II a.

7. K. 11242: 577. Fragment of body with rim of mouth of cloven vessel. On the exterior mat impressions. The fragment composed of two sherds joined together. The fracture appears plainly in the reproduction. CC: II a.

8. K. 11242: 707. Fragment of cloven vessel of brick-red ware. The cut here goes straight through the wall of the vessel. CC: II a.

9. K. 11242: 717. Fragment of bottom of cloven vessel. Faulty cut, which shows that the cut was made from the inside. Brown ware. Soot spot on the exterior. CC: II b.

Plate 9.
Half natural size.

1. K. 11242: 566. Fragment of body of brick-red ware covered on both sides with thick brown slip. Cord impressions on the exterior (fig. 2 negocoll positive). CC: II b.

2. K. 11242: 478. Fragment of neck of pale brick-red ware. On the exterior basket impressions which also continue on the neck (fig. b negocoll positive). CC: II b.

3. K. 11242: 559. Fragment of body of brown ware. Cord impressions. Soot spots on the exterior and in places on the interior. CC: II b.

4. K. 11242: 4. Fragment of body of pale-brown ware. On the exterior impressions of plaited work (fig. b negocoll positive). CC: II a.

5. K. 11242: 727. Fragment of body of thin, brown ware. Mat impressions on the outside, which is coated with soot. Soot spots also appear on the inside and fracture surfaces (fig. b negocoll positive). CC: II b.

6. K. 11242: 567. Fragment of body of yellowish-brown ware. The tone of the exterior brown. Cord impressions. CC: II b.

7. K. 11242: 249. Fragment of a tripod of brick-red ware with brownish surface layer. The exterior covered with basket impressions in »wicker-work» (fig. b negocoll positive). CC: II b.

8. K. 11242: 664. Fragment of body of pale-brown ware. Cord impressions on the exterior (fig. b negocoll positive). CC: II A.

473

Plate 10.
Natural size.

1. K. 11242: 16. Fragment of neck of brick-red ware with flamy exterior in yellow and red. Indented moulding below the mouth. Basket impressions (fig. b negocoll positive). CC: II b.

2. K. 11242: 558. Fragment of body of brown ware with reddish surface layer. On the exterior cord impressions (fig. b negocoll positive). CC: II b.

3. K. 11269: 27. Hsin Tien C. Small fragment of body and neck of brown ware. Basket or textile impressions (fig. b negocoll positive). CC: II a.

Plate 11.
Natural size.

1. K. 11242: 7. Fragment of body of brick-red ware with yellowish-brown slip on both sides. Cord impressions on the exterior (fig. b negocoll positive). CC: II a.

2. K. 11242: 667. Small fragment of body of brown ware with soot coating on the exterior. Cord impressions (fig. b negocoll positive). CC: II.

3. K. 11231: 3. Small fragment of body of brown ware (fig. b negocoll positive). CC: II b.

Plate 12.
Half natural size.

1. K. 11242: 3. Fragment of vessel of pale-brown ware. Below the ear a dark spot. On the inside of the neck brownish-purple colour. The exterior decorated with Kamm impressions (partly applied on relief bands) and opposed pairs of stamped ornaments. CC: III.

2. K. 11242: 834. Fragment of vessel of pale-brown ware. The exterior covered with mat impressions; similar impressions can also be traced on the inside. Exterior décor of relief lines with or without Kamm impressions. CC: III.

3. K. 11242: 857. Fragment of vessel of dark greyish-brown ware. On the exterior mat patterns and décor of relief lines and Kamm impressions and stamped ornaments in the form of angles. On the lower part of the neck the points of these have been directed upwards and downwards alternately. Coating of soot on both exterior and interior. CC: III.

4. K. 11242: 848. Small fragment of body of pale-brown ware. On the exterior mat impressions and relief ornamentation in meander pattern. CC: III.

5. K. 11242: 4. Small fragment of upper part of body. Dirty-brown ware. Exterior décor of relief lines and Kamm impressions. Soot marks both on the exterior and the interior. CC: III.

6. K. 11242: 845. Fragment of vessel with piece of bottom. Brownish-yellow ware. On the body mat impressions and décor of relief lines. CC: III.

7. K. 11242: 844. Small fragment of body of brown ware. Exterior relief in meander pattern. Traces of soot on both sides. CC: III.

8. K. 11242: 846. Fragment of bottom and body of greyish-brown ware. Mat impressions on the body and relief décor in meander pattern. CC: III.

9. K. 11242: 777. Small fragment of body of dirty-brown ware. Mat impressions and décor of relief lines on the exterior. CC: III.

10. K. 11242: 838. Fragment of vessel of brick-red ware with brownish tone on the exterior. Décor of Kamm lines and on the handle stamped triangles and rhombs. CC: III.

11. K. 11242: 6. Small fragment of neck of pale brownish-yellow ware. The inner-

474

side painted over with brownish-purple colour. On the exterior décor of Kamm impressions and stamped ornamentation in the form of chevrons. CC: III.

12. K. 11242: 839. Fragment of vessel of brownish-yellow ware. On the body mat impressions. The handle and neck ornamented with Kamm impressions. On the latter also stamped ornamentation in the form of triangles with the points directed alternately upward and downward. Soot marks on the exterior. CC: III.

13. K. 11242: 842. Small fragment of neck of brownish-grey ware. Decoration in the form of relief band with Kamm impressions and between them rows of short lines. Soot coating on the exterior. CC: III.

14. K. 11242: 841. Fragment of neck and body of brown ware. Traces of mat impressions and décor of Kamm impressions on the exterior. On the handle two ornamented knobs, one of which is missing. CC: III.

Plate 13.
Half natural size.

1. K. 11242: 858. Fragment of vessel of brownish-yellow ware. On the exterior soot marks and mat impressions. On the inner-side faint traces of the same impressions. Décor of Kamm impressions. The handle fragmentary. CC: III.

2. K. 11242: 1. Fragment of vessel of pale-brown ware. On the body and handle mat impressions and soot marks. Décor of Kamm impressions, relief lines and incised ornamentation of short zigzag lines. CC: III.

3. K. 11242: 7. Fragment of vessel of pale light-brown ware. On the exterior mat impressions. Décor of relief band and Kamm impressions. On the body and handle two pairs of knobs provided with a round incision. On both sides of the neck and on the upper part of the body surface painting in reddish-purple tone. CC: III.

4. K. 11242: 835. Fragment of pale-brown ware. On the body mat impressions. Décor of imposed band and stripes in relief and Kamm impressions. Also ornamental knobs with round incisions. Soot coating on the exterior. CC: III.

5. K. 11242: 8. Fragment of vessel of pale greyish-brown ware. On the exterior mat impressions and décor of relief band and Kamm impressions. On the handle and neck also double stamped impressions and on the latter two ornamental knobs with same kind of stamped impressions. On the inner-side of the neck (see fig. b) décor of broad painted lines in brownish-purple tone. On the upper part of the handle traces of the same colour. The exterior for the rest coated with soot. CC: III.

6. K. 11242: 27. Fragment of vessel of pale-yellow ware with reddish spots. Basket impressions on the exterior. CC: III.

7. K. 11242: 843. Small fragment of neck of brown ware. On the exterior décor of relief lines, Kamm and other stamped ornamentation in the form of three parallell lines. On the interior painted triangles in brownish-purple colour. Soot coating on the exterior. CC: III.

8. K. 11242: 847. Fragment of body of brown ware. On the exterior mat impressions. Décor in the form of a relief band with short oblique Kamm impressions. CC: III.

9. K. 11242: 855. Small fragment of body of yellowish-brown ware. On the exterior mat impression and relief band with Kamm impressions. CC: III.

10. K. 11242: 854. Fragment of body of same type as the preceding. Dirty-grey ware. CC: III.

11. K. 11242: 5. Fragment of neck with handle of a large vessel. Dirty-brown ware. Décor of continuous lines in zigzag pattern, and on the handle also two ornamental knobs. CC: III.

475

Plate 14.
Half natural size.

1. K. 11242: 575. Fragmentary vessel of pale-brown ware. On the exterior relatively coarse mat impressions. The neck and the upper part of the body smooth. The handle ornamented with two knobs with indentation in the centre. One knob missing. Soot spots on the exterior. CC: III?

2. K. 11242: 719. Fragment of vessel of brown ware. On the exterior (and also on the inner-side of the handle) mat impressions. Traces of the same impression also on the interior. CC: III.

3. K. 11242: 726. Fragment of vessel of pale greyish-yellow ware. Flamy tone on the exterior which has mat impressions. Traces of the same impressions also on the inner-side. Immediately below the mouth, edging of white indented moulding. CC: III.

4. K. 11242: 724. Fragment of vessel of pale-brown ware. Mat impressions on the exterior. Immediately below the mouth, short borders of indented moulding. CC: III.

5. K. 11242: 12. Fragment of vessel of brick-red ware. The tone of the outside greyish. The body and neck covered with mat impressions on the exterior. Immediately below the rim of the mouth a short border of indented moulding. Heavy soot coating on the exterior. CC: III.

6. K. 11242: 758. Fragment of vessel of pale-grey ware. On the exterior mat impressions. Immediately below the smooth rim of the mouth, indented relief band CC: III.

7. K. 11242: 771. Fragment of neck of brick-red ware. On the exterior mat impressions and soot marks. Immediately below the rim of the mouth, relief band resembling cord. CC: III.

8. K. 11242: 721. Fragment of vessel of brownish-yellow ware. Mat impressions on the exterior. Faint traces of the same impression on the inner-side as well. Immediately below the mouth, border of indented moulding. The exterior coated with soot. CC: III.

9. K. 11242: 770. Small neck fragment of yellowish-brown ware. On the outside mat-impressions. Below the rim of the mouth indented relief band. CC: III.

10. K. 11242: 789. Small fragment of dirty-brown ware. On the outside mat impressions. CC: III.

11. K. 11242: 783. Fragment of not demarcated bottom. Mat impressions even on the bottom. CC: III.

12. K. 11242: 837. Fragmentary vessel of brown-red ware. The exterior, which shows mat impressions, is covered with a coating of soot. The neck decorated with a border of indented moulding bordered above by vertical Kamm impressions, below by stamped chevron ornamentation with points turned upwards and downwards alternately.

Plate 15.
Natural size.

1. K. 11242: 798. Lump of pale yellowish-red clay. Obliquely bored hole, which does not pass through the centre.

2. K. 11242: 827. Fragmentary animal sculpture of burnt clay. Brown ware.

3. K. 11242: 748. Lump of burnt clay of pale yellow colour. The surface uneven.

4. K. 11242: 744. Fragment of greyish-brown clay. The upper side perforated with small holes, which do not go through the whole wall.

5. K. 11269: 10. Hsin Tien C. Clay object in mushroom shape.

6. K. 11242: 205. Fragment with a knob ornamented with fold-like incisions. The colour of the ware pale yellowish-brown.

476

7. K. 11242: 207. Fragment of ring-shaped foot. Brick-red ware. Exterior coated with soot.

8. K. 11242: 203. Fragmentary, entirely hollow leg of a little tripod. The colour of the ware pale-brown.

9. K. 11242: 749. Fragment of spinning whorl. Brick-red ware of high quality; the colour of the surface layer paler than the core. On the side reproduced, faintly discernable mat impressions. Diam. 70 mm.

10. K. 11242: 751. Fragment of spinning whorl of conical form. The quality of the ware coarser than in the preceding one. The colour pale yellowish-brown. Diam. 59 mm.

11. K. 11242: 821. Fragment of clay ring. Grey ware. Rounded triangular section.

12. K. 11242: 800. Fragment of clay ring. Grey ware. Triangular section.

13. K. 11242: 824. Fragment of clay ring. Grey ware. Triangular section.

14. K. 11242: 822. Fragment of clay ring. Greyish-black ware with black, shiny polished exterior. Triangular section.

15. K. 11242: 825. Fragment of clay ring. Oval section.

Plate 16.
Natural size.

1. K. 11242: f. Point of bone needle. — 2. K. 11242: a. Point of bone needle. — 3. K. 11242: e. Point of bone needle. — 4. K. 11242: 826. Fragment of bone needle or something similar. — 5. K. 11242: c. Fragment of bone needle. — 6. K. 11242: ö. Fragmentary bone needle. — 7. K 11242: Ä. Fragmentary bone needle. — 8. K. 11242: Z. Fragmentary bone needle with eye. — 9. K. 11242: b. Point of bone needle. — 10. K. 11242: Å. Bone needle with fragmentary eye. — 11. K. 11242: d. Bone needle with eye. — 12. K. 11242: 829 a. Fragment of bone needle with eye. — 13. K. 11242: 832. Awl with attachment score. — 14. K. 11242: T. Awl. — 15. K. 11242: g. Awl. — 16. K. 11242: P. Awl. — 17. K. 11242: Q. Awl. — 18. K. 11242: V. Awl. — 19. K. 11242: X. Awl. — 20. K. 11242: 819. Fragment of Awl. — 21. K. 11242: 828. Bone implement. — 22. K. 11242: N. Weaving implement. — 23. K. 11242: 831. Bone implement resembling chisel. — 24. K. 11242: S. Weaving stick. — 25. K. 11242: O. Weaving stick. — 26. K. 11242: R. Weaving stick. — 27. K. 11242: 829. Bead.

Plate 17.
Two-thirds of natural size.

1. K. 1383. Stone-axe. Edge fragmentary but has probably been polished. L. 180 mm. Br. 57 mm. at the edge. Thickness 45 mm. at the middle.

2. K. 1338. Neck fragment of axe. Narrow sides hewn.

3. K. 1384. Small axe of green-stone. Partly polished. L. 110 mm. Br. 50 mm. Thickness 27 mm.

4. K. 1379. Fragmentary axe of polished green-stone. The narrow sides also polished. Br. 66 mm. Thickness 30 mm.

Plate 18.
Two-thirds of natural size.

1. K. 11242: 6. Spear-head of slate. In the centre of the blade a not entirely perforated bi-conical hole. — 2. K. 11242: 801. Triangular spear-head of slate.

3. K. 1342. Fragmentary axe of ground green-stone. Hole for string.

477

4. K. 11242:758. Dagger-head of clay-stone. Edge sharpened.

5. K. 1340. Small axe of green-stone. Edge sharpened. Length 84 mm. Breadth 35 mm. Thickness 24 mm.

6. K. 1327. Chisel of ground chistose rock. Cross-section regular. Length 80 mm. Breadth 11 mm. Thickness 11,5 mm.

7. K. 1378. Chisel of ground argilaceous stone. Length 86 mm. Breadth 22 mm. Thickness 18 mm.

8. K. 1324. Axe of ground argilaceous stone. Back side fragmentary. Breadth 29 mm. Thickness 18 mm.

9. K. 11242:754. Implement of quartz. — 10. K. 1363. Fragment of spinning-whorl.

Plate 19.
Two-thirds of natural size.

1. K. 1331. Unfinished stone knife. Sandstone. L. 80 mm. Br. 50 mm. Thickness 8 mm.

2. K. 1334. Stone knife of sandstone. Corresponding inward curves on the short sides. L. 61 mm. Br. 44 mm. Thickness 11 mm.

3. K. 1355. Fragmentary stone knife of sandstone. Bored hole. L. 65 mm. Br. 44 mm. Thickness 10 mm.

4. K. 1385. Polished knife of green-stone. In the middle bi-conical hole. L. 79 mm. Br. (at the middle) 45 mm. Thickness 9 mm.

5. K. 1335. Knife of green-stone with sharpened edge. Bi-conical hole. L. 82 mm. Br. 39 mm. Thickness 6 mm.

6. K. 11242:H. Ground edged knife of slate. Bi-conical hole. Edge clearly curved towards the latter. L. 100 mm. Br. (at the middle) 46 mm. Thickness 6 mm.

7. K. 1364. Beating stone.

8. K. 1330. Stone club with double attachment scores crossing each other on the narrow sides. Br. 65 mm. Thickness 32 mm.

9. K. 11242:797. Fragment of sandstone. In the middle obliquely bored hole.

Plate 20.

1. K. 11269:7—8. Hsin Tien C. Large fragmentary vessel with straight walls. Brownish-yellow ware. On the exterior pale yellowish-grey slip. Mat impressions on the exterior. Large pieces broken off close to the rim of the mouth. Size 1/3.

2. K 11269:5. Hsin Tien C. Fragmentary urn of brick-red ware with brown surface layer. On the exterior, and to some extent also in the interior, soot marks. The outside of the body covered with basket or textile impressions. Size 1/2.

3. K. 11269:6. Hsin Tien C. Fragment of neck and body of brown ware. Soot marks both on the exterior and interior. The outside of the body covered with cord impressions. Size 1/2.

4. K. 11269:4. Hsin Tien C. Medium-sized urn of brick-red ware. Soot coating at the base on both outside and inside. The exterior covered with mat impressions. Immediately below the rim of the mouth, border of indented moulding. Size 1/3.

5. K 11269:3. Hsin Tien C. Fragmentary pot with two handles, one of which is missing. Pale brick-red ware. On the exterior and on the inner-side of the neck, pale greyish-yellow slip. The neck attached from the exterior. Soot marks both outside and inside. The body and the middle part of the handle covered with cord impressions. Above the handle at the rim of the mouth five ornamental nail impressions. Size 1/2.

478

Plate 21.

1.   K. 5428. Ning Ting Hsien. Pa Pao Tsui. Bought. Urn with funnel-shaped neck and bi-conical· body with rudimentary handles. The colour of the ware pale yellowish-brown. On the lower part of the body are seen faint traces of basket impressions. Height of the vessel 22.5 cm. Greatest breadth 13.6 cm. Diameter of mouth 12 cm; of the bottom 6.1 cm. Size 1/2.

2.   K. 6042. Ti Tao Hsien. Ma Chia Yao. Urn of pale yellowish-brown ware with gently rounded profile and provided with two handles. The lower part of the body covered with basket impressions. On both sides of the neck remains of thick, red colour. Height of vessel 29 cm. Greatest breadth 17.4. Breadth of handles 2.1 cm. Diam. of mouth 12.2 cm; of bottom 6.8 cm. Size 2/3.

3.   K. 5423. Urn with high funnel-shaped neck and bi-conical body, which has had two handles. The transition to the body marked by an incised line. The lower pail of the body covered with basket impressions. Size 2/3.

4.   K. 5433. Kansu. Bought. Urn with funnel-shaped neck and bi-conical body with gently rounded transition of the vertical profile. Brick-red ware. On the exterior yellow-grey slip and dark spots of oil or something similar. The lower part of the body covered with basket impressions, which continue on to the bottom. Height of vessel 22.3 cm. Greatest br. 14.8 cm. Diam. of mouth 10.2 cm; of bottom 7.1 cm. Size 1/2.

Plate 22.
One third of natural size.

1.   K. 11269: 1. Hsin Tien C. Large, fragmentary urn of brick-red smooth ware of highest quality. The tone of the exterior flamy in pale yellowish-brown brick-red. The body distinctly bi-conical and without handles. On its lower part basket impressions.

2.   K. 5426. Bought in Chin Chou. Medium-sized urn with funnel-shaped neck and bi-conical body provided with two small handles. Height of vessel 250 mm. Greatest br. 155 mm. Br. of handles 20 mm. Diam. of mouth 130 mm.; of bottom 90 mm. On the neck and upper part of body concentric striations, on the lower indistinct mat impressions.

3.   K. 5422. Ning Ting Hsien, P'ai Tzu P'ing. Bought. Medium sized vessel with wide mouth and bi-conical body, the greatest breadth of which lies below the middle of the vessel, which rests on a ring foot perforated with four holes. At the mouth two larger and two smaller handles. Very loose ware of bright yellowish-brown colour. The exterior smooth; now somewhat eroded. Height of vessel 190 mm. Greatest br. 212 mm. Br. of handles 19, 11, 18 and 12 mm. Diam. of mouth 140 mm; of foot 93 mm.

4.   K. 5963. Yü Chung Hsien, Hsiao Shih Hsia. Medium-sized vessel of same type as the preceding one. The profile of the body is, however, gently rounded in this case. Terracotta-coloured ware with dark spots, soot particles or something similar. Height of vessel 186 mm. Greatest br. 178 mm. Br. of handles 11 and 16 mm. resp. Outer diam. of foot c. 91 mm. The vessel is largely reconstructed.

5.   K. 5523. Bought in Lanchou. Jug with high neck and squat body. The mouth covered with a vaulted »roof» provided with a spout and a kidney-shaped hole. The transition between the neck and body marked by an incised line. The broad handle which has at the top a joint with two »rivet heads» is ornamented with two groups of incised lines. The fragmentary spout provided with two »rivet heads». Height of vessel to the rim of mouth 19.8 mc. Greatest br. 15 cm. Br. of handle 4.6 cm. Diam. of bottom 19.2. Dark grey ware with greyish core. The exterior smooth and showing faint traces of red colour. On the under-side of the bottom and of the handle indistinct mat impressions.

479

Plate 23.
Half natural size.

1. K. 5427. Bought in Lanchou. Jug of pale-brown ware with darker spots. Two-thirds of the mouth covered by a vaulted »roof», from which runs a spout approximately 18 mm. high. Height of vessel 156 mm; greatest br. 104 mm. Br. of handle 31 mm. Diam. of bottom 58 mm.

2. K. 5487. Chin Chou. Chen Chia Chai. Bought. Small amphora with 54 mm. high neck, somewhat widened at the top, and bi-conical body. Height of vessel 131 mm. Greatest br. 86 mm. Diam. of mouth c. 82 mm. Diam. of bottom 52 mm. Br. of handle 24 mm. Colour of ware pale yellowish-brown. On the inside of neck and handle faint traces of red colour. One handle and parts of neck reconstructed.

3. K. 6563. Particulars of the vessel's provenience missing. Small amphora with very high neck. Smooth ware of brick-red colour. Height of vessel 125 mm. Greatest br. 88 mm. Br. of handle 33 mm. Diam. of mouth 90 mm. Diam. of bottom 47 mm. On the neck and handle clearly pronounced marks from smoothing. One handle and part of the neck reconstructed.

4. K. 5429. Bought in Lanchou. Small amphora of pale-brown ware with reddish-brown spots. Form of body distinctly bi-conical. Height of vessel 110 mm. Greatest br. 86 mm. Br. of handles 26 and 27 mm. resp. Diam. of mouth 98 mm. Diam. of bottom 56 mm. Both handles ornamented with four lines, arranged in pairs, between which are placed three ornamental notches. Ornamentation carelessly executed.

5. K. 5467. Bought in Lanchou. Small amphora of brownish-red smooth ware. Height of vessel 108 mm. Greatest br. 67 mm. Br. of handles 30 mm. Diam. of mouth 90 mm. Diam. of bottom 50 mm. The upper part of the handles decorated with an hour-glass-like stamped ornamentation surrounded by four ornamental holes.

6. K. 5606. Kao Lan Hsien. Tzu Shih Chuang. Very small amphora of brick-red ware with large grey and greyish-brown spots. Height of vessel 74 mm. Greatest br. 74 mm. Diam. of mouth 62 mm. Diam. of bottom 45 mm. Br. of handles 22 mm. There is no distinct line of demarcation between the body and bottom and the technical quality is considerably poorer than in the others.

7. K. 5430. Bought in Lanchou. Small vessel resembling amphora of brownish-yellow, smooth ware. Height of vessel 95 mm. Greatest br. 80 mm. Br. of handles 28 mm. Diam. of mouth 72 mm. Diam. of bottom 40 mm. The demarcation of the bottom surface not so clearly defined as in the majority of the bought vessels. The upper part of the body ornamented with triangles in purple colour. One handle broken off and the rim of the mouth damaged.

8. K. 5992. Ti Tao Hsien. Yen Chia Chuang. Small vessel resembling an amphora of pale yellowish-brown ware. Height of vessel 94 mm. Greatest br. 105 mm. Br. of handles 20 mm. Diam. of mouth 104 mm. Bottom surface somewhat convex and its demarcation not very clearly defined. The transition between neck and body marked by an incised line. Small portions of the vessel reconstructed.

9. K. 5469. Bought in Yü Chung Hsien. Chin Hsien. Small vessel resembling an amphora with pear-shaped body. Smooth ware of dark brick-red colour. Height of vessel 95 mm. Greatest br. 93 mm. Br. of handles 25 mm. Diam. of mouth c. 89 mm. Diam. of bottom 68 mm. On its under-side dents, which may possibly be impressions of a plaited mat. (Cf. pl. 2, fig. 12).

Plate 24.
Natural size.

1. K. 11242: 802. Fragment of grey ware. The sherd provided with two circular, bi-conical holes. — 2. K. 11242: 780. Fragment of grey smooth ware. The sherd

provided with two small holes bored through. — 3. K. 11242: 550. Fragment of grey ware. Exterior decorated with an incised pattern of squares. — 4. K. 11242: 728. Small fragment of neck and body of grey ware. Body covered with mat impressions. — 5. K. 11242: 47. Small fragment of mouth; yellow ware with a large admixture of gravel. — 6. K. 11242: I. Sherd with painted décor in black and brown. — 7. K. 11242: 764. Sherd with painted décor in black and brown. — 8. K. 11242: 760. Sherd with painted décor in black. — 9. K. 11242: 813. Sherd with painted décor in black and reddish-brown. — 10. K. 11242: 807. Sherd with painted décor in black and dark-brown. — 11. K. 11242: 812. Sherd with painted décor in black and brown. — 12. K. 11242: 762. Sherd with painted décor in brownish-black. — 13. K. 11242: 1. Sherd with painted décor in lighter and darker brown. — 14. K. 11242: 761. Sherd with painted décor in brown. — 15. K. 11242: 752. Sherd with painted décor in brownish-black.

16. K. 11242: 809. Sherd with painted décor in brownish-black. — 17. K. 11242: 808. Fragment with handle. Painted décor in brownish-black. — 18. K. 11242: 766. Fragment with painted décor in pale brown. — 19. K. 11242: 810. Fragment with painted décor in brown. — 20. K. 11242: 765. Fragment with painted décor in brown. — 21. K. 11242: 814. Fragment of brown ware with red shade on the outside. Painted décor in violet brown. — 22. K. 11242: 811. Fragment of red ware with greyish spot on the outside. Painted décor of the same type as the above. — 23. K. 11242: K. Fragment with painted décor in brown. — 24. K. 11242: L. Fragment of red brown ware with a violet shade. Painted décor in blue-black. — 25. K. 11242: 763. Fragment with painted décor in dark purple. — 26. K. 11242: 104. Fragment of thrown foot of pale-grey ware. — 27. K. 11242: 23. Fragmentary lid of pale-grey ware. — 28. K. 11242: 773. Fragment with painted décor in dark brownish-purple.

*   *   *

Plate 25.

1. K. 12003: 1549. Small bi-conical amphora with high and wide collar. Fragments of long lugs attached to the belly and the rim. Height 130 mm. Outer diam. of the mouth 64 mm. Thickness of the wall 4 mm. Ware brownish. Surface polished. Part of the collar subsequently discoloured. Size 1/2.

2. K. 5824. Very large urn with slightly flaring collar, at the base of which is a superimposed band, 13 mm. broad, divided by diagonal incisions into rhombi. The upper part of the vessel is smooth, without any impressions. The lower part is covered with mat impressions. Below the equatorial line two lugs. Height 460 mm. Width 297 mm. Outer diameter of the mouth 170 mm. Size 1/4.

3. K. 12003: 1550. Fragmentary armlet of burnt clay, tapering towards one margin. Colour dirty-brown. Height 90 mm. Width 70—80 mm. Thickness of the wall 6 mm. Size 1/2.

4. K. 12003: 1671. Hollow lump of burnt clay. Toy? In the interior small balls rattle when shaken. Colour greyish brown. Size 1/2.

5. K. 12003: 1676. Ball of burnt clay. Colour grey. Size 1/1.

6. K. 1675. Ball of burnt clay. Colour grey-brown. Size 1/1.

Plate 26.

1. K. 2170: 44. 3 belly fragments. Brick-red ware of highest quality. Outside yellow. Upper part smooth. On lower part mat impressions. Thickness of wall 7 mm. Size 2/3.

481

2. K. 12003: 629. Belly fragment of brick-red ware with yellow surface. Base of darker colour. On the lower part mat impressions. Ware of highest quality. Thickness of wall 5 mm. Size 1/2.

3. K. 12003: 857. Lug and belly fragment of brick-red ware with grey core. Surface yellow with mat impressions. Thickness of wall 5 mm. Size 1/2.

4. K. 2170: 45. Belly fragment of brick-red ware with yellow surface. Ware of highest quality. Outside covered with mat impressions. On the upper part fragment of lug. Thickness of wall 7 mm. Size 2/3.

5. K. 12003: 893. Neck fragments of small vessel with narrow collar. Brown ware with brick-red core. On the outside of the collar, vertical scratches. Surface polished. Thickness 3 mm. Size 1/2.

6. K. 12003: 1456. Two fragments of a large vessel of brown ware. The outside covered with regular vertical cord impressions and decorated with superimposed wavy band. Thickness 8 mm. Size 2/3.

7. K. 12003: 1672. Spinning-whorl (?) or pendant of yellowish-brown clay. In the centre not entirely perforated hole, bored from both sides. On the illustrated side, intersecting cord impressions. Size 1/1.

Plate 27.

1. K. 12003: 927. Neck fragment of a large vessel with wide low collar. Coarse brown ware. Wall 12 mm. Below the rim, a band in relief with indistinct impressions. Size 1/2.

2. K. 12003: 834. 8 fragments of bowl with flaring rim. Brick-red ware of high quality. One of the fragments is discoloured from brick-red to dark brown. Thickness 4 mm. Surface carefully smoothed. Size 1/2.

3. K. 12003: 799. Marginal fragment of bowl of brownish-red ware with pale-yellow surface. Thickness 5 mm. The rim profiled. Size 1/2.

4. K. 12003: 836. 13 fragments of bowl with flaring rim and accentuated bottom. Brown ware of high quality. Average thickness 7 mm. Size 1/2.

Plate 28.

1. K. 12003: 796. 2 fragments of bowl with flaring rim. Ware of highest quality. Colour brick-red with pale spots on the outside. The smaller fragment has become brown on the inside through discoloration. Thickness 8 mm. Size 2/3.

2. K. 12003: 829. Two fragments of a bowl with flaring rim. Ware of the highest quality. Colour brick-red. The outside pale. The smaller fragment has become greyish brown through discoloration which is clearly visible in the reproduction. Thickness 5 mm. Size 2/3.

3. K. 12003: 687. Fragment of a bowl, the mouth of which has a rim. Size 2/3.

4. K. 12003: 820. Fragment of a bowl, the mouth of which has a rim. Size 2/3.

5. K. 5959. Four fragments of an urn with gently curved profile. Ware mixed with quartz. Colour pale yellowish-brown with brick-red spots. Lug missing. Thickness 6 mm. Size 1/2.

Plate 29.

1. K. 12003: 915. Fragment of collar of large vessel. Flaring rim. Ware yellow. Surface not polished (?). Thickness 11 mm. Size 2/3.

2. K. 12003: 679. Fragment of high collar with projecting flaring rim. Ware brown. Surface not polished (?). Thickness 7 mm. Size 1/2.

3. K. 12003: 680. Fragment of flaring rim. Brown ware of high quality. Thickness 7 mm. Size 1/2.

482

4. K. 12003:706. Fragment with lug. Ware greyish brown. Lug decorated with superimposed wavy band. Thickness of the wall 8 mm. Size 1/2.

5. K. 12003:810. Neck fragment of yellow ware, hard-baked but mingled with quartz. Probably slip on the outside. Collar curving outwards and provided with a rim. Thickness of the body 8 mm., of the neck 6 mm. Size 1/2.

6. K. 12003:756. Two fragments of a bi-conical vessel. Ware yellowish brown with grey core. The upper part has become grey through discoloration. Size 1/2.

7. K. 12003:859. Fragment of brick-red ware with superimposed band having three oblique fossae and forming a handle. Thickness 7 mm. Size 1/2.

8. K. 12003:755. Small sherd of brick-red ware with grey core. Bi-conical hole drilled from both sides. Thickness 5 mm. Size 1/1.

9. K. 12003:749. Fragment of yellow ware of highest quality. A hole bored from the outside. Thickness 3 mm. Size 1/1.

10. K. 12003:866. Base fragment of a vessel consisting of 53 different sherds. Ware of highest quality, brick-red in tone with grey core. Thickness 7 mm. Size 1/2.

Plate 30.

1. K. 12003:892. 3 fragments of bowl of yellow-brown ware. One of the fragments (to the right in the plate) dark grey through discoloration. Height 82 mm. Thickness 5—6 mm. Size 1/2.

2. K. 12003:804. Marginal fragment probably of a bowl. Pale reddish-brown ware. On the inside two splashes of red-brown paint. Thickness 6—8 mm. Size 1/2.

3. K. 12003:891. Marginal fragment of a bowl, contracting towards the mouth. Pale-brown ware. A piece of the distinct bottom is visible. Thickness about 6 mm. Size 1/2.

4. K. 12003:701. Marginal fragment of bowl with flaring rim. Grey ware of highest quality. Surface polished. Thickness 5 mm. Size 1/2.

5. K. 12003:684. Marginal fragment of bowl with flaring rim. Pale greyish-brown ware of highest quality. Surface polished. Thickness 3 mm. Size 1/2.

6. K. 12003:677. Marginal fragment of bowl with rim. Ware pale-grey of highest quality. The rim and the lower part of the body polished. Thickness 4 mm. Size 1/2.

7. K. 12003:890. Fragment of upper part of bi-conical vessel without collar. Brick-red ware with pale-brown core. The outside polished. Thickness 9 mm. Size 1/2.

Plate 31.

1. K. 12003:116. Small basin of yellowish ware mingled with quartz and mica. Surface rough. On the outside indistinct impressions. Below the rim a lump of clay has been pressed into the wall, probably in order to conceal a crack. Shape irregular. Height circa 75 mm. Diameter of the bottom 45 mm. Size 2/3.

2. K. 12003:910. Oblique mouth of brick-red ware with pale-brown core. Ware mixed with quartz. Thickness 5—9 mm. Size 2/3.

3. K. 12003:907. Narrow collar of yellowish coarse ware. Mica grains clearly visible on the surface. Thickness 6—8 mm. Size 2/3.

4. K. 6309. Urn of coarse brownish ware. The profile of the vessel is slightly curved and the mouth expanding. The outside from the shoulder downwards covered with vertical cord impressions. At equal intervals superimposed wavy clay bands. On the bottom clearly visible traces of basket impressions. Height 240 mm. Equatorial size 238 mm. Diameter of the mouth c:a 116 mm. Diameter of the bottom 120 mm. Size 1/3.

483

Plate 32.

1. K. 12003: 1455. 11 fragments of the upper part of a large vessel. Ware yellow with brick-red spots, well baked but to some extent mixed with mica and quartz. The outside covered with vertical cord impressions and decorated with superimposed wavy clay bands. Thickness 7 mm. Size 1/2.

2. The inside of the vessel described above. The construction of the vessel is clearly disclosed by cracks between the different coils superimposed one over the other. Size 1/2.

Plate 33.

1 a. K. 12003: 913. Neck fragment of large vessel. Coarse yellow ware. Outside and inside sprinkled with mica. Rim flaring. Exterior and rim covered with regular diagonal cord impressions. Thickness 11 mm. Size 2/3.

1 b. Clay model positive of fragment above.

Plate 34.

1. K. 12003: 1475. 2 marginal fragments of a bowl with contracting rim. Ware pale brown, well baked but mixed with quartz and mica. The outside covered with vertical cord impressions. Below the mouth a smooth zone. Inside, traces of red colour. Thickness 7 mm. Size 2/3.

2. K. 12003: 985. Marginal fragment of a bowl with contracting rim. Ware well baked but mixed with quartz and mica. The outside covered with deep vertical cord impressions. Below the rim a horizontal furrow. Thickness 8 mm. Size 2/3.

3. K. 12003: 1002. Marginal fragment. Vertical section almost straight. Coarse greyish-brown ware. Surfaces sprinkled with mica grains. On the outside, indistinct vertical cord impressions. On the part below the rim a superimposed ridge with 5 deep fossae and forming a handle. Thickness 9 mm. Size 2/3.

4. K. 12003: 1472. Marginal fragment of a bowl with contracting rim. Ware grey, well baked. Below the rim a smooth zone limited by a horizontal furrow, below which diagonal cord impressions are visible. Thickness 11 mm. Size 2/3.

5. K. 12003: 1008. 2 marginal fragments. Vertical section almost straight. Coarse greyish-brown ware. Surfaces sprinkled with mica. On the part below the rim a superimposed ridge forming a handle. Thickness 8 mm. Size 2/3.

6. K. 12003: 989. Marginal fragment of coarse pale-brown ware. The vertical section almost straight. The outside covered with cord impressions. Thickness 9 mm. Size 2/3.

7. K. 12003: 968. Marginal sherd of yellow ware with grey core. Well baked but mixed with mica and quartz. Surface rough. On the part below the rim a strongly protruding knob forming a handle. Thickness 11 mm. Size 2/3.

8. K. 12003: 1012. Marginal fragment of coarse brown ware, grey on the outside. Surface sprinkled with mica. The vertical section straight. On the rim and the outside of the wall are diagonal cord impressions. On the part below the rim are marks left by a knob. Thickness 15 mm. Size 2/3.

Plate 35.

1. K. 12003: 903. Neck fragment of pale-brown ware mixed with quartz. On the surfaces sooty spots. On the outside cord impressions. Below the rim a superimposed clay band decorated with oblique fossae. Thickness 7 mm. Size 2/3.

2. K. 12003: 904. Neck fragment of the same kind as described above. Probably pieces of the same vessel. Thickness 7 mm. Size 2/3.

484

3. K. 12003: 905. Neck fragment of brownish ware mixed with quartz. The outside sooty and dark. Around the margin is a superimposed band, decorated with crescent-shaped oblique impressions. Thickness 6 mm. Size 2/3.

4. K. 12003: 926. Neck fragment of a vessel with flaring rim. Coarse grey ware. On the outstanding rim and the body are traces of cord impressions, scarcely visible in the reproduction. Thickness 10 mm. Size 2/3.

5. K. 12003: 1016. Body fragment with lug. Ware brick-red with yellow surface, well baked but mixed with quartz. Lug ornated with superimposed wavy clay band. Thickness of the wall 6 mm. Size 2/3.

6. K. 12003: 1302. Body fragment of coarse brick-red ware. Surfaces sprinkled with mica. The outside covered with intersecting cord impressions and provided with a superimposed ridge, with oblique fossae, forming a handle. Thickness 9 mm. Size 2/3.

7. K. 12003: 1015. Body fragment with lug. Coarse yellow ware. On the outside are traces of diagonal cord impressions. Lug ornamented with a superimposed wavy band. Thickness 6 mm. Size 2/3.

Plate 36.

1. K. 12003: 936. Fragments of an urn of brick-red ware, well baked but mixed with quartz and mica. The outside is darker with sooty spots. The profile slightly curved with collar turning outwards. The exterior covered with intersecting cord impressions. Round the neck a superimposed wavy clay band. On the belly are superimposed wavy clay bands, forming a kind of decoration. Size 2/3.

2. K. 12003: 930. 3 neck fragments of an urn of coarse yellow ware with red spots. Collar slightly curved outwards. Between the collar and the body is superimposed a wavy clay band. The outside covered with intersecting cord impressions. Thickness 6 mm. Size 2/3.

3. K. 12003: 1190. Body fragment of coarse brick-red ware, dark-brown on the outside. Surface covered with irregular, partly intersecting cord impressions and decorated with superimposed, wavy clay bands, placed horizontally or vertically. Thickness 10 mm. Size 2/3.

4. K. 12003: 1267. Body fragment of coarse brick-red ware with sooty spots on the surface. The outside covered with horizontal cord impressions and decorated with a superimposed coiled snake. Head missing. The spots on the skin are denoted by oblique impressions. Thickness 9 mm. Size 2/3.

Plate 37.

1. K. 12003: 954. Fragment of small urn of coarse brown ware. Collar provided with a rim. Vertical section of the body slightly curved. The outside covered with coarse cord impressions. On the neck and the lower part of the body are superimposed horizontal clay bands. Between the horizontal zones are groups of diagonal super-imposed clay bands in pairs. Thickness 8 mm. Size 2/3.

2. K. 12003: 1019. Fragment of small vessel of coarse ware; colour yellow. On the outside are white spots. The mouth provided with a rim. Extending from the mouth to the upper part of the body is a broad lug. On the outside of the body are indistinct cord impressions. On the neck and below the lug, superimposed wavy clay bands. The entire lug decorated with superimposed wavy clay bands set close together. On the inside are traces of violet colour. Thickness 4 mm. Size 2/3.

3. K. 12003: 962. 5 fragments of the neck of a small vessel. Thin, well-baked ware mixed with quartz and mica. Colour pale-brown. Collar slightly expanding towards the mouth which is provided with a rim. Extending from the mouth to the upper part

485

of the vessel is a small lug. At the rim and on the outside are spots of soot. On the outside are indistinct oblique cord impressions. The neck decorated with a superimposed wavy clay band. Thickness 8 mm. Size 2/3.

4. K. 12003: 935. Fragment of a small thin-walled vessel of coarse pale-brown ware. Surface rough. Collar slightly curving outwards. Profile of the wall gently curved. On the upper part of the vessel a small lug. The neck decorated with a superimposed wavy clay band. Thickness 5 mm. Size 2/3.

5. K. 12003: 964. Neck fragment of a thin-walled vessel of brown, well-baked ware, mixed with quartz and mica. Surface dirty. Flaring rim, inside is a groove. Below the rim a small lug. At the neck and below the rim are horizontal furrows in pairs, forming a kind of decorative system. Between the furrow-zones a smooth section ornamented with a wedge in relief. Thickness 4 mm. Size 2/3.

6. K. 12003: 919. Neck fragment of yellow ware with brick-red core. The collar provided with a rim. Surface rough. On the upper part of the body two knobs forming a pair of mammae. Thickness 6 mm. Size 2/3.

7. K. 12003: 901. Neck fragment of pale-brown ware. The collar slightly curving outwards. Soot on the rim and the lowest part of the body. The outside is covered with intersecting cord impressions. Below the rim a superimposed wavy clay band under which are placed groups of short raised clay strings. Thickness 5 mm. Size 2/3.

8. K. 12003: 902. 3 fragments of a vessel of greyish-brown ware. The collar slightly curving outwards and provided with a rim. The wall of the body gently curved. The outside covered with cord impressions. At the neck a superimposed wavy clay band under which are placed groups of short raised clay strings. The relief decoration painted in violet. Thickness 5 mm. Size 2/3.

9. K. 12003: 900. Neck fragment of dark greyish-brown ware, porous but almost free from quartz and mica. Flaring rim. Neck decorated with groups of vertical striae alternating with horizontal groups. In the centre of the decoration a small knob. Thickness 6 mm. Size 2/3.

Plate 38.

1. K. 12003: 551. Small fragmentary vessel of coarse greyish-brown ware. Mouth slightly curving outwards. Body gently curved. On the upper part of the vessel is a small lug. On the outside and also on the bottom, traces of cord impressions. Round the neck and on the lug are superimposed wavy clay bands. On the belly, groups of small diagonally placed clay strings. Below them, on each side, a knob. Height 105 mm. Diameter of the bottom 60 mm. Thickness 6 mm. Size 2/3.

2. K. 12003: 948. Neck fragment of brown ware mixed with mica and large grains of quartz. Low collar with flaring rim. The outside covered with intersecting impressions. Round the neck a superimposed wavy clay band decorated with groups of fossae. Thickness about 7 mm. Size 2/3.

3. K. 12003: 1106. Fragment of the leg of a Li tripod of brown ware. Size 2/3.

4. K. 12003: 1053. Base fragment of coarse dark-brown ware. The bottom flat. On the outside are traces of cord impressions and superimposed wavy clay bands. Thickness of the wall about 8 mm. Size 2/3.

5. K. 12003: 1104. Fragment of a tripod leg(?) of brown ware. Size 2/3.

6. K. 12003: 1044. Neck fragment of a small vessel provided with a lug. Ware coarse and sooty on the outside. Size 2/3.

7. K. 12003: 1263. 2 fragments of brick-red ware, well baked but mixed with mica and quartz. The outside has become brown by discoloration and is sooty; decorated with a superimposed wavy clay band. Thickness 6 mm. Size 2/3.

486

8. K. 12003: 1104. Fragment of the leg of a Li tripod of brown ware of high quality. Size 2/3.

9. K. 12003: 1060. Base-fragment of coarse grey ware with brown core. The bottom flat. On the outside of the wall and on the bottom are traces of cord impressions. The body ornamented with two superimposed clay bands. Thickness 7 mm. Size 2/3.

10. K. 12003: 1103. Fragment of the leg of a Li tripod. Ware coarse, pale-brown with red spots. On the outside cord impressions. Size 2/3.

11. K. 12003: 1112. 9 base-fragments of coarse brown ware. The bottom flat. The outside of the wall and the bottom covered with oblique intersecting cord impressions. The exterior wall decorated with short superimposed clay strings. Thickness of the wall 7 mm. Size 2/3.

Plate 39.

1. K. 12003: 1110. Base fragment of porous greyish-brown ware. The outside and the bottom covered with irregular intersecting cord impressions. The same impressions also visible on the bottom of the interior. Through the wall, a hole drilled from the outside. Thickness of the wall 8 mm., remarkably homogeneous. Size 1/2.

2. K. 12003: 1075. Fragment of steamer of coarse pale-brown ware. The wall is expanding towards the rim, a piece of which is preserved. Bottom perforated. The outside covered with spots of cord impressions. Thickness 11 mm. Size 2/3.

3. K. 12003: 1079. Base fragment of Hsien steamer of brown, well-baked ware. On the outside are diagonal cord impressions. Thickness 8 mm. Size 2/3.

4. K. 12003: 1480. Base fragment of coarse greyish-brown ware. Surfaces sprinkled with mica. On the outside are horizontal cord impressions. Thickness 11 mm. Size 2/3.

Plate 40.

1 A. K. 12003: 1196. 3 fragments of coarse brown ware with sooty surface. On the outside, typical diagonal intersecting cord impressions. Thickness 11 mm. Size 2/3.

1 B. Clay model positive of the fragments described above.

2 A. K. 12003: 1388. Fragment of a big vessel of yellow ware mixed with mica. The outside is ornamented with a broad clay band and covered all over with typical diagonal intersecting cord impressions. Thickness 12 mm. Size 2/3.

2 B. Clay model positive of the fragment described above.

3 A. K. 12003: 1197. Fragment of coarse brick-red ware with brown surfaces. The outside is covered with typical diagonal intersecting cord impressions. Thickness 11 mm. Size 2/3.

3 B. Clay model positive of the fragment described above.

Plate 41.

1. K. 12003: 1143. Fragment of brown ware with brick-red core. Surfaces sprinkled with mica. On the upper part of the outside sparse diagonal cord impressions, on the lower part the same kind of impressions but intersecting. Thickness 10 mm. Size 2/3.

2. K. 12003: 1070. Fragment of well-baked brick-red ware mixed with mica and quartz. Surfaces probably covered with a thin slip. On the outside impressed network. Thickness 9 mm. Size 2/3.

3. K. 12003: 1462. Body fragment of a large vessel of pale-brown ware. The outside covered with diagonal intersecting cord impressions. Thickness 8 mm. Size 2/3.

4. K. 6309. Bottom of the urn reproduced in Plate 31, fig. 4. Distinct basket impression. Size 2/3.

487

Plate 42.

1. K. 12003: 395. Two fragments of the belly of a large bi-conical vessel of pale-brown ware of high quality. The upper part of the vessel (to the equatorial line) polished. The belly is ornamented with a painted décor in black consisting of a system of fine concentric lines horizontally grouped and bounded at equal distances by heavy vertical strokes. In the middle of the horizontal zone are two fine oblique lines. The horizontal line-groups are bounded by heavy lines. The lower part of the vessel undecorated. Thickness 6 mm. Size 2/3.

2. K. 12003: 115. Fragment of the upper part of bi-conical vessel of red-brown ware of high quality. Painted décor with heavy vertical stripes at the equatorial line bounded by two horizontal lines. Thickness 5 mm. Size 2/3.

3. K. 12003: 397. Two fragments of the body of a bi-conical vessel of pale-brown ware of highest quality. The outside polished. Black painting: on the upper part three parallel lines and two big circle-dots. The equatorial line bounded by four concentric lines, and below them fragments of a zigzag line. Thickness 7 mm. Size 2/3.

4. K. 12003: 396. 8 fragments forming the upper part of a big, bi-conical vessel of pale-brown ware, partly discoloured to darker brown. The outside polished all down to the lowest part. Black painting: on the upper part concentric circles and various figures bounded at the equatorial line by three parallel lines, and below them a wavy line. Below this polished and painted part of the body, a rough zone ornamented with a superimposed wavy band. Thickness 10—12 mm. Size 2/3.

5. K. 12003: 160. Belly fragment ornamented with a group of concentric circles, in the centre a horizontal line. Size 2/3.

Plate 43.

1. K. 12003: 171. Neck fragment of pale-brown, partly discoloured ware of highest quality. Low collar with flaring rim. Collar and outside of the body polished. Painted décor in black. Thickness 8 mm. Size 2/3.

2. K. 12003: 255. Neck fragment of brick-red ware of highest quality. The outside is pale and not very carefully smoothed. Painted, black décor, forming a zone of parallel lines; to the lowest one is attached a spot(?). Thickness 8 mm. Size 2/3.

3. K. 12003: 896. Fragment of coarse ware mixed with quartz and mica. On the outside are traces of intersecting cord impressions. Superimposed ridge with vertical fossae, forming a handle. Traces of cord impressions also on the ridge. Below the handle, two parallel lines painted in black. Thickness about 8 mm. Size 2/3.

4. K. 12003: 895. Four fragments of a large vessel, the upper part of which is made of carefully worked clay. The ware of the lower part is coarser and mixed with quartz. Colour yellow with brick-red spots. The profile of the vessel is only slightly curved. The upper part is carefully smoothed externally and decorated with a pattern of parallel lines and circle segments. The transition to the lower part is marked by a furrow, above which is a ridge with oblique impressions of a cone-shaped implement. Below the furrow, a line of incised holes. Lower part covered with intersecting cord-like impressions. Thickness 7—8 mm. Size 2/3.

5. K. 12003: 405. Fragment made of the same two kinds of clay as those mentioned above. Profile bi-conical. The upper part decorated with black painting forming a pattern of circle segments and parallel lines. On the lower part, vertical cord impressions. Thickness 7 mm. Size 2/3.

488

Plate 44.

1. K. 12003: 894. Two fragments of pale-brown ware. The upper part of high quality, surface smoothed and decorated with a painted pattern consisting of horizontal lines and circle segments. The lower part of coarse ware. The transition to the lower part marked by a ridge decorated with oblique impressions made by a comb-like implement. Below the ridge, groups of impressed holes(?). Thickness: upper part 5 mm., lower part 9 mm. Size 1/2.

2. K. 12003: 897. Fragment of the same type as above. Surface of the outside is smeared over with a layer of clay, under which vertical cord impressions are visible. Traces of a now lost handle. Thickness 7 mm. Size 1/2.

3. K. 12003: 244. Neck fragment of brick-red ware mixed with quartz. The outside pale-yellow and decorated with a painted pattern consisting of parallel lines, between which is a zone of vertical lines. Thickness 5—7 mm. Size 2/3.

4. K. 12003: 256. Neck fragment of pale-brown ware. The outside decorated with a painted pattern consisting of circles and dots. Thickness 7 mm. Size 2/3.

5. K. 12003: 253. Neck fragment of pale-brown ware with grey core. The outside smoothed and decorated with parallel lines, between which is a zone with drop-shaped spots. Thickness 6 mm. Size 2/3.

6. K. 12003: 143. Neck fragment of pale-brown ware of high quality. The mouth curving outwards. The neck decorated with parallel lines. Thickness 5 mm. Size 2/3.

7. K. 12003: 249. Neck fragment of small vessel. Quality of the ware high. Colour pale-brown. The flaring rim decorated with a pattern in black paint. On the outside of the neck, traces of concentric circles. Thickness 5 mm. Size 2/3.

8. K. 12003: 246. Neck fragment of brick-red ware of high quality. Rim flaring. The outside of the collar decorated with thick parallel lines. Thickness 5 mm. Size 2/3.

9. K. 12003: 389. Rim fragment of a vessel with contracted mouth, below which is a hole for tying up a crack. Quality of the ware high. Colour pale-brown. The outside decorated with a pattern of concentric circles. Thicknes 5 mm. Size 2/3.

10. K. 12003: 254. Neck fragment of large vessel. Coarse pale-brown ware. Colour of the outside brighter. Surfaces rough. The outside of the neck decorated with heavy parallel lines in black paint. Thickness of the body 10—12 mm., of the neck 8 mm. Size 2/3.

11. K. 12003: 240. Neck fragment of large vessel with flaring rim. Quality of the ware high. Colour brown. The outside of the neck decorated with a pattern of parallel lines and circle segments. Thickness 7—8 mm. Size 2/3.

Plate 45.

1. K. 12003: 278. Fragment of large vessel of pale-brown ware. Upper part made of well purified clay; the outside carefully smoothed. Lower part made of coarse ware, its outside rough, showing traces of cord impressions. Upper part decorated with black painting. Below the ornamented zone, a lug. Thickness 8 mm. Size 2/3.

2. K. 12003: 281. Fragment of yellow ware, brown inside. Quality of the clay high. The outside is smooth (now partly eroded) and decorated with a black-painted pattern consisting of parallel lines and circle. Small lug. Thickness 6 mm. Size 2/3.

3. K. 12003: 282. Fragment of thin, pale-brown ware. On the outside is a small lug. Thickness 4 mm. Size 2/3.

4. K. 12003: 277. Fragment of pale-brown ware with lug, ornamented with a superimposed wavy clay band. Above and below the lug are traces of painted parallel lines. Thickness 5 mm. Size 2/3.

489

5. K. 12003: 267. Fragment of a small bowl of brick-red ware. Surface pale-yellow. The outside decorated with groups of concentric circles. Thickness 6 mm. Size 2/3.

6. K. 12003: 367. Four fragments of a bowl of yellow ware of high quality. The mouth provided with a rim. Both outside and inside decorated with a painted pattern of parallel lines. Four holes for tying up cracks. Thickness 7 mm. Size 2/3.

Plate 46.

1 a. K. 12003: 158. Two fragments of the upper part of a bowl of yellow ware of highest quality. The flaring rim decorated with pattern of circles and oblique lines. There is also a pattern of parallel lines below the rim. Thickness 6 mm. Size 2/3.

1 b. The inside of the same bowl. Traces of decorative painting.

2. K. 12003: 368. Two fragments of a bowl. Ware good, but the surfaces not very carefully treated. The mouth provided with a rim which is painted black. Thickness 6 mm. Size 2/3.

3. K. 12003: 217. Fragment of a bowl. Quality of ware good. Colour pale-brown. The outside decorated with a pattern of black lines. The inside ornamented with triangles and parallel lines. Thickness 6 mm. Size 2/3.

4 a. K. 12003: 219. The inside of a bowl of highest quality. Colour pale greyish-white. Painted decoration of wedges and parallel lines. On the left side is a hole for tying up a crack. Thickness 6 mm. Size 2/3.

4 b. The outside of the same fragment. Colour pale-yellow. Painted pattern consisting of groups of lines and circle.

5 a. K. 12003: 209. The inside of a bowl. Ware pale-brown. Surfaces smoothed. The inside decorated with wedges. Colour of the décor brown. Thickness 7 mm. Size 2/3. 5 b. The outside of the same.

Plate 47.

1 a. K. 12003: 203. Eight fragments of a bowl with flaring rim. Quality of the ware high. Colour pale-grey. Painting executed in a brown colour. Rim ornamented with a pattern of dots alternating with oblique lines. On the outside of the body, groups of lines. Thickness 5 mm. Size 2/3.

1 b. The inside of the same bowl. The decorative painting consists of curved lines, parallel lines and trellis pattern.

2 a. K. 12003: 191. Fragment of a bowl of pale-yellow ware of high quality. Surfaces smoothed. The flaring rim and the outside decorated with the same pattern as in fig. 1. Thickness 5 mm. Size 2/3.

2 b. The inside of the same bowl. Decorative pattern consisting of curved or straight parallel lines.

3 a. K. 12003: 375. Fragment of a bowl of reddish-brown ware. Quality of the ware high. Surfaces smoothed. The rim and the outside of the body ornamented with black lines forming a decorative pattern. Thickness 6 mm. Size 2/3.

3 b. The inside decorated with diagonally placed parallel lines. Size 2/3.

4. K. 12003: 103. Fragment of bowl contracting towards the mouth. Inside decorated with a marginal zone of parallel horizontal lines with trellis-work below. Size 2/3.

5. K. 12003: 234. Rim fragment, the inside of which is decorated with red-brown triangle-shaped figures. Size 2/3.

Plate 48.

1. K. 12003: 369. Fragment of a bowl of greyish-brown ware. Quality good. The rim decorated with heavy oblique lines. The outside of the bowl ornamented with heavy

490

parallel lines, and below them diagonal lines forming a decorative pattern. Colour of the paint dark brown. On the inside, traces of painted lines forming a garland, now partly eroded (?). Thickness 5 mm. Size 2/3.

2. K. 12003: 167. Fragment of a bowl with flaring rim. The ware of high quality. Colour pale-yellow. On the rim are triangles in black paint. On the outside of the body, a painted pattern consisting of parallel lines. Thickness 6 mm. Size 2/3.

3. K. 12003: 170. Two fragments of a bowl with a rim. Ware of high quality. Colour pale-brown. The rim covered with black paint. On the outside a decorative pattern in black paint, consisting of a large spot surrounded by a circle and groups of curving lines. The inside ornamented with two heavy parallel lines. Thickness 7 mm. Size 2/3.

4 a. K. 12003: 275. Fragment of a bowl. Ware pale-brown on the outside; the inside almost brick-red; core of a grey colour. The inside decorated with hour-glass-shaped patterns surrounded by groups of spots. Size 2/3.

4 b. The outside of the same fragment. Traces of black colour on the rim. The body decorated with groups of circle segments between horizontal lines. On the left side a small knob. Thickness 5—8 mm. Size 2/3.

5 a. K. 12003: 228. Fragment of a bowl with a rim. Quality of the ware high. Colour pale-yellow. The inside is coated with grey pigment. Surfaces smoothed. The inside decorated with groups of vertical and horizontal intersecting lines forming a chessboard pattern. Thickness 5 mm. Size 2/3.

5 b. The outside of the same fragment. Décor consisting of groups of circle segments Below the rim hole drilled from the outside.

6 a. K. 12003: 169. Fragment of a bowl of pale-brown ware of high quality. The inside decorated with horizontal lines and spots alternating with groups of large circles in which are placed two pairs of round spots separated by three vertical lines. Thickness 5 mm. Size 2/3.

6 b. The outside of the same bowl. Surface eroded? Traces of painted décor consisting of diagonal lines. Size 2/3.

P l a t e 49.

1. K. 12003: 421. Three fragments of the belly of a large vessel. Quality of the ware high. Colour pale-brown. Black décor consisting of thick lines and groups of thin lines alternating with trellis pattern. Thickness 5 mm. Size 2/3.

2. K. 12003: 404. Body fragment of a large vessel. Quality of the ware high. Colour pale-brown. The outside decorated with a black pattern consisting of a dentated band from which groups of smaller lines radiate; between them large round spots. Size 2/3.

3. K. 12003: 603. Fragment of grey ware of good quality, the inside decorated with trellis pattern in black paint. Thickness 3 mm. Size 2/3.

4. K. 12003: 108. Belly fragment of pale-brown ware of good quality. The outside decorated with thick intersecting lines and groups of thin lines. Thickness 5 mm. Size 2/3.

5. K. 12003: 466. Fragment of pale-yellow ware. Quality high. The outside polished and decorated with parallel lines and trellis pattern. Thickness 5 mm. Size 2/3.

6. K. 12003: 97. Fragment of brick-red ware. Quality high. The outside decorated with heavy parallel lines and rounded dots. Thickness 4 mm. Size 2/3.

7. K. 12003: 114. Fragment of pale-brown ware. Quality high. The outside decorated with groups of concentric circles and dots. Traces of holes for tying up a crack. Thickness 6 mm. Size 2/3.

491

8. Belly fragment of bright-brown ware of highest quality. The outside polished and decorated with a painted pattern consisting of pairs of diagonal lines alternating with heavy strokes. Thickness 6 mm. Size 2/3.

9. K. 12003: 101. Fragment of grey-brown ware. Quality high. The outside polished and decorated with concentric circles and dot. Thickness 8 mm. Size 2/3.

10. K. 12003: 116. Fragment of pale-brown ware. Quality high. The outside polished and decorated with oblique and horizontal lines. Thickness 6 mm. Size 2/3.

11. K. 12003: 422. Fragment of grey-brown ware. The outside polished and decorated with curved lines and a dentated band. Thickness 8 mm. Size 2/3.

12. K. 2170: 3. Fragment of brown ware. The outside polished and decorated with curved lines and a dentated band. Thickness 8 mm. Size 2/3.

13. K. 12003: 530. Small fragment of yellow ware. The outside polished and decorated with thick line and a dentated band. Size 2/3.

14. K. 12003: 413. Fragment of brick-red ware. The outside pale-yellow and decorated with concentric circles. Thickness 7 mm. Size 2/3.

15. K. 12003: 105. Two fragments of pale-yellow ware of highest quality. The outside decorated with concentric circles of varying thickness. Thickness of the ware 6 mm. Size 2/3.

16. K. 12003: 418. Fragment of pale-brown ware, of highest quality. The outside polished and decorated with parallel lines. Thickness 6 mm. Size 2/3.

Plate 50.

1. K. 2170: 1. Two bowl fragments of brown ware with grey core. The mouth provided with a rim curving outwards. The profile of body slightly curved. The flattened rim ornamented with oblique lines. The body decorated with a unique design in black and white consisting of heavy parallel lines, between which are fine lines alternating with circular dots with white spots; below this a white horizontal line and a zone filled with small curved lines alternating with a triangle surrounded with white dots. Below the triangle a small knob. Thickness 5 mm. Size 1/2.

2. K. 2170: 5. Bowl fragment of pale-yellow ware of highest quality. The flattened rim curving outwards. Surface polished. The rim ornamented with oblique lines alternating with triangular figures and circular dots. The outside decorated with a zone of oblique lines bordered by a horizontal line. On the inside a line of triangles near the mouth; below them, curved lines and dots. Thickness 5 mm. Size 1/2.

3. K. 2170: 6. Fragment of bowl of pale-yellow ware. The outside is almost white and decorated with garlands of thick and thin lines. In the centre a curved line. On the inside, traces of carelessly executed painted triangles. Cf. Pl. 2: 8. Thickness 6 mm. Size 1/2.

4. K. 2170: 4. Fragment of a bowl of pale-brown ware of highest quality. The flattened rim curving outwards and decorated with a design (not reproduced here) of circular dots surrounded with dentated circles, triangles and trellis pattern. The inside ornamented with triangles ending in circular dots and surrounded with circular dots. Thickness 4 mm. Size 1/2.

5. K. 12003: 189. Marginal sherd of greyish-brown ware. Quality high. Rim painted brown. On the outside a design in brown consisting of circle segments and dots. Thickness 5 mm. Size 2/3.

6. K. 2170: 8. Fragment of brick-red ware of high quality. The outside pale and decorated with a black design and thick lines part of a garland and a circle. The zone between the heavy lines filled with fine lines. The circle intersected by a horizontal line. Thickness 5 mm. Size 1/2.

492

7. K. 12003:163. Bowl fragment of pale-yellow ware of highest quality. The outside polished. The inside ornamented with two curved lines below the rim; below them traces of a horizontal line. On the flaring rim is a design in black consisting of circular dots and oblique lines. On the body curved lines. On the left side are holes for tying up a crack. Thickness of the body 3 mm. Size 2/3.

8. K. 12003:222. Marginal sherd of yellow ware of high quality. The inside decorated with triangles, their points ending in a dot. The outside undecorated. Thickness 6 mm. Size 1/2.

9. K. 12003:75. Sherd of brown ware of highest quality. The outside polished and decorated with concentric circles and oblique lines. Thickness 4 mm. Size 2/3.

10. K. 2170:9. Belly fragment of rich brown ware. The inside brown. Quality of the ware high. The outside polished and decorated with black pattern consisting of horizontal lines and a zone of wavy lines. Thickness 5 mm. Size 1/2.

11. K. 12003:165. Marginal sherd of pale brick-red ware of highest quality. The flaring rim decorated with a black design of oblique wavy lines and dots. Thickness of the body 6 mm. Size 2/3.

12. K. 2170:12. Bowl fragment of pale-yellow ware of high quality. Surface polished. On the outside a black painted line. The inside decorated with triangles, their points ending in a dot. Below the triangles a zone of parallel lines. Thickness 5 mm. Size 1/2.

13. K. 12003:180. Bowl fragment of brown ware. Highest quality. Inside decorated with parallel lines and circular dot. On the flattened rim zigzag belt and wedges. Size 2/3.

14. K. 12003:166. Rim fragment of pale-yellow ware. Quality high. Surface polished. The inside decorated with a black pattern consisting of circle segments. On the flattened rim, oblique lines and dots. Thickness 4 mm. Size 2/3.

15. K. 12003:192. Rim fragment of pale-brown ware. Surface polished. The flattened rim decorated with irregularly shaped triangles in a zigzag line. Size 2/3.

16. K. 2170:2. Belly fragment of pale-brown ware. Quality high. The outside polished and decorated with a black design of horizontal parallel lines. On the upper part, where the lines curve, are oblong dots. Thickness 4 mm. Size 2/3.

17. K. 12003:196. Bowl fragment of grey-brown ware. The rim and outside polished. On the flattened rim a brown pattern with trellis work. Size 2/3.

18. K. 12003:161. Rim fragment of pale-brown ware. Surface polished. The flattened rim decorated with dark triangular zone in which a circle-dot is inscribed. At each side of the triangle-shaped figure groups of oblique lines. Size 2/3.

19. K. 12003:217. Bowl fragment of pale-yellow ware. Inside decorated with design in pale black: at the rim a triangle, below which a group of horizontal lines and circle dot. Outside ornamented with black lines (reproduced on Pl. 46,3). Thickness 6 mm. Size 2/3.

20. K. 12003:211. Rim fragment decorated with triangle-shaped figures and oblique bands. Size 2/3.

21. K. 2170:4. Rim fragment of high quality. Black design consisting of circular dot surrounded by concentric circle segments; to the left a black section the middle of which is filled with trellis work. Size 2/3.

22. K. 2170:5. Inside of bowl. Black design consisting of pointed triangles at the rim, below them circle segments and dot. Size 2/3.

23. K. 2170:7. Bowl fragment of pale-yellow ware of high quality. Outside decorated with black design consisting of groups of horizontal lines. On the upper part a couple of oblong dots between the lines. On the lower part traces of the same kind of dot. Thickness 5 mm. Size 1/2.

493

Plate 51.

1. K. 12003: 238. Bowl fragment of pale-brown ware of high quality. Outside polished and decorated with black design of horizontal lines at equal distance. Thickness 6 mm. Size 2/3.

2. K. 2170: 10. Fragment of pale-yellow ware of highest quality. Outside polished and decorated with black pattern of circle segments and a triangle in which is inscribed a circle-dot. Thickness 5 mm. Size 2/3.

3. K. 12003: 7. Fragment of grey-brown ware of high quality. Outside decorated with black design of horizontal lines intersected by two drop-shaped dots. Thickness 6 mm. Size 2/3.

4. K. 12003: 74. Inside of bowl fragment. Ware of highest quality. Colour brick-red. Inside decorated with design of two black horizontal zones with pairs of lines between. The only decoration of the outside is a black band. Thickness 4 mm. Size 2/3.

5. K. 12003: 20. Small sherd of pale-yellow ware, of highest quality. Outside polished and decorated with black design of horizontal band and »arrowhead»-shaped figures. Thickness 4 mm. Size 2/3.

6. K. 12003: 383. Fragment of small bowl. Ware of high quality. Two small holes for tying up a crack. Thickness 4 mm. Fig. a) Outside. Colour dusty brown. Black design of triangle-shaped figure filled with parallel lines and below the triangle horizontal band. In the angle between the triangle and the band, traces of knob. Fig. b) Inside. Colour brick-red, at the rim black design of triangles bordered by horizontal band. Size 2/3.

7. K. 12003: 134. Bowl fragment: rich brown ware with grey core. Surfaces polished. Both outside and inside decorated with black design of horizontal bands and groups of vertical lines. Thickness 4 mm. Fig. a) Outside. Fig. b) Inside. Size 2/3.

9. K. 12003: 79. Fragment of brick-red ware of highest quality. On the inside a black design. Thickness 4 mm. Size 2/3.

10. K 12003: 266. Fragment of a base of pale-yellow ware of high quality. The inside polished and decorated with a black design: in the centre is a circle in which is inscribed a cross formed by two groups of fine lines; between the arms of the cross, and in the middle, circular dots. Outside the circle a trellis pattern and vertical lines. Thickness of the ware 9 mm. Size 2/3.

11. K. 12003: 259. Base fragment of pale-yellow ware of high quality. The inside decorated with a black design of curved lines radiating from a large circle in the middle of the bottom. Thickness 6 mm. Size 2/3.

12. K 12003: 268. Base fragment. The ware of highest quality. Colour reddish-brown on the outside, on the inside a yellowish-white slip. The inside decorated with a pattern of black curved lines. Thickness 6 mm. Size 2/3.

13. K. 12003: 265. Base fragment of brick-red ware of highest quality. The inside decorated with a black design consisting of zones filled with a trellis pattern. Thickness 5 mm. Size 2/3.

14. K. 2170: 29. Small fragment of a handle of pale yellowish-brown ware. On the outside, oblique intersecting lines forming a chessboard pattern. Size 2/3.

15. K. 12003: 624. Fragment of a handle caressly made of yellowish-brown ware. On the outside is a brown painted décor: on the upper part oblique lines, on the lower half vertical lines. Size 2/3.

16. K. 12003: 625. Fragment of a handle of pale-yellow ware. On the outside a décor of reddish-brown lines. Size 2/3.

17. K. 12003: 210. Marginal fragment of bowl with slightly curved profile contract-

494

ing towards the mouth. Ware yellowish-white with grey core. Both exterior and interior decorated with reddish-brown zigzag lines. Thickness 7 mm. Size 2/3.

18. K. 2170: 11. Object (probably fragment of a handle) of yellow-brown ware. Surfaces polished. On the concave side a black design of thick parallel lines, between which is a zone with finer lines surrounding an oblong spot. On the convex side a group of thick parallel lines on the upper part. Size 2/3.

19. K. 12003: 80. Small fragment decorated with red-brown dot. Size 2/3.

Plate 52.

1. K. 2170: 48. Mace head of granite. Deep groove all around the body, at one side crossed by another broad groove, evidently for fastening purposes. Size 1/2.

2. K. 2170: 46. Disc-shaped pendant of white marble provided with a bi-conical hole near the margin. Thickness 3 mm. Size 1/2.

3. K. 12003: 1771. Fragment of diorit? Provided with a deep furrow on the upper side. Marks of wear in the bottom of the furrow. Size 1/2.

4. Signed only L. H. T. Unfinished axe. Edge broken. Size 1/2.

5. K. 12003: 1706. Small axe of dark, dense schistose rock. Neck broken. Surfaces carefully polished. Cross section square. Breadth 18 mm. Thickness 11 mm. Size 2/3.

6. K. 1524 and K. 1531. Two fragments of dark, dense, schistose rock. Neck broken. Size 2/3.

7. K. 1519. Small, thin axe of schistose rock. Length 73 mm. Breadth 39 mm. Thickness 7 mm. Size 2/3.

8. K. 12003: 1704. Fragmentary axe of grained (?) schistose rock. Broad-sides polished. Size 2/3.

9. K. 12003: 1743. Small axe of schistose rock. Neck broken. Breadth 40 mm. Thickness 10 mm. Size 2/3.

10. K. 1549. Fragmentary stone artifact of schistose rock. Surfaces hammered. Size 1/2.

11. K. 12003: 1732. Slate-knife. On the lateral sides two notches for tying. Edge rounded. Thickness 9 mm. Size 2/3.

12. K. 12003: 1731. Fragmentary slate-knife with oblong hole in the centre. Thickness 7 mm. Size 2/3.

13. K. 3220. Fragmentary slate-knife with two bi-conical holes. Side »wing-shaped». Thickness 6 mm. Size 2/3.

14. K. 12003: 1728. Slate-knife with bi-conical hole. Sides »wing-shaped». One of them provided with ten narrow indentations. Thickness 4 mm. Size 2/3.

15. K. 12003: 1746. Irregularly crescent-shaped knife made from a flake of dark, schistose rock. Edge sharpened only at the polished side. Back thick. Thickness (the centre) 15 mm. Size 2/3.

16. K. 1520. Fragmentary slate-chisel. Thickness 5 mm. Size 2/3.

17. K. 12003: 1757. Chisel, irregularly shaped. Size 2/3.

18. K. 12003: 1734. Fragmentary chisel of schistose rock. Size 2/3.

19. K. 12003: 1733. Long chisel of schistose rock. Size 2/3.

Plate 53.

1. Big fragmentary hoe of diorite (?). Two corresponding lateral recesses for attachment. Thickness 33 mm. Size 2/3.

2. K. 12003: 1786. Crescent-shaped grinding stone made from a sandstone block. Surface carefully smoothed. Size 2/3.

495

3. K. 2170: 20. Half of an armlet of white marble with a tinge of yellowish rose. Regularly cut, only slightly tapering towards the margins. The outside polished, on the inside traces of red pigment. On the margins groups of small incisions. At one side a hole bored from the outside. Outer diameter 80 mm. Thickness 6 mm. Size 1/2.

4. K. 270: 21. Fragment of an armlet of white marble with innumerable small pores representing a corroded mineral. Slightly tapering towards one margin. Cross-section lenticular. Thickness about 8 mm. Size 1/2.

5. K. 2170: 23. Fragment of an armlet of white sugar-grained marble. The cross-section is concave on the outside and correspondingly convex on the inside. Thickness 7 mm. Size 1/2.

6. K. 5855: 1. Axe shaped from a large bone. Outside convex, inner-side concave. Edge sharpened on the inner-side. Neck broken. Breadth at the edge 63 mm. Size 2/3.

7. K. 5855: 2. Fragmentary needle with trace of the eye. Size 2/3.

8. K. 5855: 3. Fine intact needle with eye. Size 2/3.

9. K. 5855: 4. Two fragments of a small needle with eye bored from one side. Size 2/3.

10. K. 5855: 5. Fragment of the pointed end of a needle. Size 2/3.

11. K. 5855: 6. Fragmentary needle. Size 2/3.

12. K. 5855: 7. Fragment of a needle. Size 2/3.

13. K. 5855: 8. Intact needle with bi-conical eye. Size 2/3.

14. K. 5855: 9. Fragment of a needle-point. Size 2/3.

15. K. 5855: 10. Fragment of needle with bi-conical eye. Size 2/3.

16. K. 5855: 11. Fragment of the point of a bone knife with furrow for fastening flint flakes. Size 2/3.

18—24. K. 5855: 12—18. Bone awls. Size 2/3.

25. K. 5855: 19. Fragment of bone implement. The point rounded; no edge. Size 2/3.

26. K. 5855: 20. Bone knife. The blade has on the convex side a furrow for fastening flint-flakes. The opposite side is concave. The upper part has the shape of a narrow handle. Size 2/3.

27. K. 5855: 21. Bone knife, on the straight side provided with a furrow for fastening flint-flakes extending along the entire side. The opposite side is curved. Size 2/3.

28. K. 5855: 22. Fragmentary bone implement. Below the knob-shaped top a square hole bored from one side. Size 2/3.

29. K. 5855: 23. Small bead of white marble. Size 1/1.

Plate 54.
Natural size.

1. K. 12003: 1664. Fragmentary ring of white marble with small pores representing a corroded mineral. — 2. K. 12003: 1638. Fragmentary clay ring. — 3. K. 12003: 1637. Fragmentary clay ring. — 4. K. 2170: 856. Fragmentary clay ring. — 5. K. 2170: 37. Fragmentary slate ring. — 6. K. 12003: 1745. Fragmentary slate ring.

7. K. 12003: 1558. Small fragmentary urn-shaped vessel of greyish-brown clay.

8. K. 12003: 1668. Fragmentary armlet of white marble with small pores representing a corroded mineral.

9. K. 2170: 30. Bone needle with bi-conical eye. Point very fine.

10. K. 2170: 31. Bone implement made from a thin plate split from a large bone. At the top two bi-conical holes. At the lower end one hole of the same type. Between the top holes and the four marginal indentations and between the lowest indentations marks of wear are clearly visible.

496

11. Flat bone implement. At the top a hole bored from one side. Near the point five pits. On the reverse side, one pit of the same kind slightly higher up.

12. K. 2170: 26. Slender bone-knife with furrow for fastening flint-flakes. The furrow is clearly visible in fig. b. The upper part serves as a handle.

13. K. 2170: 25. Bone knife with furrow for fastening flint-flakes. The blade is slightly curved. The handle is provided at the top with a hole. The furrow is clearly visible in fig. b.

14. K. 2170: 41. Pendant (?) of grey slate. Cross-section rectangular. Both ends obtusely pointed. 15 mm. from the top a furrow cut round three sides. Attempt at indentation at the other end on the short side. This cutting is scarcely discernible in the plate.

Plate 55.

1. K. 2353: 10. T. S. Hs. C. L. T. Collar fragment of brown ware of high quality. The outside decorated with a belt of incised parallel lines, between which are vertical lines of varying density. Thickness 6 mm. Size 1/2.

2. K. 2353: 7. T. S. Hs. C. L. T. Fragment of stone ring. Cross-section triangular. Size 1/2.

3. K. 2353: 25. T. S. Hs. C. L. T. Neck fragment of bright-yellow ware. The clay is pure but »soft», probably not burnt at a high temperature. The narrow mouth provided with »a double ring». On the neck traces of impressions. Thickness of the neck 7 mm. Size 1/2.

4. K. 2353: 42. T. S. Hs. C. L. T. Interior of fragmentary bowl. The margin rings-haped on the inside. Pale-brown ware of high quality. Thickness 7 mm. Size 1/2.

5. K. 2353: 21. T. S. Hs. C. L. T. Interior of fragment of pale-brown ware of high quality. The margin annular on the inside. Thickness 5 mm. Size 1/2.

6. K. 2353: 23. T. S. Hs. C. L. T. Interior of fragmentary bowl. Ware of high quality. The outside bright-brown and polished, the inside pale-yellow with a brick-red spot. Thickness 7 mm. Size 1/1.

7. K. 2353: 8. T. S. Hs. C. L. T. Fragment of amphora with high collar and softly curved body. Pale-brown ware of high quality. The handle decorated with long recess. Height of the collar 45 mm. Length of the handle 75 mm., breadth 33 mm. Thickness of the body 6 mm. Size 1/2.

8. K. 2358: 43. T. S. Hs. C. L. T. Fragment of small amphora of reddish-brown ware of high quality. Thickness 3—4 mm. Size 1/2.

9. K. 2353: 24. T. S. Hs. C. L. T. Handle of greyish-brown ware. On the outside, an incised ornament consisting of two crossed crescents. Thickness 5 mm. Size 1/2.

10. K. 2353: 38. T. S. Hs. C. L. T. Leg of a tripod. Ware coarse. Colour dirty-brown. The outside covered with textile impressions. Thickness about 10 mm. Size 1/2.

11. K. 2353: 22. T. S. Hs. C. L. T. Fragment of pale-yellowish ware, not very coarse, but quartz grains are visible. On the outside are fine intersecting cord impressions. Thickness 7 mm. Size 1/1.

12. K. 2353: 34. T. S. Hs. C. L. T. Urn fragment of coarse dirty greyish-brown ware. The margin provided with a rim. The outside of the body covered with textile impressions. Thickness 5—7 mm. Size 1/2.

13. K. 2353: 9. T. S. Hs. C. L. T. Fragment of big handle. Ware not very coarse, but quartz grains are discernible. Colour pale-yellowish brown. The outside ornamented with vertical furrows. Thickness 8 mm. Size 1/2.

14. K. 2353: 41. T. S. Hs. C. L. T. Base fragment of pale-brown ware of high quality. On the outside basket impression. Thickness 5 mm. Size 1/2.

497

15. K. 2353: 3. T. S. Hs. C. L. T. Ring of grey clay. Cross-section triangular. Size 1/1.

16. K. 2353: 37. T. S. Hs. C. L. T. Leg of a Li tripod. Ware coarse. Colour dusty greyish-yellow. Varying thickness; medium 9 mm. Size 1/2.

Plate 56.

1. K. 2353: 32. T. S. Hs. C. L. T. Small sherd of bright-brown ware of Yang Shao type. The ware of high quality. The rim circular on the inside. The outside carefully smoothed and decorated with garland-shaped ornamentation in greyish paint. Size 1/1.

2. K. 2353: 36. T. S. Hs. C. L. T. Fragment of funnel-shaped foot(?). Ware porous but not coarse. Colour grey. On the outside horizontal scratches. Thickness 5 mm. Size 1/2.

3. K. 2353: 28. T. S. Hs. C. L. T. Fragment of pale-brown ware of high quality. On the outside irregular zones of cord impressions bordered with smooth belts. Thickness 4 mm. Size 1/1.

4. K. 2353: 39. T. S. Hs. C. L. T. Fragment of big collar with slightly flaring rim. Ware not coarse, but to some extent mixed with quartz. Surfaces pale-yellowish grey. Core reddish-brown. Thickness 5 mm. Size 1/2.

5. K. 2359: 24. Y. Ch. Hs. H. S. H. Fragment of small amphora. Ware of high quality. Colour pale yellowish brown. Surface not very carefully smoothed. Collar high and slightly flaring. Body gently curved. At the margin and on the belly, traces of a long handle. On the collar, horizontal scratches. On the belly, indistinct basket impressions (probably »wicker-work»). Basket impressions also on the bottom. Thickness 3 mm. Size 1/2.

6. K. 2359: 25. Y. Ch. Hs. H. S. H. Three fragments of the belly of a bi-conical vessel. Ware not very coarse but to some extent mixed with lime and quartz. Surface pale-yellow. Core brick-red. Below the equatorial line a lug. On the lower portion basket impressions. Thickness 6 mm.

7. K. 2359: 18. Y. Ch. Hs. H. S. H. Small fragment of pale-brown ware. Outside polished and decorated with black pattern. Thickness 4 mm. Size 1/1.

8. K. 2359: 1. Y. Ch. Hs. H. S. H. Four fragments of the upper part of an urn with high collar. Rim slightly flaring. Quality of the ware high, but the surface not carefully smoothed. Colour dusty yellowish-brown. Diameter of the mouth 140 mm. Height of the collar 90 mm. Thickness of the body 5—7 mm. Size 1/2.

9. K. 5280. Y. Ch. Hs. H. S. H. Amphora with wide mouth and bulging belly. Colour pale-brown. Outside carefully smoothed. On the upper part of the body an incised horizonal line, below which a belt of zigzags. Above the line, ring-shaped incisions at irregular intervals. The upper part of the handles decorated with a rhombic recess. At the base of one of the handles three ring-shaped incisions, at that of the other one only two. Height 178 mm. Breadth 169 mm. Diameter of the mouth (from one handle to the other) 155 mm. Thickness 5 mm. Size 1/3.

10. K. 2359: 16. Y. Ch. Hs. H. S. H. Small sherd of grey-brown ware. Impression of coarse textile. Thickness 5 mm. Fig. a. negocoll positive. Size 1/1.

11. K. 2359: 32. Y. Ch. Hs. H. S. H. Belly fragment of pale-brown ware with brick-red core. Quality high. Upper part of the outside polished and decorated with black design in the form of broad bands under which is a wavy line. Thickness 6 mm. Size 1/2.

498

Pl. 1.

1a

14

2

3

1b

5

4

6

7

9

8

13

10

11

12

Pl. 2.

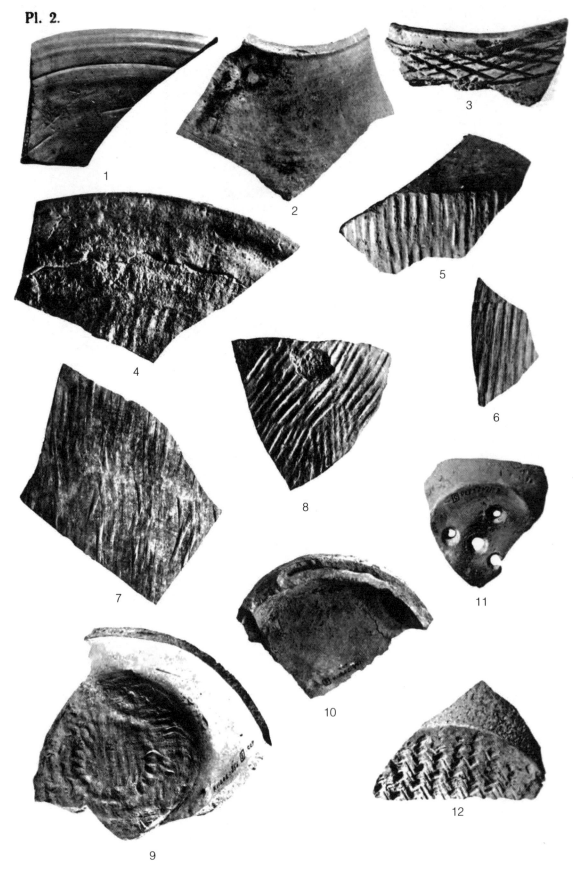

Pl. 3

1

2

3

5

4

Pl. 4.

1

2

3

4

5

6

7

8

9

10

11

12

13

11

15

16

17

18

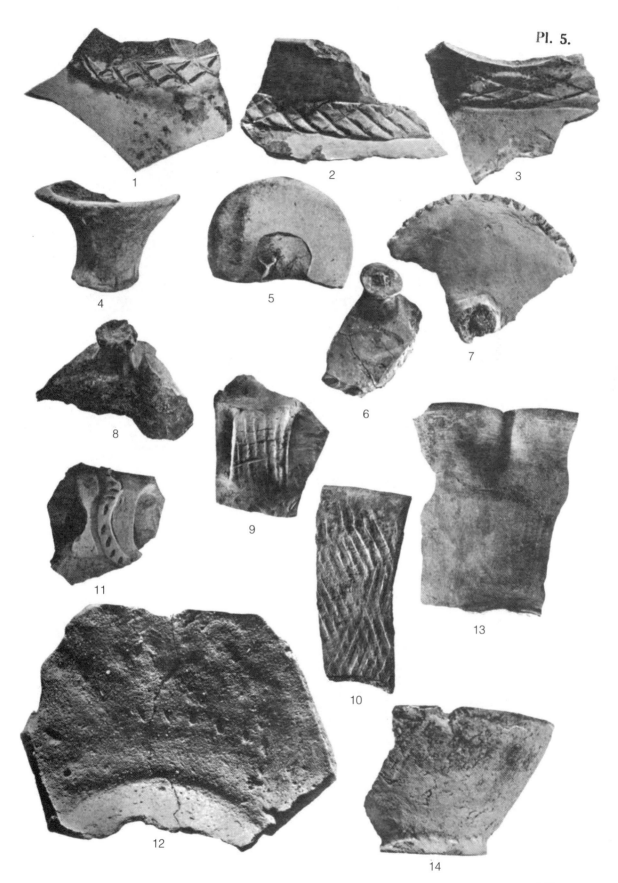

Pl. 5.

1

2

3

4

5

6

7

8

9

10

11

12

13

14

Pl. 6.

1

2

4

3

5

6

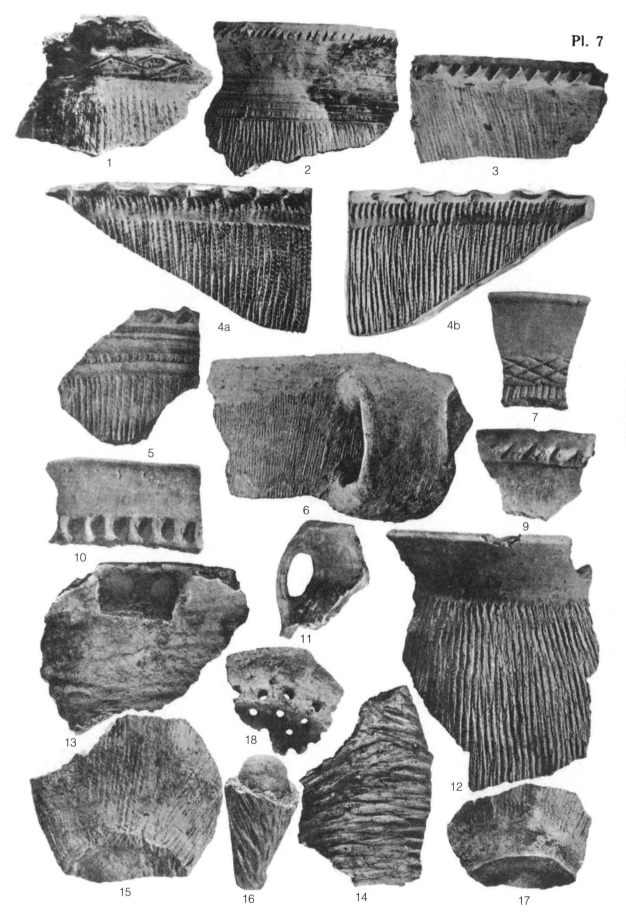

Pl. 7

1 2 3 4a 4b 5 6 7 9 10 11 13 18 12 15 16 14 17

Pl. 8.

1

2

3

4

5

6

7

8

9

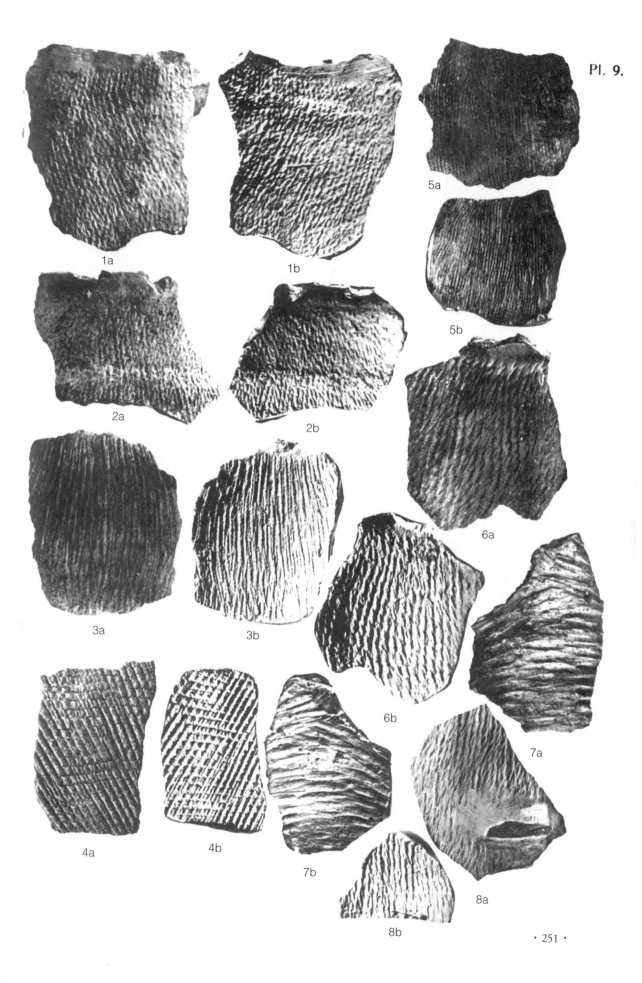

Pl. 9.

1a

1b

5a

5b

2a

2b

3a

3b

6a

4a

4b

6b

7a

7b

8a

8b

Pl. 10.

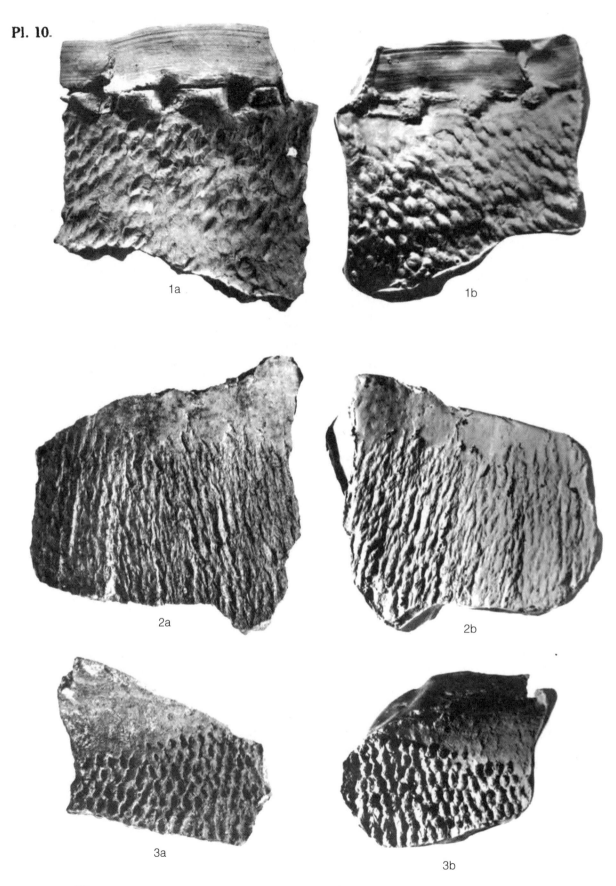

1a

1b

2a

2b

3a

3b

Pl. 11.

1a

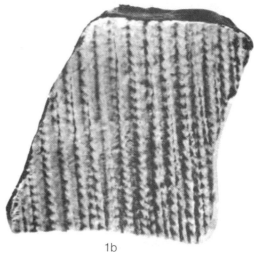

1b

2a

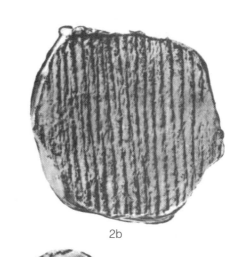

2b

3a

3b

Pl. 12.

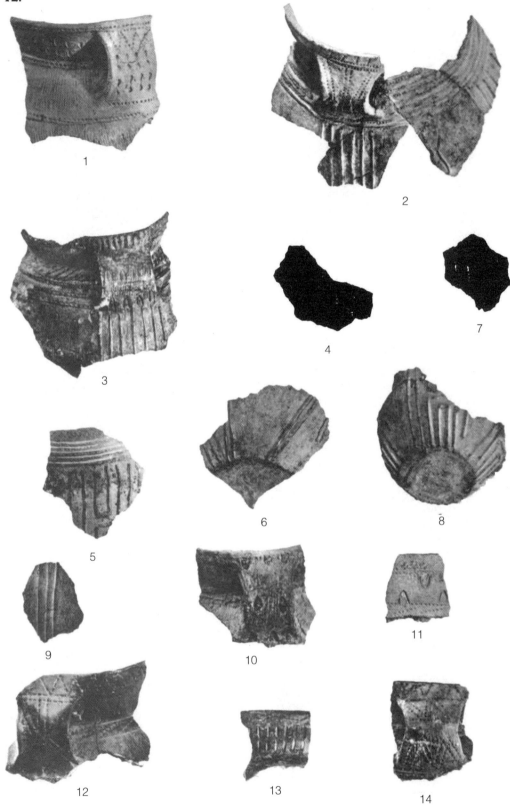

1

2

3

4

7

5

6

8

9

10

11

12

13

14

Pl. 13.

1

2

3

4

5a

5b

6

7a

7b

8

9

10

11

Pl. 14.

1

4

5

2

3

12

6

9

10

7

8

11

Pl. 15.

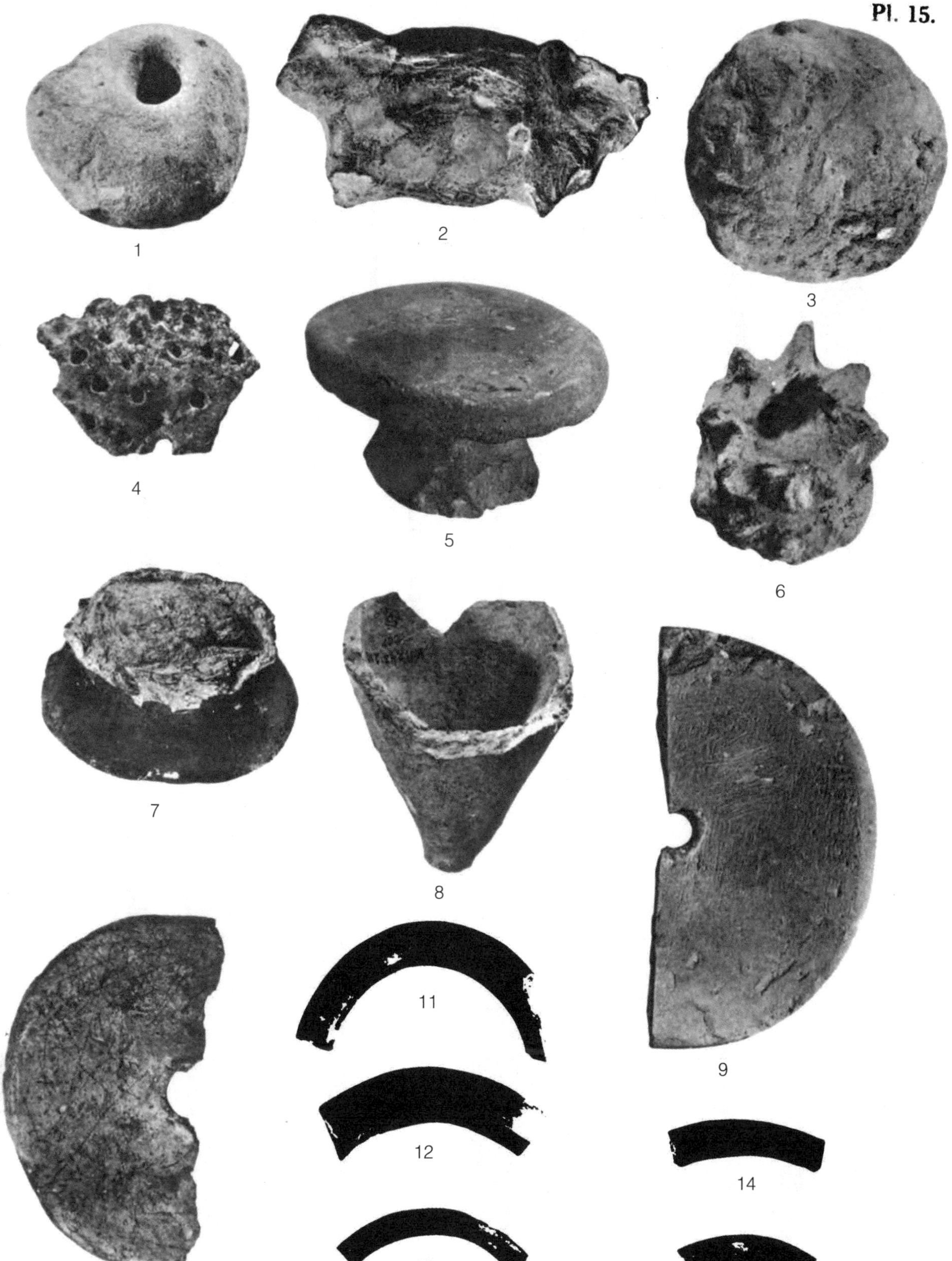

1

2

3

4

5

6

7

8

9

10

11

12

13

14

15

Pl. 16.

1   2   3   4   5   6   7   8   9   10   11   12

13   14   15   16   17   18   19   20

21   22   23   24   25   26   27

Pl. 17.

1

2

3

4

Pl. 18.

Pl. 19.

1

2

3

4

5

6

7

8a

9

8b

Pl. 20.

3

5

1

2

4

Pl. 21.

1

3

2

4

Pl. 22.

1

2

5

4

3

Pl. **23.**

Pl. 24.

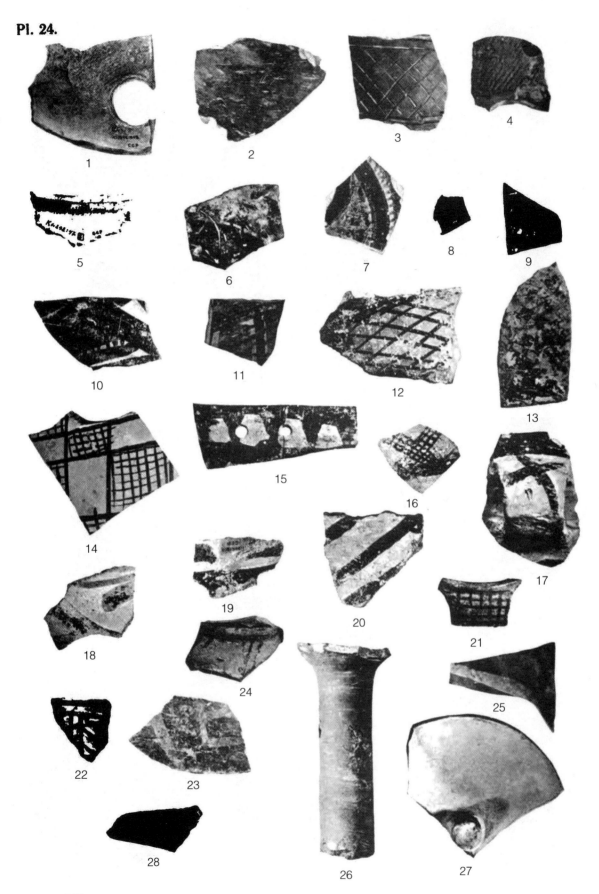

Pl. 25.

3

1

4

5

6

2

Pl. 26.

1

2

3

4

5

6

7

1

2

3

4

Pl. 27.

Pl. 28.

1

2

3

4

5

Pl. 29.

1

2

3

5

6

4

7

8

9

10

Pl. 30.

1

2

3

4

5

6

7

Pl. 31.

1

2

3

4

Pl. **32.**

1

2

Pl. 33.

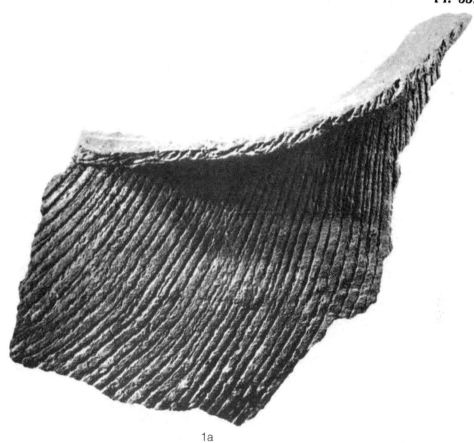

1a

1b

Pl. 34.

1

2

3

4

5

6

7

Pl. 36.

1

2

3

4

Pl. 37.

1

2

3

4

5

6

7

8

9

Pl. 38.

1

2

3

4

5

6

7

8

9

10

11

Pl. 39.

1

2

3

4

Pl. 40.

1b

1a

2b

3a

2a

3b

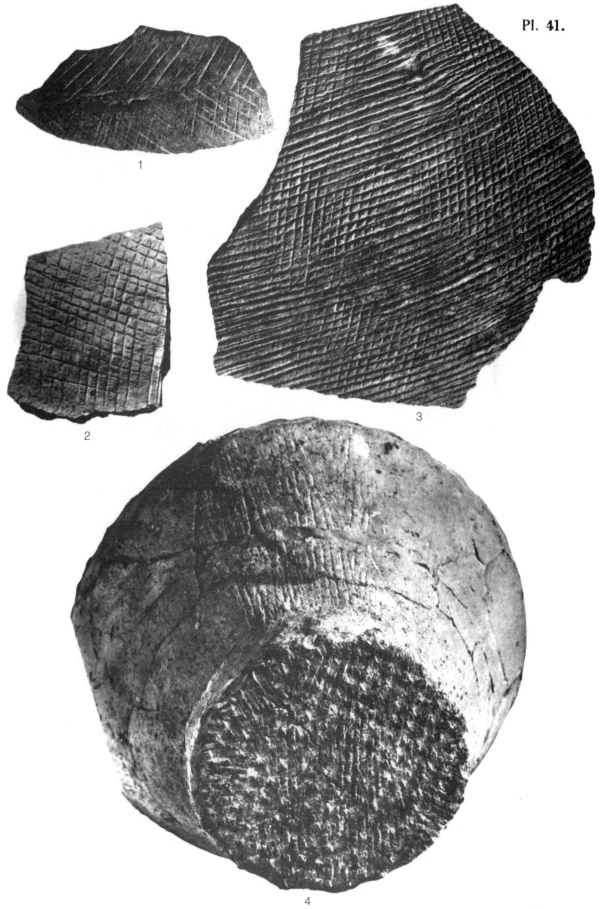

Pl. **41.**

1

2

3

4

Pl. 42.

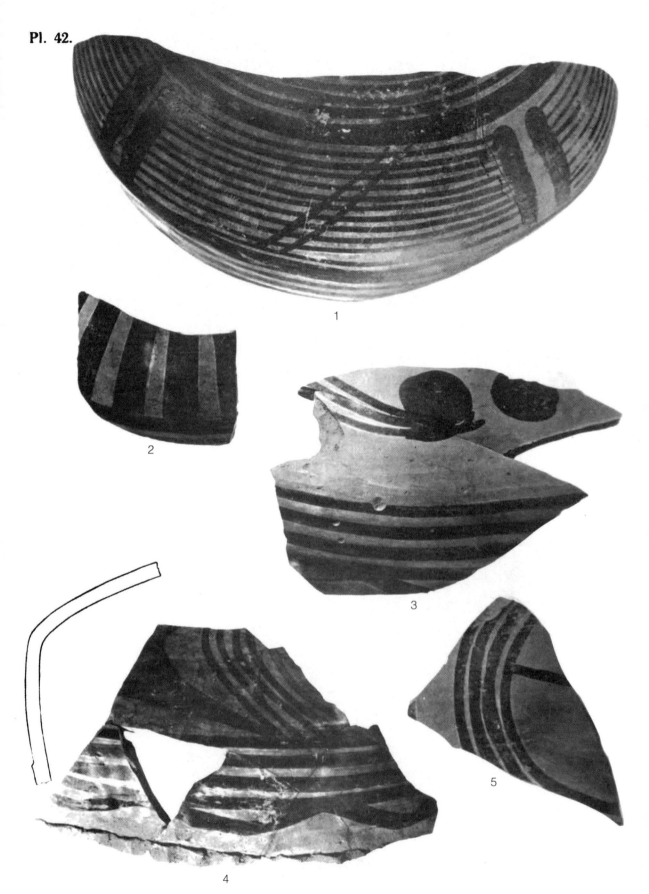

1

2

3

4

5

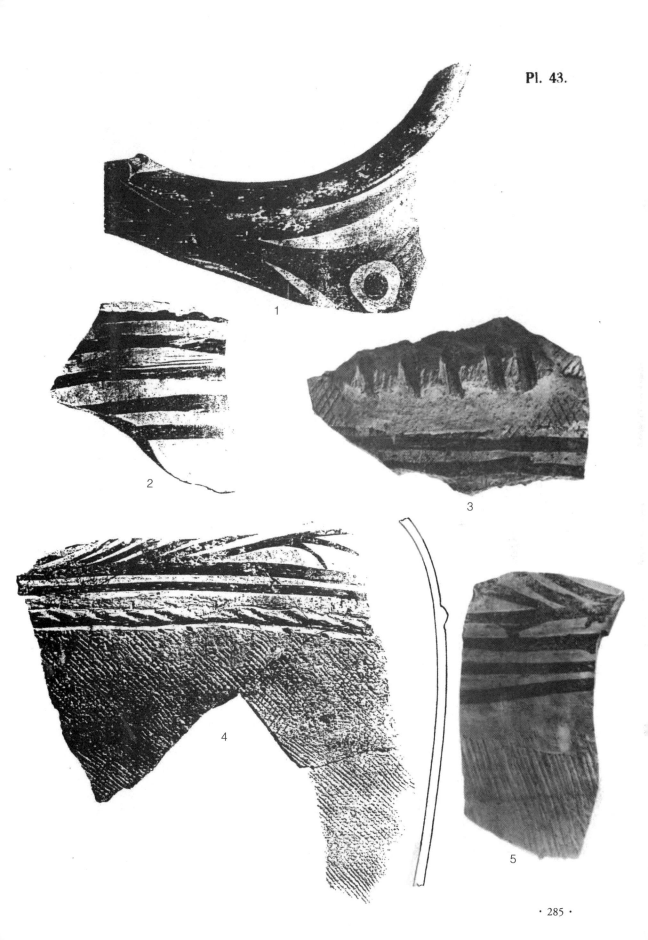

Pl. 43.

1

2

3

4

5

Pl. 44.

Pl. **45.**

1

3

2

4

5

6a

6b

Pl. 46.

1a

1b

2

3

4a

5a

4b

5b

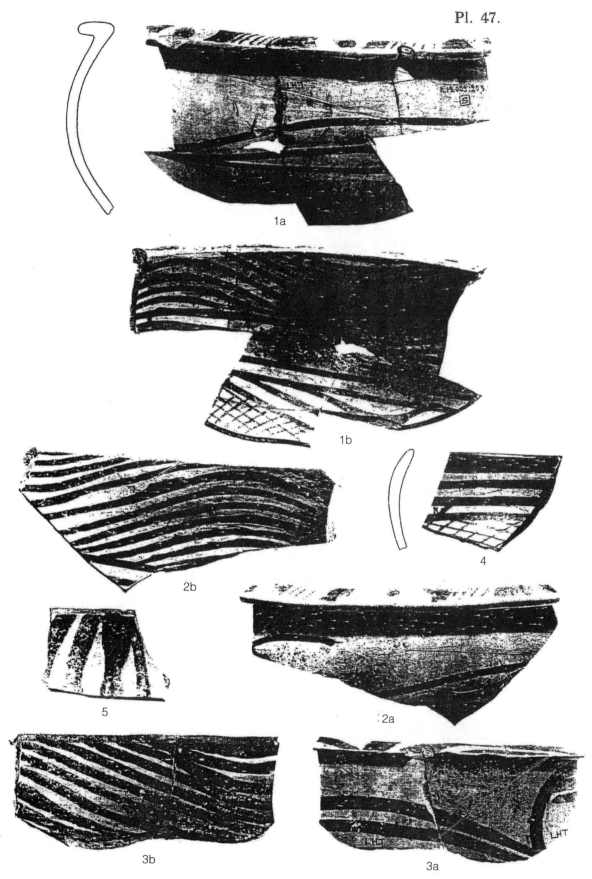

Pl. 47.

1a

1b

2b

4

5

2a

3b

3a

Pl. 48.

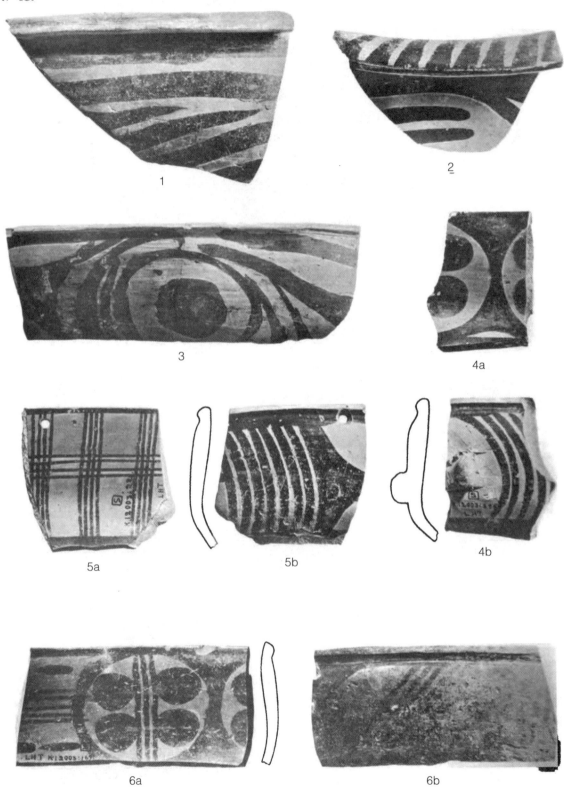

1

2

3

4a

5a

5b

4b

6a

6b

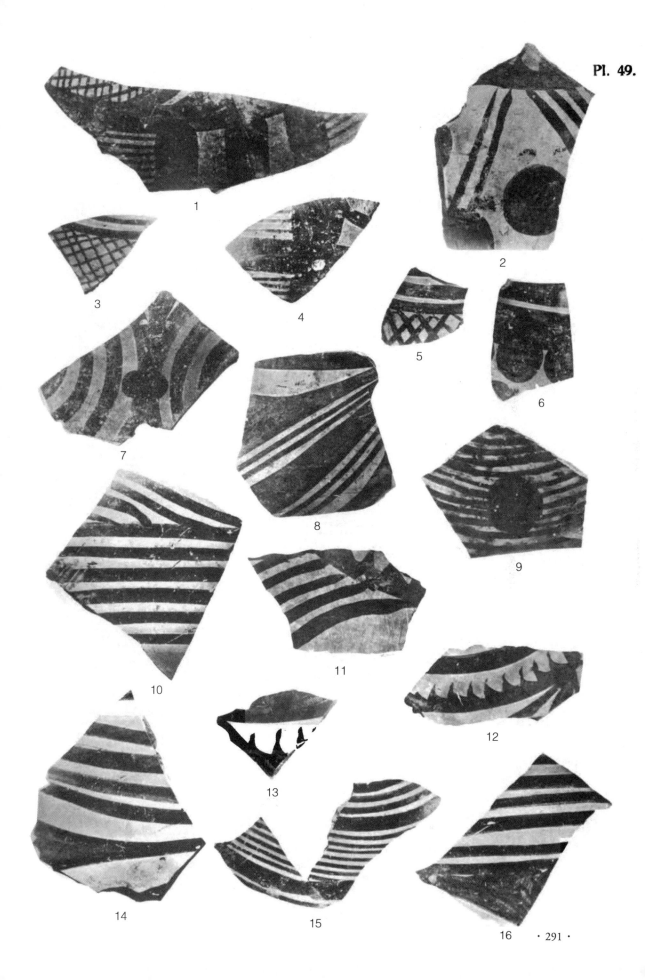

Pl. 49.

1

2

3

4

5

6

7

8

9

10

11

12

13

14

15

16

Pl. 50.

1

2

3

4

5

6

7

8

9

10

11

12

13

14

15

16

17

18

19

20

21

22

23

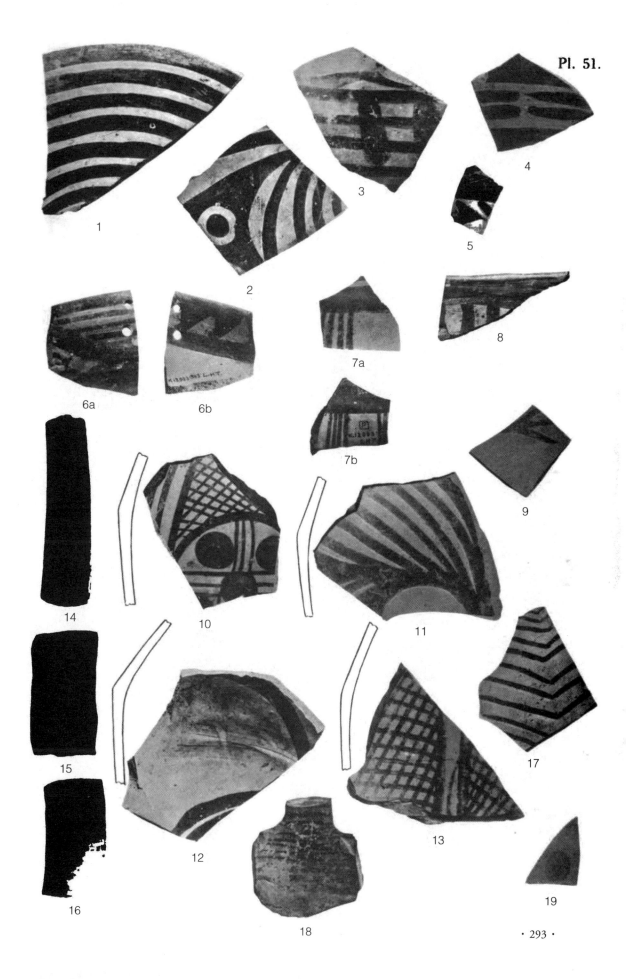

Pl. 51.

Pl. 52.

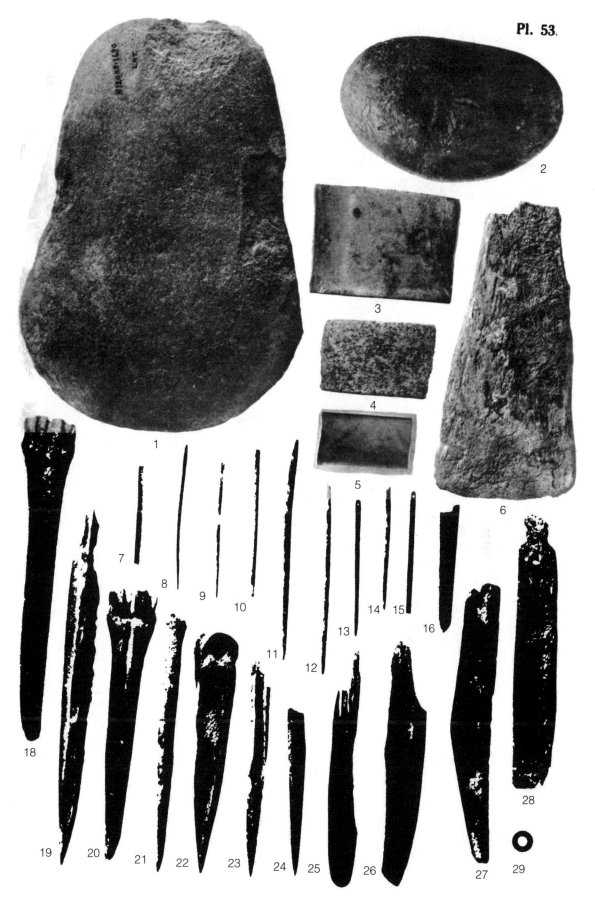

Pl. 53.

1

2

3

4

5

6

7

8

9

10

11

12

13

14 15

16

18

19

20

21

22

23

24

25

26

27

28

29

Pl. 54.

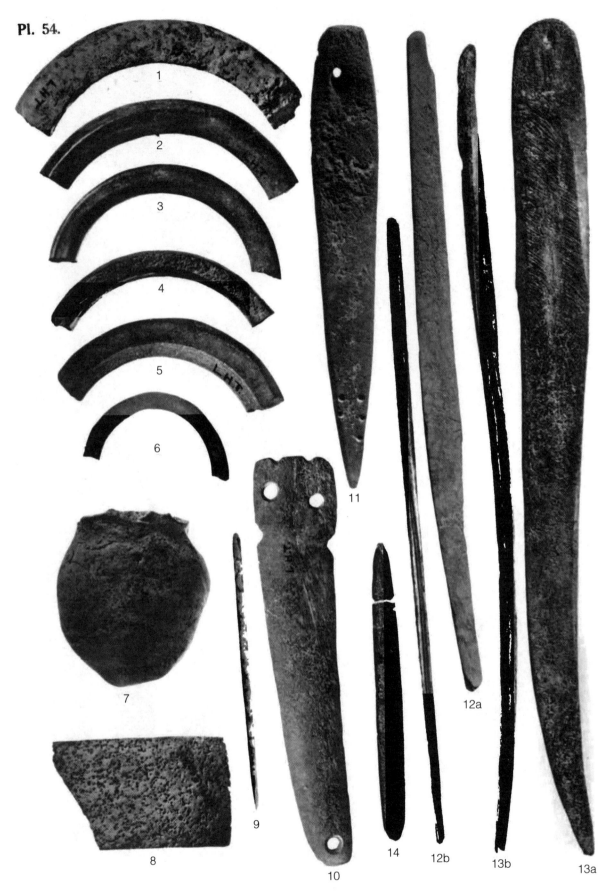

1

2

3

4

5

6

7

8

9

10

11

12a

12b

13b

13a

14

Pl. 55.

Pl. 56.

附录一

玛吉特·比林-阿尔提：
甘肃齐家坪与罗汉堂（斯德哥尔摩，1946）

钓田、正哉

　　瑞典考古学家安特生教授在中国史前文化研究方面的著作早已为人熟知，但作为具体调查事实的报告，值得一提的是1943年出版的瑞典远东古物博物馆（STASIATISKAMUSEET）刊物第15辑。正如梅原博士在本刊第30卷第4期中所述，这份出版物提供了初步但富有洞察力的概述，对于每个遗址更详细的报告仍值得期待。随后，在1945年、1946年和1947年的同一刊物中，接连公开了3份报告，期盼已久的安特生教授的研究成果几乎齐备，极大地造福了学术界。由于各种原因，中国史前时代遗址的发掘调查工作阻碍重重，这一广袤地区至今仍缺乏系统性的发掘案例。因此，上述教授的发掘文物如今被视为新鲜而重要的原始资料，在学术界占据着至关重要的位置。在深入研究这份报告时，我们必须对教授长达30年之久的文物整理工作表示敬意和赞赏。

　　现在，我将介绍玛吉特·比林-阿尔提女士所报告的位于甘肃宁定县的齐家坪遗址，该遗址安特生在《中华远古之文化》中已有描述，遗址中发现了磨制石斧、石刀、粗糙灰色绳纹陶器等中国史前时代常见的文物、一组被称为"篦点纹陶"的陶器，以及薄而精美的灰黄色双耳罐形陶器。当时，安特生博士根据这组篦点纹陶器与北欧陶器存在的相似之处推测了它们之间的关联，同时根据罐形器上的彩绘推断出与其他甘肃彩陶的关系，将其作为时间最早的陶器之一，其年代非常古老。理由是，遗址中发现了大量石斧类物品，但却并未发现金属器，同时出现仰韶文化彩陶散布在齐家坪遗址表面的现象，但这些都不足以支持确定年代。安特生甚至在1943年的报告中再次重申了他的观点。然而，除了这种层位关系的不足之外，在发掘的罐形器中发现了金属器的痕迹。因此，在1927年至1928年间首次目睹这些物品的梅原教授，公开反对将齐家坪视为甘肃最古老时期的观点，从那时起，这个问题就备受争议。这本书提到与上述问题相关的一点，即在包含层的深处发现了带有格子纹的彩陶片，此外还发现了15块彩陶片，这些彩陶片与中晚期仰韶文化甚至与朱家寨彩陶相吻合，接着在提到的粗糙灰色绳纹陶器中，详细说明了齐家坪和朱家寨之间的相似之处，并通过插图说明了这两者在时间上并没有太大的差距。此外，还有一些器物被认为是齐家期的物品，从陶土和制作等方面来看，这些器物更接近于金属时代，可能与商代青铜器有联系。因此，有人推测这些器物是在安阳金属工艺盛行时期受到技术影响而产生的低级文化产品。作为证据，报告中还举例说明家畜种类很丰富等。关于报告中提到的层位情况，虽然我们对其有比以往更详细的了解，但并没有任何决定性的证据，仅仅证明了齐家坪期与仰韶中晚期以及朱家寨期有所接触，而齐家期的重要性及其与仰韶初期的关系尚无法明确。从层位来看，齐家坪是不是甘肃最古的遗址尚无法确定。此外，对于提到的家畜种类丰富这一点，在今天资料匮乏的情况下，轻率地下结论确实令人怀疑。因此，在这里，本报告针对齐家期被视为甘肃史前时代最古老的类型的反对观点，其主要根据来自双耳瓶式陶器所展示的事实。关于这一点，与商代青铜容器的相似之处，梅原博士早已指出，特别是与商代青铜器的原型之一的黑陶相比，可以说与其极为相似，甚至可以说是黑陶本身的一种器形。最近在《中国考古学报》（原名《田野考古报告》）第3册中，夏鼐先生在甘肃省半山墓葬遗址的魏家咀村阳洼湾古墓进行了发掘，揭示了齐家期比半山期乃至马厂期更晚的层位事实，这一点令人期待。因此，从本报告书及其他方面来看，安特生博士将齐家期视为甘肃史前时代最古老期的假设已被调查人员撤回。未来的问题应该集中在栉目纹陶器和粗糙绳纹灰色陶器，特别是它们与河南的关系。然而，正如报告所述，这些事实的记录在这一方面具有新的重要意义。

　　在本报告的后半部分提到罗汉堂，该遗址已经在《黄土的儿女——中国史前文化研究》中有极为简短的记载。此外，在1943年的报告中，本遗址出土的彩陶纹样中包含了半山期流行的 "丧纹"的早期形式，而且在器形上也可以发现与齐家期完全相同的情形，因此有观点认为本遗址的年代应当接近齐家坪，属于仰韶初期。虽然这些观点部分被认同，但其与齐家坪出土品相似的容器在器形上已经有了显著进步，因此不太可能是如此古老的物品。此外，在彩陶片中（图版43）还包含了似乎属于仰韶期独立系列的内容，而且在着色技法上使用白陶衣，被认为更加先进，这进一步质疑了安特生博士的观点。在本报告中，首先关于彩陶，通过图版可清楚发现其与马家窑和朱家寨的相似之处，而在无彩纹陶器方面，小型双耳壶、席纹瓮、无装饰碗等在齐家坪的类似之处更加明显。这些事实本书首次展示，应当慎重对待。尽管安特生博士早就主张齐家坪和罗汉堂遗址具有相似性，但他并未提供新的见解。然而，如果把齐家坪与殷墟联系起来，那么罗汉堂的时代也必须相应地推迟，因此基于这种情况，须确立一种新的观点，即将罗汉堂视为齐家坪的前身。

　　报告者谨慎地指出，罗汉堂、马家窑和朱家寨出土的陶器相似之处，应等待马家窑遗址的详细报告，然后再确定时间的先后。然而，现有的证据是否足以解决这个问题呢？这里涉及未来的一个问题。此外，从彩陶和河南仰韶村、秦王寨以及山西西阴村的相似性来看，甘肃、河南这两个地区的彩陶群之间的联系引人深思，这个问题将产生何种影响，这是阅读本报告时应思考的一个重要问题。

　　最后，报告者通过一些陶器片（如插图11）与鄂尔多斯的青铜器相互比较，将罗汉堂出土的石刃嵌入骨镰的原型视为金属器，他们使用的是鄂尔多斯式的刀，这作何解释？比如说，如果考虑后者，鄂尔多斯式刀在西伯利亚和蒙古的草原地区长期存在的事实是公认的。至于石刃嵌入的工艺，或许应该考虑到这种工艺在古埃及、美索不达米亚等古代东方文明世界中早已存在的情况。

　　根据这份报告，甘肃“六期”说被修正，不再将齐家文化期视为最古老的时期，这一修正是由考古学家提出的。通过这些描述，这份报告提供了丰富的资料，我们需要重新思考甘肃和河南两地史前文化之间存在的关联，这始终是一个关系薄弱的领域。这份报告将成为中国史前史时代研究的重要基石，值得引起广泛关注。

附录二

信件一：

中央地质调查所和安特生有关
《齐家坪遗址与罗汉堂遗址考古报告》的通信

上黎家坡33号
湖南省长沙市
1938年3月30日

安特生教授：

留心转交安南法国远东学院
河内，中南半岛

我很高兴从您3月8日写给翁文灏的信中获悉，您现在在安南法国远东学院学习，并计划在那里停留数周。

去年11月23日，地质调查所所有负责地质博物馆工作的员工，除了盛先生（注：盛莘夫，知名地质学家、古生物学家），都从南京迁到了长沙。由于事出突然，我们缺乏搬运设备，大部分的出版物，包括您有关"史前遗址"的专著中未装订的图表，以及博物馆的部分藏品，都未能搬出，实在令人遗憾。盛莘夫先生现在还在南京，我们从他2月9日的来信中了解到，日本装甲部队曾占领地质调查所的建筑物，里面的家具、博物馆的箱子全部被他们点燃，玻璃窗和易碎物品一概被砸得粉碎，燃料研究大楼东翼被空袭摧毁，不过截至当天，调查所的其他楼房还未被摧毁。这封信是从南京逃离出来的难民从上海邮寄过来的。

就在我们从南京撤离的前一周，按照您的要求，我以挂号信的方式，将您专著中第一部分的二次校样和其余部分的首次校样寄到了上海国际饭店，不知是否已经安全寄达。杨森教授和比林-阿尔提的专著以及您专著中的图版都随我们搬运到了长沙。由于没有用于书籍、地图和光刻版的印刷设备，调查所的副所长黄汲清博士昨天已经派人前往香港协商书籍出版事宜。预计一两周内就能定下来。

如果事态严重，我们将从长沙迁到四川重庆以北的北碚；如果情况尚好，我们将暂且留在长沙。

我本人向您问好，并代表黄博士向您致以问候。

致敬

周赞衡（注：知名古生物学家）

信件二：

安特生和中央地质调查所有关
《齐家坪遗址与罗汉堂遗址考古报告》的通信

1939 年 5 月 15 日

周赞衡先生

中央地质调查所

亲爱的周先生：

我们在遥远的地方，一直深切地同情并关注着贵国为维护民族独立而进行的英勇斗争。圣诞节前，我用瑞典文出版了一卷《战火纷飞中》，其中后半部分写的是战后重建问题。林耀华（译者注：著名人类学家）已承诺以英文出版这一部分，但很长时间以来我都没有他们的消息。

我写信是为了我们投给《中国古生物志》的三部专著的印刷事宜，包括我本人有关史前遗址的论述，比林–阿尔提夫人有关齐家坪的专著以及詹斯关于辛店陶器的专著。

您可否给我们出一个关于这三部著作的报告：

1.您一定还记得，我论文中的地图是很久之前在北京印制的，我相信它们应该保存在南京地质调查所的大院里。您知道它们的下落吗？整个原稿已经定稿，我读过其中较大部分的两次校样和最后的三分之一部分的第一份校样。这个文本现在怎么样了？所有的图版都寄给您去复制，但我知道这部分工作在您离开南京之前还没有开始，这些图版现在在哪里？还保存完好吗？

2.从您去年 3 月 30 日从长沙寄来的信件中，我得知您已将这些原稿，包括詹斯和比林–阿尔提的专题论文，安全送到了长沙。请告知我所有这些资料是否都还安全，您是否已经安排印刷？您知道，比林–阿尔提和詹斯及我本人都非常关注这些稿件的出版问题，如果能告知我们目前的情况，将不胜感激。

今年冬天，我有可能前往中南半岛开展实地考察，届时，我非常乐意前往您所在的重庆或昆明，并迫切地想和您及黄汲清博士商讨我们为《中国古生物志》撰写的考古专著的发表问题。有一段时间，我们一直在考虑由我们自己出资在本国发表，但现在你们的抗日战争似乎出现有利的转机，可能不久就回到正轨，还是由您那边发表。无论如何，我非常希望能再次见到您和黄、翁两位博士，以便理顺所有这些发表事宜。

　　请通过航空邮件给我回信，告知我这些专著的命运、您目前的地址以及去拜访您的可能性。

　　　　致敬

附言：由于我不知地质调查所的总部目前的地址，这封信我至少寄出了四份：

1.寄往您去年3月30日给我写信的长沙地址。

2.寄往四川重庆以北的北碚，即您在信中提到的将来可能设立地质调查所总部的所在地。

3.致重庆经济事务部王文厚。

4.致中央研究院傅斯年博士，该机构现在应该设在云南昆明。

我希望这些地址中能有一个能转给您。

33 Shang Li Chia P'o,
Changsha, Hunan Province,
March 30, 1938.

Prof. J. G. Andersson,
c/o Ecole Francaise d'Extreme-Orient,
Hanoi, Indo-Chine.

Dear Prof. Andersson,

    I have pleasure to learn from your letter of
March 8 to Dr. W. H. Wong that you are now studying in
the Ecole Francaise d'Extreme-Orient, Hanoi and will stay
there for several weeks.

    All the staff members of the Geological Survey
except Mr. S. F. Sheng, in charge of the Geological Museum,
removed from Nanking to Changsha on November 23rd last year;
as it happened all of a sudden we had no facilities to remove
the most part of our own publications including the unbound
charts of your monograph on "Prehistoric Sites" and a part of
the museum collections, for which we feel very regretful. Mr.
Sheng is still in Nanking now, and from his letter of February
9th brought to and mailed from Shanghai by some refugee from
Nanking we learn that the Survey buildings have once been occupied by the Japanese cavalry troops and furnitures and museum cases
have all been burnt up by them for making fire and glass windows
and things easily breakable have all been smashed to pieces. The
eastern wing of the building for fuel researches has been destroyed by air raids, while the other buildings of the Survey remained
undemolished up to that date.

    At your request I have sent you by registered mail the
second proof of the first portion and the first proof of the remaining one of your monograph to Park Hotel, Shanghai, just one
week before our evacuation from Nanking. I should like to know
whether it has safely reached you or not. The other two manuscripts of Prof. Janse and Bylin-Althin's monographs together
with the photographic plates of your monograph have been brought
with us here in Changsha. As there are no facilities for book,
map and heliotype printings, Dr. T. K. Huang, the Vice Director
of the Survey, sent a man to Hongkong yesterday to see if there
is any possibility to print our books there. We will decide the
matter in a week or so.

    If conditions become still worse than now, we may
remove again from Changsha to Peibay, north from Chungking,
Szechuan. Otherwise we will stay here for the time being.

    With kind regards from Dr. T. K. Huang and myself,

Very sincerely yours,

Tsanheng C. Chow

May, 15th 1939.

Mr. Tsanheng C. Chow,
The National Geological Survey of China.

Dear Mr. Chow.

From a far distance we have been following with profound sympathy the heroic struggle of your nation for maintaining your national independence. By Christmas time I published in Swedish a volume __Under brin-nande krig,__ the second half of which is devoted to the reconstruction period and the war. Kegan Paul has undertaken to publish in English the second part of the book, but for quite a time I have not heard from them.

I herewith approach you about the printing of our three mono-graphs for the Palaeontologia Sinica, my description of the prehistoric sites, Mrs. Bylin-Althin's monograph on Chi Chia P'ing and Janse's monograph on the Hsin Tien pottery.

Will you please give me a report about each of these monographs:

1: You will remember that the maps for my paper were printed long time ago in Peking and were stored, I believe, in The Geological Survey compound in Nanking. Have you any news about their fate? The whole manuscript was set and I had read two proofs of the larger part and the first proof of the last one third. What has happened with this text? All the plates were handed to you for reproduction, but I understand that this part of the work had not begun before your departure from Nanking. Where are now these plates and are they still in good condition?

2: From your letter written in Changsha, March 30 last year, I learn that the manuscripts etc. of the Janse and Bylin-Althin monographs were brought by you safely to Changsha. Please tell me whether all these materials are still safe and whether you have been able to arrange for them being printed. You will realise that two authors as well as I myself are very anxious about these publications and we will highly appreciate any comunication as to the present state of these affairs.

It is possible that I will be able to go to French Indo-China fore some field work there during this winter and I would be quite pleased to proceed to Chungking or Kunming where you will be by that time. I am most anxious to discuss with Dr Huang and yourself the mode of publication of the following archaeological monographs for the Palaeontologica Sinica. Some time we have been considering the possibility of publishing them here at our expense but now your fight against the Japanese seems to take such a favourable turn that you may very soon be back in nermal conditions. At any rate I would highly appreciate to meet again Dr. Wong, Dr. Huang and yourself in order to straighten out all these publication matters.

Kindly send me by airmail a reply telling about the fate of our monographs and about your present address and the possibilities of going to visit you.

With kindest regards

Yours very truly

P.S.　As I do not know where is at present the headquarters of the Geological Survey I dispatch not less than four copies of this letter:

1: to Changsha address from where you wrote me 30 March last year.

2: to Peibay north from Vhungking Szechuan, the place which you gave in that letter as the possible future headquarters of the Geological Survey.

3: to Dr. Wong Wen-hau, Ministry of Economy Affairs, Chungking.

4: to Dr. Fu Ssu-nien, Accademia Sinica, which institution I now suppose to be lokated in Kunming, Yunnan.

       I hope that one or the other of these addresses will carry forward to you.

附录三

人名地名英汉对照

Anyang　安阳

Ch'I Chia P'ing　齐家坪

Ch'I Li Tun　七里墩

Ch'ia Yao　卡窑（卡约）

Chih Kou Chai　池沟寨

Chin Chou　秦州（今天水市）

Chin Wang Chai　秦王寨

Chu Chia Chai　朱家寨

Hsin Tien B　辛店乙址

Hsi Chun Tsun　西庄村

Ho Yin Hsien　河阴县（今荥阳一带）

Honna　河南

Hou Kang　后岗

Hsiao Shih Hsia　小石峡（榆中县小石峡甘草镇钱家坪村小石峡社）

Huang Ho　黄河

Kansu　甘肃

Kao Lan Hsien　皋兰县

Kuei Te Hsien　贵德县

Lanchou　兰州

Lo Han T'ang　罗汉堂

Ma Chang　马厂

Ma Chia Yao　马家窑

Ning Ting Hsien　宁定县（今广河县）

P'ai Tzu P'ing　排子坪（今齐家镇）

Pan Shan　半山

Pu Chao Chai　不召寨

Shanxi　山西

Shensi　陕西

Ssu Wa　寺洼

T'ao Sha Hsien　洮沙县（今临洮县太石镇）

the Hui Tsui sites　灰嘴遗址

the T'ao/the T'ao river　洮河

Ti Tao Hsien　狄道县（今临洮县）

Ulan Chada　乌兰哈达（今内蒙古赤峰市）

Yang Ho Tsun　杨河村

Yang Shao Tsun　仰韶村

Yen Chia Chuang　阎家庄

Yü Chung Hsien　榆中县